The Emergence of Humans

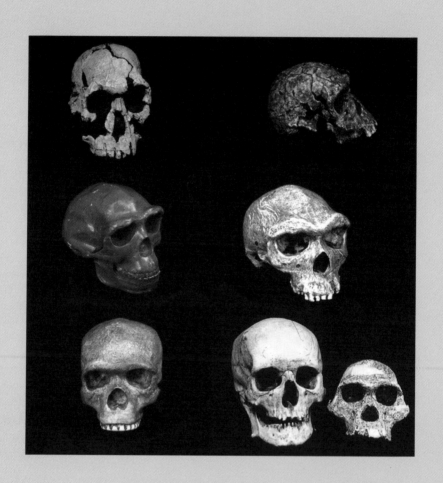

The Emergence of Humans

An Exploration of the Evolutionary Timeline

Patricia J Ash

The Open University in the South, Oxford, UK

David J Robinson

Department of Life Sciences, The Open University, Milton Keynes, UK

A John Wiley & Sons, Ltd., Publication

This edition first published by John Wiley & Sons, Ltd, 2010
© 2010 by John Wiley & Sons, Ltd

Wiley-Blackwell is an imprint of John Wiley & Sons, formed by the merger of Wiley's global Scientific, Technical and Medical business with Blackwell Publishing.

Registered office: John Wiley & Sons Ltd, The Atrium, Southern Gate, Chichester, West Sussex, PO19 8SQ, UK

Other Editorial Offices:
9600 Garsington Road, Oxford, OX4 2DQ, UK
111 River Street, Hoboken, NJ 07030-5774, USA

For details of our global editorial offices, for customer services and for information about how to apply for permission to reuse the copyright material in this book please see our website at www.wiley.com/wiley-blackwell

The right of the authors to be identified as the authors of this work has been asserted in accordance with the Copyright, Designs and Patents Act 1988.

Library of Congress Cataloguing-in-Publication Data
Ash, Patricia, 1948-
    The emergence of humans : an exploration of the evolutionary timeline / Patricia Ash, David Robinson.
        p.   cm.
    Includes bibliographical references and index.
    ISBN 978-0-470-01313-7 (cloth)
        1. Human evolution.   I. Robinson, David, 1949-   II. Title.
    GN281.A83   2010
    599.93'8—dc22
                                                                        2009041779

A catalogue record for this book is available from the British Library.

ISBN 9780470013137 (HB)   ISBN 9780470013151 (PB)

Set in 10.5/12.5 Minion Regular by MPS Limited, A Macmillan Company, Chennai, India
Printed in Singapore by Markono Print Media Pte Ltd.

First impression—2010

Contents

Preface

Discoveries of fossils of our human ancestors have always been able to generate press and public interest and that interest has, if anything, increased in the early years of the twenty-first century. Human fossils are big news and those who discover them can acquire big reputations. Contrary to what we might expect, new discoveries are not filling in gaps in a well worked out history of the rise of humans. Some of the most recent discoveries have substantially changed the picture of our evolutionary past, a picture that we thought was becoming clearer. The discovery in 2003 of a possible new species of human from Flores in Indonesia, that was living as recently as 18 000 years ago looks set to alter many of our assumptions about the evolution of the human species. Not surprisingly, the discovery is controversial and it is interesting to see how the discovery of a new fossil often brings argument and dissent in its wake. The study of human fossils can often seem a more disputatious scientific discipline than most of the others, but in part this is because there is so much interest in the subject amongst non-specialists that the legitimate argument and debate that takes place in science is carried out in a more public arena. With a fossil record that is so sparse, firm answers to questions are often impossible and what evidence there is can be interpreted in different ways. This book is an introduction to the scientific study of human evolution.

We intend this book for undergraduate students who are studying human evolution as part of a Natural Sciences degree, or who might subsequently decide to specialize in Anthropology. We do not cover all the background information that would be needed for an Anthropology course, as our primary concern is to illuminate the *evolution* of human species. The book is based on an undergraduate course we have designed and taught, a course with a target audience of first or second year equivalent undergraduates with some previous knowledge of biology. To help students with a limited biological background, we have included some basic information about evolution, genes and inheritance. Some detailed anatomical information is included in the book, but for more comprehensive information, reference to specialized Anthropology works would be necessary.

The Emergence of Humans Patricia Ash and David Robinson
© 2010 John Wiley & Sons, Ltd

There are lots of instances recounted in this book where more than one interpretation of the evidence is possible. We have tried to steer an objective path through the conflicts and do justice to different views. For example, the number of known species of human is debated in the scientific literature, with the extreme ends of the distribution being 25 species and 4. Students need to be aware of the debate and the scale of the resulting uncertainty, but won't find in this book a definitive statement of what we believe to be the 'right' number. Inevitably in a few cases we have had to follow a particular view but have given our reasons for so doing.

We will travel along the timeline of human evolution, starting with the first primates. Then, from the point where the ancestral line leading to humans diverged from the chimp line, we shall follow the evolutionary history of humans up to the point where all other species had died out and only one species remained. In doing so, we hope to highlight some of the areas of uncertainty and show why such uncertainty exists.

About the structure of this book

This book is designed to be both used as a textbook by students in a taught course and to be studied by distance learners in courses where the book is the core of their learning. We have defined a set of learning outcomes for the book and offer questions both in the text and at the end of chapters. The questions within the text provide an opportunity for students to pause and self-test their understanding. The questions at the end of the chapters are linked to the learning outcomes and enable students to test for themselves whether they are making progress in meeting particular outcomes.

Key references for each chapter are indicated by superscript numbers in the text and are listed in the further reading at the end of each chapter. These will enable students to follow up particular subjects dealt with in that chapter and include publications up to April 2009, when this text was completed. For ease of study, we have only included key citations within the text.

There are many techniques drawn from other disciplines that are available to those studying human evolution. Molecular biology, physics and genetics have all proved to have application in this field and an understanding of some techniques is necessary in understanding how evidence is obtained. Techniques are not covered in a separate section: rather each is introduced at the point in the text where it is first needed. For a comprehensive coverage of techniques students would need to refer to a more detailed text.

Patricia J. Ash
David J. Robinson

Learning outcomes and key skills for the book

A Knowledge and understanding:

A1 Understand modern evolutionary theory and simple genetics, and use your knowledge to describe the emergence of humans.

A2 Gain an overview of the evidence used for the interpretation of human evolution.

A3 Interpret new evidence and intercalate it with established lines of evidence.

A4 Recognize, and describe, the evolutionary significance of named fossils.

B Cognitive skills:

B1 Evaluate and use evidence, including data, to support theories and arguments.

B2 Attempt to classify an appropriate range of Pleistocene hominins on the basis of similarities and differences.

B3 Distinguish between a causal and a correlational relationship e.g. between assemblages of fossil hominin bones, animal bones and stone tools, which may be the result of taphonomy rather than hominin activity.

B4 Interpret and draw evolutionary trees for primates.

B5 Understand the use of models based on social structure of living primates for suggesting social structures for extinct hominins.

C Key skills:

C1 Monitor and check own progress using self assessment.

C2 Identify a line of reasoning and main points of an argument and recognize opinion and bias.

C3 Collate, summarize and interpret text and images from web resources.

C4 Communicate using written material, tables, charts and diagrams.

Acknowledgements

This book was conceived after preparing a course at The Open University and we would particularly like to thank people involved with the course, especially Brian Richardson and Tracey Carlton. Our special thanks go to Becky Efthimiou (Life Sciences) who has provided administrative support at all the production stages. We are grateful to the University for permission to use drawn artwork from other courses.

In addition to the Open University collection of casts of key specimens, we have had access to casts in the Nottingham University collection and for this we are extremely grateful to Peter Davies who originally assembled the collection and Peter Whitworth for technical help. Sue Scarborough, also at Nottingham University, gave a lot of helpful advice to us in the early stages.

We would like to thank Richard Jurd (University of Essex) for reviewing and commenting on the first drafts and providing so many constructive comments. Erik Sieffert (University of Oxford and University Oxford Museum of Natural History) provided very detailed and invaluable comments, particularly on the Chapters on Primate and anthropoid origins and we are very grateful to him.

Special thanks are due to our patient editors at Wiley, Celia Carden, Robert Hambrook and especially Nicky McGirr who encouraged us to develop the book in the first place and has been so supportive during the writing, reviewing and production stages.

This book was started while one of us (DJR) was a visiting professor in the Centre for the Studies of Higher Education at Nagoya University as a guest of Professor Terumasa Ikeda.

Finally we both owe a huge debt to Peter Davies for his continuing support, advice and intellectual stimulation over many years.

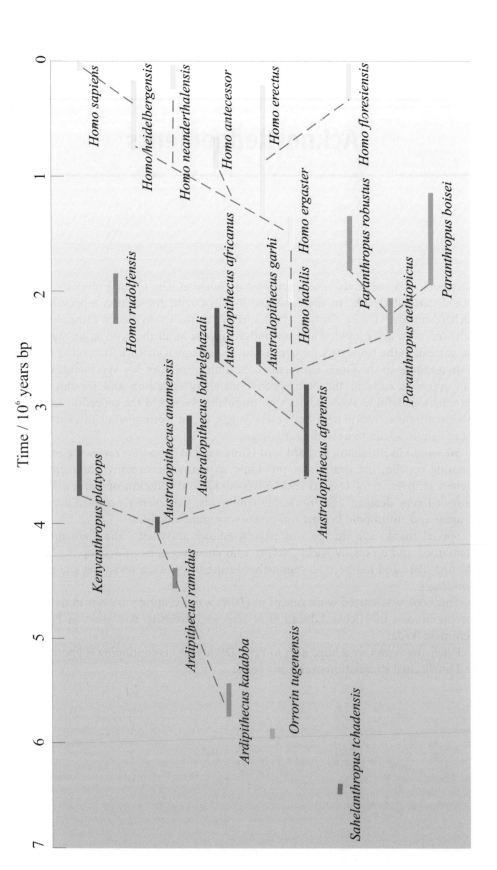

Time / 10⁶ years bp

Introduction to the Emergence of Humans

We are eminently curious and for some the biggest question in the world is – who are we and where did we come from. For many of us our ancestry is an ongoing fascination and perhaps there are very few of us who, if given the opportunity to learn more about our past, would profess no interest at all. We are the only animal, as far as we are aware, that can contemplate its own past. Why we should have this interest, and in some cases an overwhelming passion, for finding our ancestors and filling in our evolutionary tree, is not clear. Maybe we can feel more secure about our place in nature if we know how we reached it. What is clear, particularly from recent research, is that our place is not quite what we thought it was. There have been other human species in existence, some of them our recent contemporaries. We share a lot of our biology with our closest living relatives, the great apes, but recently with the completion of the mapping of the human genome we seem to be closer to them. Comparison of the chimp and human genome shows that there is an average substitution level of about 1.2% in single copy DNA, so the short-hand statement that we are 99% chimp isn't too far from the truth, at least as far as the base structure of our genome is concerned. However, other genetic differences between humans and chimps, for example in the number of copies of genes, are greater than 1%. The short-hand statement is sometimes rendered as '99% ape', but this is not really correct as we should be grouped with the apes ourselves, rather than placed in some special position in the evolutionary tree. In the past there were several species of human but now there is only one. There were many species of ape in the past too, but most are extinct and the outlook for the future of the remaining species is not good. Maybe the human species will at some time in the future be the last ape?

What is it that defines a human? It is likely that we would all feel able to answer that question to some degree by referring to our behaviour, our social structure, our intellectual capacity or our brains. Probably we would select the size of our brain as perhaps the defining feature. Maybe we would also add habitual bipedal locomotion,

The Emergence of Humans Patricia Ash and David Robinson
© 2010 John Wiley & Sons, Ltd

although it is becoming apparent that it isn't exclusively a human trait (see discussion of *Oreopithecus* in Section 5.5). Certainly there are a lot of aspects of our behaviour which do not seem to be unique to us, we share some basic features of our social structure with apes and our brain is similar to those of some primates, though larger at 1500 g – 2.1% of body mass. However, on its own, the size of the brain does not equate with, for example, intelligence. The elephant has a brain mass of around five times that of a human (7500 g), but of course has a larger body mass. As far as we can tell, it is not five times as intelligent as humans. Mice have a brain mass of 0.4 g but that equates to 3.2% of body mass, a greater proportion than in humans. So neither absolute nor relative mass is a good guide and although the human brain is larger, by volume, than a chimp brain, the brain of an extinct human species, *Homo neanderthalensis*, is 11% larger than ours.

We recognize that cognitive capacities in humans are much greater than in other animals and that this provides a clear distinction between us and our closest relatives, the other living great apes. Is this difference in capacity something that can be correlated with the comparative anatomy of the brains? Cognitive functions such as planning and organization are located in the frontal cortex of the brain and so we might expect that this area would be more highly developed in humans than in apes. In fact, this is not the case and both humans and apes share a large frontal cortex, though one that is larger than that of gibbons or macaques. So if the difference does not lie in the cortex, could it be that another unique feature of humans, the production and recognition of speech, is reflected in the structure of the brain?

Two areas of the brain are associated with communication, **Broca's area** and **Wernicke's area** (Figure 0.1). Broca's area is associated with language and part

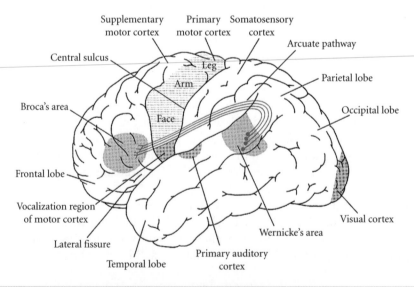

Figure 0.1 The position of Broca's and Wernicke's areas in the human brain.
Source: Biology Brain and Behaviour Book 2. © The Open University.

of Wernicke's area, the **planum temporale**, with audible and visual communication. Although both hemispheres of the brain have these two areas, the size of each is asymmetrical with the left being larger than the right. When the homologous area has been examined in chimps, gorillas and bonobos using **MRI** (Magnetic Resonance Imaging) scans this same asymmetry is present. The asymmetry of the planum temporale is also present in chimps. So again, anatomical features of the human brain that might under-pin human distinctiveness are also present in at least some of the great apes.

Clearly there must be differences between the chimp and human brain, which studies in neuroanatomy and neurophysiology will eventually elucidate, but already it seems apparent that the greater cognitive capacities in humans result from changes within specialized areas rather than new and distinct areas of the brain.

There is a picture of human evolution that was clearly in the minds of earlier anthropologists and still persists in some minds today, despite the huge body of evidence to the contrary. That picture is of a species, *Homo sapiens*, that is the terminal member of a straight line heading back through time to an ape that represents our last link to other animals. The picture has within it some assumptions. The line from apes to humans is seen as a progression or advance. Since it is a linear progression, there has been a smooth transition between one evolutionary stage and the next and, behind this assumption, is the implication that there has only been one species of human around at any one time in that progression. This assumption also leads to the idea that humans occupy a special position in the natural world, distinct from all other animals. Using the word progression implies that evolution has direction, moving towards a better or more complex state. However, evolution has not resulted in organisms becoming universally more complex. Taken as a whole, the biosphere has not become more and more advanced and complicated. The only way in which evolution can be perceived as having direction is in the fact that time has a direction. There is also an illusion of direction because evolution can build only on what already exists. So it might appear that evolution is a process of gradual improvement. Actually, since the pressures on an organism exerted by natural selection can change or even reverse with time, for example as climate changes, an apparent improvement might become detrimental subsequently. The important point to understand is that evolution has no goals and so an older idea that primate evolution was somehow preparing the way for the appearance of humans is incorrect. Although we have imposed a linear element on the story of human evolution by following a timeline, and hence also a line that follows climatic changes, the evolutionary tree of humans is a bushy one rather than a linear one, with a number of side branches.

1

The First Human Fossils

Just over 150 years ago there were no recognized fossils of ancestral human species and human remains that had been discovered were all attributed to our own species. When, in 1823, geologist and clergyman the Reverend William Buckland described the post-cranial skeleton of an anatomically modern, but undoubtedly ancient, human from Goat's Hole at Paviland on the Welsh Coast of the United Kingdom, it was possibly the first, and certainly the earliest, human fossil known at that time. That Buckland did not recognize it as such, preferring to believe that the skeleton was an intrusion into earlier, antediluvian deposits, was a reasonable conclusion when set against the intellectual background of the time.

Box 1.1 The Paviland find

Paviland cave is on the Gower Coast of Wales. On 27 and 28 December 1822 the tusk and part of the skull of an elephant were excavated from the cave by two local amateur geologists and a landowner. They also excavated many small bones and informed William Buckland, Professor of Geology at Oxford, of their finds. He visited the cave on 21 January 1823 and discovered parts of a human skeleton, together with some ivory rods and fragments of worked ivory. Worked flints were also found. The bones and the ivory were reddened by ochre. The skeleton became known as the Red Lady, although subsequently it was shown to be the skeleton of a male. Although Buckland was not inclined to regard the skeleton as dating to before the flood, it was associated with the bones of extinct mammals. Subsequent dating of the skeleton suggests an age of 24 000 years.

The Emergence of Humans Patricia Ash and David Robinson
© 2010 John Wiley & Sons, Ltd

Worked flints and stones were well known before the nineteenth century and were recognized as being associated with human activities. However, during the first half of that century interest in the age of the tools was increasing. John Frere, a member of the Society of Antiquaries, is generally regarded as the first person to publish a description of tools with the conclusion that they came from a period much earlier than a time when humans were thought to have existed. This conclusion was based on the fact that worked flints that he found in a quarry at Hoxne in Suffolk were in an undisturbed layer of gravel below, and thus older, than some marine shells and bones of extinct mammals. In his letter to the Society in 1797, Frere wrote:

> The flints were evidently weapons of war, fabricated and used by a people who had not the use of metals. They lay in great numbers at the depth of about 12 feet in a stratified soil which was dug into for the purpose of raising clay for bricks. Under a foot and a half of vegetable earth was clay 7½; feet thick, and beneath this one foot of sand with shells, and under this 2 feet of gravel, in which the shaped flints were found generally at the rate of 5 or 6 in a square yard. In the sandy beds with shells were found the jawbone and teeth of an enormous unknown animal. The manner in which the flint weapons lay would lead to the persuasion that it was a place of their manufacture, and not of their accidental deposit (Lyell, 1863).

Further discoveries of tools were made, notably in the Somme Valley from 1841 by M. Boucher de Perthes, who described them as 'antediluvian' on the basis of the undisturbed strata that they came from being below some alluvial deposits which had been regarded as derived from the great flood. Bones from extinct mammals were also present. Following a visit by Charles Lyell and Joseph Prestwich to Abbeville and Amiens in 1859, they published more information about the finds and their geological position and Lyell dealt extensively with the subject in his 1863 book, *The Antiquity of Man*. So by the time that Darwin's *On the Origin of Species* was published over 50 years of work on stone tools had shown the age of the human line to be much greater than had previously been thought. Against this background, human fossils could be set in context.

One of the first specimens of a human species other than *Homo sapiens* to be found was not recognized as such for several years. On 3 March 1848 Lieutenant Edmund Flint presented a skull to the Gibraltar Scientific Society. It had been exposed by an explosion during blasting at the Forbes Quarry in Gibraltar. Looking at it now (Figure 1.1) it is clear that it is a different species, but that is the advantage of hind-sight. At the time there was no expectation that other species of humans had existed and for the next 16 years it remained in obscurity.

In 1856 workmen at a lime quarry in the Neander valley on the river Düssel in Germany discovered part of a skull (Figure 1.2), and bones from the post-cranial skeleton of an unusual looking human. They showed the bones to an amateur naturalist who recognized them as a significant find and showed the bones to an anatomist. They jointly described the find the following year and concluded that the skeletal remains were of an individual of an ancient human race that was different from modern humans. This was a controversial view at the time and other explanations were advanced. For example, it was suggested that the remains were of a diseased human who suffered from rickets. However, despite the alternatives, the view of the authors of the publication prevailed and their description of the remains of what came to be known, in 1863, as *Homo neanderthalensis* marks the inauguration of the

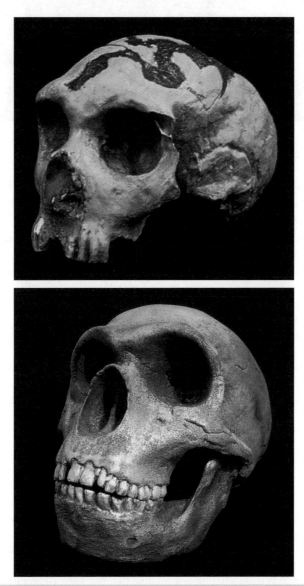

Figure 1.1 The Gibraltar skull. (a) A cast of the specimen found in 1848 at Forbes Quarry in Gibraltar. (b) A reconstruction of the Forbes Quarry skull with a lower jaw from another specimen.

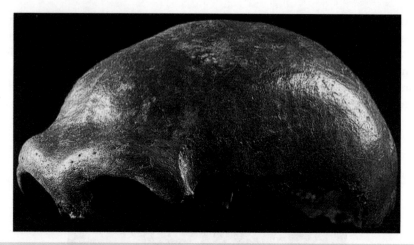

Figure 1.2 The Neander skull cap.
Reproduced by permission of the LVR-Landesmuseum Bonn.

science of palaeoanthropology, though that name was not applied to the science until the second half of the twentieth century.

Much later, in 1936, after a lot of debate, the **cranium** of a child that had been discovered in 1830 in Engis Cave near Liege in Belgium was also identified as belonging to a Neandertal. So just as the theory of evolution by natural selection was engaging science, fossil material was accumulating that would enable scientists to place humans in the evolutionary tree.

Charles Darwin did not include a treatment of humans in his first major work, *On the Origin of Species by Means of Natural Selection* (1859). In 1871 he published *The Descent of Man*, in which he dealt both with the genealogy of man and sexual selection. The book contains many fascinating insights, but for our interest in human evolution, there is one very striking section entitled 'On the Birthplace and Antiquity of Man'. In this section there is the following very prescient inference about the place where humans evolved:

> We are naturally led to enquire, where was the birthplace of man at that stage of descent when our progenitors diverged from the Catarhine[1] stock? The fact that they belonged to the stock clearly shows that they inhabited the Old World; but not Australia nor any oceanic island, as we may infer from the laws of geographical distribution. In each great region of the world the living mammals are closely related to the extinct species of the same region. It is therefore probable that Africa was formerly inhabited by extinct apes closely allied to the gorilla and chimpanzee; and as these two species are now man's nearest allies, it is somewhat more probable that our early progenitors lived on the African continent than elsewhere (Darwin, 1874).

---

1   The Old World Monkeys, apes and humans.

Box 1.2 The Gibraltar skull

The Gibraltar Scientific Society, whose members were mostly, if not exclusively, serving soldiers, met on 3 March 1848 in the Garrison Library on the Rock. The secretary was Lt Edmund Flint, RA and in the minutes of that meeting there is the following: 'Presented a Human Skull from Forbes Quarry, North Front, by the secretary'. With hindsight, we can see the importance of this meeting, but it was not recognized as such at the time and we do not know exactly how or where the skull was found. Lt Flint was later promoted to Captain. He died of apoplexy in 1857 (Rose and Stringer, 1997) and whatever details of the circumstances of the find that he knew died with him. The skull presumably remained in the care of the society until 1864, when the army officer who was governor of the military prison, included it in a consignment of fossils that he sent to George Busk at the Royal College of Surgeons in London in the summer of that year. Busk, working with Hugh Falconer (Vice President of the Royal Society), made the connection between the Gibraltar skull and the finding of the Neander fossils. Writing to J D Hooker in the evening on 1 September 1864 Charles Darwin wrote:

> Both Lyell & Falconer called on me & I was very glad to see them. F. brought me the wonderful Gibralter skull (Darwin, 1864).

So, by the time that Darwin completed *The Descent of Man*, he had certainly seen one significant human fossil. Comparison of the Neander remains with the Gibraltar skull in 1864 showed that they belonged to the same species. The skull still holds its position as one of the finest and most complete skulls of a Neandertal ever found. Perhaps if it's true importance had been recognized at the time of discovery, the Rock of Gibraltar, rather than the Neander river would have given it's name to the species we now know as *Homo neanderthalensis*.

So although such specimens of fossil humans as had been found by this time came from Europe, as also had fossils of the Miocene ape *Dryopithecus*, Darwin argued that Africa was probably the place from which humans emerged – and he was right. However, it wasn't until well into the twentieth century that fossil evidence from Africa first appeared and, as you will read in Chapter 5, there was substantial scepticism in scientific circles about the human nature of the finds.

A picture which showed *Homo sapiens* evolving from an ancestral ape was one that Darwin and Huxley could recognize and believe in. They may have differed over whether the mechanism of evolution was always a steady accretion of small changes, but the idea of an evolutionary line back to the apes upon which the few fossils then known could be placed was one that they both could agree with. Thus the fossil from the Neander River could be forced into the human line as a variant of *H. sapiens*.

Box 1.3   Why Neandertals are so called

In 1680 Joachim Neander, a German theologian and poet, died in Bremen. He had been a teacher in Dusseldorf between 1674 and 1679 and during that time he had found inspiration for his poems when walking through the valley of the Düssel. In the early nineteenth century the valley was renamed Neander in his honour. Subsequently, open-cast mining in Neander's peaceful valley exposed the Neander fossils. The German for valley was 'thal' and so the fossils became *Homo neanderthalensis* but when the German language was modernized early in the twentieth century, 'thal' was changed to 'tal' and so today the common name of the species is Neandertal but under the rules of nomenclature, the specific name can't change and so retains the 'h'.

With this picture as our starting point, we are going to describe the route from early primates to modern humans along a time-line from past to present. In doing this, we shall reveal an evolutionary line that is far from linear, often indistinct, getting longer as new finds emerge – and is still challenging to our assumptions today.

First, however, to provide a background to the study of human evolution we need to consider in the next chapter how fossils are formed, the processes of evolution and natural selection, genetics and populations.

Summary

Stone tools were recognized from the eighteenth century onwards, but although some had recognized their antiquity, it was only by the time of the publication of *On the Origin of Species*, that the tools were generally accepted as being produced by humans who lived alongside mammals that were now extinct. Early discoveries of human fossils were not recognized immediately as being of separate species. The first discovery of a specimen of a Neandertal in Gibraltar in 1848, waited 16 years before being recognized, by which time a fossil from the Neander valley found in 1856 had been described as a new species. By the time that Darwin's book *The Descent of Man* was published in 1871, he was able to suggest a possible origin for the human line in Africa.

Questions and activities for the introduction and chapter 1

Question 1.1

Explain why neither relative nor absolute brain size is a good measure of intelligence. (*Learning Outcome B1*)

Question 1.2

Construct a table showing the key dates in the development of the understanding that humans had an ancestry on a geological rather than historical timescale. *(Learning Outcome C4)*

References

Darwin, C. (1864) Letter to J D Hooker on evening of 1 Sept, in *Darwin Correspondence Project Transcript of Letter*, vol. 4605. http://www.darwinproject.ac.uk/darwinletters/calendar/entry-4605.html. (Accessed 26/10/09)

Darwin, C. (1874) *The Descent of Man*, facsimile 2nd edn, Prometheus, New York.

Lyell, C. (1863) *The Antiquity of Man*, http://www.gutenberg.org/etext/6335. (Accessed 26/10/09)

Rose, E. P. F. and Stringer, C. B. (1997) Gibraltar woman and Neanderthal Man. *Geology Today* **13**(5): 179–184.

2

The Geological Context

The physical environment in which evolution takes place is determined, over time, by climate and geographical position. The geological process of plate tectonics, which slowly changes the position of continents relative both to each other and to their position on the globe, has an influence on the climate of each. As continents touch, land bridges are created over which species can migrate; as they move apart, populations of the same species become isolated and subsequently diverge. In recent times, geologists have come to the view that major events in the distant past, like large-scale volcanic eruptions, have had a more profound influence on life on earth than was previously thought. Although probably not part of the story of human evolution, the impacts of extra-terrestrial objects on the earth have been sufficiently powerful to have had an evolutionary impact too. So, geological processes influence evolution. The history of the life and environments of the past is preserved in the rock strata, generally the younger being on top of the older ones, but the strata don't always offer a continuous record at a particular place. Cross-correlation with strata at other locations may fill in the gaps and so geological study can establish a timescale for the history of the Earth, though with some uncertainty. The rocks in which fossils are found can be dated using knowledge of how the rocks were formed and how their isotope content has changed with age. In this chapter we consider plate tectonics, the geological time scale, fossilization and dating methods.

2.1 The geological time scale

The history of the Earth is divided up into periods of varying length, which were delineated and named largely in the nineteenth century. The timing of large-scale changes in the flora and fauna set the division between periods. At the time, the geologists had

The Emergence of Humans Patricia Ash and David Robinson
© 2010 John Wiley & Sons, Ltd

no way of assigning an absolute date to the periods and they didn't have a figure for the age for the Earth. They were able to say that a particular rock formation was older than another, thus assigning a *relative* age to each. Doing this for a large number of formations produced a succession through time that gave a reasonable historical sequence, but did not have a reliable absolute date anywhere to anchor the sequence in elapsed time.

Sedimentary strata in different locations can be related through comparison of their fossils. If two rock formations contain the same assemblage of fossils, this faunal correlation suggests that the two formations fall within the same age band. Faunal correlation is a useful technique in dating human fossils. A further aid to relative dating comes from the periodic reversals of the direction of the Earth's magnetic axis. During a 'normal period' such as the one that we are in at present, a compass needle is north seeking. When a 'reversal' occurs, the same needle would become south seeking. Reversals do not have a regular pattern or duration. A change in direction may occur after 100 000 years or several million. The important feature for geologists is that igneous rock (and some fine-grained sedimentary rock) preserves a record of reversals. Fine grains or crystals containing iron become oriented in the Earth's magnetic field as the rocks form. This orientation can be detected, showing the direction of the Earth's magnetic field at the time of formation of the rock. The sequence of reversals can be used to cross-correlate rock formations and there is a geomagnetic polarity time scale which has been constructed using absolute dating techniques. The history of reversals over the last 4 Ma is shown in Figure 2.1.

Although the duration of the period when humans have been around is now recognized as being longer than originally thought, and it may be longer still as new discoveries are made, at 7 million Figure 2.2 illustrates this, with the period of human evolution occupying just 0.15% of the column.

Humans are part of the primate group of animals, which first appeared in the Palaeocene epoch. To tell the story of the emergence of humans this epoch is where we must start and Table 2.1 shows a more detailed geological time scale from the start of the Palaeocene until the present, with some significant events indicated.

2.2 Movement of the continents

The surface of the earth is built of plates which are in motion relative to each other and to the interior of the Earth. Although very slow, by comparison with a human lifetime, the movements become significant when considering evolution over long time periods. Different plates are moving at different rates. For example, the spreading rate at the Arctic ridge is less than 2.5 cm per year, but in the Pacific near Easter Island the spreading rate is more than 15 cm per year. Rates of movement in the past can be derived from faunal correlation by comparing formations on each side of a boundary and if the fossils correlate, the separation distance of the two formations can provide a rate of movement.

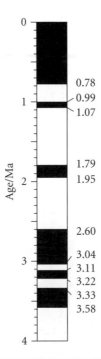

Figure 2.1 Changes in polarity of the Earth's magnetic field during the last 4 Ma. Normal is shown in black and reversed in white.

♦ What additional piece of information would be required to measure a past separation rate?

♦ An absolute date for the rocks in the formation, or a date estimated from the absolute date of rocks above or below the formation.

Satellite technology now allows very accurate measurement of current separation rates.

Around 65 Mya, at the end of the Cretaceous, the final period of the Mesozoic era, the geography of the continents was very different from the way it is now (Figure 2.3).

The super continent **Laurasia** was located in the northern hemisphere. North America was separated from South America but joined to Europe. India, isolated in the ancient Indian Ocean, and situated south west of Asia, was moving slowly towards the Asian landmass. Australia was very close to Antarctica. The land was covered with forests of coniferous trees, giant cycads and tree ferns, which were being replaced gradually by dense stands of broad-leafed trees. Climates were tropical or subtropical. Dinosaurs, including large predators, were diverse and abundant, as were flying reptiles, pterosaurs. Birds and mammals were also present, but we would not recognize these animals today. During the Eocene Laurasia started to break up. The southern

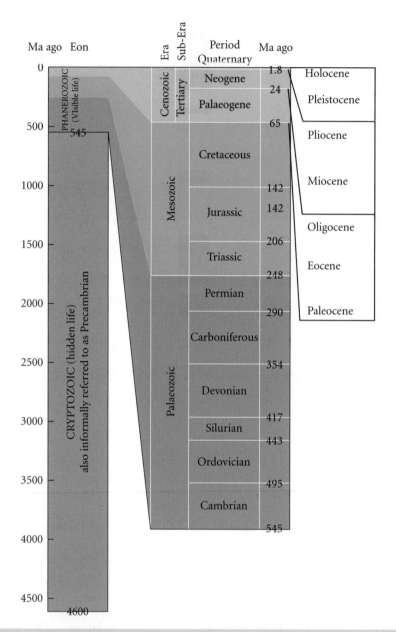

Figure 2.2 Geological column. Modified from Fossils and the History of Life P 22. © The Open University.

super continent, Gondwanaland, continued fragmenting, with Australia and South America in the process of breaking away. The mean global temperature at a peak during this epoch was al most 14 °C higher than today, the poles were free of ice but the temperature was starting to cool, the cooling getting more rapid at the end

Table 2.1 Epochs of the end of the Mesozoic era, and the Cenozoic era and major events

Era	Sub-era	Epoch or Period		Date (Mya)	Events
Cenozoic	Quaternary	Holocene		0.01–0	Extinctions of other species leave *Homo sapiens* as sole hominin
		Pleistocene		1.8–0.01	Ice age; emergence of *Homo sapiens*
	Tertiary	Pliocene		5.2–1.8	Hominin radiation; emergence of australopiths and *Homo*
		Miocene	Late	10.0–5.2	First hominin?
			Middle	16.0–10.0	Hominoid radiation
			Early	23.8–16.0	Early apes and Old World monkeys appear
		Oligocene		33.7–23.8	Anthropoid radiation
		Eocene	Late	37.0–33.7	First anthropoids
			Middle	50.0–37.0	Adapid and omomyid radiation
			Early	54.8–50.0	First adapids and omomyids
		Palaeocene		65–54.8	Radiation of placental mammals
					Plesiadapiformes and first primates
Mesozoic		Cretaceous		144–65	First placental mammals. Extinction of dinosaurs ~65 Mya

of the Eocene. As time passed, the continents got drier and the dense tropical forest became more patchy.

By the start of the Oligocene epoch, Australia and South America had separated from Antarctica, which was starting to develop an ice covering. There was a dramatic loss of species as the Earth cooled more rapidly. It is estimated that almost 20% of species became extinct. India now made contact with Europe and Asia and mammals moved freely across the continents.

Australia and South America remained isolated during the Miocene (Figure 2.4) but towards the end of the epoch Africa joined Europe at a time when sea levels were falling and the Mediterranean Sea was dry. Dry grasslands became much more widespread, as did herbivorous mammals. The climate cooled and dried further during the Pliocene and became more seasonal. It was a period when large herbivores abounded. The start of the Pleistocene epoch marks the start of the period known as the Great Ice Age, when there were five separate periods when ice and glaciers advanced and retreated. After the last retreat, 15 000 years ago we are now in an interglacial period, the Holocene epoch. These climate changes and continental movements are highly significant in the story of human evolution.

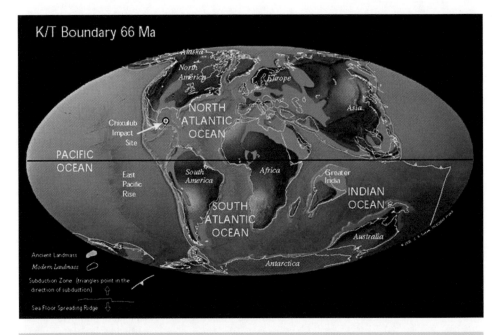

Figure 2.3   World map at the end of the Cretaceous period, 65 Mya.
Source: http://www.scotese.com/K/t.htm

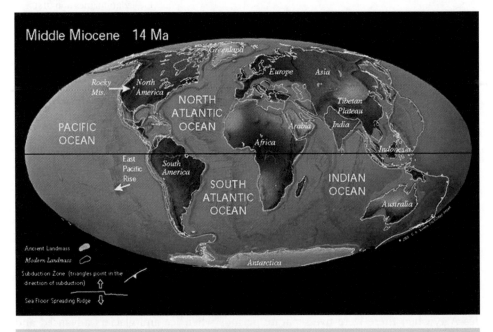

Figure 2.4   World map in the middle of the Miocene epoch, 14 Mya.
Source: http://www.scotese.com/miocene.htm

2.3 Fossilization

The process of fossilization provides us with an imperfect record of the animal or plant that is preserved. To be preserved an animal has to be buried by some means shortly after death, before too much natural decomposition and disassembly has taken place. The body of a human could not lie out in the open for very long before scavengers would scatter parts of it and reduce it to unrecognizable fragments.

♦ How might a human body come to be buried rapidly?

♦ The body would have to end up in a place where there was rapid deposition of sediment, perhaps a river or lake. Another possibility is burial by ash from a volcanic eruption. Finally, there might be deliberate burial.

Since rapid burial is very uncommon in nature, terrestrial animals are very rarely fossilized and so those fossils that we do find represent a very small, random sample. It is very rare for any information about soft tissues to be preserved and even when hard parts such as bones are fossilized, many changes may have taken place, not least distortion after burial. The eminent anthropologist Tim White described graphically a skull that he is still reconstructing more than 10 years after he discovered it as: 'road kill'.

The study of the processes by which organisms and groups of organisms become preserved as fossils is called **taphonomy**. By understanding the processes it is possible to gain a better understanding of the biases that are present in the fossil record. For example, is a particular fossil more common in the fossil record because preservation processes favour it, or because it was common in life? The anthropologist will study both the human fossils themselves and also the assemblages of the remains of other animals associated with the human fossils and it is in this context that taphonomy is important. Of course forensic taphonomy and anthropology have direct and strengthening links, as the results become available from work carried out by forensic scientists on decomposition.

2.4 Dating

Fossils of our human ancestors can tell us about their skeletal structure and may give some indication of the structure of the brain from traces on the inside of the skull bones. Bony areas where muscles were attached can give an indication of the size of the muscles and, with modern face reconstruction techniques; we may even get a general idea of how the human looked in life. Any tools or other fossil animals found associated with the human may shed light on their way of life, though often caution is needed in interpreting assemblages, as will become apparent in later chapters. But it is how we are to place fossils in their evolutionary context that is the first concern and to do that the date of the fossil is a crucial piece of information and dating fossil humans is not easy.

The study of the succession of rocks is known as **stratigraphy** and the basic principles of stratigraphy which were identified by Charles Lyell in 1830 are pretty much the same as the principles that we recognize today. When rocks are formed, for example by sedimentation in the sea, the younger layers overlay the older layers and the layers are originally laid down horizontally. Of course subsequently geological processes may distort the layers, sometimes even folding them so that they are upside-down. The processes that form and shape rocks today are largely the same as those in the past and proceed at the same rate as in the past, which is essentially Lyell's principle of **uniformitarianism**.

Box 2.1   Sir Charles Lyell

Charles Lyell (1797–1875) was born in Scotland. Although he initially made a career in law, he had been much influenced by William Buckland, while studying at Oxford, and abandoned law in favour of geology after only a brief period of work in the 1820s. By 1830 he was Professor of Geology at Kings College London. Lyell's first book *Principles of Geology*, published in three volumes between 1830 and 1833, was his most influential. In it he established the principle of uniformitarianism; that the present is the key to the past. The book had a great influence on Charles Darwin, who took Volume 1 with him on the Beagle and had Volume 2 sent to him in South America. Although Lyell became a close friend of Darwin and a long-time correspondent, he didn't embrace evolution in his *Principles* until the 10th edition. In 1863, Lyell published *Geological Evidences of the Antiquity of Man*. This book compiled the evidence for human antiquity. It linked anthropology and archaeology through the geological evidence and had as profound an influence on young geologists as had his *Principles* on a previous generation.

So when a fossil is discovered in a layer of rock (a bed), it is possible to place that fossil within a geological context that will give a relative date – younger than the layers below and older than the layers above. If these layers of rock can be linked to other rock formations it is possible to build up a sequence of beds whose relative ages are known. To then fix these relative ages in time, an absolute date for one or more of the beds is required. There are several absolute dating methods that are in use. Each has advantages and limitations, and note that absolutely does not mean the same as precise; all dates have an uncertainty associated with them that derives from the method. Fossils themselves cannot be dated directly at present, so to give a date to the fossil we have to get the date of the layer in which it was found. However, many fossils do not conveniently turn up in situ in a dateable layer.

◆ Suggest some sites other than within a layer of rock or ash, where human fossils might be discovered.

◆ You might suggest caves or places where rivers had washed out fossils.

Dating of fossils that have been removed from their original site of fossilization is more difficult, but not always impossible. Caves represent a particular problem and we consider this further in discussing South African finds, in Section 5.6. In fact, most anthropologists rely on identifying sites where weathering and erosion exposes fossils as the rarity of human fossils makes digging directly into undisturbed beds a substantial undertaking with a relatively low chance of success. It is essential to identify the bed from which a fossil originated, before it can be dated.

2.5 Dating techniques

Dating rocks using the rate of decay of radioisotopes was developed by geologists to provide absolute dates for the geological time scale. The oldest method is based on the decay of uranium in crystals, usually Zircon crystals which occur in many igneous rocks, though generally in small amounts. When a crystal of Zircon is forming at a high temperature, around 900 °C, it incorporates uranium but not lead. As it cools, the crystal structure retains the trapped uranium. There are two common isotopes of uranium, ^{238}U and ^{235}U and both are unstable, emitting alpha particles in a series of disintegrations, forming lead (Pb). The time taken for half the uranium atoms to decay to lead, the **half-life**, is different for the two isotopes. For ^{238}U, which decays to ^{206}Pb, the half life is 4.47 billion years and for ^{235}U decaying to ^{207}Pb it is 704 million years. Measuring the ratio of the amount of lead isotope to the amount of undecayed uranium isotope then gives a precise age. For example a ratio of 1 ^{207}Pb:1 ^{235}U in a rock would show that it was 704 million years since the crystals in the rock had cooled.

◆ What age would be given by a ratio of three ^{207}Pb:1 ^{235}U.

◆ 1408 million years. Imagine that there were 100 ^{235}U atoms at the start. After 704 million years there would be 50 ^{207}Pb and 50 ^{235}U. In a further 704 years half the remaining 50 ^{235}U atoms would have decayed to ^{207}Pb, giving 75 ^{207}Pb to 25 ^{235}U, a ratio of 3:1.

An example of a dating method that is well known to non-specialists is carbon dating of the material remains of living organisms. Carbon dating isn't applicable to many human fossil finds as they lie outside the time range of the method. It is actually of more use to archaeologists than most palaeoanthropologists and geologists because one of its limitations is that it can't be used routinely for dates more than 40 000 years before the present time, though special techniques can push the limit to 60 000 years ago. The technique is based on the carbon isotope ^{14}C, whose atom contains two more neutrons than that of the vastly more common stable isotope ^{12}C. ^{14}C is unstable and, over time, decays back to nitrogen. The ^{14}C isotope forms in the upper atmosphere from the interaction between cosmic rays and nitrogen. So a small proportion of the carbon dioxide in the atmosphere is ^{14}C. When plants trap carbon in photosynthesis they trap some ^{14}C which will pass along the food chain. As a result, all animals and plants have the same ratio of ^{12}C to ^{14}C. However, when the animal or plant dies, there will be no further uptake of ^{14}C and the ratio of ^{12}C to ^{14}C will change as the ^{14}C decays to nitrogen. If we know the decay rate and can measure the amount of ^{14}C left in the sample, we can calculate the time since the death of the animal or plant from which the sample came. The half-life of ^{14}C is 5730 ± 40 years.

◆ What reason(s) can you suggest for the limit of 40 000 years for the method?

◆ As the amount of ^{14}C present halves every 5730 years, older objects have smaller amounts of ^{14}C present and it becomes very difficult to make accurate measurements of very low concentrations. Also, contamination from other sources becomes much more significant when there are only low concentrations present in the sample, so there is a practical limit on the age that the technique can measure.

There are two other important techniques that have been applied in anthropology. The first method, developed to derive an absolute date from relatively young rocks, was potassium–argon, a technique specifically applicable to measurements of volcanic lavas or ash. When volcanic lava and ash cools down, it contains potassium, but no argon. Of the potassium present, a small proportion will be ^{40}K which decays to the stable isotope of argon ^{40}Ar with a half-life of 1250 million years. The amount of argon gas trapped within the rock provides a measure of the age of the rock, when compared to the amount of potassium. So two measurements are required and any sample has to be large enough to provide material for each. Young rock will not contain much ^{40}Ar. Because it is possible that some ^{40}Ar might have come from the atmosphere, the amount of ^{36}Ar is also measured. No ^{36}Ar is generated by radioactive decay in the rocks, so knowing the proportion of ^{40}Ar to ^{36}Ar in the atmosphere, a correction can be applied to the figure for the ^{40}Ar content of the lava or ash, to take account of contamination from the atmosphere.

The method was later refined for small samples. The technique is called ^{40}Ar/^{39}Ar dating. If the sample is placed in a neutron beam, ^{39}K can be converted to argon, but in this case a different isotope ^{39}Ar. The argon gas can then be driven off from the sample, for example by heating with a laser, and the ratio of the two argon isotopes will allow the age to be determined.

An early use of potassium–argon dating changed the known time scale of human evolution. A skull discovered by Louis Leakey in Olduvai Gorge was excavated from a stratum known as Bed I that had an estimated age of 600 000 years. The skull was the first of a new species, which Leakey named *Zinjanthropus boisei* – see Section 8.2. Garniss Curtis and Jack Evernden derived absolute dates for some closely related volcanic ash deposits both above and below the cranium and their mean figure of

1.75 Mya almost tripled the age of human ancestry at a stroke. Controversial though this was at the time, more recent measurements with refined techniques have only altered the date slightly, to 1.85 Mya. The bottom of Bed I is dated at 2.10 Mya and the top to 1.23 Mya.

There is a time gap between carbon and potassium–argon dating as carbon dating is possible up to a maximum of 40 000 years, while potassium–argon can be used for ages greater than 100 000. This gap has been bridged by two techniques. One is the uranium-lead technique described earlier. The second technique is **Electron-spin resonance (ESR).** Over time, minerals accumulate a number of trapped electrons that have been knocked out of their orbit by radioactive decay, and then trapped within the crystal lattice. An external magnetic field can force these electrons to vibrate (resonate) and the amount of power absorbed by the sample is directly proportional to the number of trapped electrons, which in turn is directly proportional to the age. ESR can be used to date some fossil material directly, such as teeth as long as there is a sample of the matrix from which the specimen came, so that the level of background radiation can be determined.

2.6 Habitats and environment

The dating of fossils helps to place them in a temporal and evolutionary context, but does not reveal a great deal about the way of life or conditions of the time. However, if the human fossil is found with those of other animals, then the fossil assemblage as a whole may reveal a lot about the type of habitat in which the humans lived. When the fossils of animals that are very similar to extant species are discovered, it is easy to deduce the type of habitat they occupied and thus get indirect evidence of the habitat occupied by the humans. Where there is no modern counterpart it is more difficult, but it is often the teeth and jaws that are preserved as fossils and these yield information about the type of food that the owners fed on. The tooth shown in Figure 2.5 comes from a rodent that was alive in the Late Eocene. As there isn't much wear visible, it was probably a young individual. The strong crests suggest that the animal fed on leaves and the height suggests that it also fed on fruit. We can compare it with the teeth of the present day cane rat.

From a complete assemblage of fossils it is possible to work out the range of food types that were available and hence the type of habitat that might provide these. The ancient mammal whose tooth is shown in Figure 2.5 is thought to have lived in a wooded environment surrounded by ponds and lakes containing water plants such as water lilies and pondweeds. Information about diet can also come from measuring the ratio of two stable isotopes of carbon in dental enamel, as you will read later on in Section 6.9.

Clues about ancient vegetation can come from pollen and spores. Both are microscopic and very resistant to decay. Pollen is produced by the reproductive system of flowering plants and conifers. Ferns and mosses release spores. Examples of both are shown in Figure 2.6. Although some pollen grains are quite distinctive and can be

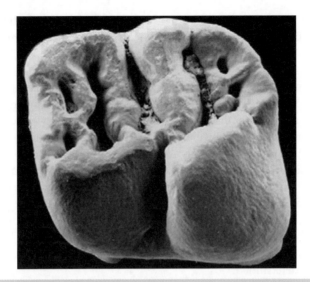

Figure 2.5   A scanning electron micrograph of a tooth of an Eocene mammal, showing a structure that indicates that this mammal fed on leaves, probably with some fruit. The nearest living animal is the cane rat.
Source: http://www.gl.rhbnc.ac.uk/schools/cabinet01/drawer07a.htm

assigned to a genus, others, such as many grasses, can only be classified in a larger group as 'grasses'. Pollen is dispersed by wind or animals and may be preserved, for example, in lake sediments. When a pollen sample is collected and analyzed it provides two broad types of evidence. Firstly, there will be pollen that has been carried over a distance in the air and giving a general picture of the vegetation over a wide area. Secondly, the sample should provide a good idea of the local plant assemblage. Both these types of evidence allow deductions to be made about the climate that existed at the time.

If there are thick sediments representing deposition over a long period, then changes in the pollen samples with time will indicate climate and habitat changes. For example in Africa, core samples from Lake Malawi have provided records from the present to 1.5 Mya. The records show that there was a drought in that part of Africa between 135 and 75 000 years ago, followed by much more humid conditions 70 000 years ago (Scholz *et al.*, 2007).

Another useful indicator of ancient environments and climate is the remains of beetles. At some fossil sites up to 200 species of beetle have been identified. Many of today's beetle species have existed for several million years, so it is possible to deduce the climatic conditions at fossil sites from a knowledge of where the species live today. Beetles are quite sensitive to climate and may have a specialized habitat, such as association with a particular plant. One species on its own may not give sufficient clues about the climate, but the beetle assemblage at a particular site should give a composite picture that is quite accurate.

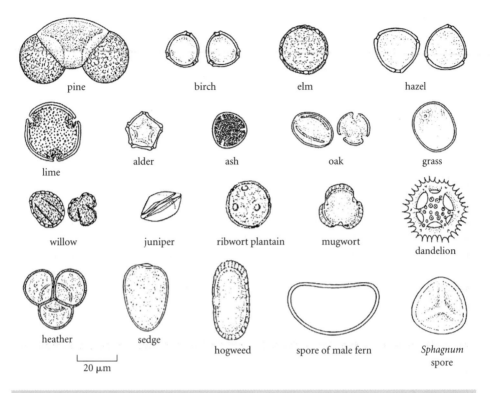

pine

birch

elm

hazel

lime

alder

ash

oak

grass

willow

juniper

ribwort plantain

mugwort

dandelion

heather

sedge

hogweed

spore of male fern

Sphagnum spore

20 µm

Figure 2.6 A variety of spores and pollen grains.
Reproduced from Wilson *et al.* (1999) P164.

2.7 Climate changes and long-term cycles

The orbit of the Earth has cyclical variations which can influence the climate. The angle between the planet's rotational axis and the orbital plane currently varies by 2.4 degrees. The time taken for the angle to change from 22.1 to 24.5 degrees and then back again is roughly 41 000 years. The effect of this change is that as the angle increases, the difference between summer and winter temperatures becomes greater and winters get cooler while summers get warmer. The effect is asymmetric in that the magnitude of the cooling of the winter is not the same as the magnitude of the warming of the summer. The maximum and minimum figures might well have been different in the past.

The orbit is elliptical and the shape of the ellipse varies over a cycle of roughly 100 000 years, this figure being the mean of several components. The overall effect is that the distances between the earth and the sun at both the closest approach and when they are the furthest apart vary cyclically. The climatic effect is to alter the relationship between the length of winter relative to summer and the length of spring relative to autumn.

A further influence on climate comes from the 'wobble' in the axis of rotation. The direction of the axis relative to the stars changes with a period of about 26 000 years.

This explanation is a very simplistic account of the cycles that influence the changing position of the earth relative to the sun. The cycles and their interactions are very complex and the influences that they have on climate are complex too. Changes in climate have played a part in the evolution of humans and an understanding of the influence of these long term cycles will help to explain the changes in climate that is revealed in the fossil record.

Summary

There are a number of geological processes that influence evolution and there are features of the Earth's orbital motion that influence climate. The continental plates have changed position on the earth's surface over time and the movement has meant that climatic conditions have changed too. Volcanic eruptions have sometimes been of sufficient magnitude to effect climate. The relative geological time scale was established in the nineteenth century and estimates of the dates of particular formations were made. With the study of radioactive isotopes came techniques for measuring the absolute ages of rocks.

Questions

Question 2.1

How many reversals of the Earth's magnetic field have there been since 4 Mya and what was the date of the last one?

Question 2.2

What advantage might beetle remains have over pollen samples as indicators of local climate? (*Learning Outcome B1*)

Question 2.3

How was it possible to determine so precisely the age of a fossil discovered in Olduvai Gorge and originally called *Zinjanthropus*? (*Learning Outcome A4*)

References

Scholz, C.A., Johnson, T.C., Cohen, A.S., King, J.W., Peck, J.A., Overpeck, J.T., Talbot, M.R., Brown, E.T., Kalindekafe, L., Amoako, P.Y.O., Lyons, R.P., Shanahan, T.M., Castaneda, I.S., Heil, C.W., Forman, S.L., McHargue, L.R., Beuning, K.R. Gomez, J. and Pierson, J. (2007) East African megadroughts between 135 and 75 thousand years ago and bearing on early-modern human origins. *Proceedings of the National Academy of Sciences*, **104**, 16416–16421.

Wilson, R.C.L., Drury, S. A. and Chapman, J. L. (1999) *The Great Ice Age*. Oxford University Press.

3

Evolution and Natural Selection

Evolution, change over time, is evident from the fact that many organisms that exist today are different from those found in the fossil record. Yet it is possible to see relationships between fossils and living forms that are a clear indicator of changes taking place with time. The changes that have taken place have been driven by varied processes, but a principal one is natural selection. In this chapter we examine the phenomenon of evolution by natural selection and the interaction with genes.

3.1 Darwin and the origin of species by natural selection

Charles Darwin (1809–1882) stands out as a giant figure in biology. His voyage on the Beagle, from December 1831 to October 1836, gave him the opportunity to observe the natural history of many Pacific and Atlantic islands and parts of South America and Australia. Yet Darwin's short spell of just 5 weeks on the Galápagos Islands subsequently had a great impact on his ideas. Amongst the descriptions of iguanas and giant tortoises in his journal, he recorded that he had seen groups of finches on the islands, all of them similar, with grey brown or black plumage, but with distinct variants of beak shape and size. The ornithologist, John Gould, told Darwin that he had classified the finches into 13 species, and that particular species were found on different islands. During their visit to the islands, the captain of the Beagle and Darwin collected specimens of the finches for detailed study. Darwin regretted later that he had not recorded the islands where he had collected them. Nevertheless, John Gould's description of the various finches and his division of them into species, provided

The Emergence of Humans Patricia Ash and David Robinson
© 2010 John Wiley & Sons, Ltd

Darwin with much food for thought. He wrote in his account of his voyage in the Beagle:

> Seeing this gradation and diversity of structure in one small, intimately related group of birds, one might really fancy that, from an original paucity of birds in this archipelago, one species had been taken and modified for different ends (Darwin, 1839).

Darwin's experiences in the Galápagos were followed by his scientific observations. At his home, Down House in Kent, he studied variation in people and other animals over many years (Box 3.1). For example, one of his important scientific investigations involved a study of fancy breeds of pigeons.

Box 3.1 Charles Darwin

Having briefly studied medicine at Edinburgh University and feeling that he was not cut out for a career as a physician, Darwin went to Christ's College in Cambridge in preparation for becoming a clergyman. He received a good scientific training at Cambridge, even though it was not part of his religious studies. When an opportunity to join an expedition came up he abandoned his studies and joined HMS Beagle as a companion to the ship's captain, Robert Fitzroy. During the voyage Darwin gradually became convinced that biological evolution had occurred, but more importantly for the future, he saw how it could have happened through natural selection. He did not publish his ideas until almost 20 years after the end of the voyage, when he and Alfred Russel Wallace, who had been reasoning along the same lines as Darwin, both had papers read at the Linnean Society in London on 1 July 1858. John Murray published Darwin's book *On the Origin of Species by Mean of Natural Selection*, on 24 November 1859 and the quiet revolution in biological thinking became a very public one. Darwin continued to work on a wide variety of biological problems, while living quietly at his Kent home, Down House. He published further work, notably *The Descent of Man* and *Selection in Relation to Sex*.

3.1.1 The idea of 'selection'

During the nineteenth century, the keeping and breeding of fancy pigeons was a popular and competitive hobby, and many peculiar breeds were available. In 1855, Darwin joined several London pigeon fancier clubs and obtained at least 8 different varieties of specially bred pigeons that he kept in a loft in the grounds of Down House. The varieties look very different from each other, and could be regarded as different species by someone who is unfamiliar with pigeon breeds. Darwin allowed several of the fancy varieties to interbreed and after just a few generations, obtained birds with a similar body shape, colour and pattern of plumage, as the rock pigeon, *Columba livia*. Darwin was convinced that all the fancy pigeon breeds were descended from the one ancestor, the rock pigeon. He knew that the fancy variants were derived from selective breeding; he had heard pigeon fanciers using the term 'selection' for describing their choice of breeding birds. Breeders had selected birds with the desired features for breeding and eliminated those with unwanted characters until a distinct breed or strain was obtained. Those breeds are maintained by careful selection of pairs of birds having the desired features.

Darwin realized that the idea of selection is a key concept for understanding evolution and the link between selection and evolution underpinned his thoughts and investigations for many years. Darwin understood that a similar process to selective breeding would explain the origin of species. The essence of Darwin's theory of natural selection is that for a species in a particular environment, those individuals having variants of features that enhance their survival, will be more likely to live long enough to produce viable offspring. This point can be illustrated by the following thought experiment.

Imagine a scenario where an ancient primate species lived in tropical rain forest, rich in a diversity of trees bearing abundant soft fruits. Gradual cooling of the climate meant that the soft fruit trees died out but tree species with tough spiny leaves and nuts with tough fibrous husks flourished. Some individuals in the primate population had unusually large molar teeth, and managed to chew the husks and nuts sufficiently to obtain enough nutrition to survive, grow to maturity and breed. Let's make two assumptions. Firstly, that large molar size was a heritable character and secondly that, on average, each individual with large molars reared two offspring to maturity. Individuals with small cheek teeth did not do well, with each individual producing less than two surviving offspring. So in an environment where soft fruit trees were depleted, individuals with the larger cheek teeth could eat the tougher fruits and survive to rear offspring that inherited this character. As the soft fruit trees declined, individuals with the enlarged molars increased in numbers in succeeding generations. Therefore the frequency of the heritable variation, large molars, in the population increased also. This is a simple hypothetical example that shows how natural selection operates.

In reality the situation would not be quite so simple but there are real examples where changes in the environment of primates have been catastrophic, for example recent conversion of African rainforests to farmland. Environmental pressures are the agents that exert selective pressure on wild species. Food or rather the lack of it is an enormous selective pressure for all animal species, including ourselves, as we shall see in succeeding chapters. The enlarged cheek teeth of our hypothetical primate can be regarded as an example of **adaptation**, a heritable feature in the structure or chemistry of an organism that helps it to survive and breed in its environment.

In Chapter 3 of *On the Origin of Species* (Darwin, 1859), Darwin set out to explain his theory of natural selection, and to discuss the necessary circumstances for natural selection to occur. Darwin was aware that an important condition for natural selection to occur is that *species produce many more offspring than can survive*, and he explored the consequences of unlimited survival of all offspring of humans and other animals. At the time that he wrote *On the Origin of Species*, the human population had doubled in about 25 years, and Darwin pointed out that if this rate of increase were allowed to continue for man, in a few thousand years, 'there would literally be no standing room for his progeny'. However, population increases of species are checked, because there is competition between individuals of the same species, as well as between different species for resources. Darwin introduced the concept of a *struggle for existence* that encompasses not just physical battles between individuals, but also other aspects, such as the need to find food and water in times of shortage, the avoidance of predators and resistance to disease. *Variations in features* between individuals may provide possibilities for improvements or reductions in the ability to survive to adulthood. Darwin appreciated that *such variations have to be heritable* in order to be acted on by natural selection, with the offspring inheriting features present in their parents.

The thought experiment above considers how an advantageous character might spread within an interbreeding population. How then, might separation of a population into more than one species occur? The Galápagos had shown Darwin that geographical separation could lead to divergence in separated populations and the formation of new species. This type of speciation is now called **allopatric speciation**. The literal meaning of allopatric is 'other country'. However, Darwin also thought that the most likely place for divergence to start was within a crowded single population, with the geographical separation following later. This form of speciation is now called **sympatric speciation** (literally 'same country'). He was well aware that constant blending of divergent characters within a population might act *against* separation, which made it more difficult to see how sympatric speciation might occur. Reproductive isolation is necessary and there are ways in which that might appear in an interbreeding population. For example, a new form might arise that was active at different times of the day, or showed a change in reproductive behaviour. There are good examples of sympatric speciation in insect populations, but there is a view amongst some biologists that normally interbreeding within a population will be at too high a rate for speciation to occur. Sympatric speciation is still a controversial area of evolutionary theory today.

Darwin was hampered by his lack of knowledge of genetics, which was a huge gap in the foundation for his theory. Although he knew that for natural selection to occur it was essential that features were heritable, he did not understand how features of parents were transmitted to their offspring. Yet what we have learned about inheritance of characters and molecular genetics since Darwin, has shown that his theory is a valid one. The modern synthesis of evolution blends Darwin's theory with genetics and molecular biology, and Darwin's ideas are supported by evidence derived from anatomy, genetics and molecular biology.

3.2 The modern synthesis of evolution

Darwin would have been interested to know that research during the twentieth century established that characters of a species are determined by genes, which are lengths of deoxyribonucleic acid, DNA, composed of two long sequences of chemicals known as nucleotides, organized as a double helix (Figure 3.1). A nucleotide molecule contains one

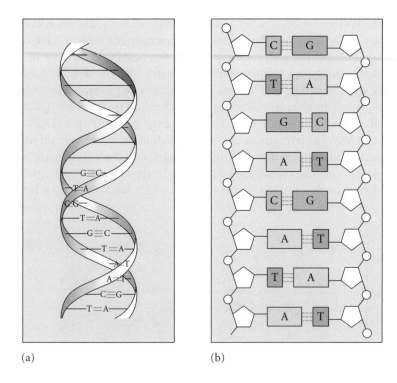

(a)   (b)

Part of base sequence from normal adult human haemoglobin, HbA

Nucleotide	CTG	ACT	CCT	GAG	GAG	AAG	TCT
Amino acid	Leu	Thr	Pro	Glu	Glu	Lys	Ser

Part of base sequence from adult human haemoglobin, HbS

Nucleotide	CTG	ACT	CCT	GTG	GAG	AAG	TCT
Amino acid	Leu	Thr	Pro	Val	Glu	Lys	Ser

(c)

Figure 3.1 (a) Part of a DNA molecule showing the double helix structure with the two strands of nucleotides linked by bases (b) Part of an unwound DNA helix, showing how base pairing obeys the base pairing rules, A-T and C (A = adenine; T= thymine; C = cytosine; G = guanine). (c) Part of the sequence of DNA codons for haemoglobin. The first sequence is from normal adult human haemoglobin A (HbA). The sequence below it is identical except for one change in the code, which produces a different amino acid. Valine is substituted for Glutamate. Haemoglobin with this substitution is HbS, the haemoglobin type present in humans with sickle-cell anaemia. (a and b) Reproduced from Human Biology Book 1 P67. © The Open University.

of four bases. Within the DNA molecule, specific trios of bases, known as **codons**, code for particular amino acids. So the genetic code is a code for protein molecules, and a gene is a string of codons, each coding for an amino acid. The sequence of codons in a DNA molecule provides a template for protein synthesis. The direct link between the genetic code and proteins reflects the crucial importance of proteins in living organisms.

The bodies of all animals are studied at various levels of organization, gross anatomy, tissue, cellular, biochemical and molecular. The gross anatomy of animals comprises organs such as liver, kidney, muscle and bone, which in turn are made up tissues composed of specialized cells. Cells and the matrix material in tissues, are made up of large molecules known as macromolecules, including carbohydrates, lipids, proteins and nucleic acids such as deoxyribonucleic acid, DNA, which holds the genetic information.

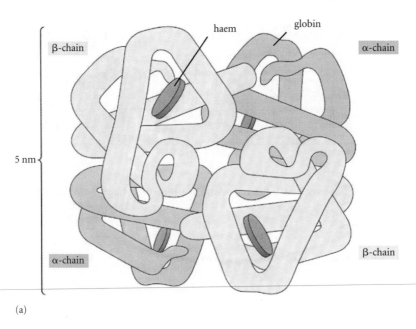

(a)

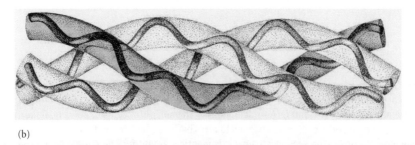

(b)

Figure 3.2 (a) Structure of haemoglobin, a globular protein in red blood cells, that can bind up to four oxygen molecules (b) structure of collagen the fibrous protein that forms the framework of bone. Reproduced from: (a) Biology: Uniformity and Diversity Book 3(1) P73. (b) Discovering Science Book 9 P.22. © The Open University.

DNA and also signalling molecules such as hormones, operate at a molecular level, initiating synthesis of proteins and cellular responses respectively. Such large molecules are organized structurally and functionally inside the body cells (Figure 3.2(a) and 3.2(b)). For all cells, proteins are of crucial importance. Globular proteins such as enzymes and haemoglobin are made of amino acid chains, wound together forming complex and specific shapes. Fibrous proteins such as keratin and collagen in contrast have a fibre-like shape, and form the structure of the outer layer of skin, hair, claws, nails, bone and the connective tissues that provide a framework for the structure of organs (Figure 3.2(b)). Muscle consists of special contractile proteins, and the skeleton is constructed on a framework of collagen.

Other macromolecules, carbohydrates and lipids, are important cellular energy stores in liver, muscle and fat. The synthesis of all macromolecules depends on enzymes, which are proteins. The molecular structure of each protein is determined by its amino acid sequence, which in turn is coded for by genes consisting of base sequences in DNA, for example the part coding sequence for the molecule haemoglobin shown in Figure 3.1(c). Protein synthesis begins by unwinding the part of the DNA molecule that contains the base sequence coding for that particular protein. The base sequence is copied on to another nucleic acid molecule, messenger RNA, (mRNA), which as its name implies, carries the information out of the nucleus and into the cytoplasm. Synthesis of mRNA from the DNA template is known as **transcription**. The codons in the mRNA are then used as a template for protein synthesis, which occurs in special organelles in cell cytoplasm known as the rough endoplasmic reticulum (Figure 3.3). Synthesis of proteins from the mRNA template is known as **translation**.

The procedure can be summarized as: DNA makes RNA makes protein, often called the Central Dogma of molecular biology, although subsequently it was shown that information could also flow from RNA to DNA.

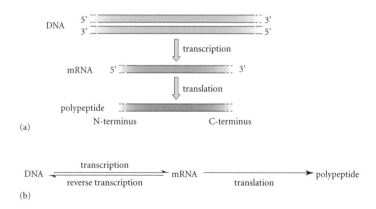

Figure 3.3 The role of mRNA in DNA transcription and translation. (a) Information flow from DNA to mRNA to polypeptide chain that will then fold to form a protein molecule. (b) A revision of the Central Dogma of molecular biology that shows reverse information flow from mRNA to DNA. Reproduced from Biology: Uniformity and Diversity Book 3(2) P35. © The Open University.

3.2.1 DNA makes mRNA makes protein

So far our description suggests that the structure of proteins is immutable but this is far from being the case. In individuals of every species, there are mutations, which are spontaneous changes in bases in codons.

◆ What would be the effect of a spontaneous change in a base in a codon within a gene?

◆ It is likely that the codon could code for a different amino acid, causing a change in the amino acid sequence of the protein coded for by the gene.

Harmful and lethal mutations are rare. Although most mutations have little apparent benefit or harm associated with them, mutant genes provide the raw material for natural selection. A harmless or slightly harmful mutation in individuals living in a particular environment may become beneficial should the environment alter. A well-known human example is the mutant haemoglobin gene that is the cause of sickle cell anaemia. The replacement of just one base in the gene coding for haemoglobin, causes the replacement of one amino acid, glutamine, with another, valine (Figure 3.1(c)). The change in amino acid alters the structure of the haemoglobin molecule so that it no longer folds into the correct shape.

Each individual has two copies of most genes, one copy inherited from the father and the other inherited from the mother. If an individual has two copies of the sickle cell gene, full-blown sickle cell anaemia develops. The mutant haemoglobin molecules cannot fold correctly and the red blood cells have a characteristic sickle shape that gets jammed inside tissue capillary beds causing intense pain. The oxygen carrying capacity of sickle cell haemoglobin is poor, causing lassitude and collapse in the affected person. In contrast individuals bearing just one copy of the sickle cell gene do not develop sickle cell anaemia. There is a slight reduction in the oxygen carrying capacity of haemoglobin, but the individual has a high resistance to malaria. For populations living in many parts of Africa where malaria is endemic, the sickle cell gene is relatively common, because of the selective advantage it provides in an environment where there is malaria. In contrast, for people of African descent who live in the United States, there is no advantage in having the sickle cell gene, and frequency of the sickle cell gene is declining there.

Now consider the mutant gene in rats that enables them to survive death by poisoning from intake of the anticoagulant warfarin. When warfarin was first used as a rat poison in the 1950s, rats had no resistance to the poison and entire populations of rats died out to the delight of farmers, those working in food processing industries and indeed anyone who had problems with rats. However it wasn't long before rats with resistance to warfarin were discovered living happily in environments where warfarin was present. The mutant gene for resistance was very rare in the rat population, but the presence of warfarin meant that only those few rats having the mutant gene could survive. In an environment without warfarin, having the mutant resistance gene conferred no advantage, indeed these rare mutant rats were at a disadvantage as the biochemical pathway that confers resistance is 'wasteful' in that it uses up precious energy. For wild animals the slightest disadvantage can compromise survival. The mutant gene for warfarin resistance is known as a **dominant gene**, which is expressed even if there is just one copy. So any rat with one copy of the warfarin resistance gene, inherited either from the mother or the father, will be resistant to the poison.

The presence of warfarin in the environment exerts a strong selective pressure; rats that do not have the resistance gene die if they eat warfarin. The original small population of rats bearing the mutant gene increased rapidly because the huge birth rate of rats meant rapid proliferation of resistant rats and the near 100% death rate of the non-mutant rats removed competition for resources.

3.3 Inheritance of characters

Each individual has a set of genes that determine appearance, metabolism and indeed the entire set of heritable features. An organism's appearance and the observable characteristics are known as the **phenotype** of the organism. We saw in the previous section that a gene is a length of DNA that codes for a particular protein. The overall set of genes of an individual is known as the **genotype** and individuals inherit their genotypes from their parents. DNA does not exist as molecules floating around inside cells. The DNA is condensed into thread like structures known as chromosomes inside cells. Humans have a total of 46 chromosomes, 23 pairs with one member of each pair derived from the mother and the other derived from the father (Figure 3.4). Each chromosome contains a characteristic set of genes. For example chromosomes 9 and 11 carry genes involved in determining hair colour. Some genes determine single characters and these have been used as models for understanding gene inheritance. Gregor Mendel's research (published in 1866), involved crossing strains of pea plants which had easily identifiable features, such as long or short stems, and counting the numbers of offspring with each of the features. The ratios of offspring bearing the features enabled Mendel to work out the principles of inheritance that still apply today, to animals as well as plants. Mendel was unaware of the existence of genes but we can now apply what we know about genes to the ratios established by Mendel's experiments. Within an individual each gene exists as two copies, which may be identical, or different. Different versions of specific genes are known as **alleles**. Note however that the genes that determine male sex that are present as one copy only on the male Y chromosome (Figure 3.4) and 'pair' with the female genes on the female sex chromosome X. The huge variety of combinations of alleles in a species, complemented by new mutations, provides the raw material for natural selection.

For simplicity we now examine the inheritance of one dominant mutant gene that causes **achondroplasia**, failure of the normal growth mechanisms in long bones resulting in short limbs and short stature. The gene is located in chromosome 4, and as we saw in Section 3.2.1, a mutant gene arises by means of a change in the base sequence. Most cases of achondroplasia known today arise as a result of new mutation, so babies having the condition are usually the first known in a family. Studies of families that have several members with achondroplasia, have shown that this mutant

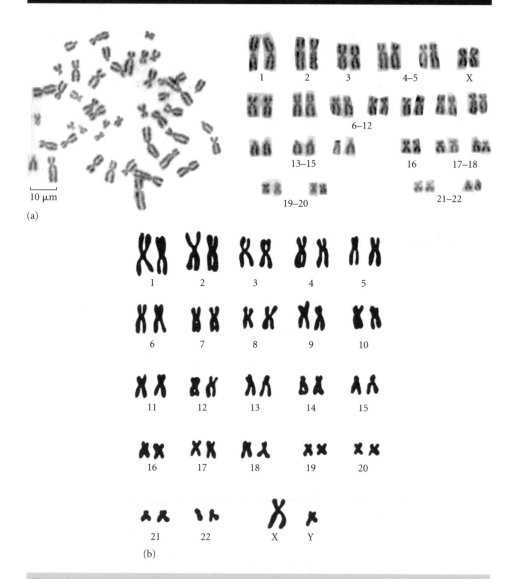

Figure 3.4 The 23 pairs of human chromosomes. This type of preparation is known as a karyotype and is made by photographing human cells that are dividing. Individual chromosomes are cut out of a digital photograph on a computer screen, and the chromosomes rearranged in pairs and numbered as shown. The karyotype in (a) is from a female while that shown in (b) is from a male, as can be seen from the presence of the Y chromosome. A male has the sex chromosomes XY, and a female has sex chromosomes XX. Reproduced from (a) and (b) Discovering Science Book 9 P.77. © The Open University.

gene is dominant. The relative proportions of offspring born with a genetic condition can be worked out by means of a simple Punnet square (named after the scientist who devised this method). The columns and rows are headed respectively by the possible genotypes of the maternal and paternal gametes. The genotypes of the parents

Table 3.1 (a) Inheritance of achondroplasia. The mother has genotype *Aa*, and has achondroplasia; the father has normal stature and his genotype is *AA*. The presence of the gene *A* causes achondroplasia. The mother produces 50% eggs with the genotype *a*, that codes for normal skeletal growth and 50% with genotype *A* that codes for achondroplasia. The father produces spermatozoa with genotype *a* only

So genotype of parental generation, P: mother *Aa* × father *aa*		
Maternal gametes: 50% *A* and 50% *a* Paternal gametes: 100% *a* Punnet square for offspring, **F1 generation:**		
Genotypes of gametes	Egg *a*	Egg *A*
Sperm *a*	*Aa*	*Aa*

Table 3.1 (b) The mother and father have genotype *Aa*, and both have achondroplasia. The mother and father produces 50% gametes with the genotype *a*, that codes for normal skeletal growth and 50% with genotype *A* that codes for achondroplasia

So genotype of parental generation, P: mother *Aa* × father *Aa*		
Genotypes of gametes	Egg *A*	Egg *a*
Sperm *A* Sperm *a*		

are written as simple letters; by convention the dominant gene is given a capital letter and the recessive gene the lower case version of that letter. Table 3.1(a) shows that if the father has two copies of the normal gene, denoted as '*a*', all his sperm will have the '*a*' genotype. If the mother has one copy of the normal gene for growth, '*a*', and one copy of the achondroplasia gene, '*A*', half of her egg cells will have genotype '*a*' and half will have genotype '*A*'. The Punnet square demonstrates that there is a 50% chance that each child they have will inherit the achondroplasia gene, and will be affected by achondroplasia. The ratio of offspring in the offspring, denoted as the F1 generation, is 1 : 1.

◆ Study Table 3.1(b) and fill in the Punnet square to work out the genotypes of the offspring of two parents with achondroplasia, each having one mutant a gene and one normal A gene. What are the relative proportions of genotypes in the offspring?

◆ There is a 25% chance that each child will have two achondroplasia genes and a 50% chance that each child will have just one achondroplasia gene. One in four of the offspring will be of normal stature and not have an achondroplasia gene.

Table 3.2 (a) Punnet square for calculating proportions of genotypes of offspring from parents each with one mutant *TYR* gene for albinism, b. The *TYR* gene for normal pigmentation is denoted as *B*

P generation: parent genotypes: father *Bb* × mother *Bb*		
Genotypes of gametes	Egg *b*	Egg *B*
Sperm *b*	*bb*	*BB*
Sperm *B*	*Bb*	*BB*

Table 3.2 (b) Punnet square for calculating proportion of offspring from a father with one albino gene, *Bb*, and a mother with two albino genes, *bb*

P generation: parent genotypes: father *BB* × *Bb*		
Genotypes of gametes	Egg *b*	Egg *b*
Sperm *b*		
Sperm *B*		

Use of the Punnet square for working out ratios of genotypes of offspring provide us with the same ratios as were observed by Mendel in his studies of pea plants. A single recessive gene in an individual is not expressed if the other copy of the gene is dominant. Albinism is a rare recessive genetic condition in which pigment is lacking from the iris of the eyes and in most types of albinism, also skin, and hair. About 1 in 17 000 people in the United Kingdom is affected by albinism. Other mammals have albinism too. For example a male albino gorilla, Floquet de Neu, lived at Barcelona Zoo for 27 years and fathered 27 children, none of whom inherited his albinism. Floquet de Neu did not have truly white hair; his hair was blonde, as is the case for most people who have albinism. The genes that determine pigmentation of skin and hair are found on several chromosomes, but for simplicity we will focus on chromosome 11, and the *TYR* gene, which codes for the enzyme that stimulates synthesis of melanin. A recessive mutation in the *TYR* gene causes complete albinism in which there is no pigment in skin, hair or eyes. Individuals with just one copy of the *TYR* gene albino gene will have normal skin, hair and eye pigmentation. Table 3.2(a) shows the genotypes of the offspring of two people who each have an albino gene and a normal *TYR* gene for skin pigmentation.

◆ Examine the Punnet square in Table 3.2(a). What are the relative proportions of offspring who would inherit albinism? What percentage of offspring would have one copy of the albinism gene?

◆ Twenty-five per cent of children would have two copies of the gene for albinism and would have albino features; 50% of the children would have one copy of the albinism gene and would have normal pigmentation; 25% of children will not carry the albinism gene.

♦ Complete the Punnet square in Table 3.2(b) and work out the relative proportions of albinism and normal pigmentation in the offspring.

♦ Fifty per cent of children will have two copies of the albinism gene and will have albino traits; 50% of children will have one copy of the albinism gene and will have normal pigmentation.

We can see from our Punnet squares that inheritance of individual characters obeys relatively simple rules, which were discovered by Mendel. Furthermore, we can appreciate how an important criterion in Darwin's list of requirements for natural selection is fulfilled. Genetic characters are hereditary and determined by genes. Genes can be either dominant or recessive; a third category is incomplete dominance. The sickle cell gene shows incomplete dominance as those people who have just one copy have a slight anaemia that is not usually life threatening, but prevents establishment of the malaria parasite. Hence the sickle cell mutant gene has a high frequency in many human populations in Africa, even though it is lethal in those individuals who have two copies.

In this section we have examined single mutations in single genes. Bear in mind that primate genomes contain many thousands of genes, organized within chromosomes. For example, the human genotype is contained in 46 chromosomes, which are 23 pairs, each pair comprising one chromosome from the mother and one from the father. Of course in a pair of chromosomes, both the maternal and paternal versions (with the exception of the sex chromosomes in males) have the same set of genes, but are likely to have different versions or alleles of many of these genes. For example, paternal chromosome 11 may have the normal gene for haemoglobin; the maternal chromosome 11 may have the mutant haemoglobin gene that causes sickle cell anaemia. Each member of each pair of chromosomes has many alleles different from the other chromosome of the pair. Hence there is a huge genetic variation in eggs (oocytes) and sperm, leading to great variation in people. Even within families no two individuals look the same, not even siblings, but they may have particular features in common, or look completely different!

The process of formation of eggs and sperm, gametogenesis, reshuffles the parental alleles resulting in **recombination**, providing another major source of variability in populations of humans and other primates. So particular combinations of alleles are not likely to be inherited but the advantage of such variability is that during hard times, for example, drought and consequent lack of food, a few individuals may have a combination of genes that enable them to survive until the food supplies are re-established, ensuring survival of the population.

3.4 Population genetics

Now we have examined the mechanisms of inheritance we can consider how this science is linked to Darwin's theory of evolution by natural selection.

♦ Which type of favourable mutant gene would spread most rapidly through a population of animals, dominant or recessive? Explain your reasoning.

♦ A dominant gene would spread more rapidly than a recessive gene because both individuals with just one or two copies of the gene would be more likely to survive and produce offspring thereby increasing the rate of spread of the gene.

The process by which the frequency of a mutant gene increases so much within a population of animals that it becomes the norm, is known as **gene fixation**. In fact a change in the proportions of phenotypes in a population can be regarded as a salient feature of evolution by natural selection. To illustrate this imagine a hypothetical population of primates living in an Oligocene forest around 30 mya. The simplified scenario is that initially the forest where the primates lived had dense stands of trees bearing soft juicy fruits. As the climate became drier, the soft fruit trees died off and were replaced by the hardier tree species bearing hard nuts encased in fibrous husks. In the population there was a recessive gene mutation which, in individuals who were homozygous for the mutation, resulted in large cheek teeth. Initially, the proportion of individuals with large cheek teeth was small. We will designate the mutant gene as 'l'. The normal or '**wild-type**' gene can be designated as 'L'. The total reservoir of genes in a population of animals is known as the gene pool, and most of the genes for molar tooth size would be the wild type 'L' allele. There would be just a few of the mutant genes 'l' and they would rarely come together in the same individual to produce a homozygous recessive individual with large cheek teeth. So, initially there would be few individuals with the large molars and their numbers might be maintained at a low level because they had no particular advantage in comparison to those having the small cheek teeth, as long as the major part of their diet was soft fruit. As the environment changed and the consequent soft fruit shortage became severe the mutant 'l' gene would increase in frequency, as individuals able to eat the hard fruits would be more likely to survive and produce offspring. In other words the mutant individuals are more likely to survive to breed than the wild types; that is to say, the mutants have a greater fitness than the wild type monkeys. Large cheek teeth confer an advantage in an environment where the major foods available for primates are fruits and nuts with hard shells and fibrous husks. The offspring of the individuals with the larger cheek teeth in turn would be more likely to survive and breed, so in this environment they have increased **fitness**. So natural selection acts on phenotypes thereby changing the frequencies of alleles in the gene pool of a population.

How do the principles of genetics, inheritance and natural selection help us with interpreting the fossil evidence for the evolution of humans? Palaeoanthropologists look at the suite of characters found in particular fossils and work out how they can be linked to other fossil and living species. The more characters that can be identified the more reliable, and objective, are the proposed evolutionary relationships. In particular, we look for characters that are the result of common descent. Such characters are defined as being **homologous**, and they are important as being those that can be used to help determine evolutionary relationships. To identify homology we look for particular features in related species that are derived from the same structure. The forelimbs of vertebrates are variable in appearance and function, but they are all derived from the same structures (Figure 3.5). So the forelimb of a lemur, the arm of a human and even the flipper of a seal are homologous characters. The bones of the forelimb of vertebrates are variable in appearance and function, but they are all derived from the same structure, the **pentadactyl** (five digit) limb. The five digits of the human hand include four fingers and an opposable thumb. In contrast to the fingers of the human hand, those of a bat are enormously elongated, and the thumb is short with a curved claw. The flipper of a porpoise is supported by a pentadactyl limb with very short and robust humerus, ulna and radius, and the digits are apparent but the three central digits have increased numbers of finger bones, known as phalanges.

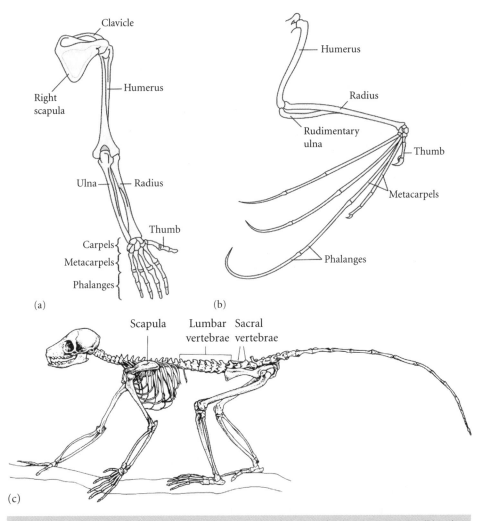

Figure 3.5 The pentadactyl limb of vertebrates. The skeleton of (a) a human arm, (b) a bat wing and (c) a lemur.
Source: (a) and (b) Studying Mammals P36. © The Open University. (c) Rogers (1986) P.165.

◆ Examine the forelimb skeleton of the ringtail lemur, and compare with the human arm (Figure 3.5).

◆ The long bones of the lemur forelimb, the humerus, ulna and radius, are thin. In contrast the long bones of the human arm are relatively robust. Otherwise the forelimb skeletons of the two species are similar, each having similar relative lengths of humerus, radius/ulna and hand.

Where similar selective pressures result in similar adaptations in different animal groups, the adaptive features are described as being **convergent**, or **analogous**. For example, the eyes of primates and other mammals are very similar in structure to the eyes of squid, which are marine predators. Squid are invertebrates, classified in the phylum Mollusca, which also includes snails and slugs. The herbivorous snails and slugs have tiny simple eyes whereas the large eyes of squid are an adaptive feature for a predator that hunts by sight. Good vision is also important for primates who rely on vision for finding and hunting or collecting food and this group also has relatively large eyes. The eyes of squid and mammals are regarded as examples of convergence, as molluscs and mammals are not closely related in evolutionary terms. Convergence illustrates the power of natural selection. Similar selective pressures, relating to searching for food by sight, link to similar adaptive features.

◆ Which groups of characters, convergent or homologous, can be used to construct evolutionary trees? Explain your answer.

◆ Only homologous characters can be used, because by definition, they link species and groups together in an evolutionary sequence.

The distinction between convergent evolution of analogous characters and the development of homologous characters is no longer so simple. Application of molecular analyses of DNA base sequences has shown that some characters thought to be analogous do have a very ancient origin and share the same or similar genes. Convergent evolution of the eye in molluscs and vertebrates is a classic example. Molecular studies have shown that the *Pax-6* gene coding for the transcription factor *Pax-6* is found in the compound eyes of insects, the eye of the squid and vertebrate eyes. Transcription factors are specialized protein molecules that switch on transcription of specific genes. Each transcription factor has a unique protein structure that allows it to bind to a specific gene and to switch on transcription. *Pax-6* may be a universal molecule in animals that controls development of the eye. Researchers demonstrated that when the mouse *Pax-6* gene is integrated into the genome of the fruit fly *Drosophila*, additional eyes are produced where the mouse *Pax-6* gene is expressed. Similar studies have demonstrated that squid *Pax-6* gene inserted into the *Drosophila* genome also generates additional eyes where it is expressed. The salient point here is that the same transcription factor, *Pax-6*, is essential for development of the eye in many animal groups, including vertebrates, insects and molluscs. So the molecule that controls development of the eye is probably ubiquitous in the animal kingdom. Mutations in the *Pax-6* gene can have serious effects. Some mutations cause aniridia, absence of the iris, often associated with faulty development of the retina and impaired vision.

Currently most researchers in palaeoanthropology use cladistics as the system for determining classification schemes for primates based on identifying sets of common homologous characters in fossil species. We shall return to the principles and use of cladistics in the following chapter.

3.5 Geographic isolation and speciation

The variability between individuals in populations can be of great advantage to a species in that this increases the likelihood of some individuals surviving when there is a change in the environment. Large-scale changes in climate cause long-term changes in vegetation cover. Imagine the scenario of a large tropical forest occupied by several species of **arboreal** (tree-dwelling) primates (Figure 3.6). Over thousands of years, climate

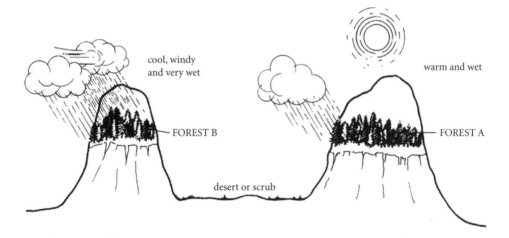

Figure 3.6 Effect of large-scale climate changes on a population of arboreal primates. Two stands of forest that were originally part of a continuous forest are isolated from each other. Over several hundred thousand years the climate had become very dry, so that gradually the forest trees at low elevations died out, and were replaced by desert scrub land. None of the forest animals remain in the desert and were replaced by other species that moved into the developing desert ecosystem. However forest persists on the tops of two mountains at high elevations, where condensation of moisture, especially at night, produces sufficient water to sustain the trees. The climatic conditions in each stand of forest are different in that one mountain top, B has a colder windier climate than the other, A, meaning that the range of tree species in the two forests are not the same. The animal populations in the two stands of forest are isolated from one another. Reproduced from A Science Foundation Course Unit 21 P.23. © The Open University.

change resulted in a cooler and drier climate, causing reduction of forest cover and its replacement by areas of tropical grassland, savannah and scrub desert. Tracts of forests remain on higher ground, on the slopes of two mountain ranges. One of the primate species continues to survive in the forested areas in the mountains, but dies out in the lowland area. Now there are two populations of primates isolated from each other by grassland and scrub desert (Figure 3.6). Over time, differences in the environment on the two mountain ranges become more marked and link to climate changes. One mountain range, B, has a cooler climate than the other, A. Fruit trees bearing soft fruit are more common on the slopes of A but trees bearing hard fruits have become dominant on the slopes of B. Climate changes and the changes in the environment in the slopes of the two mountain ranges link to changes in the phenotype of the two primate populations. Eventually the primates living on the slopes of B have a larger body size than the population on Mount A. The primates on B also have thicker fur than those on A. When differences between the two populations have become so great that the two groups can no longer interbreed, speciation has occurred. Speciation linked to isolation is known as allopatric speciation. While the isolation of populations of animals places them at risk of extinction (because numbers may be small and genetic variability restricted) it also provides opportunities for speciation. The term **adaptive radiation** is used to describe the process of speciation in the descendants of a single species resulting in a diversity of species, each occupying a particular **niche**. The term niche describes the 'space' that an animal occupies within its environment, including the food that it eats, and habitats that it occupies for example, forest canopy, burrow and river bank.

The idea that changes in the environment are the drivers for speciation and adaptive radiation is intuitive and palaeoantologists have been investigating. Elizabeth Vrba (Yale University) proposed the habitat theory, which states that species' responses to climate change are the driver of evolutionary change. Climate change may result in physical barriers or the emigration of populations of animals across barriers, which in turn create isolated populations. Vrba studied ancient populations of African antelopes dated from the late Pliocene to the early Pleistocene, a time of climate change involving global cooling and shift to lower rainfall, resulting in replacement of forest with grasslands. Vrba found that species were disappearing from the record and being replaced by new species. Some of the species had migrated out of cooler areas into warmer areas, coping with climate by migration and effectively tracking it. Such activities may be interpreted incorrectly as evolutionary changes. Nevertheless, Vrba (1993) identified that there were extinctions and also evolution of new species, including hominins. She interpreted the fossil evidence as supporting her turnover pulse hypothesis, which proposed that the late Pliocene climate changes drove a concentrated episode of extinction and speciation about 2.5 mya, described as a turnover episode or pulse. More recent research that focused on fossil finds in the Turkana-Omo basin (Behrensmeyer *et al.*, 1997), suggests that there was no significant pulse at 2–2.5 mya, but rather, a prolonged period of turnover from 3.0 to 2 mya. Other hypotheses for the driver of human evolution are habitat-specific, with each focusing on a particular habitat, and linking adaptations to the features of the habitat. For example, the savannah hypothesis proposed that drier and open environments were the drivers for adaptation during the early evolution of hominins from the late Miocene to the early Pleistocene. However, an extensive review concluded that there is no overall environmental explanation for the evolution of hominins from their ancient primate ancestors (Potts, 1998). The position remains the same today.

As we progress along the evolutionary timeline from the earliest known primates to *Homo* we will examine as far as possible the environmental context for fossil finds. We begin by considering the adaptive radiation of a group of animals regarded by some researchers to be ancestral to true primates, and by others as being a 'sister' group, a branch that diverged from the ancestral group of primates.

Questions

Question 3.1

Explain the 'central dogma' of molecular biology. (*Learning outcome A1*)

Question 3.2

Summarize, as a bulleted list, the aspects of natural selection as defined by Darwin. (*Learning outcome A1*)

Question 3.3

A mutant gene appears in a population which, when expressed, confers greater fitness on the individual. Explain what fitness means in this context. Would the mutant gene spread faster if it was recessive rather than if it was dominant? (*Learning outcomes A1 and C1*)

References

Behrensmeyer, A.K., Todd, N., Potts, R., and McBrinn, G. (1997) Late Pliocene Faunal Turnover in the Turkana Basin, Kenya and Ethiopia. *Science*, **278**, 1589–1594.

Darwin, C. (1839) *The Voyage of the Beagle*, 2nd edn, 1844. London: Henry Colburn.

Darwin, C. (1859) *On the Origin of Species by Means of Natural Selection*. London: John Murray.

Potts, R. (1998) Environmental hypotheses of hominin evolution, in *Yearbook of Physical Anthropology*, Vol. 41, pp. 93–136.

Rogers, E. (1986) *Looking at vertebrates*. Harlow: Longmans.

Vrba, E. S. (2005) Mass turnover and heterochrony events in response to physical change. *Palaeobiology* **31**(2): 157–174.

4

65 – 40 mya: Primate and Anthropoid Origins

The warm conditions found in the Eocene period provided ideal conditions for growth of extensive tropical and sub-tropical forests. Primates with some characteristics similar to those of modern species first appeared around 55 mya, although an earlier group of Palaeocene species have a few primate characteristics. The geographical distribution of early primates was rather different from that of modern primates and they flourished in the forests of North America, Eurasia and Africa. However, at the end of the Eocene epoch the global climate was cooling and the geographical range of the primates reduced.

If the amount of diversity seen in primates today is taken as a guide, then there are fewer species of primate known from the fossils than would be expected. The fossil record of primates is not extensive and it is very patchy. However, it has been estimated that barely 7% of all primates that ever existed are represented in the fossil record (Martin, Soligo and Tavare, 2007), so the real diversity of ancient primates is likely to be greater than the fossil record suggests. It is not possible to identify precisely the place where the first primates appeared and there is some doubt, as you will discover, about exactly which of the very early groups of mammals, are closest to the origin of primates. The fossil record indicates that the earliest known placental mammals may have appeared as long ago as 125 mya, and that the earliest known primates appeared about 56 mya. However, the genetic evidence suggests an earlier date for the origin of primates (Martin, Soligo and Tavare, 2007), around 60–65 mya, and even up to 80–90 mya! Furthermore, there

The Emergence of Humans Patricia Ash and David Robinson
© 2010 John Wiley & Sons, Ltd

is controversy about when and where the earliest anthropoid appeared and we shall be exploring some of the available evidence. The suborder Anthropoidea is of interest with regard to the emergence of humans, because anthropoids include apes and humans as well as New World and Old World monkeys.

♦ Over what time span were (i) mammals and (ii) primates, coexisting with dinosaurs?

♦ (i) If mammals emerged about 125 mya, then they would have coexisted with dinosaurs up to 65 mya, a time span of about 60 million years. (ii) If primates emerged at some point between 80–65 mya then they would have coexisted with dinosaurs up to 65 mya, a time span of about 0–60 million years.

The order Primates are classified within the clade Euarchonta, which is a subdivision of the Superorder Euarchontoglires (Figure 4.1). A **clade** is a group of species that includes the common ancestor of the group and its descendants. The other subdivision of the Euarchontoglires, Glires, comprises the Rodentia and Lagomorpha, forming a **sister group** to the Euarchonta.

Superorder	Euarchontoglires
Glires	Order: Rodentia: rodents
	Order: Lagomorpha: rabbits, hares
Euarchonta	Order: Scandentia: tree shrews
	Order: Dermoptera: colugos (flying lemurs)
	Order: Plesiadapiformes
	Order: Primates

The view of Bloch *et al.* (2007) is that the order Plesiadapiformes, which they define as stem primates, underwent adaptive radiation at the end of the Cretaceous about 65 mya, and that Euprimates and Plesiadapoidea had emerged from this radiation by about 62 mya. Euprimates would then be a sister group to the Plesiadapoidea (Bloch *et al.*, 2007). The evidence for this interpretation was a cladistical analysis using evidence from fossil crania, post-cranial bones and teeth. Various outgroups were used, including Scandentia, Dermoptera and *Asioryctes* (a late Cretaceous mammal) However, according to the fossil record, the first primates had appeared during the early Eocene by about 55 mya either in Africa or possibly Asia. So the existence of a 'ghost lineage' of primates that lasted about 7 million years was proposed. However, recent research using a statistical method (Tavare *et al.*, 2002) based on a model of diversification pattern indicates a common ancestor for primates emerged 81.5 mya. A more recent update of this research proposes that primates emerged as long ago as 80–90 mya (Martin, Soligo and Tavare, 2007). The authors suggest that the end of the Cretaceous extinction event could have stalled the initial adaptive radiation of primates, an intriguing explanation. In that case, the ghost lineage suggested by Bloch *et al.* could represent the start of a second diversification of primates that occurred after the Cretaceous mass extinction event.

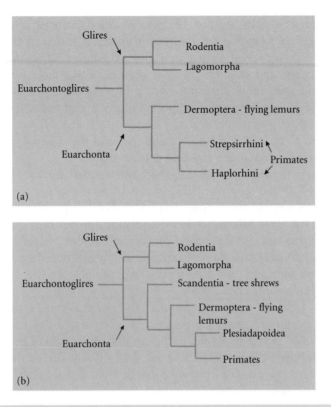

Figure 4.1 (a) Simplified evolutionary tree for primates (adapted from Martin, 2008); (b) simplified evolutionary tree for primates that includes a group within the extinct Plesiadapiformes, the Plesiadapoidea (Bloch, *et al.*, 2007).

Other views of primate origins based on DNA studies interpret the evidence differently, and do not include the Plesiadapiformes. Nevertheless, there is argument about which of the two groups, tree shrews and colugos, are the most closely related to primates. As a result, research has focused on looking for a sister group relationship between primates and another group.

♦ Explain why the identification of a sister group for primates would help to clarify the ancestor of primates.

♦ By definition two sister groups share a common ancestor, which would have diverged into two sister groups. Therefore, there would be some clues to the identity of the common ancestor.

Two hypotheses have been proposed for identifying the common ancestor. The Primatomorpha hypothesis asserts that colugos and primates are sister groups and so had a common ancestor. In contrast, the Sundatheria hypothesis is that tree shrews and colugos together form a sister group to primates. A recent investigation of the molecular evidence identified shared indels in Primates, Colugos and Scandentia. Indels are insertions and deletions in gene sequences that code for proteins. The researchers found seven indels that supported colugos as the closest living relatives of primates. No indels were found that supported the view that tree shrews and colugos together form a sister group to primates. So, according to this evidence, primates and colugos are likely to be a sister group because they had the closest evolutionary relationship in terms of shared indels (Janecka *et al.*, 2007).

However research studies on SINES, short interspersed nuclear elements (short DNA sequences 100–500 base pairs long inserted into the genome) provided a different view (Kriegs *et al.*, 2007). The data confirmed the position of Glires as the sister taxon for the Euarchonta, but left the relationship between the three groups, Scandentia, Primates and Dermoptera unresolved. Other research studies have reached different conclusions. An investigation of cytogenetic evidence from a study of chromosomes, indicated that tree shrews and colugos together formed a sister group to the primates (Nie *et al.*, 2008).

So, currently, we do not know the details of the evolutionary origin of primates. Robert Martin recently reviewed the evidence and concluded that it is essential that colugos are included in any discussion of the evolutionary origin of primates (Martin, 2008). Currently, given the uncertainty about the early division of the three groups, tree shrews, colugos and primates, no group can be identified as being the most closely related to the Primates.

We begin by examining some ancient groups of mammals suggested by researchers as being close to the ancestors of primates.

4.1 The Scandentia and the Plesiadapiformes

From about 65 mya there was a substantial adaptive radiation amongst the mammalian groups. Primates originated around 65–81.5 mya, (Table 4.1), but older primate-like fossils have been found, that were more similar to squirrels and tree shrews. However we have no way of knowing which of these, if any, was the ancestor of primates. Extant tree shrews, found in South-East Asia are squirrel-like, and most of them are terrestrial. Most tree shrews do not have grasping hands and feet and all their digits have claws (Table 4.2), with the exception of the pen-tailed tree shrew, *Ptilocercus*. Nevertheless, similarities of some anatomical features in tree shrews and primates, as well as some molecular evidence, led to the suggestion that a group of ancient tree shrews were the ancestors of primates. However as we have seen, not all of the molecular evidence supports this view. Furthermore similarities between tree shrews and primates (Table 4.2) can be interpreted as convergent evolution of functional features related to an arboreal lifestyle.

Sargis (2004) suggests that the common ancestor of tree shrews probably had the grasping hands and feet characteristic of primates. He points out that the extant pen-tailed tree shrew, *Ptilocercus* has grasping hands and feet and that this species provides

Table 4.1 Summary of classification of geological time spans

	Time span/ Mya	Notes
Eon		
Cryptozoic	4 000 (4 billion)–543	
Phanerozoic	543–Present	
Era		
Palaeozoic	543–248	Explosion of diversity of multicellular animals. Vertebrates and arthropods colonize land. Dinosaurs abundant at end of era in Permian period
Mesozoic	248–65	Dinosaurs dominant land fauna up to ~65 mya. Earliest known mammals appeared in Jurassic ~125 mya
Cenozoic	65–present	
Period: Only those periods relevant to emergence of mammals, primates, apes and hominins are included		
Cretaceous	144–65	The most recent period of the Mesozoic. Modern mammal and bird groups appeared. Dinosaurs were dominant up to end of the Cretaceous when they died out in massive extinction event. Emergence of mammals ~125 mya, and primates ~65–80 mya
Campanian	83.5–70.6	Dinosaurs dominate land fauna; small shrew-like mammals include marsupials and placental species. Genetic evidence suggests origin of primates ~80 mya
Maastrichtian	71.3–65.5	Most recent epoch of the Cretaceous period. Extinction of dinosaurs at end of Cretaceous
Tertiary	65–2	Adaptive radiation of primates including monkeys, apes and hominins
Epochs		
Palaeocene	65–56.5	Earliest era of Tertiary period. Insectivore-like mammals. Adaptive radiation of mammals, for example, Plesiadapiformes. Origin of anthropoids ~56 mya
Eocene	55.5–35.5	Emergence of euprimates. Global warming for 100 kya from 55 mya. Anthropoid radiation
Oligocene	35.5–23.8	Anthropoid radiation
Miocene	23.8–5.3	Emergence and radiation of apes
Pleistocene	5.3–2.0	Emergence of hominins and *Homo*

a useful model for Plesiadapiformes, which he regards as early primates. The grasping abilities of *Ptilocercus*, which are not so pronounced as those of primates, could be similar to the primitive state for the Euarchonta (Sargis, 2004).

Plesiadapiformes existed during the Palaeocene and were primate-like mammals similar to tree shrews, with small brains and no adaptations for fast leaping. Fossil

Table 4.2 Comparisons of the features of tree shrews and primates

Feature	Primates	Tree shrews
Skull	Short snout	Trend for shortening of snout
Orbits	Large forward facing orbits	Relatively small lateral orbits but arboreal species have forwardly rotated orbits and vision area of brain is well developed
Post-orbital bar	Post-orbital bar present (Figure 4.4)	Post-orbital bar present (but is present in many mammal groups)
Brain size	Large brain size	Relatively small brain size
Teeth	Reduced number of teeth in some species	Reduction in teeth but this happened in other groups of mammals too
Digestive tract	Caecum present housing bacteria that break down plant food	Caecum present housing bacteria that break down plant food
Incisors	In most catarrhines & platyrrhines, the incisors broad and spatulate, but much variation between species.	Incisors resemble canine teeth; lower incisors project forwards
Offspring at birth	Precocial[a]	Altricial[b]
Gestation period	Long in comparison to body size	Relatively short in comparison to body size

[a]The term **precocial** means young that are sufficiently mature in behavioural and anatomical terms to fend for themselves to some extent.
[b]The term **altricial** means young that are extremely immature and cannot feed or look after themselves.
Source: Adapted from Robert Martin, 1990, The Field Museum, Chicago.

discoveries have provided clues about what these animals looked like. The best-known example is *Plesiadapis* found in France, and North America and dated at around 65 mya. *Plesiadapis,* from North America, may have reached Europe by crossing a North Atlantic land bridge, the Thulean that included Greenland (Smith, Rose and Gingerich, 2006). The animal had a rodent-like skull and hands with claws and features of the skeleton suggest it was a competent tree climber, similar to tree squirrels. *Plesiadapis* lacked a post-orbital bar, had a small brain with relatively large olfactory lobes, a relatively long snout, large incisors and a diastema (Figure 4.2b). *Plesiadapis* also had claws not nails. Primate-like features of *Plesiadapis* include the molars, and the postcranial morphology. Ancient lake deposits at Menat in France yielded two skeletons of *Plesiadapis* with skin and hair remains as carbonaceous film, which showed that this animal had a long bushy tail (Figure 4.2a).

Studies of the fossil anatomy of other plesiadapiformes suggest a diversity of niches and indicate a small part of the adaptive radiation of the group. One group, known as picrodontids, found in North America, has enlarged lower molars with wide shallow crowns and long knife-like incisors similar to those of fruit bats suggesting that these animals were feeding on juicy fruits. Another group, carpolestids, had enlarged incisors, huge blade-like lower premolars that worked against the enlarged rasp-like upper premolars, suggesting a diet of tough fibrous fruits, nuts and shoots.

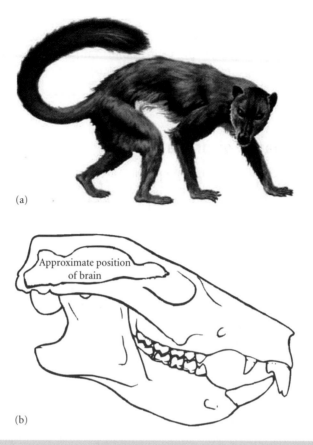

(a)

(b)

Approximate position of brain

Figure 4.2 (a) A sketch of how *Plesiadapis* may have appeared in life; (b) sketch of side-view of skull of *Plesiadapis cookei* (Late Palaeocene, Clarks Fork, Wyoming). Note the rodent-like features, the large incisors and the diastema between the incisors and cheek teeth. The orbits are on the sides of the head.
Source: (a) Reproduced with permission from Simon and Schuster Publishing Co. (b) Reproduced by permission of the University of Michigan Museum of Paleontology, based on Gingerich and Gunnell (2005) P 189.

One fossil skeleton of *Carpolestes simpsoni* found in Wyoming and dated at 55 mya shows some of the features regarded as characteristic for both primates and Plesiadapiformes (Bloch and Boyer, 2002). For example, the animal had teeth that suggest a diet of flowers, seeds and fruit, typical of primates. Opposable big toes indicate that *Carpolestes* was an efficient tree climber. Other important features are the long fingers and opposable hallux with a nail, not a claw.

As the Paleocene ended, and the Eocene began, there was warming of the climate – rainforest was widespread. From about the middle of the Eocene, climates at higher latitudes were cooling and drying gradually, leading inevitably to changes in vegetation. By about 50 mya, the Plesiadapiformes became extinct as the true primates were diversifying. This version of events is accepted by those researchers who interpret the specialized features of Plesiadapiformes as meaning it is impossible for them to be ancestral or close to the origin of true primates. In contrast, Bloch and Boyer (2002) suggest that *Carpolestes* acquired the specialized grasping foot like that of primates, from a common ancestor, and that the similarities between Plesiadapiformes and Euprimates suggest a shared arboreal ancestry.

4.2 The emergence of primates

True primates, sometimes known as euprimates, appear in the fossil record from about 58–55 mya. It is useful at this point to consider the features that define a primate. As pointed out by Robert Martin (Field Museum Chicago), it is difficult to select a set of clear-cut defining features. Nevertheless Martin compiled a list of primate features, which we summarize here. In primates, locomotion is hind limb dominated, and the centre of gravity of the body is always close to the hind limbs. Locomotion style varies from brachiation in gibbons, to vertical clinging and leaping in tarsiers, knuckle walking in gorillas and chimpanzees, and bipedal walking in *Homo*, and occasionally, chimpanzees. Primates typically have grasping hands and feet with opposable thumbs and big toes, claws are replaced by nails, (but in some species claws are present on certain digits, for example aye-aye, marmosets). Finger and toe pads are ridged, which helps with grasping. Brain size is increased in comparison to other mammal groups, slightly so in lemurs, lorises and tarsiers, and more so in monkeys and apes. The sense of smell is reduced, and the snout is shortened to varying degrees – compare lemurs with long snouts and wet noses, with great apes and humans with flat faces and dry noses. Primates have a lower rate of reproduction than other mammal groups with longer gestation periods and interbirth intervals; single births are common. The age of reproductive maturity in primates is relatively greater than in other mammal groups. The typical habitats for most primates are tropical and sub-tropical forests.

A particular evolutionary feature of primates that is visible in the structure of the skull is the change in orientation of the eyes when compared with other mammals. Vision is well-developed, with varying degrees of convergence of the eyes providing stereoscopic vision. The forward pointing eye sockets are surrounded by additional bones in the skull, particularly the post-orbital bar (Figure 4.3a) in Strepsirrhines (also known as prosimians, for example lemurs and Adapiformes, a group of Palaeocene primates discussed in Section 4.3). In anthropoids the post orbital bar is expanded forming a protective bony cup for the eye (Figure 4.3b).

Given the long list of primate features, it is not surprising that there is dispute between palaeontologists about the selective pressures that shaped the primate adaptation. The first explanation suggested for the primate adaptation was the **arboreal hypothesis**, proposed by Grafton Elliot Smith and Frederic Wood Jones. They suggested that primate adaptations link to their arboreal life. The grasping hands and feet of primates link to their effective locomotion via branches and creepers. The development

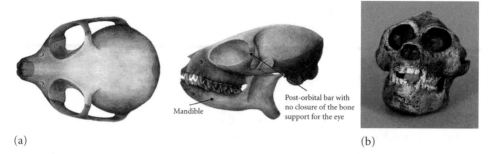

(a)   (b)

Post-orbital bar with
no closure of the bone
support for the eye

Mandible

Figure 4.3 (a) Sketch of skull of *Teilhardina asiatica* showing the post-orbital bar and the gap in the bony support for the eye; (b) a cast of the skull of *Aegyptopithecus* (an early anthropoid from the early Oligocene in the Fayum Depression, Egypt) showing closure of the gap in the bony protection of the eye. (a) Reproduced, with permission, from Ni, X., Hu, Y., Wang, Y. and Li, C. (2005). A clue to the Asian origin of Euprimates. Anthropological Science 113, P4. © The Anthropological Society of Nippon.

of the eyes and their location at the front of the face, and reduction in olfactory sense organs point to vision being a more effective way of finding food and spotting predators in tree canopies. Overall, Smith and Jones proposed that primates have superior adaptations for arboreality in comparison to other arboreal mammals.

♦ Drawing on your general knowledge name other tree-dwelling mammals that do not have the adaptations seen in primates.

♦ Squirrels and some tree shrews do not have forward-facing eyes, or grasping hands and feet yet they are successful arboreal mammals.

The existence of well-established and successful arboreal mammals that are not primates led Matt Cartmill at Duke University to criticize the arboreal hypothesis (Cartmill, 1974). He pointed out that most arboreal mammals do not have the adaptations characteristic of primates. Squirrels have a long snout, laterally positioned eyes and hands and feet that are not grasping. Their arboreal skills are at least equal to those of primates and often superior. Cartmill suggested the **visual predation hypothesis**, which links the eyes positioned at the front of the face, and grasping hands and feet of primates to their habit of stalking insect prey, then grabbing them with the hands, while the grasping feet secure the body to the tree branch. Indirect evidence supporting this hypothesis comes from observations on other species. Forward facing eyes are found in predators such as cats and owls that rely on vision to find their prey and need to judge distance accurately in order to capture it. Other arboreal predators such as chameleons have grasping hands and feet, which they use to anchor themselves to a branch or twig while they catch an insect with their long prehensile tongue.

Cartmill proposed that the features of primates are convergent to those observed in animal groups that are either predators or arboreal feeders, or both.

♦ Link features characteristic of primates that can be viewed as being convergent with those in other named animals or animal groups.

♦ The large forward-facing eyes of primates are convergent with similarly positioned eyes in carnivores such as cats and owls. Grasping hands and feet of primates are features convergent with the grasping hind feet observed in chameleons.

Cartmill suggests that ancestral primates, arboreal predators of insects and small vertebrates, may have resembled tarsiers or mouse lemurs. Tarsiers are small (80–150 g) arboreal haplorhine primates found in the rainforest in East Asia. They have elongated hindlimbs, used for leaping and for clinging to branches. Some species, for example Phillipines tarsier, *Tarsius syrichta*, have very large eyes, an adaptive feature for a nocturnal predator. Their diet comprises small vertebrates and insects, which they catch by jumping on the prey and grasping it with their hands. Mouse lemurs are found in Madagascar. They are small arboreal primates that feed on insects, spiders, fruit and flowers. The smallest species is the pygmy mouse lemur, which weighs just 31 g. Ravosa *et al.* (2000) proposed that the evolution of the post-orbital bar in primates links to the movement of the orbits to the front of the face and the increase in size of the orbits. Furthermore, the rigidity and support provided to the lateral margins of the orbits by the post-orbital bar preserves acute vision while the animal is picking up and chewing food with the teeth. These features are advantageous for animals that are nocturnal predators, a point that lends support to the visual predation hypothesis.

Palaeoanthropologists have found fossils of ancient primates dating back to ~55–60 mya. *Altiatlasius* found in Late Palaeocene sediments in Morocco, and dated at 56 mya was claimed to be an early primate. *Altiatlasius* is related to prosimians and early anthropoids, but no detailed conclusions can be reached about the classification of this species (Fleagle, 1999). The fossils consist of molars, which have some features in common with those of early primates, but some researchers claim this species is a plesiadapiform. *Altiatlasius* is a primitive stem anthropoid (Section 4.7) based on phylogenetic analysis of 360 morphological characters (Seiffert *et al.*, 2005). Fossil teeth (a few upper molars and lower premolars), of another ancient primate, *Algeripithecus minutus* were discovered in Middle Eocene sediments at Glib Zegdou, Algeria (Fleagle, 1999). The molars are broad and cube-like, suggesting a **frugivorous** diet, and the size of the teeth indicates that *Algeripithecus* was about the size of a marmoset.

At an early stage of their evolution, primates split into the families Adapidae and Omomyidae. Both groups appear quite suddenly in the Eocene fossil record in both Europe and North America suggesting that they immigrated from Africa or Asia. As we shall see later, Asia is the more likely site of the origin of the two groups. Fossil remains of adapiformes have similarities to lemurs and lorises and include large species that were probably diurnal. Their dentition suggests that they were leaf and fruit eaters. Omomyiforms resemble tarsiers and the huge orbits of some species suggest that at least some of them were nocturnal, resting in trees during the day in a vertical position, rather like extant tarsiers. Modern tarsiers are arboreal, nocturnal and are vertical clingers and leapers, so bear similarities to omomyiforms in habits and anatomy. However, fossil omomyiforms are not the same as modern tarsiers, which are highly specialized animals, for example the spectral tarsier and the Phillipine tarsier, which are not considered to resemble species living 40–50 million years ago.

Some palaeoanthropologists consider adapiformes to be the ancestors of anthropoids, the group that includes lemurs, catarrhine monkeys and apes and humans (Figure 4.4a). Others view omomyiforms as the ancestors of tarsiers and the anthropoids (Figure 4.4b). Another view is that anthropoids share a common ancestor with *Tarsius* a genus grouped within the prosimians (Suborder Prosimii or Strepsirrhini). On the other hand, anthropoids could be derived from a very early split between the Prosimii and Anthropoidea. (Figure 4.4c). Fossil evidence from Africa and Asia, e.g. *Altiatlasius* dated at 56 mya, provides some support for this view. However the actual details of the evolutionary tree for the origin of anthropoids are not known for cer-

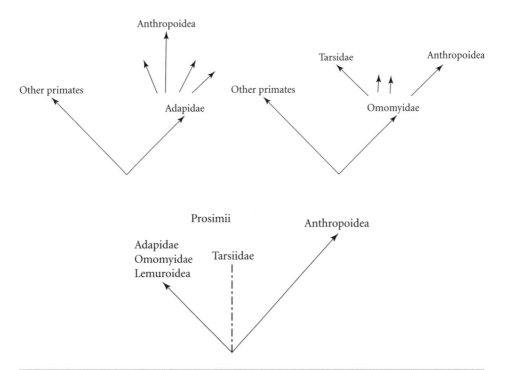

Figure 4.4 Suggested evolutionary relationships of Omomyidae and Adapidae. Adapted from information in Dagosto (2002), P126–7.

tain, and other variants have been proposed. We shall return to the arguments later in Section 4.6. By the Eocene, both groups, Prosimii and Anthropoidea, had grasping hands and feet. They had nails instead of claws, on some or all digits, and their eyes were rotated forwards, providing stereoscopic vision, linked to increased complexity of visual sensory pathways.

4.3 Ancient primates

In order to gain some understanding of the diversification of primates we need to investigate research that shed light on the climate and topography of our planet 55 mya. Geologists identified a period of intense global warming from 55.5 mya that lasted about 100 000 years at the beginning of the Eocene epoch. The start of the global warming was identified as the Palaeocene – Eocene (P/E) thermal maximum, which was marked by tropical moist climates. Even the Arctic regions had a temperate to sub-tropical climate. The global warming at the onset of the Eocene was accompanied by diversification of trees, shrubs and other flowering plants. In turn the diverse plant life provided abundant food resources for mammals, including primates and this was an important factor in their evolution. Robert Sussman's **angiosperm radiation theory** asserts that the radiation of primates was linked to the radiation of flowering plants, which provided a huge variety of flowers, nectar and fruit as well as leaves (Sussman, 1990). Sussman argues that there was co-evolution of plant eaters and plants whereby primates (as well as fruit bats and plant-eating birds), were important seed dispersers. Primates thrived and diversified in the forests that developed in the warm tropical climates of the Eocene. If the estimate of the date range for the emergence of primates made by Robert Martin is correct, the radiation of primates in the early Tertiary (Table 4.1) would have been the 'second wave' of primate evolution (Martin, Soligo and Tavare, 2007).

Many fossil primates have been discovered in Europe, Asia and the United States, but we only have space to describe a few representative examples here. One of the oldest known species dated about 55 million years old (early Eocene), discovered by Ni and his colleagues (Ni *et al.*, 2005, 2004), in sediments in the Hengyang basin, China, is the omomyid, haplorhine *Teilhardina asiatica* (Figure 4.5). The animal had an estimated body mass of <28 g, and the skull is just 25 mm in length. The braincase has no sagittal crest, and a brain size small in comparison to extant primates. Although the orbits are not totally forward facing they are close to convergent and the snout is slightly shortened (Figure 4.3a). The dentition is regarded as primitive with four upper premolars (Box 4.1).

Large canines and pointed premolars with sharp shearing crests suggest an insectivorous diet. *T. asiatica* is considered (Ni *et al.*, 2004) as being close to a stem euprimate. *T. asiatica* resembles *T. belgica*, discovered in Dormaal, Belgium, and the two may be part of a sister group positioned at the base of the omomyid/tarsier-anthropoid clade. It is interesting that there are also at least five American species of *Teilhardina*, including *T. americana and T. brandti*, discovered in the Willwood formation in Wyoming.

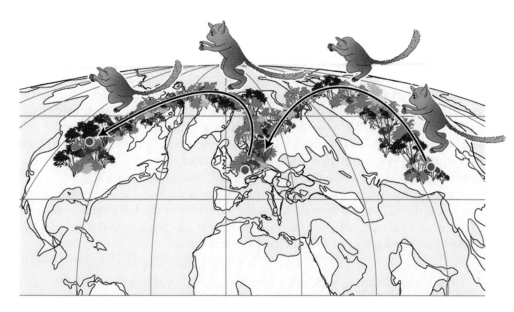

Figure 4.5 Sketch map of route of dispersal of *Teilhardina* through Asia, Europe and North America, including the Thulean land bridge.
Adapted from Smith *et al.*, (2006) P11224.

T. asiatica is considered to be the most primitive species because of its dentition, and in having relatively smaller orbits than the other known *Teilhardina* species which suggest a diurnal lifestyle. How did *Teilhardina* manage to be so widely distributed? The world map of about 65 mya shows that China and Belgium were in the same land mass, so overland migration was feasible. Yet by 55–65 mya, America and Europe were separated by ocean, with Greenland between, indicating that primates would have needed to swim across the sea to reach America, an unlikely feat. However, during the early Eocene, up to about 50 mya, North America and Western Europe were connected via Greenland by the Thulean landbridge (Figure 4.5). Around 55 mya the area supported primates, reptiles such as crocodile and lizards, and also trees and herbaceous plants. The start of the Eocene 55.5 mya, coincided with the Palaeocene/Eocene thermal maximum (PETM), comprising about 100 000 years of intense global warming (Smith, Rose and Gingerich, 2006). The climate in the Thulean landbridge and over the rest of the northern hemisphere, was warm, temperate and frost-free. A well-vegetated landbridge would have provided a habitat suitable for primates as well as a dispersal route linking Asia, Western Europe and America.

The use of new, precise, dating techniques by Smith *et al.* (2006) has identified *T. asiatica* as the oldest of the *Teilhardina* species and provided a method of tracing their dispersal routes out of Asia. *Teilhardina* had reached Europe at about 5 000 to 12 000 years after the Paleocene/Eocene (P/E), boundary dated at about 55.5 mya. *Teilhardina* reached North America by at least 25000–15000 years after the P/E boundary. Although this appears to be a rapid dispersal rate, as living mammals disperse at a rate of about 1–10 km year^{-1} it would have taken *Teilhardina* about 20 000 years to reach North America, moving in an east to west direction from Europe, and crossing by the Thulean landbridge. Given the warm climate and increased humidity during the PETM, the vegetation on the northern landbridges, which include the Beringia and Thulean would have been evergreen forest. This would be suitable habitat for primates as well as other mammals, birds and insects. The expansion of animal populations into new territories would have resulted in their dispersal and their expansion into North America. Once *Teilhardina* reached North America, fossil evidence suggests diversification into at least five other species of omomyids.

There are many uncertainties about primate evolution and an important question is whether *T. asiatica* does represent the condition of the last common ancestor of primates. Ni *et al.* (2004, 2005) had suggested that their discovery of *T. asiatica* had revived the hypothesis of an Asian origin for euprimates.

♦ Outline the evidence provided by Smith *et al.* that supports Ni *et al.*'s view that *T. asiatica* with its primitive anatomy and as the oldest known primate from Asia, suggests an Asian origin for primates.

♦ The use by Smith *et al.* of precise dating techniques with a baseline of the PETM that could identify differences as small as tens of thousands of years confirmed *T. asiatica* as the oldest known species of *Teilhardina*. The primitive dental anatomy supports this view. Subsequently in the evolution of the primates, dentition was reduced (Box 4.1).

Ni *et al.* argue that if *T. asiatica* is close to being the common ancestor for primates, then this would have been a small diurnal insectivore relying on vision to find and capture insect prey. They point that this reasoning is inconsistent with Bloch and Boyer's view that euprimates could have evolved from a *Carpolestes*-like ancestor (Section 4.2) that was a fruit-eater, that did not rely mainly on vision to find food, but had well-developed olfactory senses.

More omomyiform fossils dated from 55–33 mya have been found in Asia (55–45 mya), Europe (55–33 mya), North America (55–34 mya) and Africa (Kirk and Simons, 2001, Fayum depression 33–36 mya). Most of the fossils are bones and teeth, and many are of poor quality. Known omomyiform species weighed <450 g and their teeth suggest diets of fruit, gum, sap, insects and small vertebrates. Omomyiformes with sharply crested teeth are assumed to have been insectivorous; those with small blunt molars are likely to have eaten soft ripe fruits.

A total of about 69 species of omomyids have been found in North America, an indication of the huge diversity of primates in that area. We have only the space to examine a few examples here. They include *Tetonius*, found in the Willwood formation in the Bighorn Basin by Jacob Wortmann in 1881. *Tetonius* had grossly enlarged and forward pointing lower incisors, similar to those of living primates that feed on gum, using their lower incisors to gouge out tree bark to gain access to gum (Figure 4.6). In 1991, Christopher Beard and his colleagues (Carnegie Museum of Natural History,

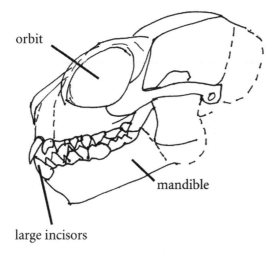

orbit

mandible

large incisors

Figure 4.6 Side view of skull of *Tetonius*, an omomyiforme. Like other omomyiforms, *Tetonius* was a small animal with large incisors and small canines. Note the large eyes which suggest that this species was nocturnal. Adapted from Fleagle (1999) P 358.

USA) discovered six skulls of *Shoshonius*, in Wyoming (the same location where *Notharctus* fossils have been found). The researchers noted that *Shoshonius* has some features characteristic of tarsiers. As in tarsiers, the snout is reduced, and the orbits are large. The large orbits suggest a nocturnal lifestyle, and the sharp crested molars suggest a diet of insects and small vertebrates. Overall *Shoshonius*, like *Tetonius*, appears to be very specialized. These are all small primates; the skull of *Shoshonius* for example, is only 2.8 cm long.

Overall, few omomyiform fossils have been found in Asia and they include those such as *Macrotarsius*, found in fissure fillings close to Shanghai. These primates are similar to the fossils found in North America and Beard suggests that they reached Asia by crossing the Beringia land bridge about 45 million years ago.

Eocene omomyiforms in Europe were very different from those in Asia and North America. One possible cause was that Europe was isolated from Asia for part of the Eocene by a stretch of ocean east of the Ural Mountains. The flooding of the Thulean land bridge in the early Eocene at about 50 mya completed Europe's isolation.

♦ Why would flooding of the Thulean land bridge be linked to the difference in the omomyiforms found in Europe and North America and Asia?

♦ A stretch of ocean between Europe and Asia would have blocked dispersal of primates between the two continents. So once Europe and North America were separated by an unbridged ocean, there was no more dispersal of omomyiforms between the two continents. Hence adaptive radiation of primates proceeded independently in the three continents, resulting in communities of primates made up of different species.

The European omomyiforms are known as microchoerids, and about 11 species are known. One example is *Necrolemur*, which was discovered in 1873 in limestone fissure fillings in Quercy, southern France. *Necrolemur antiquus* had relatively long hindlimbs, characteristic of leaping primates, and large orbits suggesting that it was nocturnal. The cheek teeth were broad with blunt cusps, indicating fruit eating, and the striations on the lower front teeth suggest that these teeth were used for grooming. The front teeth are interpreted by some authorities as being three pairs of canine teeth, although Fleagle (1999) interprets the front two teeth as incisors and the third tooth as a canine. The front dentition suggests that *Necrolemur* also fed on gums, which are sugary exudates from trees. Extant primates such as the pygmy marmoset use their front teeth to cut into tree bark to access the gums that exude out of the holes. *Necrolemur* is dated at late Eocene and to early Oligocene. The dentition of other microchoerids found in Europe suggests they were insectivorous, for example *Pseudoloris*. Christopher Beard speculates on the evolutionary relationships of omomyids and suggests that *Teilhardina* may have given rise to the European microchoerids and the later North American omomyiforms.

Adapiformes are considered to show more **primitive** characters than any other fossil primates so far discovered, in that their tooth and jaw anatomy is so generalized. Most primates have three premolars on each side of their upper and lower jaws, but in contrast, some early adapiformes have four. The first known primate fossils were dug up from gypsum quarries in Paris by workmen, who handed them over to George Cuvier (1769–1832), the founder of the science of paleontology. Cuvier named the fossils *Adapis parisiensis*. Some years later, about 1870, more well-preserved fossils of *Adapis* were discovered in limestone fissures in Quercy, France. Limestone fissures form where limestone is exposed to weather, especially rain. As rainwater, which is slightly acid, percolates through cracks in limestone, it dissolves away the rock forming larger and larger cracks, which grow into large fissures. The fissures accumulate mud and debris, including animal bones taken there by predators or washed in by floodwater. Therefore, as we shall see at later points on the timeline, limestone fissures can be rich sources of fossils. The skull anatomy of *Adapis* suggests that the animal was a leaf eater, in that there are substantial attachments for jaw muscles (temporalis muscle) including sagittal and nuchal crests (Figure 4.7). Leaves require much chewing to extract their sugars, proteins, vitamins and minerals. The upper and lower molars of *Adapis* have sharp crests resembling the molars of leaf-eating monkeys – during chewing, the crests slice the leaves. *Adapis* had a long snout and **endocasts** demonstrate large olfactory lobes, suggesting that sense of smell was important. The skeletal anatomy of adapiformes indicates an evolutionary relationship between them and lemurs and lorises. Adapiformes lived from ~55–10 mya and fossils have been found in North America, Asia and Europe. There is evidence of a major adaptive radiation of the group in Europe with about 50 species so far known.

Adapiformes discovered in the United States include *Notharctus* species, such as *N. venticolous*, dated at around 50 mya. *Notharctus* has the typical adapid features of forward facing eyes and therefore binocular vision. The brain is relatively large, the

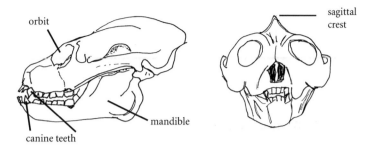

Figure 4.7 Lateral and front views of skull of *Adapis,* an adapiform. Adapiformes have small incisors and large canines. Adapted from Fleagle (1999) P358.

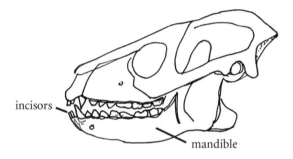

Figure 4.8 Sketch of side view of skull of *Notharctus,* an adapiform. Beard (2004) suggests that *Notharctus* was a leaf eater. Adapted from Fleagle (1999) P358.

snout is reduced and teeth include small vertical incisors (Figure 4.8). The grasping hands have digits with nails not claws, opposable thumbs, and big toes. Limbs are flexible, there is a long tail and supple back. *Northarctus* has long hind limbs suggesting the animal could leap from tree to tree. The long hindlimbs and relatively short forelimbs are similar in proportion to those of lemurs, but the forelimbs of *Notharctus* are more robust than those of living lemurs. Beard suggests that *Notharctus* was a leaf eater, with cheek teeth having strong crests (Beard and Wang, 2004). The sudden appearance of *Notharctus*-like primates in North America, along with other mammals, supports dispersal from Asia, which was joined to North America during the Eocene (Figure 4.5).

The evolutionary relationships between the groups Omomyiformes and Adapiformes and modern primates are unclear and still debated. Their relationships are considered further in Section 4.6. Some palaeoanthropologists view Omomyiformes as ancestral to tarsiers and as having some anthropoid-like features.

The Adapiformes are considered by some as being ancestral to Strepsirrhines, which include lemurs, galagos and lorises. However the relationships between the early primates and extant species remain a matter of current debate as more fossil and genetic evidence becomes available.

4.4 Dentition of ancient primates

By now you may have noticed that teeth and jaw bones are the commonest primate fossil remains found. The reason is that the lower jaw consists of very dense bone and the structure of teeth makes them even harder, (Figure 4.9a) so both of these are more likely to be preserved as fossils than the rest of the skeleton. Teeth can provide palaeontologists with much information about the diet of fossil primates.

Study of dentition of living primates provides information about the structure of teeth associated with particular diets. For example, leaf-eating monkeys have teeth with sharp cutting edges, known as crests; as the upper and lower teeth meet during chewing, the cutting edges of the crests slice the leaves and/or insects. Smaller insect eating primates have similar teeth. Monkeys with rounded blunt cheek teeth, molars and premolars, tend to eat soft fruits. Bearded saki monkeys that eat hard fruits and nuts that have to be bitten and chewed in order to access the nutritious kernel have large molars with broad ridged surfaces, which are used to grind down hard foods. Jaw muscles, the temporal and masseter, are well-developed in the bearded saki, and pronounced jaw muscle attachments can be seen on the cheek bones and lower jaws. Studying teeth of fossil primates and comparing them with those of modern primates can tell us about the feeding habits and diet of the fossil species.

Fossil primate dentition can also provide information about evolutionary relationships between primate groups. However, there are pitfalls linked to convergence; for example, species that chew hard foods tend to have similar traits, adaptive features which can be linked to heavy chewing. So groups of species that have similar diets, but are not related in evolutionary terms would have similar teeth. Nevertheless, comparisons of dental formulae in fossil primates and living species provide evidence for evolutionary relationships between groups as we shall see in this and later chapters. For ease of comparison between species, the number and types of teeth in a species are described by the dental formula (Box 4.1). *Adapis*, for example, has a dental formula of 2/2 1/1 4/4 3/3, a total of 40 teeth. Anthropoids have fewer teeth. New World monkeys, (classified in the Infraorder Platyrrhini) have the dental formula 2/2 1/1 3/3 3/3, a total of 36 teeth, whereas Old World monkeys (Infraorder Catarrhini), have just 32 teeth, with dental formula 2/2 1/1 2/2 3/3. The situation is not quite so simple, as the upper dentition of tarsiers is 2/2 1/1 3/3 3/3, the same as that of New World monkeys although the lower (mandible)dentition of tarsiers is even more reduced at 1/1 1/1 3/3 3/3.

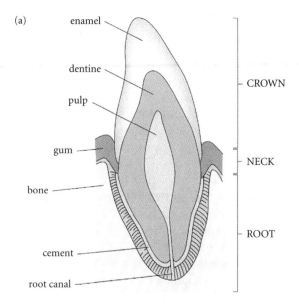

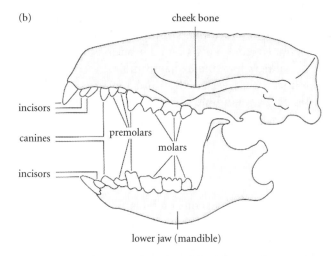

Figure 4.9 (a) Generalized structure of a mammalian tooth, a vertical section; (b) side view of skull and lower jaw of European hedgehog to show types of mammalian teeth. Reproduced from (a) Studying Mammals P. 29. © The Open University. (b) Reeve, N. (1994) Studying hedgehogs, Poyser Natural History Series.

♦ Examine Figure 4.9a and write down the dental formula for the hedgehog.

♦ The dental formula of the hedgehog is 3/2 1/1 3/2 3/3 (a total of 36 teeth).

♦ In comparison to *Adapis*, an adapiform, which teeth have been lost in (i) New World monkeys, and (ii) Old World monkeys?

Box 4.1   How we make sense of fossil teeth

During their lifetime, mammals have two sets of teeth. The first teeth to erupt are known as milk teeth; they fall out and are replaced by the adult teeth during the late juvenile stage of life. In adult life, a mammalian tooth comprises three regions, the crown, the neck and root (Figure 4.9a). The crown is the visible part of the tooth that emerges from the gum; the gum encloses the neck of the tooth, and anchors the tooth in the gum. The outer layer of the crown is enamel made of calcium phosphates and fluorides, which resists damage from hard food and protects the delicate inner layers. Much of the tooth is made of dentine, which is similar to bone in structure in that it consists of a fibrous framework in which are embedded crystals of calcium salts. Mammals have several kinds of teeth, (Figure 4.9b), which perform different functions in feeding. The incisors are situated at the front of the jaw and used for biting and grasping. The canine teeth behind the incisors are sharp and pointed and used for grasping and biting food and used as weapons by fighting males. Premolars and molars behind the canines are used for chewing and grinding the food so that it is broken up into pieces small enough for swallowing.

The numbers of each type of tooth in the upper and lower jaws can be shown in shorthand by the **dental formula**. The formula describes the number of incisors, canines, premolars and molars on each side of the upper and lower jaws. For example, tree shrews have the dental formula 2 incisors 1 canine 3 premolars 3 molars in the upper jaw (**maxilla**), and 3 incisors 1 canine 3 premolars 3 molars in the lower jaw (**mandible**), abbreviated as 2/3 1/1 3/3 3/3.

♦ (i) New World monkeys have lost one premolar in each side of both the upper and lower jaws, giving 3 premolars in each side of the upper and lower jaws. (ii) Old World monkeys have lost 2 premolars in each side of both the upper and lower jaws, giving 2 premolars in each side of the upper and lower jaws.

♦ The colobus monkey, an Old World monkey, has a dental formula: 2/2 1/1 2/2 3/3. Compare the dentition of the tree shrew and the colobus monkey.

♦ The dental formula of the tree shrew is 2/3 1/1 3/3 3/3. In comparison to the tree shrew, the dentition of the colobus monkey is reduced. The monkey has only 2 incisors on each side of the lower jaw whereas the tree shrew has 3 on each side of the lower jaw. The premolars are reduced to 2 on each side of the upper and lower jaws of the monkey, whereas the tree shrew has three premolars on both sides of the upper and lower jaws.

However, note that *Tarsius* also has reduced dentition, having a dental formula 2/1 1/1 3/3 3/3. The reduction in dentition has proved of importance in the discussion of the origin of the anthropoids. The suborder Anthropoidea includes the Old World and New World monkey superfamilies and also the Hominoidea, the group that includes apes and humans.

4.5 The most ancient anthropoid?

In 1992, while excavating mid-Eocene sediments in Jiangsu Province China, Christopher Beard (Carnegie Museum of Natural History) found parts of a minute fossil lower jaw containing one premolar, and two molars. He recognized it as belonging to a tiny primate, estimated body mass, 100 g, which he named *Eosimias sinensis.* Just three years later, in 1995, fossil finds in a deep gully in the Yuanqu Basin, China, by Beard's team provided detailed information about the dentition of *Eosimias.* One of the team, Wen Chaohua, found both halves of a perfectly preserved lower jaw of *Eosimias* in a block of freshwater limestone that he had split apart with a pick. All the teeth are intact, and include enlarged canines, thin sharp pre-molars and molars with pointed cusps. The dental formula of *Eosimias* is 2/2 1/1 3/3/ 3/3, characteristic of anthropoids and tarsiers. The jaw is monkey-like, as the chin is deep and robust and the canine teeth project above the other teeth, as seen in many monkeys (Figure 4.10). *Eosimias* is important because its similarities to the omomyiformes suggest that it is closely linked to tarsiers and anthropoids. *Eosimias centennicus* is dated at about 45 mya, and if its classification is accepted, it is one of the oldest known anthropoids.

◆ Consider the dates for *Eosimias* and *Altialasius* and explain how they affect the arguments that anthropoids originated either in Asia or Africa.

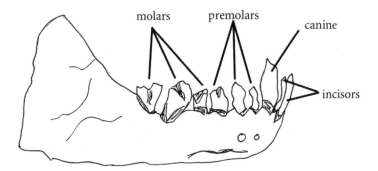

Figure 4.10 Sketch of lateral view of mandible (lower jaw) of *Eosimias centennicus. Adapted from* Beard and Wang (2004) P407.

♦ In some ways the anatomy of *Eosimias* supports the view that it is an anthropoid. The age of the fossils, ~45 mya means it is one of the oldest known undisputed anthropoids. However, the tooth anatomy of *Altialasius*, the age of which is estimated at 56 mya, indicates that it is the oldest known stem anthropoid. Therefore anthropoids are unlikely to have originated in Asia if the oldest species are found in Africa.

Elwyn Simons has provided a number of arguments against the classification of *Eosimias* as an anthropoid. One argument put forward (Miller and Simons, 1997) is that an early anthropoid, *Proteopithecus sylviae*, discovered in sediments in the Late Eocene Quarry at L-41, at Fayum in Egypt has anthropoid features, none of which are present in *Eosimias*. The argument will continue, as more evidence is discovered. The overall view of Simons though is that *Eosimias* is likely to be an anthropoid. A recent discovery in Gujerat State in India has been identified *Anthrasimias*, dated at, 55–54 mya, as an anthropoid (Bajpai *et al.*, 2008), which complicates the picture.

4.6 Evolutionary relationships of adapiformes, omomyiforms and anthropoids

There is disagreement amongst palaeoanthropologists about which, if any, of Adapiformes and Omomyiformes were the group that were ancestral to the early anthropoids (Figure 4.4). Adapiformes have primate features, a post-orbital bar, forward-facing eyes, and reduced snout. Features adapiformes have in common with anthropoids include small lower incisors with $I_1 < I_2$. Most omomyids do not have this feature but some do, including *Teilhardina belgica*. Their incisors are vertically orientated. Omomyiform have several features in common with anthropoids including a short face, large orbits with a narrow gap between them, and tooth rows that are close to parallel. The incisors are orientated vertically, and canines are interlocking and larger in males. In some species the two halves of the mandible are fused. So we have many loose ends in this chapter which cannot be tied up simply because there is insufficient evidence to do so. The evolutionary relationships between Adapiformes, Omomyiformes and Anthropoidea are especially difficult to tease out and are explored further in Chapter 5, in which we begin by examining some Late Eocene Adapiformes discovered in the Fayum depression in Egypt.

A suite of characteristic features of fossil skull anatomy, if available, provide evidence for verifying that a fossil is an anthropoid primate. The dental formula of anthropoids is a useful starting point, but not unique to the group, as we saw in Box 4.1. The orbit and middle ear of primates have unique features that are regarded as tarsier-anthropoid **synapomorphies**, derived features that are shared by two or more groups with a shared ancestry. We saw in Section 4.2 that early primates have a bony post-orbital bar running from the cranium to the zygomatic arch (Figure 4.3a). In anthropoids and tarsiers, this bar is expanded into a post-orbital septum, which is a thin sheet of bone separating the orbit from the temporal fossa (Figure 4.3b). In all primates, the petrosal bone forms the floor of the air-filled middle ear chamber, the tympanic cavity, of tarsiers, forming an 'auditory bulla'. In tarsiers and anthropoids, an accessory chamber, develops from the auditory tube and remains there throughout life.

♦ Given the known characteristic primate and anthropoid features of the skull, why is it difficult to identify some fossil skulls, for example, as primate or anthropoid?

♦ Most fossil skulls are incomplete so if important diagnostic features are missing it is not possible to identify the skull fragments as primate or anthropoid.

Kay *et al.* report in their review of Anthropoid origins (Kay, Ross and Williams, 1997) that the common features of tarsiers and anthropoids have been interpreted as suggesting that living anthropoids and *Tarsius* are sister taxa within the **Haplorhini** (Table 4.3), suggesting that these two groups are more closely related to each other than to omomyiformes. Kay *et al.* discount the hypothesis that the two groups have evolved from different omomyid ancestors. They point out that phylogenetic analyses of recent and fossil species indicate that a haplorhine–strepsirrhine split had occurred in the early Eocene and that *Eosimias* and other eosimiids are primitive anthropoids. There was a shift from a nocturnal way of life to diurnal at the base of the tarsier–eosimiid–anthropoid clade.

Table 4.3 Example of primate classification

Primates
Suborder Prosimii (Suborder Strepsirrhini)
Family: incertae cedis
Atlanius; Altiatasius?

Infraorder Lemuriformes
Superfamily: Adapoidea
Examples (Eocene forms):
Notharctus; Adapis; Adapoides; Wadilemur; Aframonius; Anchomomys

Superfamily: Lemuroidea
Examples:
Lemur (for example ring tailed lemur); *Varecia* (for example ruffed lemur)
Indri (the largest extant lemur); *Megaladapis* (extinct by 500 years ago)
Daubentonia (aye-aye); *Propithecus* Verreaux's sifaka

Superfamily: Lorisoidea
Examples:
Galago bushbabies; *Progalago* Miocene species;
Otolemur Thick-tailed bushbaby; *Perodictus* potto;
Pseudopotto Martin's false potto; *Loris* loris; *Arctocebus* Angwantibo

Infraorder Tarsiiformes
Superfamily: Omomyidae
Examples (Eocene forms):
Teilhardina; Tetonius; Shoshonius; Necrolemur; Pseudoloris; Microchoerus

(*Continued*)

Table 4.3   (Continued)

Suborder Haplorhini
Infraorder Tarsii
Superfamily: Tarsoidea
Family Tarsiidea
Tarsius Tarsius extant; *Afrotarsius* Oligocene species

Suborder Anthropoidea
Infraorder incertae cedis
Superfamily incertae cedis
Examples (Eocene forms):
Altiatasius? 56 mya
Eosimias China A stem anthropoid 42–45 mya
Pondaungia; Biretia; Algeripithecus

Infraorder Platyrrhini
Superfamily Ceboidea: New World monkeys
Family Atelidae: examples
Carlocebus (Miocene); *Propithecia (Miocene)*; *Cacajao* uakari
Callicebus titi monkey; *Protopithecus a* Pleistocene monkey (10–100 kya)
Alouatta howler monkey; *Ateles* spider monkey; *Lagothrix* woolly monkey

Family Cebidae: examples
Aotus owl monkey; *Dolichocebus* a Miocene monkey *from S. America*
Cebus capuchin; *Saimiri* squirrel monkey

Infraorder Catarrhini
Superfamily Propliopithecoidea
Family Propliopithecidae: examples
Propliopithecus Early Oligocene, Fayum depression, Egypt
Aegyptopithecus A stem catarrhine Early Oligocene, Fayum depression, Egypt

Family Oligopithecidae
Examples:
Oligopithecus Early Oligocene Fayum depression, Egypt
Catopithecus Late Eocene Fayum depression, Egypt

Superfamily: Cercopithecoidea Old World monkeys
Family Cercopithecidae: examples
Dolichopithecus; Cercopithecoide; Rhinocolobus; these are
Pliocene colobus monkeys
Procolubus Red colobus monkey; *Colobus* colobus monkey
Dinopithecus Giant baboon Late Pliocene
Macaca macaque monkeys; *Papio* baboon
Cercopithecus Guenon monkeys; *Chlorocebus* Vervet monkeys
Mandrillus Drill; *Miopithecus*; Talapoin monkeys
Simias pig tailed leaf monkey
Superfamily: Hominoidea[a]

[a]See Table 5.1 for detailed classification of the Hominoidea.
Source: Adapted from Fleagle (1999), P577–80.

4.7 Classification of Primates

Biologists attempt to take what is known about the evolutionary relationships between animals when classifying particular groups. There have been many attempts at the classification of primates. Known fossil species are included in classification schemes where this is feasible. Table 4.3 provides a simplified classification scheme derived from one prepared by Fleagle (1999). Not all classification levels are included.

♦ Examine the classification of primates in Table 4.3. Name the major extant groups, Superfamilies, of extant primates included in the Anthropoidea.

♦ The superfamilies within the Anthropoidea include: Ceboidea (New World monkeys); Cercopithecoidea (Old World monkeys); and Hominodea (apes and humans).

Fossil evidence indicates that the common ancestor of anthropoids originated either in Asia or Africa. The discovery by Beard and his colleagues of *Eosimias* dated at 45 mya identified one of the oldest known stem anthropoids, providing evidence for the origin of anthropoids in Asia. Beard interprets *Eosimias* as the sister group of all anthropoids, which implies an Asian origin. The oldest known stem anthropoids found in Africa are *Algeripithecus* known from about 10 teeth, and *Altiatlasius* known from 10 molars. However, if we accept that *Algeropithecus* dated at 45 mya, and *Altiatlasius* dated at 56 mya are stem anthropoids, then the anthropoids would have a very long evolutionary history in Africa. Elwyn Simons and his team discovered many ancient anthropoids in the Fayum depression in North Africa (Chapter 5) but these appeared abruptly in the fossil record at ~35–30 mya, leaving a long gap that weakened the support for an African origin for anthropoids (Simons, 1995; Simons *et al.*, 2007). We will see in the following chapter that this gap was partly filled in 2005 by the discovery of more anthropoid fossils at Fayum dated at 37 mya.

Summary

Clearly many questions remain about the emergence of the early primates and the evolutionary relationships between the colugos, tree shrews, plesiadapiformes and primates. What is clear is that the evolutionary tree for the early primates is very bushy. Fossil evidence reveals that Eocene primates had a much wider geographical distribution than do living primates, as their early evolutionary history was played out over four continents, Asia, Africa, America and Europe. As we shall see in Chapter 5 the radiation of anthropoids and the emergence and radiation of the Hominoidea also resulted in many branches forming a very bushy evolutionary tree.

Questions and activities

Question 4.1

Summarize Robert Martin's definition of a primate as a set of bullet points. For each, assess how far Martin's criteria define humans.

Question 4.2

Examine the sketches in Figure 4.11 of the mandible (lower) jaws of three ancient primates, *Adapis*, *Notharcus* and *Cantius*, and write down the dental formula for the lower jaw of each of these species.

Question 4.3

In the year 2000, tiny ankle bones of a fossil primate *Eosimias* were found by Professor D. Gebo and colleagues in an Eocene limestone quarry close to the Yellow River in China, about 560 miles southeast of Beijing.

1 Outline a dating technique that you would recommend as being appropriate for finding out the date range for the fossils. (Hint: *Refer to Section 2.4*)

2 Explain why accurate dating is so important for fossil primates in the context of human evolution.

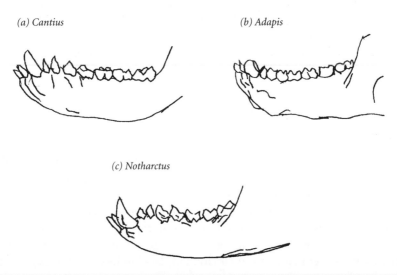

(a) Cantius

(b) Adapis

(c) Notharctus

Figure 4.11 Sketches of mandibles of three adapiformes, (a) *Adapis*; (b) *Notharcus*; and (c) *Cantius*. Adapted from Fleagle (1999).

References

Bajpai, S., Kay, R.F., Williams, B.A., Das, D.P., Kapur, V.V., and Tiwari, B.N. (2008) The oldest Asian record of Anthropoidea. *Proceedings of the National Academy of Sciences*, **105**, 11093–11098.

Beard, C. (2004) *The Hunt for the Dawn Monkey*. University of California Press.

Beard, K.C. and Wang, J. (2004) The eosimiid primates (Anthropoidea) of the Heti formation, Yuanqu basin, Hanxi and Henan Provinces, People's Republic of China. *Journal of Human Evolution*, **46**, 401–32.

Bloch, J.I. and Boyer, D.M. (2002) Grasping primate origins. *Science*, **298**, 1606–1610.

Bloch, J.I., Silcox, M.T., Boyer, D.M., and Sargis, E. (2007) New Palaeocene skeletons and the relationship of plesiadapiforms to crown-clade primates. *Proceedings of the National Academy of Sciences*, **104**, 1159–1164.

Cartmill, M. (1974) Rethinking primate origins. *Science*, **184**, 436–443.

Dagosto, M. (2002) The origin and diversification of anthropoid primates, in *The Primate Fossil Record* (ed. W.C.Hartwig), Cambridge University Press, Cambridge, pp.125–132.

Fleagle, J.G. (1999) *Primate Adaptation and Evolution*, New York: Academic Press.

Gingerich, P.D. and Gunnell, G.F. (2005) Brain of *Plesiadapis cookei*. Contributions from the Museum of Palaeontology, University of Michigan. **31** (8), 185–195.

Janecka, J.E., Miller, W., Pringle, T.H., Wiens, F., Zitzmann, A., Helgen, K.M., Springer, M.S., and Murphy, W.J. (2007) Molecular and genomic data identify the closest living relative of primates. *Science*, **318**, 792–794.

Kay, R.F., Ross, C., and Williams, B.A. (1997) Anthropoid origins. *Science*, **275**, 797–804.

Kirk, E.C. and Simons, E.L. (2001) Diets of fossil primates from the Fayum Depression of Egypt: a quantitative analysis of molar shearing. *Journal of Human Evolution*, **40**, 203–229.

Kriegs, J.O., Churakov, G., Jurka, J., Brosius, J., and Schmitz, J. (2007) Evolutionary history of 7SL RNA-derived SINEs in supraprimates. *Trends in Genetics*, **23**, 158–161.

Martin, R.D. (1990) *Primate Origins and Evolution*. Princeton, NJ: Princeton University Press. 840pp.

Martin, R.D. (2008) Colugos: Obscure mammals glide into the evolutionary limelight. *Journal of Biology*, **7**, Article 13.

Martin, R.D., Soligo, C., and Tavare, S. (2007) Primate origins: Implications of a Cretaceous ancestry. *Folia Primatologica*, **76**, 277–296.

Miller, E.R. and Simons, E.L. (1997) Dentition of *Proteopithecus sylviae*, an archaic anthropoid from the Fayum Depression,Egypt. *Proceedings of the National Academy of Sciences of the United States of America*, **94**, 13760–13764.

Ni, X., Hu, Y., Wang, Y., and Li, C. (2005) A clue to the Asian origin of Euprimates. *Anthropological Science*, **113**, 3–9.

Ni, X., Wang, Y., Hu, Y., and Li, C. (2004) A euprimate skull from the early Eocene of China.*Nature*, **427**, 65–68.

Nie, W., Fu, B., O'Brien, P., Wang, J., Su, W., Tanomtong, A., Volobouev, V., Ferguson-Smith, M., and Yang, F. (2008) Flying lemurs – The 'flying tree shrews'? Molecular cytogenetic evidence for a Scandentia-Dermoptera sister clade. *BMC Biology*, **6**, 18.

Ravosa, M.J., Noble, V.E., Hylander, W.L., Johnson, K.R., and Kowalski, E.M. (2000) Masticatory stress, orbital orientation and the evolution of the primate postorbital bar. *Journal of Human Evolution*, **38**, 667–693.

Sargis, E.J. (2004) New views on tree shrews: The role of Tupaiids in primate supraordinal relationships. *Evolutionary Anthropology*, **13**, 56–66.

Seiffert, E.R., Simons, E.L., Clyde, W.C., Rossie, J.B., Attia, Y., Bown, T.M., Chatrath, P., and Mathison, M.E. (2005) Basal Anthropoids from Egypt and the Antiquity of Africa's Higher Primate Radiation. *Science*, **310**, 300–304.

Simons, E.L. (1995) Skulls and anterior teeth of *Catopithecus* (primates:Anthropoidea) from the Eocene and anthropoid origins.*Science*, **268**, 1885–1888.

Simons, E.L., Seiffert, E.R., Ryan, T.M., and Attia, Y. (2007) A remarkable female cranium of the early Oligocene anthropoid *Aegyptopithecus zeuxis* (Catarrhini, Proliopithecidae).*Proceedings of the National Academy of Sciences*, **104**, 8731–8736.

Smith, T., Rose, K.D., and Gingerich, P.D. (2006) Rapid Asia-Europe-North America geographic dispersal of earliest Eocene primate *Teilhardina* during the Paleocene-Eocene Thermal Maximum. *Proceedings of the National Academy of Sciences*, **103**, 11223–11227.

Sussman, R. (1990) Primate origins and the evolution of angiosperms.*American Journal of Primatology*, **23**, 209–223.

Tavare, S., Marshall, C., Will, O-., Soligo, C., and Martin, R.D. (2002) Using the fossil record to estimate the age of the last common ancestor of extant primates. *Nature*, **416**, 726–729.

References

5

40 – 8 mya: Anthropoids and Hominoids

During the Early to Late Middle Eocene, about 40–36 mya, the global climate was warm and tropical forest was widespread over the planet. Adaptive radiation of the primates increased their diversity and anthropoids appear more frequently in the fossil record in Africa. From the mid-Eocene there was a gradual change at higher latitudes to drier climates and cooler temperatures. The cooling continued well into the Oligocene, and by about 32 mya, it had triggered a mass extinction event in which primates had disappeared from northern latitudes and were restricted to the equatorial forest that remained. **Hominoids** emerged during the Late Oligocene and as global warming set in during the Miocene, their subsequent adaptive radiation led to a diversity of Miocene apes in Africa, Europe and Asia. Their subsequent decline in range and diversity links to further cooling of global climate in the Late Miocene.

5.1 Introduction

The warm climate of the Eocene and the associated evergreen tropical forests persisted until this epoch was drawing to its end. At this time, a dramatic change in climate, involving significant global cooling was established. This major change linked to a rapid Antarctic glaciation, (Liu *et al.* 2009), a profound drop of about 30°C in sea temperatures and a concomitant drop in mean global surface temperature (GMST) from the high temperature peak in the Eocene. As GMST cooled, by about 36 mya, tropical forest had become restricted to the equatorial belt. Primates became extinct in Europe and North America as grasslands and open woodlands replaced the tropical

The Emergence of Humans Patricia Ash and David Robinson
© 2010 John Wiley & Sons, Ltd

forests. Therefore, it isn't surprising that an Oligocene site in North Africa, the Fayum Depression, which at that time had retained the equatorial forest, was the home for a rich variety of primates including galagids, adapids and early anthropoids. Oligocene sites in India and Pakistan have also yielded fossil primates, including Strepsirrhines such as *Bugtilemur* dated at 30 mya.

Primates also colonized South America during this period possibly by island hopping on vegetation rafts, and moving along continental shelves across the Atlantic Ocean, which was not as wide during the Oligocene as it is now. Once in South America the anthropoids that had arrived there were isolated from those in the Old World and their adaptive radiation formed the groups of New World monkeys (Table 4.3).

More global cooling during the Miocene diminished the tropical forest cover, which was replaced by savannah grassland in some parts of Africa. The dominant primates in the Miocene were apes, which had undergone substantial adaptive radiation resulting in diverse species in Africa, Asia and southern Europe. However, by 10 mya ape species were declining in number as adaptive radiation of monkeys in Africa and South America, was reaching its peak. Adaptive radiation of cercopithecine monkeys in Africa was accompanied by their spread into Eurasia. During the Oligocene and Miocene, prosimians in Africa declined, with the notable exception of Madagascar where their adaptive radiation resulted in an eclectic group of lemur species, occupying a diversity of niches.

Initially we examine some of the Late Eocene and Early Oligocene primates discovered in the Fayum Depression and Asia. Elwyn Simons, Erik Sieffert and colleagues have spent many years excavating sites in the Fayum Depression and discovered a variety of fossil primate species. The site includes sediments dating from about 37 mya.

5.2 Radiation of the anthropoids and other primates

Anthropoid origins are uncertain, and currently the available evidence is equivocal with regard to an Asian or African origin. It is likely though that anthropoids emerged in the Eocene. Nevertheless, future fossil finds could well change the balance of the evidence.

◆ Where were the earliest anthropoid fossils discovered? Write an outline description of the fossil remains.

◆ The earliest known primates that had anthropoid features were discovered in Africa. The detailed anatomy of fossil molars of *Altiatlasius* found in Morocco, and dated at ~55 mya suggests that it is a primitive stem anthropoid (Section 4.7). Fossil teeth (upper molars and lower premolars), of an ancient primate, *Algeripithecus minutus* found in early-Middle Eocene sediments at Glib Zegdou, Algeria suggest that it was an early anthropoid dated at ~45 mya.

Erik Seiffert has pointed out that as crown primates, primates of 'modern aspect' (Euprimates) are of Asian or Laurasian origin, the date attributed to *Altiatlasius* suggests an early immigration of primates into Africa or parallel radiation of anthropoids in Africa and Asia that are so far unknown because of the lack of fossil evidence (Seiffert *et al.*, 2005a). The discovery of *Eosimias* (Section 4.7) complicates the picture. *Eosimias* discovered in China (Section 4.5), dated at 40–45 mya is recognized by some palaeoanthropologists as an anthropoid, and close to the origin of this group. Other researchers doubt that *Eosimias* is an anthropoid.

Fossils of early anthropoids continue to be discovered in Southeast Asia. Jean-Jacques Jaeger *et al.* (2004) discovered fossils of an ancient primate when they were excavating Eocene sediments dated at 37 mya close to the village of Bahin in Myanmar. The group discovered fragments of an upper and lower jaw that were similar to those of *Eosimias*. The new species, named *Bahinia pondaungensis* had an estimated body weight of about 400 g in life and like *Eosimias*, had a shortened muzzle, vertical incisors and strong canine teeth. The upper molars of *Bahinia* have a well-developed **cingulum** surrounding the crowns, and cutting crests suggesting a diet of small animals such as insects and fruit. *Bahinia* has the same dental formula as *Eosimias*, 2/2 1/1 3/3/ 3/3, and detailed morphological features of the teeth led Jaeger to place the species in the same family, the Eosimiidae. *Bahinia* is considered by Jaeger to be a basal anthropoid, with affinities to the tarsiids rather than to adapiforms or omomyids. The finds of *Bahinia* and other ancient Asian anthropoids suggests that from ~40 mya, there was an adaptive radiation of anthropoids in Asia as well as in Africa during the Eocene. However, not all palaeoanthropologists accept that *Bahinia* is an anthropoid. There is a close resemblance between *Bahinia* and *Notharctus* and it has been suggested that the large face and small laterally placed orbits of *Bahinia* support the view that it is a strepsirrhine (prosimian) not an anthropoid (Rosenberger and Hogg, 2007).

Other primate fossils found in Myanmar include two species of *Pondaungia* and one species of *Amphipithecus*. Fossils of these species were found in the Ponduang formation of Myanmar dated in the Middle to Late Eocene, dated at about 37.2 mya. *Pondaungia* and *Amphipithecus* are adapiforms not anthropoids (Gunnell *et al.*, 2002). However other researchers assert that *Pondaungia* is an early anthropoid and that this species is sexually dimorphic and *Amphipithecus* is the female (Jaeger *et al.*, 2004). These species are likely to be a small sample of the diversity of Asian primates living in tropical forest in Asia during the Middle to late Eocene.

Fossilized remains of trees and pollen tell us that there was dense cover of tropical forest in North Africa during the late Eocene and early Oligocene, including the now arid and desolate Fayum Depression in the Egyptian desert. Here the dense forest was close to an inland sea. Elwyn Simons (Duke University Primate Centre) and his colleagues have been excavating sediments in the Fayum Depression, Egypt since the early 1960s. Recent excavations at Fayum (Seiffert *et al.*, 2005a), in the Birket Qarun locality (BQ-2) led to the discovery of two species of *Biretia*, *B. fayumensis* and *B. megalopsis*, both dated at 37 mya. *Biretia* species are early African anthropoids, of about the same age as *Bahinia*. *Biretia* was very small, *B. fayumensis* weighing just 160–273 g, a value estimated from tooth size comparisons with extant primates. *B. megalopsis* was bigger than *B. faymensis* and had large orbits suggesting that it was nocturnal. *Biretia* is classified in the order Parapithecoidea, (one of the orders of ancient anthropoids found at Fayum). The parapithecids were marmoset-like animals, with dentition characteristic of leaf eaters, all with the New World monkey dental formula, 2/2 1/1 3/3 3/3. The shared derived features of the teeth in *Biretia* and the more recent Parapithecoidea suggest a diverse and ancient clade of parapithecids, that could include *Algeripithecus*.

As more fossil species are discovered, a picture of the diversity of Late Eocene and Early Oligocene anthropoids and other primates is emerging. Fossil discoveries in sediments dated more recently than 37 mya at Fayum indicate radiation of several primate groups in equatorial Africa. More than 11 primate genera have been discovered in Locality 41 (L-41), Jebel Qatrani, in sediments containing other mammalian genera known to be characteristic of Eocene deposits in Europe, Tunisia and Oman. This evidence, with supporting palaeomagnetic evidence indicates that the L-41 sediment is Late Eocene. A more precise date range was obtained by Erik Seiffert when he re-examined the chronological evidence and made comparisons with strata elsewhere in North Africa (Seiffert, 2006). The revised age estimates of the sediments provided an Early Oligocene date of 34.8–33.7 mya for quarry L-41.

There is insufficient space for consideration of all of the primate species and the fossil discoveries, so representative examples are considered to provide a picture of their diversity. Primate fossils discovered at quarry L-41 include a right mandible with teeth from the canine to M3, attributed to *Anchomomys milleri* a non-adapiform stem strepsirrhine (Simons, 1997). Maxillary fragments attributed to the cercamoniine adapiform *Aframonius dieides* were also found in L-41 and added important information to the find of a mandible of the same species three years earlier (Simons and Miller, 1997). Seiffert has described fossils of the late Eocene strepsirrhine primate, *Wadilemur elegans*, which include a right mandible with teeth, P3 – M3, identified as a primitive stem galagid lorisiform (bushbabies and galagos) (Seiffert *et al.*, 2005b).

♦ What is a strepsirrhine?

♦ A strepsirrhine is a member of the suborder Strepsirrhini, also known as the suborder Prosimii. This group includes lemurs and lorises (Table 4.3).

The diversity of the primates found at L-41, suggests that early African anthropoids evolved as part of a large African primate radiation during the Eocene. Prior to 2005, Simons and his team had discovered 11 species of fossil anthropoids dating from 34 to 29 mya, and classified them in three families. The parapithecids were marmoset-like animals (including *Biretia*), with dentition characteristic of leaf eaters, all with the New World monkey dental formula, 2/2 1/1 3/3 3/3. Parapithecids are described variously as early or stem anthropoids. The three known species of *Apidium* are also parapithecids. The hind limbs of *Apidium phiomense* were longer than the fore-limbs and this primate was able to leap **quadripedally** between trees (Fleagle and Simons, 1995). The grasping hind feet helped *Apidium* to avoid falling out of trees. Limb anatomy also suggests *Apidium* could run quadripedally along branches. The squirrel monkey *Saimiri sciureus* is suggested as having similar behaviour to that of *Apidium*. Fleagle and Simons (1995) suggested that features of the skeleton are similar to those of *Saimari* and that it resembles a hypothetical ancestral platyrrhine.

◆ What is a platyrrhine?

◆ A platyrrhine is a member of the Infraorder Platyrrhini, the New World monkeys. Extant species include the woolly monkeys, spider monkeys as well as squirrel monkeys.

The propliopithid and oligopithecid families were larger animals than the parapithecids, and were mostly fruit-eaters. *Catopithecus browni*, an oligopithecid found at Fayum, and dated at 34 mya has three premolars in each side of both upper and lower jaws, and derived features such as complete bony eye sockets. *Proteopithecus sylviae* dated at 34.8–35 mya is a stem anthropoid with the New World dental formula of 2/2 1/1 3/3 3/3. Body size was small, with brain size estimated at just 2.7 cm³. Both species had relatively small orbits, suggesting that they were diurnal. Both species show sexual dimorphism in the size of their canine teeth, with males having canines considerably larger than those of females (Simons, *et al.*, 1999). Sexual dimorphism of canine teeth in social species provides clues to social structures of groups of primates (Section 5.4).

The propliopithecid, *Aegyptopithecus*, dated at 29–30 mya, was the largest fossil anthropoid discovered in the Fayum, with males weighing up to about 6 kg found in the Fayum Depression. The cranium is flat, and without a forehead; the orbits face forwards (Figure 5.1a). The dental formula of *Aegyptopithecus* is 2/2 1/1 2/2 3/3. The small forward incisors have a flat biting surface, contrasting with larger pointed canine teeth. There is a gap, the **diastema**, between the second incisor and canine in the upper jaw (Figure 5.1b). The enlarged canine teeth in the upper jaw fit in the diastema between the canine and first premolar in the lower jaw. The molars are not particularly enlarged, but they have grinding surfaces, including a broad extra ridge known as a cingulum, that surrounds the main cusps. The **foramen magnum** in the basicranium is quite far back, typical for a quadripedal animal (Figure 5.1c). The **hallux** is opposable and the foot appears as if it was used for grasping.

Aegyptopithecus is important as it may represent the basic anthropoid condition before the split between Old World and New World monkeys. Recent research in which CT scans of three *Aegyptopithecus* skulls were carried out, revealed **paranasal sinuses** similar to those found in humans and apes (Rossie *et al.*, 2002). We shall see in Section 5.5 that this discovery has implications for views on the origin of the Hominoidea, the group that includes apes and humans.

Early to Middle Oligocene sites in India and Pakistan have also yielded fossil primates (Marivaux *et al.*, 2001). So far five fossil primates have been discovered in Late Eocene-Early Oligocene sediments in the Bugti Hills, Balochistan, Pakistan They include *Guangxilemur singsilai* identified from fossil premolars and molars, and were

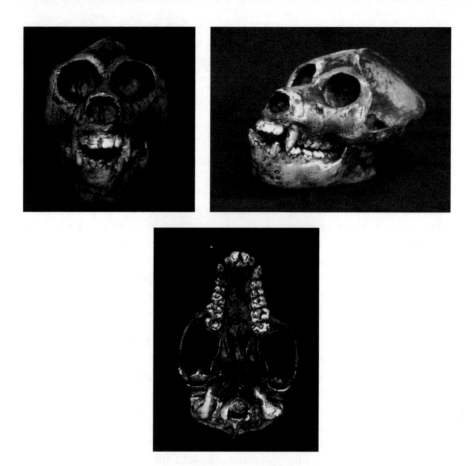

Figure 5.1 (a) Front view of a cast of the skull of *Aegyptopithecus*. (b) Side view of skull of *Aegyptopithecus*. (c) Basicranium of *Aegyptopithecus*.

dated at about 30 mya. *Guangxilemur* was identified as an adapiform. *Bugtilemur* was a small strepsirhine primate that would have weighed about 80–100 g, about the size of *Cheirogaleus*, a dwarf lemur. *Bugtilemur* is of special interest as the tooth anatomy of this species is so similar to that of the dwarf lemur, which is very different to the other lemur species in Madagascar. However, Madagascar and the Indian subcontinent separated about 88 mya whereas the origin of lemurs is estimated at about 62 mya.

◆ Suggest how lemurs might have reached the Indian subcontinent.

◆ A small group may have drifted there across the ocean on a vegetation raft.

We do not know if this was feasible, or even if the journey was in the opposite direction from the Indian subcontinent to Madagascar. Nevertheless, Asia also needs to be considered as a location for the early evolution of lemurs.

Now that we have examined a diversity of primates that lived from about 40 to 30 mya it is useful to consider how the evolutionary relationships between these diverse ancient species can be determined.

5.3   Use of cladistics for identifying evolutionary relationships in primate groups

Cladistics is the technique of choice for identifying the most likely evolutionary relationships between the various groups of primates. So before we proceed any further with our timeline we are digressing to examine the principles of cladistics. The underlying assumption of cladistics is that the members of a defined group, for example, the order Primates, have a common evolutionary history, which makes them more related to each other in evolutionary terms than members of another group, for example, order Lagomorpha (rabbits and hares). The members of the group, known as a clade, are assumed to have evolved from a common ancestor. The divergence of groups within the clade, known as **cladogensis**, is assumed to have involved splitting of each lineage into two further sub-groups. Changes in characters within lineages of a clade took place over time. Cladistics involves the examination of the suite of characters in individual species, both fossil and living to find out common characters within groups that can be used to determine phylogeny.

However, certain common characters of animals in two groups may not be linked to evolutionary relationships between those groups. Most insect species possess wings, but that does not imply an evolutionary relationship with birds. The structure of a bird's wing is derived from part of the bony internal skeleton of vertebrates, the vertebrate five-digit limb. In contrast the insect wing develops as an outgrowth of the cuticle, the external arthropod skeleton. So we cannot use the common possession of wings to indicate an evolutionary relationship between birds and insects. Possession of wings in birds and insects is regarded as an example of convergence and in cladistics convergent characters are known as **homoplasies**. Whether characters are defined as convergent depends on the level of hierarchy of the groups that are being compared. Birds and insects are classified in the Kingdom Animalia which reflects their evolutionary history, in that it is likely that all animals evolved from an ancestral multicellular group, possibly dating back to >100 mya. So at least in terms of the time scale of a billion years there is an evolutionary relationship between vertebrates and invertebrates. Such evolutionary relationships are confirmed by analyses of DNA sequences, which have identified genes common to fruit flies, mice, apes and humans. For example, genes that code for the human eye have DNA sequences common to genes that code for the very simple eyes of flatworms, compound eyes of insects and the eyes of apes and humans.

So when undertaking a cladistic analysis the first task is to identify the level of phylogenetic relationships that are of interest. If we want to look at relationships between ancient primates and the first known anthropoids, we need to focus on characters identified in the fossil remains and those characters that are known to define anthropoids. Therefore, we would not for example, select multicellularity as a character. Identifying the relevant characters for a cladistical analysis is not straightforward and can be controversial. The principle of cladistic analysis is to identify a suite of shared characters in the group that are unique to that group, and to look for those characters in species that may be related. The principle is the same whether the characters are anatomical, physiological, biochemical, or molecular.

We have already seen how certain common characters in two groups identified as homoplasies cannot be used to suggest an evolutionary relationship between those two groups. Common characters identified as resulting from common phylogeny are known as homologous characters and only such characters can be used to work out evolutionary relationships between groups. Each of the homologous characters of any organism may be of two types, **primitive** and **derived**. The term primitive has been mis-used so much in the past that it is no longer used by many biologists, who use the term **plesiomorphic** instead. Features described as primitive are those that were present in an ancestral group of animals and continue to be present in living species of the group. For example, possession of nails in living primates is considered to be a primitive feature (**plesiomorphy**) in relation to ancient primates. Ancestral primates had nails rather than claws on at least some of their fingers and toes, as we have seen in fossils of the plesiadapiform, *Carpolestes*. Derived features, or **apomorphies**, are defined as those that evolved later in a group. A post-orbital bar is considered to be a derived feature for early primates that distinguishes them from a sister group, Plesiadapiformes (Section 4.2). However, in relation to living primates, the post-orbital bar is regarded as a primitive feature, as it is found in the earliest true primates. The possession of nails in living primates would be regarded as derived in relation to other groups of mammals such as tree shrews and rodents. So, the possession of nails is a **shared derived character** found in primates, distinguishing them from other mammal groups such as tree shrews. The term synapomorphy is used in cladistics to mean a shared derived character. Identifying a feature as primitive or derived is described as deciding on the feature's **polarity**.

Having identified polarity for the characters, the next stage is to sort the groups that share synapomorphies. If there are anomalies or conflicts, the principle of **parsimony** is used. This approach involves selection of the simplest possible interpretation of the features of the species so that they are collected into groups by using the smallest possible number of steps.

◆ Summarize the principles involved in building a **cladogram**.

◆ Select the groups that are considered to have evolutionary relationships. Each group should include sub-groups or clades.

◆ Identify the defining characters of the animals within the selected groups.

◆ Examine each character and decide on polarity for each – is the character primitive or derived?

♦ List the derived characters and compare their incidence in the various groups.

♦ Now using the comparisons, construct a cladogram as a series of branches. At each branch, one of the animal groups that doesn't share a common character with the rest of the group branches into its own clade.

The cladogram built up in Figure 5.2 illustrates the application of the principles. The groups involved are all classified within the phylum Chordata, which itself is defined by the possession of a notochord and a dorsal nerve cord. Note that all groups and species are placed at endpoints, not on **nodes**, which are the branches where there are splits of the cladogram lines into two lines. Each node has to have a list of synapomorphies identified as common to all the groups that lead off from that node.

So, in order to construct a cladogram for the lamprey, trout, toad, lizard, rat monkey and modern human, *Homo*, a set of selected synapomorphies, shared derived characters, are listed (Table 5.1) and the presence or absence of each character in each group is recorded. The numbers of characters identified for each group are counted and the cladogram constructed. Bear in mind that although the construction of *this* cladogram in Figure 5.2 demonstrates the principles, it is greatly simplified.

In this cladogram, the lamprey represents an **outgroup**.

Although a cladogram is not quite the same as an evolutionary tree, it is assumed that it represents an estimate of phylogeny. So cladograms are also used to represent evolutionary trees, as in Figure 5.3.

Table 5.1   Sets of synapomorphies and their presence (x) or absence in each of seven groups of chordates

	Lamprey	Trout	Toad	Lizard	Rat	Monkey	Homo
Dorsal nerve cord	x	x	x	x	x	x	x
Vertebral column		x	x	x	x	x	x
Heart: two chambers	x	x	x				
Heart: three to four chambers				x	x	x	x
*Amniote egg				x	x	x	x
Placenta					x	x	x
Gills	x	x					
Lungs			x	x	x	x	x
Orbits face forwards						x	x
**EQ > 5.0							x
Skin naked	x		x				
Two pairs of limbs			x	x	x	x	x
Skin with scales		x		x			
Skin with hair/fur					x	x	x
Totals for each group	4	5	6	7	8	9	10

* An egg protected by membranes, in contrast to those of fish and amphibians.
** Encephalisation Quotient.

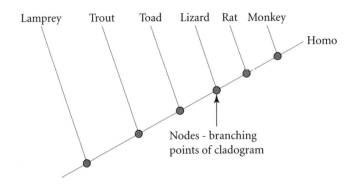

Figure 5.2   Cladogram prepared from data in Table 5.2.

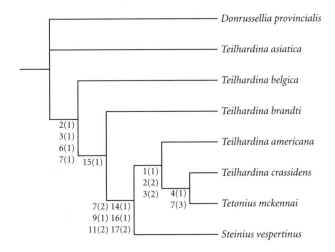

Figure 5.3   Cladogram for early primates. Adapted from Smith, Rose and Gingerich (2006) P11227.

Now examine the tree in Figure 5.3, which was constructed as a cladogram, derived from the most parsimonius tree. Recall from Chapter 4, that Smith *et al.* had reported that of the various species of the primitive omomyiform *Teilhardina*, *T. asiatica* is the oldest known species. The researchers carried out a cladistic analysis of 17 dental characters, including changes in the width of molars and premolars and in the shapes of the canine teeth. The adapiform *Donrussellia provincialis* was selected as the out-group. This species has the dental formula 2 1 4 3 so is similar to *Teilhardina* in possessing four premolars.

Donruselia, which represents the outgroup, is placed above the line that had split forming *T. asiatica*, representing the sister group for the other *Teilhardina* species. *T. belgica* is the sister group to the line giving rise to *T. brandti*, *T. American*, *T. crassidens* and *T. mckennai*. *Stenius vespertinus* is more primitive than *T. america* and dated at 1–2 million years later than *americana* so may have arisen from a different Eurasian ancestor.

In Section 5.5 we examine the adaptive radiation of hominoids during the Oligocene and Miocene, and how cladistics has thrown some light on their evolutionary relationships. However, at this point, before moving on to the origin and radiation of the Hominoidea it is useful to pause to investigate the social structures of extant primates.

5.4 Social structures in primate groups

One difficulty with the study of extinct species is that their fossil anatomy and paleoenvironment provides at best small clues to their behaviours. One defining characteristic of primates is their tendency to live in social groups. Studies of social groups in living primate species can help to provide some understanding of the social behaviours of extinct species. Most extant monkeys and all apes are social animals and have an extraordinary diversity of social structures. A social group provides opportunities for intense social interaction, including planning, deception and forming alliances. There are also opportunities for the young to learn from other members of the group, especially their mothers.

Savannah baboons live in large groups of up to 200 individuals. One large male who is dominant to all other males in the group has first choice of females in oestrus. The male is much larger than the female who has no defence against him. Within a large group there are likely to be several females in oestrus at the same time, so other large males will also have opportunities to mate with them. This type of mating system where a male has opportunities to mate with many females is defined as **polygynous**. In social groups with a polygynous mating system, males tend to be much larger than females. Males compete with each other for females using their large canine teeth as warning signals and weapons.

♦ The canine teeth in male *Catopithecus browni* and *Proteopithecus sylviae* were much larger than those of females. Suggest the type of social group and mating system that may have been characteristic of these two fossil monkeys.

♦ Evidence from observations of the social structures of extant primates can be used to link sexual dimorphism to social structure. Male savannah baboons live in a social structure having a polygynous mating system. Males have much larger bodies and larger canine teeth than females. The males' canine teeth are used as threats and weapons to establish dominance over other males in the group for access to females for mating. So extrapolating from the extant savannah baboon, it is likely that *Catopithecus browni* and *Proteopithecus sylviae* males were living in a social group structure in which the mating system was polygynous.

Similar principles can be applied to the Miocene apes. We have very few extant ape species, in comparison to the great diversity of Miocene apes. Nevertheless having some understanding of social groups of living ape species helps in suggesting hypotheses for the structure of the social groups of Miocene apes.

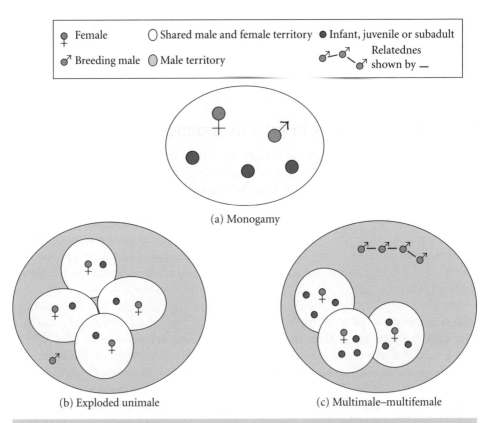

Figure 5.4 (a) Social group of gibbons, depicted as a map. (b) Single male orang utans defend a group of females and their offspring but females may be distributed over a wide area, a situation known as 'exploded unimale'. (c) In chimpanzee social groups, several related males mate with and defend a group of females and their offspring. This is a multimale-multifemale group with female territories. Adapted from Studying Mammals © The Open University.

The simplest social structure is monogamy, in which males and females live as single pairs. This is the typical social structure for gibbons, and a group consists of a male and female, with on average two offspring, one very young and suckling, and the other a juvenile (Figure 5.4a).

In contrast to gibbons, orangutans have an extreme form of polygyny in which one male's territory includes the overlapping territories of two or more adult females. The female with her offspring is the core of the group. She has her own defined home range, which overlaps with the ranges of other females in the group. Each male defends his territory, which includes the ranges of the females he has access to for mating (Figure 5.4b). Adult males weigh 80 kg, more than twice as much as females, which weigh up to 40 kg. Males have distinctive secondary sexual characteristics, enlarged canine teeth, long fur and fleshy inflatable cheek pads, both features linking to their competition with other males for females. Males use their large body size and teeth as weapons and air in their inflated cheek pads can resonate, making their calls audible for up to a kilometre distance. Warning calls help to prevent physical conflicts, but a resident male will fight fiercely if he meets a male intruder.

African apes live in different social structures to those of the Asian apes. Chimpanzee social structure is based on **multimale polygyny**. Chimpanzees live in loose groups of 15–80 animals, including mature males, females and offspring of various ages (Figure 5.4c). Each female has a core area which may overlap with that of other females. A female lives and travels with her offspring, but can join other females and their offspring. Such a social structure is known as '**fusion-fission**'. Contact between the scattered members of the group is maintained by distance calls, known as pant hoots. Baby chimpanzees are cared for by their mothers, and are weaned at 4–5 years old. After a long juvenile phase, lasting about 8–11 years, they become sexually mature.

Young adult female chimpanzees may transfer or be kidnapped into other communities, but males remain in their own group. So all males in a group are closely related, and co-operate to defend their community's range against males of neighbouring groups. Within their community, males associate with each other and form dominance relationships, whereby one individual becomes the alpha male. The dominant position of the alpha male is maintained by the support of his allies. Males compete with each other for females using their sharp enlarged canines as weapons. Male chimpanzees are about 25–30% larger than the females, a typical situation where males compete for access to females. All male chimpanzees are dominant to all females.

Two features of sexual dimorphism, enlarged canine teeth and large body size in males, observed in fossil ape species provide clues to their social behaviours.

5.5 The hominoidea

Fossil evidence suggests that anthropoid monkeys were not so abundant or widespread during the Miocene, as they were during the Eocene. Their decline began in the late Eocene and continued in the Oligocene as the climate was cooling. Climate change and warming in the Miocene resulted in increasing aridity and development of steppe grassland, but there were still some moist forests persisting in Europe and Asia. Anthropoid monkeys were still present in Africa and a split between Old World and New World monkeys occurred at the end of the Miocene. Overall, though, the fossil evidence suggests a decreasing range for Miocene monkeys in the Miocene. In contrast, there was a tremendous adaptive radiation of apes, which became more diverse and numerous than anthropoid monkeys. At least 100 fossil species are known and they were discovered in Africa, Europe and Asia. Apes are classified in the Superfamily Hominoidea (Table 5.2), which also includes humans.

Fossil evidence suggests that Miocene apes living in Africa were the earliest known hominoids (Figure 5.5), and their anatomy and dates support an African origin for the clade. Although the primate fossil record in Africa is quite rich from 36–32 mya,

Table 5.2   Classification of Hominoidea

Superfamily Hominoidea	
Family Hylobatidae	*Hylobates; Symphalagus*
Family Afropithecidae	*Afropithecus; Heliopithecus*
Family Hominidae	
Subfamily Kenyapithecinae	*Kenyapithecus*
	Griphopithecus
	Maboko hominid?
Subfamily Dryopithecinae	
Tribe Dryopithecini	*Dryopithecus*
Tribe Oreopithecinae	*Oreopithecus*
Subfamily Ponginae	*Pongo*
	Sivapithecus
	Gigantopithecus
	Lufengopithecus
Subfamily Homininae	
Tribe Gorillini	*Gorilla*
Tribe Panini	*Pan*
Tribe Hominini	*Ardipithecus*
	Australopithecus
	Kenyanthropus
	Paranthropus
	Homo
Incertae sedis: *Graecopithecus*	
Hominidae: Incertae sedis	*Otavipithecus*

this is not the case for the time span 32–21 mya. This means that the precise divergence time for cercopithecoids and hominoids cannot be obtained from the fossil record. *Kamoypithecus hamiltoni*, identified as a hominoid by its dentition, is dated at 27.5–24 mya but there is argument about whether this species is hominoid. As only a few fragments of jaw have been found, and there is insufficient material there to confirm *Kamoypithecus* as a hominoid, more fossil evidence will be needed to do this (Leakey, Ungar and Walker, 1995). Otherwise, either *Proconsul* dated at ~20 mya or *Morotopithecus* dated at ~20.6 mya are the oldest known hominoids. Genetic evidence indicates an earlier origin for the hominoids. Gene sequences of 150 000 base pairs from two cercopithecoids, rhesus macaque, and anubis baboon, and two hominoids, chimpanzee and modern human have been compared (Steiper, Young and Sukarna, 2004). Each 150 000 base pair set was trimmed to five nonrepeat DNA sequences, each known as a contig set, and a molecular clock was applied comparing the hominoid with the cercoptihecid contigs in a set. The analysis gave divergence dates for cercopithecoids and hominoids of from each contig ranging from 29.2 to 3 mya (Figure 5.5).

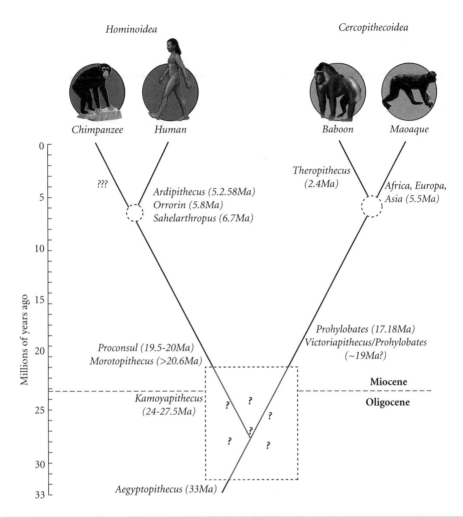

Figure 5.5 Phylogeny of four hominoid taxa, including the dates and names of fossil taxa relevant to divergence between hominoids and cercopithecoids. Aegyptopithecus is placed at the root of the phylogeny at 33 mya. Note the estimated divergence time of Prohylobates (gibbons) at ~18–17 mya. Reproduced, with permission, from Steiper M E, Young N M and Sukarna T Y (2004) Genomic data support the hominoid slowdown and an early Oligocene estimate for the hominoid-cercopithecoid divergence. Proceedings of the National Academy of Sciences 101 no 49 P17022 © (2004) The National Academy of Sciences, U.S.A

♦ How does the date range for the hominoid-cercopithecoid split derived from the genetic data compare with that suggested by the fossil data? What problems arise from your comparison?

♦ The date range obtained with the genetic study is considerably older than that estimated from the fossils' dates, which could be 27.5–20.6 mya assuming that *Kamoypithecus* is a hominoid. The sparse fossil record for primates from 32 to 21 mya means that there is no way so far of checking the fossil record for agreement with those dates.

Fossils of *Morotopithecus* were discovered in Uganda in the 1960s by Bishop and colleagues, and include a large palate and a partial face. In 1994 and 1995, Gebo and MaClatchy discovered fragments of the femur and vertebrae (Gebo *et al.*, 1997). Measurements of the fossils and comparison with measurements on living apes, suggest a body size close to that of a large adult female chimpanzee, about 50 kg for *Morotopithecus*. The lumbar vertebrae of *Morotopithecus*, unlike those of *Proconsul*, have processes and small muscle attachments that would have restricted movement of the lower back. These features suggest a similarity to apes, unlike the adaptations linked to quadrupedal locomotion *in Proconsul*. MaClatchy and others describe two partial femurs and part of a shoulder bone they discovered. The robust femur, relatively much thicker than that of any living apes, indicates that the limbs were carrying a heavy load. The glenoid fossa, the 'socket' of the shoulder joint is broad and curved allowing a wide range of movement for the arms, as seen in living suspensory primates. They interpret the fossils as indicating an arboreal ape, practising careful vertical climbing, suspensory movement through trees and quadrupedalism (MaClatchy *et al.*, 2000). If Rossie *et al.*'s (2002) view that *Proconsul* is a stem catarrhine, a monkey, and not a stem hominoid, is accepted, then *Morotopithecus* may be the oldest known hominoid.

Three species of *Proconsul* are arguably amongst the earliest members of the Hominoidea. *Proconsul* fossils were found in Miocene deposits on the islands of Rusinga and Mfangano in Lake Victoria, Kenya. The islands formed during the Miocene, as the now dormant volcano Kisinguri erupted lava flows and ash. The alkaline soils supported dry deciduous woodland between volcanic eruptions and also favoured the preservation and fossilization of bones and teeth. Many fossil bones of Miocene apes and other animals have been found in the volcanic deposits on the islands. Rusinga Island was the location of the first known skull of *Proconsul* discovered in October 1948 by Mary Leakey. Mary and her colleague Heselon Mukiri found 30 fragments of the skull and jaw, enough to put together to make a near complete skull of *Proconsul heseloni* (KNM-RU 7290). The cranium is slightly domed with a forehead and large and forward facing orbits are (Figure 5.6). The face is prognathous, projecting forward into a snout.

The mandible is deep with both jaws bearing large teeth. As in all apes, the dental formula of *Proconsul* is 2/2 1/1 2/2 3/3. The molars on both jaws have flattened grinding surfaces. The incisors project forwards, and the canines in particular are long and sharp. The body size of *Proconsul heseloni* is estimated at ~10 kg, about the size of a small female baboon (Walker and Shipman, 2005). Although the skull is incomplete, it was possible to estimate brain size at ~167 cm^3. Relative brain size is a more useful measure, which is expressed as the encephalization quotient, EQ (Box 5.1), a measure of brain size in relation to body size. Estimates of EQ for *P. heseloni* are ~1.5, suggesting that relative brain size is close to the mean value for surviving anthropoids. Compare the value of EQ for *P. heseloni* with that for chimpanzee, 2.0, and for *Homo sapiens*, 5.8.

Walker's team re-visted Rusinga and Mfangano islands several times, and discovered many more fossils of *Proconsul*, representing four species. The largest, *Proconsul*

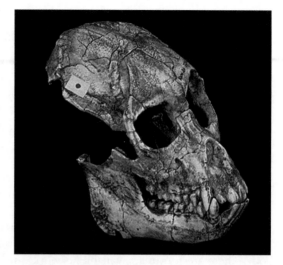

Figure 5.6 Skull of *Proconsul heseloni* discovered at Rusinga.

major weighed about 63.4–86.1 kg and just a few postcranial fossils have been found at Napak in Uganda and Songhor, Kenya. The smallest species, weighing ~10 kg was *P. heseloni*, found at both Rusinga and Mfangano. *P. africanus* also found at Rusinga and Mfangano, was larger weighing from 9.3 to 13.6 kg, and showed some anatomical differences from *P. heseloni*. The fossil remains of nine individual skeletons of *P. africanus* were found by Walker's team at Kaswanga on Rusinga. They included milk teeth and long bones of two juveniles, identifiable because the **epiphyses** (growth plates) of the long bones had not fused indicating that the individuals were still growing. Of the remains of the seven adults two appeared to be females as their canine teeth were smaller than those of the males. Fossils of a third species, *Proconsul nyzanae* were discovered at Kaswanga on Rusinga, and also at Mfangano where a partial skeleton was found. *P. nyzanae* is distinguished by an estimated body mass of 28–46.3 kg. Research carried out on the partial skeleton by Carol Ward (University of Missouri-Columbia) revealed that *P. nyzanae* had at least six lumbar vertebrae, and that the processes of these vertebrae allowed considerable movement and flexibility in the lower back. A long flexible back is a characteristic feature of monkeys. In contrast apes have a rigid lower back, which cannot be bent because of interlocking vertebral processes, and relatively small muscles in the lower back. Carol Ward's comparative study of the sacral vertebrae of tailed monkeys, tailless apes and *Proconsul nyzanae* indicated that *Proconsul*, like apes, did not have a tail. The kneecap of *Proconsul*, like that of apes, was wide and shallow, slotted in a wide shallow groove permitting a wide range of motion. The long hand bones resemble those of monkeys. So, the evidence suggests that *Proconsul* had a mix of monkey-like and ape-like features (Figure 5.7). *Proconsul's* skeletal anatomy suggests slow careful movement in trees, including quadrupedal movement with the body oriented horizontal to a branch, or the ground (Walker and Shipman, 2005).

Box 5.1   Relative brain size of primates

Palaeoanthropologists are interested in drawing comparisons between relative brain sizes in fossil primate species. Our own species has a very large brain size in comparison to other hominoids and as we follow the time line we will see that increasing brain size was an important feature in the evolution of humans. Brain size on its own cannot be used as a simple measure of increasing brain size in *Homo*. It is important to take body size into account too, as brain size increases with body mass in primates as a whole. Palaeoanthropologists use an index, the **encephalization quotient,** EQ to express the relative real size of a primate's brain in comparison to the size that would be expected in a primate of similar body mass. For example, a fossil primate of body mass estimated at 20 kg might be expected to have a brain size of 200 cm³. Encephalization Quotient (EQ), is defined as the ratio of the mass of the brain to the expected mass of the body. There are formulae available to work out EQ. For example the formula devised by Jerison (1973) has been used in many cases:

$$EQ = M_{brain}/0.12M_{body}^{2/3}$$

Estimated size of *P. heseloni* = 167 cm³ and assuming brain density of 1 g cm⁻³, then brain mass = 167 g. Walker estimated body mass of *P. heseloni* at 10 kg, so substituting values into formula gives:

$$EQ = 167g/(0.12 \times 10\,000^{2/3})g$$

$$= 167g/107g$$

$$EQ = 1.56$$

Compare this to the EQ value of about 5.8 for modern humans, Jerison (1973) calculated EQ values for a number of Cenozoic primate-like animals and primates. Plesiadapids have calculated EQ values of 0.2–0.62, and Eocene and Oligocene primates values of about 0.39– 0.97.

The finds of fossils of nine individual *Proconsul africanus* found at Rusinga suggest a family group, but we cannot be certain because the collections of fossil bones could have been accumulated over many hundreds of years, a tiny period in geological time but representing many generations of *Proconsul*.

◆ What process could have led to accumulation of *Proconsul* bones over hundreds of years?

Figure 5.7 Reconstruction of *Proconsul africanus* dated at about 18 mya based on finds before 1959 by M Leakey, and in 1980 by Alan Walker and Martin Pickford. (Reproduced from Lewin 1999, P90).

♦ The site may have been used over many years by carnivores such as big cats, for killing and eating their prey, or even for caching.

Nevertheless, tantalizing evidence for the social structure of *Proconsul* groups includes the larger canine teeth in males than in females, suggesting sexual dimorphism.

♦ What does sexual dimorphism of canine teeth suggest about the social structure of *Proconsul*?

♦ Chimpanzees live in multimale-multifemale groups, and males compete with each other for dominance and access to females. The males have enlarged canines, used both for weapons and as threats. Sexual dimorphism of canines in *Proconsul* suggests similar behaviours in males of this ancient species.

Apes and humans live within complex social structures, so there is much interest in evidence that throws light on social structure in fossil species.

Walker and his team conclude that the Rusinga fossils form a 'crucial link between the early primates of forest habitats and human forerunners living in a more open country habitat'. However, not everyone agrees that *Proconsul* is a 'human fore-runner' or indeed an ancestor of apes. Rossi *et al.* carried out CT scans of the skull of *Aegyptopithecus* (an early anthropoid dated at ~34–29 mya, Section 5.2). They were interested in the view that frontoethmoid sinuses in *Proconsul* and other

Miocene apes are synapomorphies. Sinuses are air-filled cavities in the bones of the face that are lined with epithelium. The frontal sinuses are located on both sides of the forehead, and ethmoid sinuses are located between the eyes. CT scans of three faces of *Aegyptopithecus* demonstrated the presence of ethmoid sinuses and also small extensions of the sinuses into the frontal bones. Rossi *et al.* interpret these as homologous precursors to the large frontal sinuses in African apes and humans, suggesting that it is a primitive retained character in *Proconsul*. They suggest that the argument for *Proconsul* being an ancestral hominoid is weakened.

From about 25 mya, there was a widespread adaptive radiation of Miocene apes with fossil species discovered in Africa, Europe and Asia, but none in America or Australia. Important discoveries of other Miocene apes from Africa, include *Afropithecus* and *Turkanopithecus*. Richard and Meave Leakey, working with Alan Walker, discovered two new species of Miocene apes at Kalodirr on the west side of Lake Turkana (Leakey, Leakey and Walker, 1988). They found a robust skull, a jaw and postcranial fragments, of a previously unknown species, *Afropithecus turkanensis*. These fossils were dated at 17.5–17 mya. Measurements of the fossil bones suggested an estimated body mass of ~50 kg. The skull comprises a complete face and upper jaw, and resembles that of a gorilla. The face shows marked prognathism, with a long narrow snout and robust and **procumbent** (forward-projecting) incisors (Figure 5.8a). The canine teeth are small, rounded and tusk-like, and those of males may have been larger than those of females. There is a 6.5 mm diastema between the second incisor and the canine tooth. Walker and Shipman (2004) suggest that *Afropithecus* was a seed-eater, using its procumbent incisors for biting into hard fruits and peeling off the husks of seeds and the thick-enameled molars for crushing hard seeds, such as nuts. The procumbent incisors and the diastema resemble in some ways those of cavy-like rodents for example, agouti, (Figure 5.8c) which use the incisors for grasping, peeling and biting into nuts, even those as hard as brazil nuts.

Afropithecus is similar to *Morotopithecus*. It is interesting to note at this point that there is a view amongst some researchers that *Morotopithecus* and *Afropithecus* should be classified in the same genus. The rationale is that the dental characteristics of the two species are so similar that the differences between them are within the range that would be expected between individuals of the same species (Patel and Grossman, 2006).

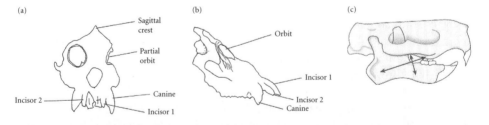

Figure 5.8 Comparison of skull of *Afropithecus* and cavy type rodent. (a) and (b) Outline of partial skull of *Afropithecus*. (c) Side view of skull of cavy-like rodent. (c) Reproduced from *Studying Mammals* P.53. © The Open University.

Leakey *et al.* (1988) interpret the fossils as suggesting that *Afropithecus* was slow-moving and arboreal, because of similarities in the postcranial fragments to the postcranial skeleton of *Proconsul nyanzae*. The face of *Afropithecus* bears similar features to that of *Aegyptopithecus*, but the skull of *Afropithecus* is much larger. Walker and Shipman speculate that *Aegyptopithecus* could be ancestral to *Afropithecus* or that the face of *Afropithecus* was a primitive feature for African apes and monkeys. They also suggest that *Afropithecus* could have wandered out of Africa and reached Eurasia by 16 mya.

The second Miocene ape discovered at Kalodirr by the Leakeys was *Turkanopithecus kakolensis* (Leakey, Ungar and Walker, 1995). The fossils include a skull dated at 18–16 mya. and there are distinct brow ridges.

♦ Which apes were likely to have co-existed with *Turkanopithecus*?

♦ Both *Proconsul* and *Afropithecus* were likely to have co-existed with *Turkanopithecus*.

The canine teeth of *Turkanopithecus* are relatively large suggesting that the fossil is male. The face is very different from that of either *Afropithecus* or *Proconsul*, in that the muzzle is squared and the nasal opening broad. The orbits are set wide apart.

Genetic studies on humans and living great ape species have suggested that the great ape and **hominin** clades (Table 5.2) diverged about 16 to 11 million years ago, during the Middle Miocene. *Morotopithecus* dated at ~20 mya is far too ancient to be considered as either a hominin ancestor or as a sister taxon of the Homininae. So Miocene apes dated at the Middle Miocene are of particular interest. *Kenyapithecus* is a fossil ape dating from ~14 mya. The first fossils were discovered in 1961 by Louis Leakey at Fort Ternan in Kenya, and named as *K. wickeri*. Later in 1965 and 1993 further excavations on Maboko Island in Lake Victoria yielded more finds, dated at ~15.5 mya but with more derived features including a robust mandible and anterior dentition with procumbent orientation of the lower incisors (McCrossin and Benefit, 1993). These features had suggested a different species, which Leakey named as *Kenyapithecus africanus*. In 1993, at Tugen Hills, Kenya, Boniface Kimeu found more fossils of *Equatorius*, including a jaw with thickly enamelled teeth, vertebrae, ribs and bones from forelimbs including wrists and hands. The remains are dated at 15 mya. It was the discovery of more finds of Middle Miocene hominoid fossils at Kipsaramon at Tugen Hills that led to the recognition of the genus *Equatorius* (Ward *et al.*, 1999), as well as the realization that the fossils named previously as *K. africanus* bear close resemblances to those of *Equatorius*. Therefore, fossils named as *K. africanus* were also grouped into the new genus, and all were named as *Equatorius africanus*. The anatomy of the fossil bones indicates that *Equatorius* was not closely related to living apes. From the fossil anatomy it appears that body size of *Equatorius*, about 27 kg, was similar to that of a male adult baboon. The front and hind limbs of *Equatorius* were of equal length, indicating quadrupedal locomotion, and the structure of the vertebrae indicates a flexible vertebral column. The humerus has a small posteriorly orientated flattened head. Both hands and feet were grasping, indicating arboreality, but these animals also spent time on the ground as dense tropical forest became more open inresponse to increased aridity. Primitive features include the molar size sequence, $M_1 < M_2 < M_3$ and in the upper jaw, thick tooth enamel, low-crowned canines relative to those in the lower jaw. Some features of the hind-limb bones are primitive in that they are similar to those of *Proconsul* and *Afropithecus*. Derived features of *Equatorius* include reduced premolar and molar cingulae and relatively long premolars. In the postcranial skeleton, derived features include straight robust clavicle (collar bone), and robust ulna. The more recent *K. wickeri*, is interpreted as having more derived features than *Equatorius* and as a later species within the stem hominoid radiation in the Miocene.

By around 25 mya, India had collided with Asia and Asia was joined to Europe forming a large land mass. Africa was separated from Europe and Asia but by the mid-Miocene, 16–14 mya, a land connection had developed between Africa and Asia, which allowed migration of hominoids into Asia. Miocene apes in Africa were therefore able to disperse into Asia and Europe. Fossils of an ape named as *Griphopithecus alpani* were discovered at Pasalar in Turkey, as well as a second un-named species. The Turkish fossils include 11 mandibles and maxillae and >1000 teeth. Other fossils found at the same site are 2 maxillae and 59 teeth which look identical to those of *Kenyapithecus*. These fossils were assigned to *Kenyapithecus*, because of shared derived features of the anterior dentition. *Griphopithecus* retains primitive characters seen in early Miocene African apes and bears a close resemblance to *Equatorius africanus* found on Maboko Island and Kipsaramon. Andrews deduces that during the Middle Miocene there was emigration of the African apes out of Africa as the Tethys Sea had closed, forming a land link between Africa and Eurasia. Steven Ward also suggests that *K. wickeri* dated at 14 mya may have migrated out of Africa, to Eurasia and given rise to *Griphopithecus*. The environment during the Middle Miocene in both Turkey and Africa was deciduous woodland. Small apes such as *Limnopithecus* existed at the same time.

Griphopithecus has been found in sites in Europe, including Engelweiss in Germany, Sandberg in the north west of Bratislava, and Slovakia. Begun suggests collecting the known *Griphopithecus* species, as well as *Kenyapithecus* and *Equatorius* into a group, 'griphopiths'. However he acknowledges that the phylogenetic relationships between them are poorly understood (Begun, 2007). The oldest fossils are those from Germany and Turkey, dated at 16.5–16 mya and those from Slovakia and Africa are more recent at ~15 mya. Griphopiths from all locations have shared derived characters that make them unique and very different from the Early Miocene apes. Their jaws are robust and the molars have thick enamel with low cusps, relatively little dentine, and reduced cingulae. The molars are remarkably similar to those of *Kenyapithecus wickeri* and also similar to those of *Equatorius*. Nevertheless, the similarity between *Kenyapithecus wickeri* and *Equatorius* derives from a generalized ape morphology in the Middle Miocene (Stringer and Andrews, 2005). Study of microwear patterns in the teeth of *Griphopithecus* shows patterns that are very close to those of *Pongo* (King, Aiello and Andrews, 1999). The researchers conclude that *Griphopithecus* ate a similar diet to *Pongo*, soft fruits and occasionally hard or unripe fruits as well as nuts. During the Middle Miocene, Pasalar had a seasonal climate and the mammals living there were species typically found in subtropical monsoon woodland. The post-cranial skeleton of *Equatorius* shows indications of terrestriality but not quadrupedal locomotion.

Postcranial anatomy of *Griphopithecus* indicates that it could be both arboreal and terrestrial. Evidence from Middle Miocene sediments suggests that the forests where *Griphopithecus* was living appeared not to have had sufficient tree cover for a large ape to move swiftly through the trees.

Other fossil apes were also living in Europe in the Middle Miocene. *Pierolapithecus cataluna* dated at 13–12.5 mya was discovered in Spain by Moya-Sola *et al.* (2004). The fossils include cranial dental and postcranial remains. This species has elongated molars and its long sloping face is similar to that of *Afropithecus*. The cheek bones are located high in the face. Postcranial fossils include parts of the hand, which has short fingers, which would not allow suspensory movement and behaviours. Certain derived aspects of the post cranial skeletal anatomy suggest an upright **orthograde** posture. The term orthograde is used to describe upright ape locomotion either when climbing or walking bipedally, for example, to collect fruits from high branches. The thorax is broad and shallow and the stiff lumbar skeleton suggests a vertical posture and the ability to climb in an upright position. So *Pierolapithecus* has a curious mix of primitive and derived features not seen in extant apes where suspensory behaviours are linked with upright posture.

Other Miocene apes discovered in Europe include *Dryopithecus* and *Oreopithecus*. Researchers have focused on *Dryopithecus*, as a sister clade to African apes and humans. *Dryopithecus* species lived in swamp forests in Europe from 14 to 9 mya, spanning the Middle and Late Miocene. Four species have been identified so far. Fossils have been found in France, Germany, Greece, Spain and Hungary. Finds of fossils of *Dryopithecus* at Rudabanya, Hungary (Kordos and Begun, 2002) provided information about both the anatomy and locomotion, and studies of the palaeoecology revealed the Late Miocene swamp forest environment in which *Dryopithecus* was living (Kordos and Begun, 2002). The phalanges of *Dryopithecus* were highly curved, with attachment sites for robust flexor muscle and these features of the forelimbs indicate that *Dryopithecus* was arboreal and suspensory. Parts of fore limbs that were found included a broad distal humerus, with a large trochlea and an ulna with a well developed keel that would have articulated with the trochlear notch of the humerus. So the elbow joint of *Dryopithecus* resembles that of modern great apes in that it allows a wide range of movement with resistance to tearing and breaking, essential for animals that climb and are suspensory. The skull is relatively light with flat cheeks which are directed forwards (Figure 5.9).

Features of the teeth of *Dryopithecus* suggest this ape was a fruit eater. The incisors are both of similar size and relatively small, as are the canine teeth. The size of the canines in males is reduced relative to those of other hominoids such as *Afropithecus*. The teeth of *Dryopithecus* are thinly enamelled, and the premolars and molars have blunt and rounded surfaces, with cusps and wide basins consistent with a diet of soft fruits. The behaviour of *Dryopithecus* was probably similar to that of an extant great ape. *Dryopithecus* resembles juvenile African great apes in that the front part of the maxilla is orientated vertically and not elongated as it is in adult great apes.

However, the post-cranial skeleton has resemblances to orang utans, especially elongated hind limbs and elongated fingers on the hands. So *Dryopithecus* appears to have been arboreal and to have spent little time on the ground. Interesting fossil

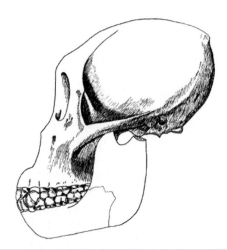

Figure 5.9   Side view of skull of *Dryopithecus brancol* discovered at Rudabanya. Reproduced from Kordos and Begun, 2002, P54.

finds at the same site were teeth of the Miocene catarrhine pliopithecoid monkey *Anapithecus hernyaki*, which in life would have weighed about 15 kg. A few postcranial fragments were found, including curved phalanges and some foot bones with morphology suggesting suspensory postures. Fossil remains of another pliopithecoid monkey *Epipliopithecus vindobonensis* were also found at Rudabanya. These monkey fossils are reminders that monkeys were still found outside Africa and Asia during the Miocene although their diversity and distribution were reduced considerably from that in the Eocene.

Oreopithecus is a late Miocene ape dating at around 7–9 mya. Fossils have been found in Tuscany (Agustí, Siria and Garcés, 2003) and Sardinia, Italy, and East Africa. An account of the skull, which has mostly ape-like features, has been written around a reconstruction, but here we will focus on the post-cranial skeleton. These apes lived in swamp forest habitats and their fossils were deposited in layers of coal sediments. The body mass of females was ~15 kg. Certain features of the fossils of *Oreopithecus* bones indicate that it was habitually bipedal and so not totally ape-like. For example, the spine shows **'lordosis'**, a curvature of the lumbar spine seen in humans. In contrast, curvature is not seen in the lumbar spine of *Dryopithecus*. *Oreopithecus* also has a valgus angle more similar to that of humans than that in apes (Figure 5.10). The feet of *Oreopithecus* are peculiar, as they are shorter in proportion to body mass than in apes, and are more platform-like, like those of humans. There is evidence of arboreal suspensory behaviour too in that the anatomy of the shoulder joint shows mobility.

Moyà-Solà and Köhler suggest that *Dryopithecus* was the ancestor of *Oreopithecus*, and they interpret the features linked to bipedalism in *Oreopithecus* as 'automorphies' (Moyà-Solà and Köhler 1995). An 'automorphy' is a derived character not shared with other species. A derived character is one that is a modified version of a primitive

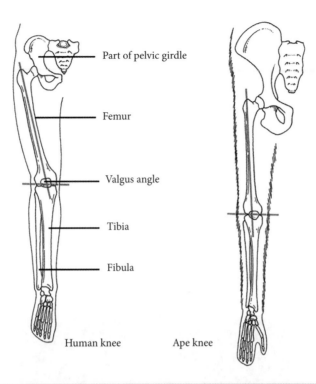

Part of pelvic girdle

Femur

Valgus angle

Tibia

Fibula

Human knee   Ape knee

Figure 5.10 The valgus angle is the angle that the femur makes with the knee. The angle in humans allows the foot to be placed directly below the centre of gravity, which give much improved bipedality when compared with an ape. Adapted from Lewin (1999) P95.

character and has therefore evolved later within the group. For *Oreopithecus* this means that features linked to bipedalism in this species, evolved in response to environmental pressures peculiar to the Mediterranean islands in which it was living. There were no land-based mammalian predators on the islands, but food resources were limited by the small size of the islands. Hence there was competition for food resources between *Oreopithecus* individuals and also with other species. Natural selection would have promoted adaptations linked to lower energy expenditure and efficiency of food collection and utilization. In *Oreopithecus* this linked to reduction in tree climbing, which is costly in terms of energy expenditure. Collecting fruit and leaves while standing bipedally, and walking for short distances between bushes or trees (as observed in chimpanzees) may have increased success in foraging for food. However, the researchers' arguments are weakened by finds of *Oreopithecus* fossils in mainland Italy too, not just in islands!

The location of the finds of *Oreopithecus* and the dates attributed to this species, indicate that this species is not on the hominid/hominin line of evolution, despite the signs of bipedalism. *Oreopithecus* demonstrates one aspect of the wide range of diversity among the Miocene apes; all were hominoids.

Apes were also living in Asia during the Miocene. Fossils of *Sivapithecus* have been found in the Siwalik Hills, India, and also in China and Turkey. The fossils are dated between 12 and 7 mya (Stringer and Andrews, 2005). *Sivapithecus* comprises several species. The skull is very similar to that of the orang utan, with its overall dished shape, broad cheeks that face forward (in most apes cheeks are pointed partly laterally) and robust lower jaw. (Figure 5.11) As with the orang utan skull, that of *Sivapithecus* is concave when viewed from the side. The orbits are close together and are elongated and oval in shape. The nasal alveolar region (that which joins the floor of the nose and the mouth) of *Sivapithecus* and orang utan are very similar. As in *Dryopithecus*, the molars of *Sivapithecus* are thickly enamelled and relatively large but they do not have the same complex patterns of ridges and curves seen in orang utan molars. The link between *Sivapithecus* and orang utan is unusual, as no direct link is known between any other fossil ape and an extant species.

The available postcranial remains indicate that *Sivapithecus* was arboreal but also partly terrestrial. There is no indication of suspensory locomotion in the fossil anatomy of *Sivapithecus*. As the habitat of *Sivapithecus* was open subtropical monsoon forest

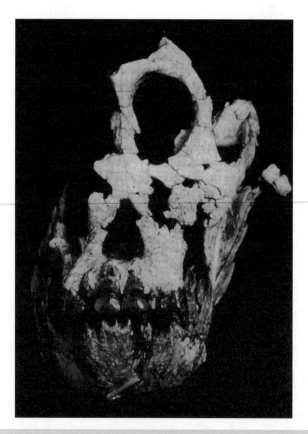

Figure 5.11   Front view of skull of *Sivapithecus*. Reproduced from Lewin (1999) P92.

interspersed with areas of open grassland, suspensory locomotion would not have been feasible.

One *Sivapithecus* species was ancestral to *Gigantopithecus*, which is also found in China, India and Vietnam. The first known fossils of *Gigantopithecus* were teeth found in Chinese medicine shops by Ralph von Koeningswald who named them. More fossil teeth and jawbones were found in Liucheng cave in Liuzhou. The jaw bones are very thick and form a deep jaw. The incisors are peg-like and close together, and the canines are blunt. The molars and premolars have thick enamel and their roots have relatively greater surface areas than extant apes (Kupczik and Dean, 2008). Overall the cheek teeth appear adapted for heavy grinding and resemble those of the giant panda. It has been suggested that *Gigantopithecus* subsisted on bamboo, grasses, fruit and seeds. The estimated height of *Gigantopithecus* in life is about 3 m, and estimated body weight is 540 kg, but careful comparisons of sets of teeth suggest that the males were much larger than the females. This giant ape may have existed between about 2 mya and 400 kya. Excavations at Tham Khuten cave in northern Vietnam revealed teeth of *Homo erectus* and *Gigantopithecus* in sediments dated at about 475 kya, suggesting the co-existence of these two species (Ciochon *et al.*, 1996).

Currently there are no hominoids in Europe, and just one species in Asia, so inevitably the question which springs to mind is why did they disappear?

An episode of climate change, the **'Vallesian Crisis'** at about 9.6 mya in the Middle and Late Miocene, resulted in colder winters and dryer summers. Climate change was initiated by the mountain building in the Alpine Himalayan area, which caused huge climate changes including increased seasonality. In turn, the climate change resulted in the loss of the subtropical forests at higher latitudes inhabited by hominoids. Research studies on plant fossils in the Late Miocene sediments in Western Europe indicate that the extinction of hominoids in Europe linked to the loss of evergreen broad-leaved subtropical woodland and its replacement by woodland dominated by deciduous trees (Agustí, Siria and Garcés, 2003). Most of the European apes, for example *Dryopithecus*, were frugivorous and ate fruits and soft vegetation. Survival in the winter was an increasing problem as neither fruit nor soft leaves were available in the winter months, so hominoids declined and became extinct. However as fossil finds in Spain indicate, the catarrhine pliopithecid monkey *Egaropithecus* survived the change in vegetation probably because this was a folivorous species. So about 9 mya there were monkeys living in the deciduous forest in Southern Europe.

The salient point is that from about 12 to 9 mya, there were many ape species living in three major continents. Moya-Sola and Kohler (1995) suggest that the ancestor of *Dryopithecus* may have been an African Miocene ape that had wandered out of Africa at about 15 mya and reached Europe and spread as far as Asia (Solà and Köhler, 1995). Adaptive radiation of the ancestral African ape resulted in evolution of different species in Europe, Asia and China. By about 9 mya, diversity of the apes were decreasing as climate change caused great changes in the forest cover of more northern regions, especially southern Europe. However, *Oreopithecus*, living in the subtropical swamp forests of Mediterranean islands and southern Italy persisted for longer, possibly up to 6 mya, because favourable climatic conditions persisted for longer there (Rook *et al.*,

2000). No fossil hominoids that could be ancestors of the chimpanzee have been found in Africa. However, the earliest hominine fossils were found in Africa – the fossil and genetic evidence supports the view that hominine clade originated in Africa, as we shall see in Chapter 6.

5.6 Conclusion

The time span from 40 to 8 mya included the late Eocene, Oligocene and much of the Miocene. There were huge changes in global climates over this relatively short time, marked by two episodes of global cooling. The first episode of global cooling from about 36 mya was caused by the build-up of the Antarctic ice cap and resulted in loss of tropical forest from most of the northern hemisphere, with tropical forest restricted to equatorial regions. The diverse primate species present in the Eocene disappeared from North America and Europe and were apparently confined to areas of forest closer to the equator such as that in the Fayum Depression and Asia. At some point in the Middle Oligocene, there was the emergence of hominoids, with *Morotopithecus* and *Proconsul* being examples of the earliest species. As the climate warmed hominoids spread to Europe and Asia, and fossil evidence has shown that there were many species, possibly at least a hundred. By about 10–9 mya however, further climate change, the 'Vallesian crisis' had caused further global cooling and diminished the evergreen tropical forests. Deciduous forest replaced the evergreen trees and hominoids and other primates no longer had access to fruits and foliage as both disappeared in the winters. So apes and monkeys disappeared from Europe and became restricted to Africa and Asia. The primate record from 40 to 8 mya demonstrates how fluctuations in climate accompanied by changes in the flora, cause extinctions of animals that specialize in utilizing specific food resources. So at this point we leave North America and Europe and focus attention on Africa and Asia for the investigation of the timeline for human evolution.

Questions and activities

Question 5.1

(a) Using the gibbon and the chimpanzee respectively as examples, explain the links between sexual dimorphism in body size and (i) monogamy and (ii) polygyny in extant ape species.

(b) How are the links that you describe used as evidence for the social structure in extinct apes known only as fossils? Outline one example in one or two sentences.

Question 5.2

(a) Examine Figure 5.12, a cladogram which shows phylogenetic relationships of early and Middle Miocene hominoids (Moyà–Solà, *et al.*, 2004). Which species and groups are defined as crown hominoids?

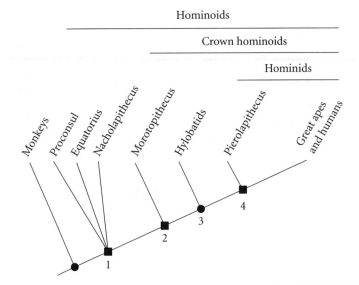

Figure 5.12 A cladogram which shows the phylogenetic relationships of early and Middle Miocene hominoids (Moyà-Solà *et al.*, 2004).

(b) Which species represents the sister group to great apes and humans?

(c) Does the cladogram tell us that *Morotopithecus* represents the ancestor of the crown hominoids? Explain your answer in a few sentences.

(d) Which groups are hominids?

Question 5.3

Consider the features of the dentition of *Dryopithecus*. Outline two aspects of the evidence from the dentition that would support the view that *Dryopithecus* subsisted on a diet of soft fruits and young leaves.

Question 5.4

Imagine a scenario in which you had discovered a partial skull and teeth of a late Miocene ape, dated at 8–9mya, and named as *Khoratpithecus piriyai* (Chaimanee et al., 2004). The incisors are missing but there is an indication of their forward projecting orientation from the empty sockets in the mandible. The cheek teeth are coated with thin enamel, and have broad surfaces that are not ridged, but have blunt rounded cusps. Examine the occlusal and lateral views of the mandible (Figure 5.13) and suggest the diet of this species, with a brief explanation of your interpretation.

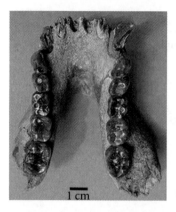 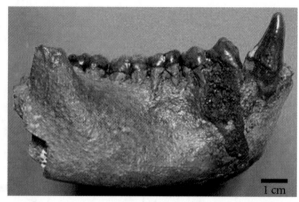

Figure 5.13 Mandible of *Khoratpithecus piriyai* (a) occlusal view and (b) lateral view. Reprinted from by permission from Macmillan Publishers Ltd: Nature (Chaimanee, *et al.*, 2004).

References

Agustí, J., Siria, A.S.D. and Garcés, M. (2003) Explaining the end of the hominoid experiment in Europe. *Journal of Human Evolution*, **45**, 145–153.

Begun, D. R. (2007) How to identify (as opposed to define) a homoplasy: examples from fossil and living great apes. *Journal of Human Evolution*, **52**, 559–572.

Ciochon, R., Long, V.T., Larick, R., González, L., Grān, R., de Vos, J., Yonge, C., Taylor, L., Yoshida, H. and Reagan, M. (1996) Dated co-occurrence of *Homo erectus* and *Gigantopithecus* from Tham Khuyen Cave, Vietnam. *Proceedings of the National Academy of Sciences of the United States of America*, **93**, 3016–3020.

Chaimanee, Y. Suteethorn, V., Jintasakui, P., Vidthayanon, C., Marandat, B. and Jaeger, J-J. (2004) A new orang-utan relative from the Late Miocene of Thailand, *Nature*, **427**, 439–441.

Fleagle, J.G. and Simons, E.L. (1995) Limb skeleton and locomotor adaptations of *Apidium phiomense*, an Oligocence anthropoid from Egypt. *American. Journal of Physical Anthropology*, **97**, 235–289.

Gebo, D.L., MacLatchy, L., Kityo, R., Deino, A., Kingston, J. and Pilbeam, D. (1997) A hominoid genus from the early miocene of Uganda. *Science*, **276**, 401–404.

Gunnell, G.F., Ciochon, R.L., Gingerich, P.D. and Holroyd, P.A. (2002) New assessment of *Pondaungia* and *Amphipithecus* (Primates) from the late middle Eocene of Myanmar, with a comment on Amphipithecidae. *Contributions from the Museum of Palaeontology*, University of Michigan, Vol. **30**, 337–372.

Jaeger, J.-J., Chaimanee, Y., Tafforeau, P., Ducrocq, S., Soe, A.N., Marivaux, L., Sudre, J., Tun, S.T., Htoon, W. and Marandat, B. (2004) Systematics and paleobiology of the anthropoid primate *Pondaungia* from the late Middle Eocene of myanmar. *Comptes Rendus Palevol*, **3**, 243–255.

Jerison, H.J. (1973) *Evolution of the Brain and Intelligence*. Academic Press, New York.

King, T., Aiello, L.C. and Andrews, P. (1999) Dental microwear of *Griphopithecus alpani*. *Journal of Human Evolution*, **36**, 3–31.

Kordos, L. and Begun, D.R. (2002) Rudabanya: a Late Miocene subtropical swamp deposit with evidence of the origin of African apes and humans. *Evolutionary Anthropology*, **11**, 45–47.

Kupczik, K. and Dean, M.C. (2008) Comparative observations on the tooth root morphology of *Gigantopithecus blacki*. *Journal of Human Evolution*, **54**, 196–204.

Leakey, M.G., Ungar, P.S. and Walker, A. (1995) A new genus of large primate from the late Oligocene of Lothdok, Turkana District, Kenya. *Journal Of Human Evolution*, **28**, 519–531.

Leakey, R.E., Leakey, M.G. and Walker, A.C. (1988) Morphology of *Afropithecus turkanensis* from Kenya. *American Journal of Physical Anthropology*, **76**, 289–307.

Liu, Z., Pagani, M., Zinniker, D., DeConto, R., Huber, M., Brinkhuis, H., Shah, S.R., Leckie, R.M. and Pearson, A. (2009) Global cooling during the Eocene-Oligocene climate transition. *Science* **323**, 1187–1190.

MaClatchy, L., Gebo, D., Kityo, R. and Pilbeam, D. (2000) Postcranial functional morphology of *Morotopithecus bishopi* with implications for the evolution of modern ape locomotion. *Journal of Human Evolution*, **39**, 159–183.

Marivaux, L., Welcomme, J.-L., Antoine, P.-O., Metais, G., Baloch, I.M., Benammi, M., Chaimanee, Y., Ducrocq, S. and Jaeger, J.-J. (2001) A Fossil Lemur from the Oligocene of Pakistan.*Science*, **294**, 587–591.

McCrossin, M.L. and Benefit, B.R. (1993) Recently recovered *Kenyapithecus* mandible and its implications for great ape and human origins. *Proceedings of the National Academy of Sciences of the United States of America*, **90**, 1962–1966.

Moyà-Solà, S. and Köhler, M. (1995) New partial cranium of *Dryopithecus lartet*, 1863 (Hominoidea, Primates) from the upper Miocene of Can Llobateres, Barcelona, Spain. *Journal of Human Evolution*, **29**, 101–139.

Moyà-Solà, S., Köhler, M., Alba, D.M., Casanovas-Vilar, I. and Galindo, J. (2004) *Pierolapithecus catalaunicus*, a New Middle Miocene Great Ape from Spain. *Science*, **306**, 1339–1344.

Patel, B.A. and Grossman, A. (2006) Dental metric comparisons of *Morotopithecus* and *Afropithecus*: implications for the validity of the genus *Morotopithecus*. *Journal of Human Evolution.*, **51**, 506–512.

Rook, L., Renne, P., Benvenuti, M. and Papini, M. (2000) Geochronology of *Oreopithecus*-bearing succession at Baccinello (Italy) and the extinction pattern of European Miocene hominoids. *Journal of Human Evolution*, **39**, 577–582.

Rosenberger, A.L. and Hogg, R. (2007) On *Bahinia pondaungensis*, an Alleged Early Anthropoid. *PalaeoAnthropology*, **2007**, 26–30.

Rossie, J.B., Simons, E.L., Gauld, S.C. and Rasmussen, D.T. (2002) Paranasal sinus anatomy of *Aegyptopithecus*: implications for hominoid origins. *Proceedings of the National Academy of Sciences of the United States of America*, **99**, 8454–8456.

Seiffert, E.R. (2006) Revised age estimates for the later Paleogene mammal faunas of Egypt and Oman. *Proceedings of the National Academy of Sciences of the United States of America*, **103**, 5000–5005.

Seiffert, E.R., Simons, E.L., Clyde, W.C., Rossie, J.B., Attia, Y., Bown, T.M., Chatrath, P. and Mathison, M.E. (2005a) Basal Anthropoids from Egypt and the Antiquity of Africa's Higher Primate Radiation. *Science*, **310**, 300–304.

Seiffert, E.R., Simons, E.L., Ryan, T.M. and Attia, Y. (2005b) Additional remains of *Wadilemur elegans*, a primitive stem galagid from the late Eocene of Egypt. *Proceedings of the National Academy of Sciences of the United States of America*, **102**, 11396–11401.

Simons, E.L. (1997) Preliminary description of the cranium of *Proteopithecus sylviae*, an Egyptian late Eocene anthropoidean primate.*Proceedings of the National Academy of Sciences of the United States of America*, **94**, 14970–14975.

Simons, E.L. and Miller, E.R. (1997) An upper dentition of *Aframonius dieides* (Primates) from the Fayum, Egyptian Eocene. *Proceedings of the National Academy of Sciences of the United States of America*, **94**, 7993–7996.

Simons, E. L., J. M. Plavcan, et al. (1999) Canine sexual dimorphism in Egyptian Eocene anthropoid primates: *Catopithecus* and *Proteopithecus*. *Proceedings of the National Academy of Sciences of the United States of America*, **96**, 2559–2562.

Smith, T., Rose, K.D. and Gingerich, P.D. (2006) Rapid Asia-Europe-North America geographic dispersal of earliest Eocene primate *Teilhardina* during the Paleocene-Eocene Thermal Maximum. *Proceedings of the National Academy of Sciences of the United States of America*, **103**, 11223–11227.

Steiper, M.E., Young, N.M. and Sukarna, T. Y. (2004) Genomic data support the hominoid slowdown and an early Oligocence estimate for the hominoid-cercopithecoid divergence. *Proceedings of the National Academy of Sciences of the United States of America*, **104**, 8731–8736.

Stringer, C. and Andrews, P. (2005) *The Complete World of Human Evolution*, Thames and Hudson, London.

Walker, A. and Shipman, P. (2005) *The Ape in the Tree*, Harvard University Press.

Ward, S., Brown, B., Hill, A., Kelley, J. and Downs, W. (1999) *Equatorius*: a new hominoid genus from the Middle Miocene of Kenya. *Science*, **285**, 1382–1386.

6

8 – 4.4 mya: Who Were the Ancestors of the Hominins?

The period from 8 to 4.4 mya was one from which until fairly recently, no human ancestors were known. The Miocene apes lived predominantly in sub-tropical forests, probably less dense than such forests are today. The hominins that appeared during this period appear to have lived in wooded, tropical forests, although the evidence of the type of environment is fairly limited. This period is now seen as being a crucial one for the development of the human line since at some time during it, the first human ancestor evolved. However, there are very few fossils from this very long period of time and any evolutionary tree is bound to be speculative.

At some point around 7 to 6 million years ago the first hominin appeared, probably evolving from the group of Miocene apes that extended across Europe, Asia and Africa. These apes were robust in form, with molar teeth that had a thick layer of enamel. They lived in a relatively open environment with a seasonal climate. The first hominins that we know of seem to have inhabited open forests and were adapted to a ground-living way of life. Defining the distinguishing features that separate the early hominins from the Miocene apes is not easy and this should not be unexpected to you as in the continuum of evolution, pinpointing the precise point at which an ape became human is very difficult.

◆ Give reasons why pinpointing this transition is problematic.

◆ You might suggest: (i) information is only available from skeletal material; (ii) clear definitions of the defining characteristics of humans are not fixed.

The Emergence of Humans Patricia Ash and David Robinson
© 2010 John Wiley & Sons, Ltd

An increase in brain size, which is one of the features of modern humans, is quite a late development, within the last 2 million years. There are anatomical features which, when combined, help to define the status of a species, but the best feature that we can use is the presence of bipedal locomotion.

The availability of genome sequence data for humans and apes has enabled geneticists to estimate the dates at which divergence in the human and ape lineages occurred. The estimates are made using the assumption that molecular changes in the genome accumulate at a regular rate like a clock. The 'molecular clock' idea was put forward in 1965 and since then has been applied widely in taxonomic studies. Although called a 'clock', the molecular clock is not a single regularly ticking clock; rather it is the smoothed rate of a large number of different rates within a complete genome. Not all parts of a genome mutate at the same rate. Some do accumulate mutations at a regular clock rate, but others have a rate that is different at different points in their evolutionary history. These examples highlight the difficulty of making estimates of time, based on the rate of accumulation of mutations in the genome. However, it is possible to use methods that take lineage-specific rates and other variables into account. Recent sequencing data from humans, chimps, orangutans, gorillas and macaques, have been used to estimate divergence times. The results are given in Table 6.1. These figures need to be borne in mind when considering the dates of candidate fossils for the status of 'first' or 'earliest' hominin.

Before considering the shape of the evolutionary tree during this period, consider the key fossil specimens.

6.1 The first hominin: Toumai?

There is naturally great interest in finding fossils of hominoid species close to the origin of the hominin line. Inevitably discussion will focus on whether such specimens are really apes that are very close to being human or the earliest true humans, but arguably the more interesting questions arise from the anatomy and the relationship between structure and function.

Table 6.1 Divergence time ranges for human and apes

Species	Speciation time (range in mya)
Hominoidea and Cercopithecoidea	30.5 (26.9–36.4)
Pongo (Orangutan)	18.3 (16.3–20.8)
Gorilla	8.6 (7.7–9.2)
Homo and *Pan* (chimp) divergence	6.6 (6.0–7.0)

Figures from Steiper and Young (2006).

Toumai, *Sahelanthropus tchadensis*, was dug out of the desert in Chad, Africa, by a team led by Michel Brunet and Patrick Vignaud of the University of Poitiers in 2001 (Box 6.1). The skull (Figure 6.1) was named Toumai, which is the name given traditionally by the local people to a child born dangerously close to the dry season. The fossil skull was not in pieces but remarkably complete; the lower jaw bone was found close to the skull. Subsequently more fossils have been recovered and there are now bones from at least six individuals.

Box 6.1 The discovery of the first fossil of *Sahelanthropus tchadensis*

Ahounta Djimdoumalbaye, an undergraduate student in Life Sciences at the University of N'Djamena was one of a team of four surveying and collecting fossils at a site called Torros-Menalla in Northern Chad in July 2001. On the morning of their last day, in misty conditions, they worked in pairs looking for fossils. Djimdoumalbaye noticed a blackish lump on the ground near a sand dune and, as he got closer he saw teeth. He picked it up and found that he was holding an ape-like skull, lacking a lower jaw but with most of the upper teeth in place. The leader of the team, French geographer Alain Beauvilain, was called over and he took photographs and established the position of the find with GPS. Around the find were other fossils of animals and they collected 141 that morning before returning to N'Djamena. They knew that if the skull was confirmed as a hominin, then they had made a major discovery. The fossil animals they had collected from the site were at least 6 million years old and probably contemporaneous with the skull. The name Toumai was suggested by the President of Chad when he was shown the skull by Michel Brunet and Alain Beauvilain, a few weeks later.

Toumai has a small cranium suggesting a small ape-like brain with a size of 360–370 cc, estimated from computer imaging. The huge brow ridges and face resemble the face of *Homo*, as does the small size of the canine teeth. The enamel on the teeth is very thick. This combination of characters is not one found in fossil apes, but equally, it is not seen in the later hominins. The front of the skull foreshadows the australopithecines (a group that will be described in Chapter 7) whilst the back of the skull is very similar to that of an ape. The jaws show that there were 32 teeth, as in the Old World monkeys, apes and humans.

The skull has been scanned using high-resolution computed tomography. The resulting digital images were then disassembled, digitally cleaned of adhering matrix and reconstructed. The reconstruction was used to assess the position of the foramen magnum relative to the orbital plane – a line joining the upper and lower margins

(a)   (b)

Figure 6.1   (a) Skull of *Sahelanthropus tchadensis*, known as Toumai. From Brunet, *et al.* (2004). (b) The discovery of Toumai was featured prominently in newspapers.

of the orbit. In humans the foramen magnum is almost at right angles to the orbital plane, whereas in the chimp it is at a more acute angle. The angle in the reconstructed skull of Toumai is closer to humans than chimps, indicating a more bipedal gait, and is in the same range as that of *Australopithecus afarensis* and *A. africanus*.

The skull is dated to the late Miocene epoch at about 7 mya. Absolute dating methods cannot be used as ashes, which could be used for potassium/argon dating, are not present at the site. Sediments suitable for relative dating by palaeomagnetism are also absent. However, there are fossil vertebrates in the strata and a great many of them have been identified, over 700 specimens of 45 taxa of mammals for example. These have been compared with East African sites and the mammalian fauna is more primitive than a Kenyan fauna from 6 mya and is similar to the fossil assemblage at another Kenyan site, Lothagam, whose age is estimated at 6.5–7.4 mya. So from the fossil assemblage the skull can be dated to around 7 mya.

At a site 18 km from the site where Toumai was discovered, which is in the same stratigraphical unit, there is an ash layer and it was hoped that this could be used for Argon dating. However, the crystals in the ash were not suitable. Instead a technique based on the ratio of two isotopes of Beryllium was used Box (6.2). Layers above and below the ash layer were dated and these could then be used to correlate with the stratigraphy at the site where Toumai was discovered. From this complex work a date of 7.04 ± 0.18 Ma emerged for *S. tchadensis*. The date is in good agreement with the age determined from the fossil mammals in the same strata. It is not, however, perfectly aligned with the mean separation date for hominins and chimps, which is 6.6 mya (range 6.0–7.0), so the big question here is whether Toumai is a hominin on, or close to, the evolutionary line to *Homo* or perhaps an ape. As all the specimens found and assigned to the genus so far are from skulls, we do not know whether Toumai was bipedal or totally arboreal.

Box 6.2 The ^{10}Be/^{9}Be Technique

The main source of ^{10}Bc is from the atmosphere and reaches the ground in rain and dew. Any that falls into water will end up in marine or freshwater sediments where it will decay with a half life of about 1.4 million years. ^{9}Be comes from a different source to ^{10}Be, entering sediments from detritus. It has been demonstrated in marine systems that when a leaching process is used to remove soluble Beryllium from sediments, the ratio of ^{10}Be to ^{9}Be in the leachate represents the ^{10}Be/^{9}Be ratio at the time of deposition. There are a number of provisos that must be attached to this statement, the most important of which is that there was no addition or subtraction of ^{10}Be in the sample subsequent to deposition.

The ^{10}Be/^{9}Be ratio is not fixed for all environments and so it is necessary to establish the starting ratio, which can be done by looking at similar present day environments in the same region. Diatoms build their silicate skeletons from components that are dissolved in the water. They trap both isotopes of Beryllium in their skeleton while they are alive and so provide a sample of the ^{10}Be/^{9}Be ratio at the time that they were alive. Calibration of the ^{10}Be/^{9}Be ratio in a particular region can be done by looking at both modern and ancient diatoms and determining the ratios. The resulting dates for the ancient diatoms can then be compared with dates obtained by other independent methods, for example fossil faunas.

♦ How does the lack of postcranial material influence our interpretation of the evolutionary position of Toumai?

♦ Our key defining character of a hominin, bipedal locomotion, can only be inferred from the position of the foramen magnum, which is not conclusive proof of bipedalism.

There are some post-cranial fossils in the collection, but they have not yet been identified and do not necessarily belong with the skull, or to a hominin (Beauvilain and Le Guellec, 2004).

Clues to the environment that Toumai occupied come from the associated fossil assemblage (Vignaud *et al.*, 2002). There are some large species of fish over 1 m long, indicating extensive areas of water. The fish populations supported both crocodiles and gavials. Fish that can survive low oxygen levels have also been found, together with amphibians, reptiles and amphibious mammals (hippos). This assemblage suggests lakes and swamp areas, but there are also elephants, Bovid and giraffes, which suggest both wooded savannah and more open savannah. Whether Toumai was at home in all of these environments is unknown at present.

So the problem that remains is: if Toumai is a hominin and not an ape, and the date of 7 mya is correct, there is a difference between the fossil date and the data from molecular analysis which suggests a divergence of *Homo* and *Pan* occurred at 6.6 mya with a range of 6.0–7.0 mya (Table 6.1).

6.2 The first hominin: *Orrorin?*

Fossil bones found in the Lukeino formation in the Tugen Hills Kenya (Senut *et al.*, 2001) comprise 12 fragments from 5 individuals. The fossils come from four distinct sites. The finds have been assigned to a new hominin genus and species, *Orrorin tugenensis* (Figure 6.2). There are fragments of two proximal left femurs, a bit of a

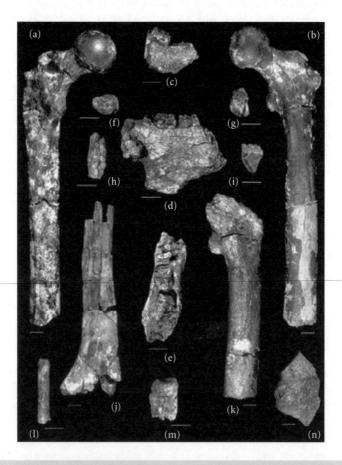

Figure 6.2   Fossil bones of *Orrorin tugenensis*.

Reproduced, with permission, from Senut, B. *et al.* (2001) First Hominid from the Miocene (Lukeino Formation, Kenya) Comptes Rendus de l'Académie des Sciences - Series IIA - Earth and Planatary Science, 332, 2, page 141 © 2001 Éditions scientifiques et médicales Elsevier SAS.

right humerus, mandibular fragments, a finger bone and a few teeth. Brigitte Senut, one of the team who found the fossils, suggests that *Orrorin* was about the size of a chimpanzee. Senut claims that the femur anatomy of *Orrorin* indicates that the species was walking bipedally, which supports the view that *Orrorin* was a hominin (Pickford *et al.*, 2002; Senut *et al.*, 2001). The humerus shows evidence of arboreal adaptations. It is possible that *Orrorin* was bipedal, but there is still debate about the gait adopted by the creature – was it human-like, or more like an australopith, or something else.

The fossils of *Orrorin* could be dated accurately because they were lying over a lava flow, dated at 6.2 mya and were topped by another lava flow, dated at 5.65 mya. However, this range still allows for nearly half a million years difference between the fossils found at the lowest of the fours sites and those at the highest. The date of 6.2–5.65 mya suggested for *Orrorin* made it at the time of its discovery, the oldest known hominin, if we accept the evidence that it was bipedal. How disappointing that although we have some teeth and jaw fragments, we do not have a skull.

Orrorin appears to have lived in open woodland that contained stands of trees of sufficient size to accommodate populations of colobus monkeys (Pickford and Senut, 2001). Some of the bones of mammals found at the site, including the hominins, have tooth marks on them, indicating the presence of predators. This environment is not the savannah that would at one time have been predicted as the place where there was selection for bipedalism and it is now becoming clear that the earliest bipedal hominins appeared in wooded areas.

Box 6.3 Finding *Orrorin*

Orrorin was not the first significant fossil that Kiptalam Cheboi had found. In 1984, working with Andrew Hill and Sally McBrearty in the Tugen Hills where he grew up he found a fragment of a jaw which resembled that of *Australopithecus afarensis*. It is now recognized as *Ardipithecus*. In late 2000 Martin Pickford and Brigitte Senut returned to the Tugen Hills and, as soon as they met up with Cheboi he showed them two pieces of jaw bone containing molars that he had found and a finger bone found by a co-worker. The fossils appeared to be hominin. He took Pickford and Senut to the site where he had found the fossils and they found four pieces of thigh bone. They recognized immediately that the finds were very ancient as they came from a sedimentary formation that lay below a basalt layer that was over 5 million years old. At the time of their discovery, they were the oldest announced hominin specimens by over a million years. In the following weeks more fossils were discovered. The find was announced at a press conference in Nairobi on 4th December 2000 and, in tribute to the year of their discovery, the fossils were dubbed the 'Millenium Ancestor'.

The *Orrorin* fossils remain controversial. CT scans at 0.5 mm intervals have been made of the femur and the results have been published but there is insufficient information available to enable a comparison with the femur of *Australopithecus afarensis*, a detailed description of which was published in 2002 by Tim White and others. An account of the 'inside' story of early hominin femora can be found in a paper by Tim White published in 2006.

6.3 Another first hominin: *Ardipithecus kadabba*

Ardipithecus kadabba was discovered in the middle Awash Valley, Ethiopia, by Haile Selassie and Giday WoldeGabriel (Haile-Selassie, 2001). The first finds were discovered in 1997 and comprise a mandible with teeth, hand and foot bones, arms, a collar bone and a toe bone (Figure 6.3). The fossils were dated at 5.2–5.8 mya by the K^{40}–Ar^{40} (potassium–argon) technique. The anatomy of the toe bone, which has a slanted surface at the rear joint, suggested to the discoverers that the animal was

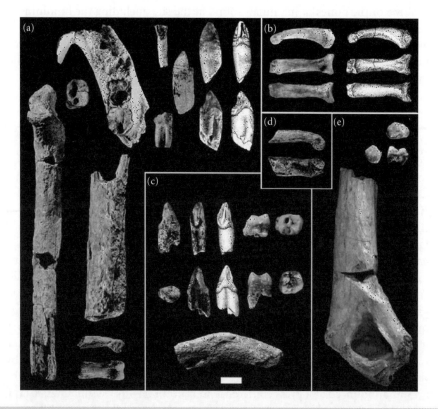

Figure 6.3   Fossil remains of *Ardipithecus kadabba*.

WoldeGabriel, *et al.* (2001). Reprinted by permission from Macmillan Publishers Ltd: Nature (Haile-Selassie, Y. Late Miocene hominids from the Middle Awash, Ethiopia. Nature 412, P179 Fig. 1), copyright 2001.

bipedal, although this view is disputed by others (Senut, 2006). The narrow front teeth and enlarged back teeth are more similar to those of other hominins than to apes. Fossil animals, found in the same layers suggest a well-watered forested habitat for the species (WoldeGabriel *et al.*, 2001). There are remains of tree-living monkeys, similar to the present day colobus monkeys.

The location and dates suggested for the fossils, along with the evidence for bipedalism, make it feasible that the species could be ancestral to the hominins.

6.4 *Ardipithecus ramidus*

The first specimens of *Ardipithecus ramidus* were discovered in the Awash region of the Afar triangle in 1992. The fossils were described by Tim White and others in 1994 and, at the time, it was the oldest and most primitive hominin known at an age of 4.4 mya (White, Suwa and Asfaw, 1994). They initially assigned the fossils to *Australopithecus*, but later transferred them to the new genus *Ardipithecus* (White, Suwa and Asfaw, 1995). Many of the features of the specimens are ape-like – the relatively large canines, the smaller molars and the thin enamel layer, for example. These features suggest a diet of soft vegetable material and fruit. However, there are a number of derived features that *A. ramidus* shares with later hominins, particularly the position of the foramen magnum, which is further forward than in apes, and the elliptical shape of the upper end of the humerus.

♦ What is the significance of the position of the foramen magnum in this species?

♦ The position of the foramen magnum would suggest that the head was on top of the spine and thus the species was bipedal.

If it is correct that *Ardipithecus* was bipedal, then the environment in which it lived is significant, because it appears to have been a forest habitat, judging from the associated vertebrate fossils.

♦ What is the implication of the forest environment?

♦ It has been suggested that bipedalism developed as the environment got drier and the habitat became more open and savannah-like. Bipedal hominins would have had a selective advantage. The evidence from *Ardipithecus ramidus* does not support that proposition.

A partial skeleton of *Ardipithecus ramidus* was discovered in 1994 and excavated over a two year period. The find has not yet been described*. The skull is crushed into hundreds of pieces and the bones are in such a fragile state that conservation and

---

*Note added in proof - A special issue of Science on 2nd October 2009 contains 11 papers describing the fossils.

reconstruction are a very long term process indeed. Micro-CT scans are being used to reassemble the specimen.

6.5 An un-named hominin from Lothagam

In 1967 a fragment of a mandible was found at Lothagam, west of Lake Turkana. The specimen is the posterior portion of a right mandible, with a first molar that is worn and has fairly thick enamel. It has been suggested that the specimen has affinities with *Australopithecus afarensis* specimens, such as those from Hadar and Laetoli (see Section 7.3). The structure of the jaw and the characteristics of the teeth suggest the close relationship, but Meave Leakey and Alan Walker (2003) have suggested that it is closer to *A. amanensis*. However, they agree that, at present, the mandible cannot be assigned to any particular hominin species. It is dated at between 5 and 4.2 mya.

6.6 Evolutionary relationships of the early hominins

Bipedality is the key feature that defines hominins and both *Ardipithecus kadabba* and *Orrorin tugenensis* appear to show adaptations that would indicate bipedality. Both are more primitive than *Ardipithecus ramidus*, which was definitely bipedal and is dated to 4.4 million years ago. If we were to accept that between 9 and 7 million years ago there was a bipedal ape, *Oreopithecus bambolii* (Susman, 2005), living as an isolated population in Italy, then we would need to consider the possibility that bipedality had arisen more than once in hominoid evolution. If this is the case, then perhaps bipedality cannot be the defining feature of hominins. While the discoverers of the fossils of the three taxa described above, and the Lothagam specimens, all claim hominin status for their finds, it is necessary to at least consider an alternative possibility. Could the common ancestors of chimps and hominins have possessed a rudimentary form of bipedalism? Maybe these specimens are actually part of the chimp evolutionary tree, or they could be a branch of the ancestral tree of both chimps and hominins – a branch that came to a dead end.

An interesting interpretation of these early species is provided by Brigitte Senut, who first described *Orrorin tugenensis*. She regards the date for the divergence of *Homo* from *Pan* as about 12 mya, with *Orrorin* being a bipedal hominin at 6 mya, on the direct line to *Homo*. She sees *Ardipithecus* as related to the chimps and *Sahelanthropus* possibly related to gorillas. The Australopiths then form an offshoot from the line proceeding directly to *Homo* and are, consequently, a lineage that died out (Senut and Pickford, 2004). This is a controversial view, as will become clear in the next chapter.

A further factor that should be considered is that although these three taxa have all been assigned to different genera, comparison between them is difficult as the remains are fragmentary. Those canine and molar teeth that have been found are similar, so one interpretation is that they are all part of a common lineage and perhaps the same genus (Haile-Selassie, Suwa and White, 2004). Variation between the teeth of the three genera is no greater than seen within extant ape genera.

So, at present, the position of these three genera in the human evolutionary tree is difficult to establish. Whatever their status, though, they are highly significant finds from a long period for which we lack a good human fossil record. As you will read in the next chapter, two distinct lines are recognizable in the evolutionary tree of Pliocene hominins and the distinctions between these – teeth size and jaw size – are very similar to those between the two groups of Miocene apes. Further fossil specimens will help to sort out the hominin evolutionary tree during this crucial and extremely interesting period of nearly 3 million years.

6.7 Conclusion

Three recently described genera of hominin fossils from Africa have started to fill in the gap between the Miocene apes and the later Pliocene hominins. All the specimens come from the end of the Miocene and at present offer a rather confused picture of evolution during some 3 million years. Even whether they represent one genus or three genera is not certain. The incomplete nature of the fossils means that it is very difficult to determine whether all were indisputably human, but without doubt all the finds are very significant additions to the story of human evolution, for they provide us with either a view of the ape lineage just prior to the emergence of a true hominin, or the very earliest part of the hominin line.

Question

Question 6.1

Ardipithecus ramidus was probably bipedal. What is the evidence for this and how is bipedality thought to be linked to the habitat type? (Learning outcome B1)

References

Beauvilain, A. and Le Guellec, Y. (2004) Beauvilain and Le Guellec reply. *South African Journal of Science,* **100,** 445–446.

Brunet, M.,F. *et al.* (27 other authors) (2004) 'Toumaï', Late Miocene of Chad, the new earliest member of the human branch." *Comptes Rendus Palevol* 3(4): 277–285.

Haile-Selassie, Y. (2001) Late Miocene hominids from the Middle Awash, Ethiopia. *Nature,* **412,** 178–181.

Haile-Selassie, Y., Suwa, G., and White, T.D. (2004) Late Miocene teeth from Middle Awash, Ethiopia, and early hominid dental evolution. Science, **303,** 1503–1505.

Leakey, M.G., and Walker, A.C. (2003) The Lothagam Hominids. In Leakey, M.G. and Harris, J.M.H. (eds.) Lothagam the Dawn of Humanity in eastern Africa. Pp. 249–257. Columbia University Press: New York.

Pickford, M. and Senut, B. (2001) The geological and faunal context of Late Miocene hominid remains from-Lukeino, Kenya. *Comptes Rendus De L Academie Des Sciences Serie Ii Fascicule a- Sciences De La Terre Et Des Planetes,* **332,** 145–152.

Pickford, M., Senut, B., Gommery, D., and Treil, J. (2002) Bipedalism in *Orrorin tugenensis* revealed by its femora. *Comptes Rendus Palevol,* **1,** 191–203.

Senut, B. (2006) Bipedie et climat. *Comptes Rendus Palevol,* **5,** 89–98.

Senut, B. and Pickford, M. (2004) La dichotomie grands singes-homme revisitee. *Comptes Rendus Palevol,* **3,** 265–276.

Senut, B., Pickford, M., Gommery, D., Mein, P., Cheboi, K., and Coppens, Y. (2001) First hominid from the Miocene (Lukeino Formation, Kenya). *Comptes Rendus De L Academie Des Sciences Serie Ii Fascicule a-Sciences De La Terre Et Des Planetes*, **332**, 137–144.

Steiper, M.E. and Young, N.M. (2006) Primate molecular divergence dates. *Molecular Phylogenetics and Evolution*, **41**, 384–394.

Susman, R.L. (2005) *Oreopithecus:* Still apelike after all these years. *Journal of Human Evolution*, **49**, 405–411.

Vignaud, P., Duringer, P., Mackaye, H.T., Likius, A., Blondel, C., Boisserie, J.R., de Bonis, L., Eisenmann, V., Etienne, M.E., Geraads, D., *et al.* (2002) Geology and palaeontology of the Upper Miocene Toros-Menalla hominid locality, Chad. *Nature*, **418**, 152–155.

White, T.D. (2006) Early hominid femora: The inside story. *Comptes Rendus Palevol*, **5**, 99–108.

White, T.D., Suwa, G., and Asfaw, B. (1994) *Australopithecus ramidus*, a New Species of Early Hominid from Aramis, Ethiopia. *Nature*, **371**, 306–312.

White, T.D., Suwa, G., and Asfaw, B. (1995) Corrigendum: *Australopithecus ramidus*, a New Species of Early Hominid from Aramis, Ethiopia. *Nature*, **375**, 88.

WoldeGabriel, G., Haile-Selassie, Y., Renne, P.R., Hart, W.K., Ambrose, S.H., Asfaw, B., Heiken, G., and White, T. (2001) Geology and palaeontology of the Late Miocene Middle Awash valley, Afar rift, Ethiopia. *Nature*, **412**, 175–178.

7

4.2 – 3.0 mya: Adaptive Radiation of Hominins

During this period the climate in general was warmer and wetter than it is now. In Africa, areas where fossil humans are found today were tropical woodland with some forest in patches bordering rivers and lakes. The peak phases of warmth occurred in between 4 and 3 mya, the Middle Pliocene. At the end of the period, around 3 mya the climate in Africa started to change, beginning to get cooler and more arid.

The period 4.2–3.0 mya seems to have been a period of adaptive radiation, with a new group of hominins emerging – the Australopithecines. Australopithecines were in the family Australopithecinae, which incorporates the genera, *Australopithecus* and *Paranthropus*. Recent changes in taxonomy, principally as a result of genetic analysis of the modern humans and modern apes, have placed the old family Australopithecinae into the subtribe Hominina (the other subtribe being the Panina). Thus the vernacular term for these genera is now 'australopiths' rather than australopithecines. The genetic data that support the close linkage between *Homo* and *Pan* are not, of course, available for most fossil taxa, including the australopiths. It is probable that the genus *Australopithecus* is paraphyletic – that is all the members of the group have a common ancestor but the group does not include all the descendants of the common ancestor. The genus *Paranthropus*, on the other hand, is monophyletic.

Australopiths have small cranial capacities by comparison with later *Homo* species, with a range from around 350 cc to just over 500 cc. There is a limited amount of

The Emergence of Humans Patricia Ash and David Robinson
© 2010 John Wiley & Sons, Ltd

fossil post-cranial material and this suggests a body shape in which the pelvis was wide and the rib cage narrowed from pelvis to shoulders. The arms were relatively longer than the legs and the gait was almost certainly bipedal, judging by the pelvis and feet.

7.1 The australopiths

So far eight species of australopith are known. All are found in Africa; none have been found elsewhere. The first discovery of an australopith was made by Raymond Dart in 1924, as he sorted through a box of rocks and fossils sent to him from limeworks at Taung, close to the Kalahari Desert (see Section 5.5). Dart identified a brain endocast, fossils of the mandible and much of the face, as belonging to 'an extinct race of apes intermediate between living anthropoids and man'. The Taung child, as the collection of fossils is known, is classified as *Australopithecus africanus,* a species with estimated dates of 2.9–2.4 mya (Box 7.1).

Table 7.1   Key australopith fossils

Australopith species		Discovery of first fossil	Date or date range	
Australopithecus	*Au. anamensis*	1994, Kanapoi, Kenya	4.17 to 4.07 mya (Leakey *et al.,* 1998)	
	Au. afarensis	1977, Hadar, Ethiopia.	3.9–3.0 mya (Kimbel *et al.,* 2004)	
	Au. africanus	1924, Taungs, South Africa.	3.2–2.0 mya (Partridge, 2000)	2.5–1.5 mya (Berger, Lacruz and de Ruiter, 2002) (see Section 5.5)
	Au. bahrelghazali	1995, Bahr el Ghazal, Chad	3.5 mya (Brunet *et al.,* 1995)	
	Au. garhi	1990, Bouri, Middle Awash, Ethiopia	2.5 mya (Asfaw *et al.,* 1999)	
Robust group *Paranthropus*	*P. aethiopicus*	1967, Omo and 1985 Lake Turkana	2.6 mya	
	P. robustus	1938, Kromdraii	1.8–1.6 mya (White, 2002)	
	P. boisei	1959, Olduvai Gorge	2.3–1.4 mya	
Possible australopith	*Kenyanthropus platyops*	1998	3.5 mya	

Box 7.1 The single species hypothesis

Loring Brace and Milford Wolpoff's single species hypothesis for the evolution of *Homo sapiens* involved steady progression up a single evolutionary ladder. The principle of competitive exclusion, which states that two species with similar adaptations cannot co-exist, was extended to the evolution of hominins. The defining feature of *Homo* was regarded as culture and this was viewed as so powerful an adaptation, that only one species of hominin could exist at any one time. If two hominin species found themselves in the same area at the same time there would inevitably be conflict between them because they both shared the same adaptation – culture – and therefore only one could be successful. Loring Brace saw the progression as happening in four stages: Australopithecines → *Homo erectus* → Neanderthals → *Homo sapiens*. The articulation of this progression has been an unfortunate one as it has led to attempts to corral all hominins into existing genera. Furthermore, the 'progression' does not accommodate specimens whose position in time does not fit, leading to arguments about the date assuming greater importance than the morphology – what the specimen actually looks like. The unfortunate legacy of the linear progression and the single species hypothesis is well described by Ian Tattersall and Jeffrey Schwartz (Tattersall and Schwartz, 2000).

Around 2.5 mya three or more species of hominins co-existed in Africa. *Australopithecus garhi*, (2.5 mya), *Australopithecus africanus* (2.9–2.4 mya) and *Paranthropus aethiopicus* (2.7–2.3 mya) were contemporary with each other (Walker *et al.*, 1986). In addition there is a jaw dated at 2.3 mya from the Hadar region of Ethiopia which is undoubtedly a species of *Homo*. The evidence for co-existence of more than one hominin species refutes the single species hypothesis, which should have disappeared some time ago. It is still prevalent in the creationist literature, as a quick web search will demonstrate.

Following the discovery of the Taung child, other specimens of australopith were found and it appeared that there were two forms. One was a robust form with large back teeth, powerful jaws and a pronounced crest on the cranium. The other form, represented by the Taung specimen, did not have these features and became known as the gracile form.

Although there are differences between robust and gracile species in the jaws, jaw muscle attachments and teeth, nevertheless, gracile and robust forms have many common features, justifying their classification, for the present, with the australopiths. The differences between gracile and robust australopiths justify placing robust forms in a separate genus, *Paranthropus*. For example, the robust forms have two cusps on the first premolar in the lower jaw (as does *Au. africanus*). The gracile forms are likely to be a paraphyletic group, whereas *Paranthropus* is almost certainly monophyletic (Chapter 8).

7.2 The first australopith – *Australopithecus anamensis*

In 1994/1995 Meave Leakey and her team discovered some hominin bones from the post-cranial skeleton and both upper and lower jaws of what they subsequently described as a new species of australopith, *Australopithecus anamensis* (Leakey *et al.*, 1995, 1998). The bones were found at Kanopi and Allia Bay in the Turkana region of Kenya. They also found a number of unattached teeth, and both the jaws and teeth are very similar to those of *Au. afarensis*. The jaws are of two sizes, showing primitive hominin characters. By contrast the post-cranial skeletal material is much more human-like, in the structure of the knee and elbow joints. Twenty years before, a fragment of humerus had been found at the same site (Patterson and Howells, 1967). It too is more human-like than ape-like. So, we have a hominin with a post-cranial skeleton that is more human than that of *Au. afarensis*, yet is earlier in time, at 4.17–4.12 mya (Kanapoi). The Allia bay finds are dated at 3.9 mya (Kimbel *et al.*, 2006). It is possible that the amalgamation of all the finds from both Kanapoi and Allia Bay is an un-natural assemblage that contains more than one species – there are, for example, two sizes of jaw, but Leakey and her team, having analysed more recent finds, conclude that there is sexual dimorphism within the species. Ian Tattersall and Jeffrey Schwartz summarize the position of *Au. anamensis* as: 'chronologically preceded *afarensis*, but was *afarensis*-like from the neck upwards and *Homo*-like from the neck down' (Tattersall and Schwartz, 2000).

In 2006 the discovery of more specimens of *Au anamensis* was announced, from the Middle Awash area of Afar in Ethiopia (White *et al.*, 2006). The finds are reliably dated to 4.1–4.2 mya and include the earliest femur of an australopith yet found, as well as dental and cranial material. The significance of the find is that previously the species was only known from the Turkana site. At the Middle Awash site two other species of hominin have been found and as the strata in the region are well dated it is possible to analyze their phylogenetic relationships with some degree of confidence. Over 500 vertebrate fossils have been found in the same strata as *Au. anamensis* and they provide a picture of a restricted range of habitats that were essentially closed or open, grassy woodland.

7.3 *Australopithecus afarensis*; a possible ancestor of *Homo*

Australopithecus afarensis is the best-known hominin species from East Africa. Since the first discovery of fossils in the Hadar region of Ethiopia in 1973 around 360 specimens have been collected at the site, 90% of the total for this species. The Hadar rock formation is exposed along the sides of the Awash River, in the Afar Depression. The story of the initial discovery made by Don Johanson and his team has become a classic of palaeoanthropology and is outlined in Box 7.2.

Box 7.2 The discovery of *Australopithecus afarensis*

In 1973 the International Afar Research Expedition started searching for fossils near Hadar, on the banks of the Awash River in the Afar region of Ethiopia. Don Johanson describes in his book '*Lucy, the beginnings of human-kind*', how he was pre-occupied in thinking about the costs of the expedition, while he was surveying and he idly kicked at what looked like a hippo rib sticking out of the sand. It turned out to be part of a tibia. Only a few yards away was a piece of femur, while nearby a further piece was discovered. These three pieces together made a knee joint and the anatomy of the joint convinced Johanson that it was from a bipedal human rather than a monkey. Until that moment, nobody had seen the knee joint of a hominin over 3 million years old and it provided what was then the oldest evidence of one of the defining features of human evolution – bipedality. The other significance, of course, was that it confirmed the wisdom of mounting the expedition to the Afar region. The following year, the hopes raised by the discovery of the knee joint were more than met.

The 1974 season started with the finding of parts of three hominin jaws, two of them found within an hour of each other. Then, on the day after Richard and Mary Leakey had visited the site, Don Johanson and Tom Gray discovered a number of hominin bones together which would later prove to have come from one individual over 3 million years old. Eventually there were several hundred pieces of bone, representing about 40% of the skeleton. This skeleton – AL 288-1 – was unique at the time of discovery in being the first skeleton of such a great age, a skeleton of an ancestral small hominin at a time when the oldest skeleton known was 75 000 years old. Although there have been spectacular finds since then, this skeleton, known as 'Lucy', remains the best known fossil human specimen, outside the scientific community. The following year brought another spectacular discovery when a large number of fossils were found in one site, representing at least 13 different individuals. They were dubbed 'the first family' by the team. The finds from Hadar, accumulated over just a four year period, provided an unprecedented number of specimens and individuals of a new species of australopith.

Almost from the moment of discovery, the taxonomic status of the species has been a cause of much debate. When Johanson reported the discovery of the first specimens, he included in the new species material from Laetoli that had been discovered by Mary Leakey (Leakey, 1976) and was around half a million years older (Johanson and White, 1979; Johanson, White and Coppens, 1978; Leakey and Walker, 1980). The fact that Hadar and Laetoli were both geographically and temporally distinct suggested to

Table 7.2 Distribution of *Australopithecus afarensis* in Africa. The stratigraphic units from which specimens have come are given in the table, with the most northerly sites to the left. From Kimbel, Rak and Johanson (2004)

Age (mya)	Hadar	Middle Awash	Koobi Fora	Laetoli
3.0	Kada Hadar			
3.2	Denen Dora		Tulu Bor (?3.3)	
3.4	Sidi Hakoma	Matabaietu		Upper Laetolil

some workers that the populations were distinct species. However, the present position is that *Au. afarensis* is biologically and statistically a valid species and that it incorporates fossil specimens for the locations given in Table 7.2. The relationship of *Au. afarensis* to other members of the genus is less clear, a problem discussed further in Section 7.7.

With the discovery of fossils from a large number of individuals came a further problem. There were very large individuals and some small ones. Did they represent two separate species or a single species. The differences between the largest and smallest were greater than between males and females of any living primate, but Don Johanson and Tim White eventually concluded that the specimens all belonged to the same species, but a markedly sexually dimorphic one.

One of the problems facing taxonomists was the lack of substantial fossil skull bones in the original finds from Hadar. However, in 1992, Yoel Rak discovered two fragments of occipital bone at the base of a steep hill made up of Hadar sequence silts and clays. Further excavation revealed other bones that together made up 75–80% of a single skull. It transpired that the first two bones found actually belonged to a second individual. Over 50 fragments of the skull (A.L. 444-2) were excavated and detailed study of the skull has enabled a cladistic analysis of the australopith to be carried out to establish the position of *Au. afarensis* in the human evolutionary tree. The methods used to reconstruct and evaluate this important find provide a valuable case study to illustrate anthropological research (Kimbel, Rak and Johanson, 2004).

A unique find was made at Laetoli in 1976 that gives us a glimpse of hominins in life – a contrast to the story left by their bones. An accidental discovery by visiting researchers at Mary Leakey's camp came about, so the story goes, when they were larking around after a day of hard work. One of them fell and discovered while getting up that there was a footprint in the exposed rock. Uncovering more of the rock revealed a variety of animal tracks. Subsequently in 1978 more of the tracks were uncovered and amongst them was a line of human footprints Figure 7.1. The footprints look surprisingly close to those of modern humans and are from an individual who is definitely bipedal. The position of the big toe matches that of humans and is very different from the footprint

Box 7.3   Endocasts

An endocast is a three-dimensional model of the interior of a cavity – in this case the cavity in the skull normally occupied by the brain. Following the death of an individual the decaying brain material may be replaced by sediment which over time becomes a solid fossil, giving a natural endocast. It was this process that produced the endocast that Raymond Dart described in the 1924 discovery of the 'Taung child' (see Section 7.5). A good natural endocast shows the surface features of the brain, such as the extent of the lobes of the cerebral cortex. However, any endocast can only show those details that have left an imprint on the inner surface of the skull, so an endocast is not a perfect representation of the whole of the brain surface.

Natural endocasts are not that common. To get an artificial cast of a fairly complete skull, latex rubber solution is poured into the skull and allowed to set. When removed, the latex cast will show the details from the internal surface of the skull. Generally, however, skulls are fragmentary and also sometimes distorted during the fossilization process. The skull of *Australopithecus afarensis* (A.L. 444-2) discovered in 1992 is distorted, with a greater disruption to the right side. In calculating the cranial capacity, a plaster endocast was cut into two halves and the left was reconstructed to give a more accurate measurement of the cranial capacity. The amount of water displaced by the re-constructed half endocast was measured, giving a corrected volume of 269 ml. Doubling this, making an assumption of symmetry between right and left, gave a figure of 534 ml for the cranial capacity of A.L. 444-2.

If a skull can be scanned using an **MRI (Magnetic Resonance Imaging)** it is possible to create a digital endocast, which of course is a non-destructive technique. To do this requires access to expensive instruments, but as it is such a sophisticated technique and yields detailed three-dimensional results, it will become the standard in the future.

left by chimps, for example. The footprints have a ridge that corresponds to the arch on the inner edge of the foot. A recent analysis of the prints (Berge, Penin and Pelle, 2006) shows that they exhibit a mixture of ape-like and human-like characteristics and although they are more human than ape, they are still distinctly different from modern humans. The probability is that they were produced by *Australopithecus afarensis* and the tracks of three individuals have been identified. The Getty Museum has recently been involved with attempts to conserve the tracks, which are being damaged by tree roots.

Figure 7.1   A cast of the Laetoli footprints.
Courtesy of Brian Richardson.

7.4 The flat-faced skull from Kenya

For at least 20 years after the discovery and naming of *Australopithecus afarensis*, it was the only genus known in the period 4–3 mya. Given the number of species in the later fossil record, this seemed anomalous and in 1998 Meave Leakey explored two sites from which un-identified hominin remains had been recovered. These sites fell within the 4–3 mya time frame. She and her team found a number of new specimens, including a very cracked cranium (KNM-WT 4000) with unusually flat facial anatomy, which they assigned to a new genus, *Kenyanthropus platyops* (Figure 7.2). The find was made at Lomekwi, to the west of Lake Turkana. The specimens lack most of the derived features of the *Paranthropus* genus, do not show the derived features associated with *Homo* and are more developed than *Ardipithecus*. Both the face and its small molars make *K. platyops* distinct from other *Australopithecus* species too. Accurate dating of the find has been possible, using the ^{40}Ar-^{39}Ar method. Two tuffs that lie above and below the stratum that the cranium was recovered from are dated at 3.57 and 3.40 mya and these provide an estimated date of 3.5 mya for the cranium.

At the time that *Kenyanthropus* was living in the Turkana area the environment would have been made up of grasslands with areas of woodland, and gallery forest – that is a narrow strip of forest alongside a river.

With the exception of the size of its brain (approx. 350 cc), *Kenyanthropus* bears similarities to the famous specimen KN-MER 1470, found in 1972 at Lake Rudolf in Kenya and dated to 1.9 mya (see Section 8.6). As you will read in Section 8.6 it is claimed that there is enough evidence to place 1470 in the same genus as *K. platyops*.

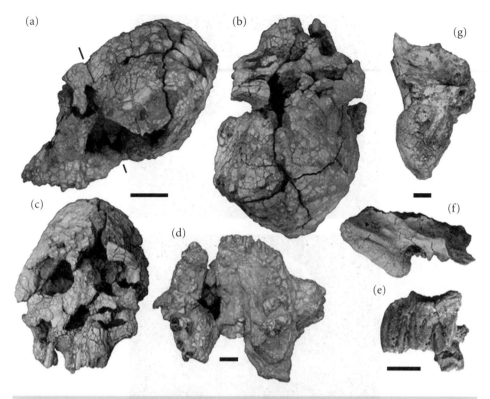

Figure 7.2   (a) *Kenyanthropus platyops*. (b) Superior view. (c) Anterior view. (d) The palate. Paratype KNM-WT 38350. (e) Lateral view. KNM-WT 40001. (f) Lateral view. (g) Inferior view. Scale bars: a–c, 3 cm; d–g, 1 cm.
Reprinted by permission from Macmillan Publishers Ltd: Nature (Leakey, M. G. F. *et al*. New hominin genus from eastern Africa shows diverse middle Pliocene lineages." Nature 410: P435) copyright 2001.

7.5 *Australopithecus africanus*

Historically, *Australopithecus africanus* was the first australopith to be discovered and named. Raymond Dart, who had worked under Professor (later Sir) Grafton Elliot Smith in the United Kingdom, went to Witwatersrand in South Africa to take up the chair in Anatomy. In November 1924 the Northern Lime Company dispatched two crates of fossil specimens from the mines and two lumps of breccia to be hand delivered at the same time by Professor Young, a geologist. The two lumps of breccia fitted together to form part of a skull and associated fossilized brain. Although there were lots of baboon skulls from the site, he recognized this one as different. It became known, on account of its small size, as the Taung 'child' (Figure 7.3).

The lime works from where the fossil came from were at Taung, close to the Kalahari Desert. Dart later reported his first view of the skull:

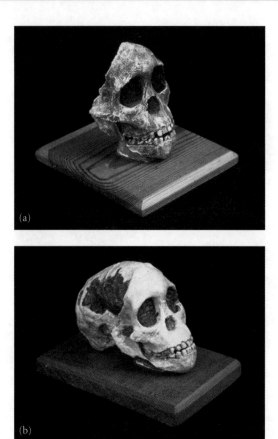

Figure 7.3 Cast of the Taung child. (a) Skull. (b) Skull with brain endocast in place.

But I knew at a glance what lay in my hands was no ordinary anthropoidal brain. Here in lime-consolidated sand was the replica of a brain three times as large as that of a baboon and considerably bigger than that of any adult chimpanzee. The startling image of the convolutions and furrows of the brain and blood vessels of the skull was plainly visible (Dart and Craig, 1959).

♦ One of the features of the skull indicated to Dart that this species was bipedal. Which feature would have indicated that?

♦ The foramen magnum in this specimen is below the brain case, as in humans, rather than at the back of the skull, as in apes.

Proportionally, the 'child' had a small brain and therefore was more ape-like, but the teeth were more like human teeth. Whether the brain shows a more human organization is still debatable, but examination of a more recently discovered specimen of *Au. africanus* (Lockwood and Tobias, 1999) provides evidence of some reorganization. Ape and human brains differ in size, of course, but there are some other differences, one of which is the volume of the primary visual striate cortex (PVC). Relatively speaking, the PVC is smaller in humans than apes. In the anthropoid apes the front edge of the PVC is defined by a prominent trough on the brain surface – the lunate sulcus. This sulcus is not always present in humans and when it is, it is not prominent and is in a more posterior position. The new skull, Stw 505, has a lunate sulcus in a more posterior position than in a chimp, suggesting that at least one australopith species underwent brain changes that gave it a more human anatomy. One consequence of this change would be an increase in part of the cerebral cortex (posterior parietal) and so it is tempting to imagine this might be linked to increased communication and tool-using.

Box 7.4   The Taung child – anatomists at loggerheads

Raymond Dart had worked with Professor Grafton Elliot Smith before becoming Professor at Witwatersrand in South Africa. However, when the first description of his new fossil was published in *Nature*, there was deep scepticism in England about the claims for the skull being from a new genus of human. The language used by the protagonists seems extreme even by present day standards. Elliot Smith called the name *Australopithecus* 'so uncouth a name' in a letter to the *Times* (Feb 17 1925). Sir Arthur Keith held the view that the skull was merely a young anthropoid ape and that both anthropoid apes and the forest environment that they lived in extended 2000 miles further south (into South Africa) than today. This provoked a furious response from Dart, in an interview with the *Times* published on 24 March 1926. He described Keith's statements as 'ridiculous' and went on 'There is not a shred of evidence ..... for these magical forests'. He suggested that 'their postulation illustrates the Bolshevistic trickery with South African geography ....' and so on. The debate about the position of *Australopithecus africanus* continued for some time. Dart had a champion at Oxford University, Sir Wilfrid Le Gros Clark, who for many years countered the highly critical views of Grafton Elliot Smith and Arthur Keith and contributed to the acceptance of the Dart's specimen – and the South African australopiths generally – as human. Some 80 years later it appears that although Dart was right in many of his views about the hominin status of the genus, it is looking increasingly likely that *Au. africanus* represents an extinct side branch of the evolutionary tree.

Following the discovery of the Taung child, Robert Broom, who had collected and studied mammal-like reptiles in South Africa hoped for a another site with hominin fossils and after a search lasting over ten years, he found fossils in the caves at Sterkfontein. Here is his description of the discovery of perhaps his most famous find:

> When the smoke of the blast blew away, we found that a beautiful skull had been broken in two. The outer part of the rock had the top of the skull, and all the lower half was exposed in the wall. As the top of the skull had been split off we could see into the brain-cavity, which was lined with small lime crystals. I have seen many interesting sights in my long life, but this was the most thrilling in my experience (Broom, 1950).

This skull, Sts 5, became known as 'Mrs Ples', the name derived from Broom's original description of the specimen as *Plesianthropus* (Figure 7.4). Broom also found

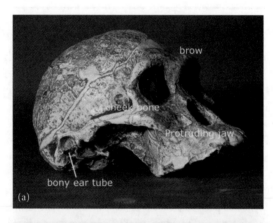

(a)

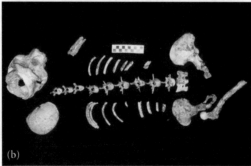

(b)

Figure 7.4   (a) A cast of the skull of 'Mrs Ples' (Sts 5) to show key features. (b) skeleton Sts 14 with the skull (Sts 5).
Source: (b) (Transvaal Museum).

some postcranial skeletal material and recently it has been suggested that these might be from the same individual as the skull (Thackeray, Gommery and Braga, 2002).

Since then other sites have been added to the list of South African caves yielding hominins.

There is a lot of variability in the specimens assigned to *Au. africanus*. For example, there is a specimen whose teeth and forwardly pointing jaw are similar to a female orang (Stw 252) and there is the rather short-faced specimen with worn teeth (Sts 71). The skull Stw505 has the largest cranial capacity by some margin and if the largest estimate of close to 600 cm^3 is correct, then it exceeds the cranial capacity of some early *Homo* specimens from East Africa that are nearly 1 million years younger (see Section 8.7).

7.6 Sterkfontein and the 'little foot' discovery

Sterkfontein in South Africa lays claim to being the richest site for fossil hominins in the world. From the caves and quarries in the area have come specimens of three different genera, over 500 specimens in all. The caves are now a World Heritage Site. In 1994 Ron Clarke was searching for bovid fossils in stored material from Sterkfontein when he came across five bones from the left foot of a hominin. Later, by chance, he discovered more bones amongst the stored material and finding that all came from the same individual, he asked two co-workers to look at the original cave to see if they could find any more. They found, *in situ*, what is probably most of the rest of the skeleton, including the complete skull of a hominin that is an australopith but cannot yet be assigned to any species. The skeleton is embedded in hard breccia and is still (2009) being extracted.

The date of the specimen has been difficult to determine. The method adopted was one in which the amount of unstable isotopes of beryllium, ^{10}Be and aluminium, ^{26}Al were measured. These isotopes are produced by the interaction of cosmic rays with the nuclei of atoms in quartz. The longer the rock is exposed, the more isotopes that accumulate. When the rock is suddenly buried, as happened at Sterkfontein no more isotopes are formed and the decay ratio ^{26}Al/^{10}Be decreases exponentially with time. The sample closest to the skeleton yields a date of 4.17 mya +/−0.35 (total uncertainty).

◆ What is the significance of the date of 4.17 mya for the probable phylogenetic relationships of the specimen?

◆ The date for the skeleton raises interesting possibilities, though of course until the complete skeleton has been extracted and studied, no definite placing of the specimen in the evolutionary tree can be made. It is earlier than *Au. afarensis* and would be a contemporary of *Au. anamensis*. If it is a new species, it shows that radiation in the australopiths at that time was greater than previously thought.

There are two types of femur present in the fossil remains from Sterkfontein that suggests that there might be two forms of australopith present. At the moment, both are regarded as being *Au. africanus*. As more details emerge from study of the Sterkfontein caves and their fossils, we can expect to derive a clearer picture of the hominin life in the area 4 million years ago.

It is important to appreciate, though, that where dating is not easy – and the Sterkfontein area presents some special difficulties – there can be differences in estimated dates. Indeed the dating of all the hominins from South African caves is difficult. The Sterkfontein caves are in dolomite, with the fossils preserved in the infills that form a tough, calcified breccia of dolomite, chert and surface soil (Partridge *et al.*, 2003). Biochronological dating – the use of other fossil species present to correlate with strata that can be dated – has been the most common method applied. Using this method, Lee Berger and his team came up with a highly controversial and much younger date for the Sterkfontein caves, which would place the little foot fossil at no older than 3.04 mya and perhaps in the range 1.07–1.95 mya. The authors of the paper Berger, Lacruz and de Ruiter (2002) suggest that *Au africanus* from Sterkfontein date from 1.5 to 2.5 mya and do not overlap, therefore, with *Au. afarensis*, *Au. bahrelghazali* and *Kenyanthropus platyops*. Accepting these dates would, of course, give a very different picture of the hominin scene across Africa!

7.7 Which species belong in the genus *Australopithecus*?

The position of *Australopithecus afarensis* in the human evolutionary tree is a matter for continuing debate. Even the naming was controversial, partly because of the use of one of the Laetoli specimens, LH4 (Figure 7.5) as the type specimen (Box 7.5), but also because there is another Laetoli specimen with a different name

Figure 7.5   A cast of the type specimen of *Australopithecus afarensis*.

(*Praeanthropus africanus*) that is almost certainly the same species. This specimen was described in 1950, so the names take priority. Thus Johanson could not use the species name *africanus* for his new *Australopithecus* species as the name *Au. africanus* already existed for the South African specimens described originally by Dart. To further complicate the situation, *Au. afarensis* might be ancestral to both *Au. africanus* and *Paranthropus*, in which case it does not belong in the genus *Australopithecus*. In that case, the name *Praeanthropus afarensis* would be the correct one, in line with the rules of nomenclature. Although this discussion of names seems, on the face of it, to be a trifle nerdish, it is of significance because the names express evolutionary relationships. Also, of course, you will not find consistency in the use of names in the literature. However, it is the relationships that in the end are of most interest to us.

Underlying the discussion of the genus names is the assumption that we are clear about the definition of each genus. This becomes particularly interesting when considering the changes that have taken place in the definition of the genus *Homo*, which we consider in Chapter 8, changes which have been made to accommodate

---

Box 7.5   Type specimens

When a new species is described, the specimen that the description was made from is termed the type specimen and is usually lodged in a museum collection so that it is available to other researchers. Subsequently, any other specimen that is assigned to the same species must have the same characteristics as the type specimen. There is variation within all species so a subjective assessment has to be made about whether slight differences are normal variation or indicative of a different species. If as a result of new specimens coming to light, an existing species is split into two, the original type and original name remain and a new type is designated for the new species. If, however it is found that two types exist for the same species, then the first one (with its description) takes priority. Problems arise with human fossils, as you will discover, when the type specimen is but a fraction of the whole skeleton, since the only points of comparison can be with the bone or bones present in the type.

---

features possessed by newly discovered fossil species added to the genus. Ernst Mayr defined a genus as being a taxon that occupies a single adaptive zone. In the case of the australopiths, *Australopithecus* includes the first hominins with developing bipedality and *Paranthropus* includes the hominins that moved into the savanna habitats and became specialized on feeding on tougher plant material.

There are similarities between *Au. afarensis* and *Au. africanus* but there are also differences. For example, although both species were bipedal, the arms of *Au. afri canus* appear to have been longer relative to the hind limbs and so to have been more ape-like, whilst *Au. afarensis* had fore limb to hind limb proportions more similar to the proportions in *Homo*. The canine teeth of *Au. africanus* are smaller, whilst the molars are larger and have thicker enamel. The mean cranial capacity of *Au. africanus* is 440 cm³, which is slightly less than that of *Au. afarensis*, which is 446 cm³. The range of measurements from five *Au. afarensis* crania is 387–534 cm³. However measurements of one particular possible *Au. africanus* skull, Stw 505 from Sterkfontein, are controversial with a figure close to 600 cm³ being suggested (Hawks and Wolpoff, 1999 with figure of 598 cm³). A study using serial CT data (Conroy *et al.*, 1998) to produce a computer model gave a lower figure of 515 cm³, still larger than the values for the six *Au. africanus* skulls measured (mean 440 cm³, range 425–485 cm³). Of course, there is still a possibility that Stw505 might be classified as a new species.

The timing of the appearance of *Au. afarensis* in the fossil record places it earlier than *Au. africanus* and cladistic analyses of the hominins consistently place *Au. afarensis* as the basal taxon of the subsequent radiation of australopiths and the genus *Homo*.

7.8 Conclusion

From 4.2 to 2.5 mya there was diversification within the hominins. The evolutionary picture at the first part of the period is becoming clearer as new finds emerge and these finds suggest a sequence from *Ardipithecus ramidus* at 4.4 mya to *Australopithecus*

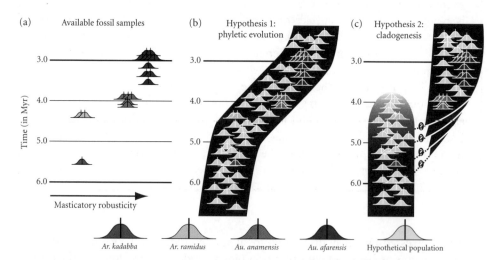

Figure 7.6 Two possible phylogenetic trees for the period 6 to 3 mya. (a). The phyletic tree, showing a single lineage evolving at varying rates. (b). The branching tree, with a speciation event producing the *Australopithecus* branch (White *et al.*, 2006. Reprinted by permission from Macmillan Publishers Ltd: Nature (White, T. D., WoldeGabriel, G., Asfaw, B., Ambrose, S., Beyene, Y., Bernor, R. L., Boisserie, J.-R., Currie, B., Gilbert, H., Haile-Selassie, Y. *et al.* (2006). Asa Issie, Aramis and the origin of *Australopithecus*. Nature 440, P887), copyright 2006).

afarensis at 3.6 mya, with *Au. anamensis* (4.2 mya) anatomically intermediate in many characters between these two species. Through the series, there is an increase in tooth size that would be related to a diet that contained an increasing proportion of hard items. This trend, together with an increase in the size of associated skull components, continues until it reverses in species of *Homo*, when presumably it lost its selective advantage as stone tools came into use.

Two possible explanations for the phylogeny exist and these have been proposed by Tim White and others. They point out that at present there are insufficient specimens to allow us to distinguish between the two phylogenetic trees, illustrated in Figure 7.6. We shall consider phylogenetic trees further in Chapter 10.

So far there are eight known species of australopiths that existed in time frames within 4.2–1.2 mya. From about 2.5–1.2 mya, at least three species of robust australopith co-existed with *Homo* species and we consider all these species in the next chapter.

Questions and activities

Question 7.1

Explain the rationale behind the single species hypothesis. On the basis of what is currently known, what evidence refutes the hypothesis? *(Learning outcome B1)*

References

Asfaw, B., White, T., Lovejoy, O., Latimer, B., Simpson, S. and Suwa, G. (1999) *Australopithecus garhi*: a new species of early hominid from Ethiopia. *Science*, **284**, 629–635.

Berge, C., Penin, X. and Pelle, E. (2006) New interpretation of Laetoli footprints using an experimental approach and Procrustes analysis: preliminary results. *Comptes Rendus Biologies*, **5**, 561–569.

Berger, L.R., Lacruz, R. and de Ruiter, D.J. (2002) Brief communication: revised age estimates of *Australopithecus*-bearing deposits at Sterkfontein, South Africa. *American Journal of Physical Anthropology*, **119**, 192–197.

Broom, R. (1950) *Finding the Missing Link*, Watts and Co., London.

Brunet, M., Beauvilain, A., Coppens, Y., Heintz, E., Moutaye, A.H.E. and Pilbeam, D. (1995) The first australopithecine 2,500 kilometers west of the rift-valley (Chad). *Nature*, **378**, 273–275.

Conroy, G.C., Weber, G.W., Seidler, H., Tobias, P.V., Kane, A. and Brunsden, B. (1998) Endocranial capacity in an early Hominid cranium from Sterkfontein, South Africa. *Science*, **280**, 1730–1731.

Dart, R.A. and Craig, D. (1959) *Adventures with the Missing Link*, Hamish Hamilton, London.

Hawks, J. and Wolpoff, M.H. (1999) Endocranial capacity of early hominids. *Science*, **283**, 9.

Johanson, D.C. and White, T.D. (1979) A systematic assessment of Early African hominids. *Science*, **203**, 321–329.

Johanson, D.C., White, T.D. and Coppens, Y. (1978) A new species of the genus *Australopithecus* (Primates: Hominidae) from the Pliocene of eastern Africa. *Kirtlandia*, **28**, 1–11.

Kimbel, W.H., Lockwood, C.A., Ward, C.V., Leakey, M.G., Rak, Y. and Johanson, D.C. (2006) Was *Australopithecus anamensis* ancestral to *A. afarensis*? A case of anagenesis in the hominin fossil record. *Journal of Human Evolution*, **51**, 134–152.

Kimbel, W.H., Rak, Y. and Johanson, D.C. (2004) *The Skull of Australopithecus afarensis*, Oxford University Press, Oxford.

Leakey, M. (1976) Fossil hominids from the Laetoli beds. *Nature*, **262**, 460–466.

Leakey, M.G., Feibel, C.S., McDougall, I. and Walker, A. (1995) New four-million-year-old hominid species from Kanapoi and Allia Bay, Kenya. *Nature*, **376**, 565–571.

Leakey, M.G., Feibel, C.S., McDougall, I., Ward, C. and Walker, A. (1998) New specimens and confirmation of an early age for *Australopithecus anamensis*. *Nature*, **393**, 62–66.

Leakey, M.G., Spoor, F. Brown, F.H., Gathogo, P.N., Kiarie, C., Leakey, L.N. and McDougall, I. (2001) New hominin genus from eastern Africa shows diverse middle Pliocene lineages. *Nature,* **410**(6827): 433–440.

Leakey, R.E.F. and Walker, A.C. (1980) On the status of *Australopithecus afarensis*. *Science*, **207**, 1103.

Lockwood, C.A. and Tobias, P.V. (1999) A large male hominin cranium from Sterkfontein, South Africa, and the status of *Australopithecus africanus*. *Journal of Human Evolution*, **36**, 637–685.

Partridge, T.C. (2000) Hominid-bearing caves and tufa deposits. in *The Cenozoic of Southern Africa*, (eds. T. C. Partridge and R. R. Maud), Oxford University Press, New York, pp. 100–125.

Partridge, T.C., Granger, D.E., Caffee, M.W. and Clarke, R.J. (2003) Lower Pliocene hominid remains from Sterkfontein. *Science*, **300**, 607–612.

Patterson, B. and Howells, F.C. (1967) Hominid Humeral Fragment from Early Pleistocene of Northwestern Kenya. *Science*, **156**, 64–66.

Tattersall, I. and Schwartz, J.H. (2000) *Extinct Humans*, Westview Press, Boulder, Colorado.

Thackeray, F., Gommery, D. and Braga, J. (2002) Australopithecine postcrania (Sts14) from the Sterkfontein Caves, South Africa: the skeleton of 'Mrs Ples'? *South African Journal of Science*, **98**, 211–212.

Walker, A.C., Leakey, R.E., Harris, J.M. and Brown, F.H. (1986) 2.5-Myr *Australopithecus boisei* from west of Lake Turkana, Kenya. *Nature*, **322**, 517–522.

White, T.D. (2002) Earliest hominids. in *The Primate Fossil record*, (ed. W.G.Hartwig), Cambridge University Press, Cambridge UK, pp. 407–417.

White, T.D., WoldeGabriel, G., Asfaw, B., Ambrose, S., Beyene, Y., Bernor, R. L., Boisserie, J.-R., Currie, B., Gilbert, H., Haile-Selassie, Y. *et al.* (2006) Asa Issie, Aramis and the origin of *Australopithecus*. *Nature*, **440**, 883–889.

8

3.0 – 1.0 mya: Emergence and Diversification of the Genus *Homo*

At some point around 2.5 mya, a speciation event resulted in the emergence of *Homo*. At least three australopith species were present in Africa at that time, including *Australopithecus garhi*, *Paranthropus boisei* and *P. robustus*. From around 2.5 to 1.2 mya, australopiths were coexisting with *Homo* species. So far at least four species of *Homo* have been described for this time period. As is already clear from earlier chapters, the classification of hominins is not fixed, and although this account will follow the most up-to-date view, other schemes are possible.

At around 2.5 mya the climate was getting colder, with an increase in the amount of polar ice. As a consequence of more water being locked up in ice, there was an overall increase in aridity. In Africa the change opened out the forests and grassland replaced wooded areas. Antelopes and other savannah species flourished. Against this background of climate change the hominins became more diverse, the first species of *Homo* arrived and tools manufactured from stone made their first appearance.

Within this period there was a change in the behaviour of the hominin population and groups of hominins began a migration that took them northwards, out of Africa and into Asia. Only *Homo* have been found outside Africa, so the assumption is that it was in members of that genus that the behavioural adaptations that favoured migration, first evolved.

The Emergence of Humans Patricia Ash and David Robinson
© 2010 John Wiley & Sons, Ltd

8.1 The Robust Australopiths

Following his description of the Taung child, Raymond Dart hoped that other specimens would turn up and so other sites were searched. Two sites, both investigated by Robert Broom, yielded specimens that were clearly related to the original specimen, but had back teeth that were larger. The skull appeared flatter with more powerful jaws and a pronounced crest on the cranium – the sagittal crest which is the attachment point for the temporalis muscles of the jaws. Broom considered that he had a new species and he named it *Paranthropus robustus* (Broom, 1938). The individuals were so obviously massive that it prompted thoughts that there might be one species of South African hominin that was highly sexually dimorphic, rather than two species. There is marked sexual dimorphism in the skull of some of the great apes; more marked in gorillas and orangs than in chimps. Male chimps may have a sagittal crest on the skull, female chimps do not. Males and females of *Au. afarensis* are very different in overall size (Stringer and McKie, 1996) with the males being up to 4 ft 10 in (1.47 m) tall while females are 3 ft 3 in (0.99 m), on average. However, it is now clear that two species are present in Southern Africa and that *P. robustus* is younger than *Au. africanus*, appearing in the fossil record at the time that *Au. africanus* was disappearing (if we discount, for the present, the contentious dating for the Sterkfontein series outlined in Section 7.6). *P. robustus* appears in South Africa around 1.8 mya and disappears some 200 kya later (White, 2002).

In 1994 a well preserved skull of an australopith was excavated at Drimolen in South Africa. Much of the skull is intact. Other hominin specimens have been discovered at the site and most of them can be assigned to *P. robustus*. An analysis of the specimens by Andre Keyser (Keyser, 2000) suggests a greater degree of intraspecific variability than previously thought and marked sexual dimorphism.

Although *P. robustus* has only been found in South African sites, other robust forms occur in East Africa and also in Ethiopia. In the next sections we consider the other robust forms and their taxonomic status.

8.2 *Paranthropus boisei*

In July 1959 Louis and Mary Leakey were working in Olduvai Gorge when they found the cranium of an individual with large jaws and big teeth that resembled the South African *Paranthropus robustus*, but was even more robust. Louis Leakey described the new specimen (OH 5) in an article in *Nature* and notwithstanding its similarities with *P. robustus*, placed it in a new genus, *Zinjanthropus*. The skull is still referred to as Zinj, but the genus name is no longer used and the specimen is placed in the same genus as the South African species – *Paranthropus boisei* (Figure 8.1).

Comparing the type specimen (OH 5) with a well preserved *P. robustus* cranium from Swartkrans (SK 48) (Figure 8.2), the brow, face and cheek bones are more massive. The anterior teeth are small and the cheek teeth are large, but OH 5 has larger cheek teeth than SK 48.

Other specimens of *P. boisei* have been found, notably a mandible from the Peninj River area on the shores of Lake Natron. This mandible, with its large chewing teeth and small incisors and canines fits well with the cranium of the type specimen OH 5, which does not have a mandible itself (Figure 8.1b).

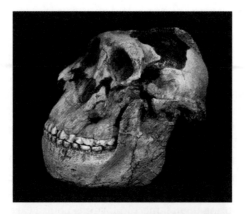

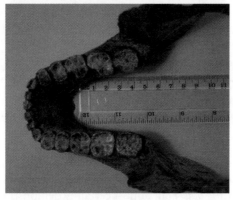

Figure 8.1 The *Paranthropus boisei* cranium was discovered in 1959. The first complete skull of *P. boisei* was not found until 1993, in Konso, Ethiopia. This is a cast of the cranium fitted to a mandible from Peninj (shown separately).

Figure 8.2 A cast of SK48, a well preserved cranium of *Paranthropus robustus* from Swartkrans.

Box 8.1   Finding 'Dear boy'

Louis Leakey was absolutely certain that he would discover the fossil of an early human, when he returned to the Olduvai Gorge in 1951. His certainty was to be justified, but not until 1959. On 17 July he had a slight fever and stayed in camp while Mary Leakey went out and searched for fossils. Shortly before noon, with the sun high in the sky, it was time to stop work, but she saw a scrap of bone projecting from the ground. Closer examination revealed two large teeth set in a jaw. It was part of a hominin skull, still in place. The excavation took 19 days. The skull was embedded in soil but broken into around 400 pieces, which had to be painstakingly re-assembled. Both were delighted with the find and referred to it affectionately as 'Dear boy'. It was to bring them fame and fortune. Louis Leakey originally thought it was a very early species of *Homo*, but placed it in a new genus, *Zinjanthropus*, from which another of the skull's nicknames – Zinj – comes. The size of the teeth and the evidence of large jaw muscles led to a further nickname – Nutcracker man – although more recent examination of the teeth of several individuals suggests a pattern of wear more consistent with a diet in which fruit predominated (Ungar, Grine and Teaford, 2008).

Two crania discovered in 1970 and 1971 at Koobi Fora in Kenya by Richard Leakey display characteristics of *P. boisei* but almost certainly demonstrate sexual dimorphism. KNMER 406 is a largely complete cranium of an adult male and although it is missing all the teeth, the tooth roots are massive. The face is very wide as a consequence of a wide flare on the arched cheek bones (the zygomatic arch). The sagittal and nuchal crests are large. The estimated brain size is 510 cc.

◆ What is the significance of the flared cheek bones?

◆ The temporalis muscles, the 'chewing muscles' of the lower jaw run up the side of the skull, inside the cheek bones. The wide flare means that the muscles were large – in fact four times the size of our own temporalis muscles.

KNMER 732 shows many of the features of OH5 and KNMER 406, but lacks the prominent crest and is smaller, although interestingly the estimated brain size is almost identical to that of KNMER 406, at 500 cc.

Although there are nearly 100 fossil specimens that are assigned to *P. boisei*, there is no postcranial material that can be unequivocally linked to the species, so in working out its lifestyle we can only reason from the skull. Most people accept that part of the diet, at least, contained seeds and nut with hard coats. Whether there were other components too is not known for certain so we can't be sure that the diet was a highly specialized one.

♦ Using your knowledge of modern primates, can you deduce anything about the social system of *P. boisei?*

♦ The presence of sexual dimorphism is associated with competition for females, in modern primates. It is probable that there was a primate-like social system in *P. boisei* and other australopiths and the sexual dimorphism suggests that there was more competition between males, such as is found in gorillas where one male controls a group of females and their offspring.

8.3 *Paranthropus aethiopicus*

In 1968 Yves Coppens, Richard Leakey and F Clark Howell led a team investigating the Lower Omo river area in Southern Ethiopia. They discovered mandibles and teeth of what was undoubtedly a very robust species of australopith, which was assigned to a new genus – *Paraustralopithecus aethiopicus*, but it was not clear to everybody that they were of a new species and possibly they really belonged with *P. boisei*. The Shungara formation that the finds came from was dated to 2.4–2.3 mya. Another significant point about this find is that stone tools are associated with the same formation, although none of the hominin finds have been at the same site, or associated with, these stone tools. They are slightly younger than the stone tools found at Gona in Ethiopia, that date from 2.6 mya. They may be linked with *A. garhi* from the same area and time period, but again there is no direct association between the finds (Semaw, 2000).

However in 1986 the picture changed when the discovery of a robust australopith skull was announced in *Nature* – the black skull. The black skull (Figure 8.3) is richly

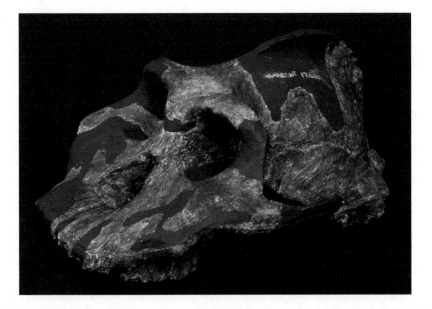

Figure 8.3 *Paranthropus aethiopicus.* A cast of the black skull.

mineralized, but the facial region is in fragments that makes reconstruction difficult. Alan Walker, Richard Leakey and others, when describing it, considered it to belong in the species *P. boisei*. The palate is very large and in this respect it resembles the specimens that were found at the Omo river, and so Walker and Leakey suggested that further work ought to be done to see if the black skull and *Paraustralopithecus aethiopicus* should be combined in one genus, which would become *Paranthropus aethiopicus*. You will find that the black skull is often labelled *P. aethiopicus*, but some workers have pointed out that it has yet to be shown to belong with the Omo specimens. Ian Tattersall and Jeffrey Schwartz commented on the reconstruction of the face and that it might be a bit flatter (Tattersall and Schwartz, 2000). Also they noted differences from the other robust forms. David Cameron and Colin Groves (2004) point to the smaller cranial capacity, larger front teeth and the date as placing the black skull anatomically between *Au afarensis* and the other *Paranthropus* species. They suggest naming it *P. walkeri* until any link with the Omo specimens has been proved or dis-proved. Also, there is another species extantx at the same time, *Austrlaopithecus garhi*.

8.4 *Australopithecus garhi*

The Middle Awash site in Ethiopia has yielded specimens of *Ardipithecus, Australopithecus anamensis* and *Au. afarensis*, all older than 3 mya. There is relatively little fossil material from the crucial period of 3–2 mya, but a further australopith, *Au. garhi*, gives us a glimpse of that period.

The first fossils of this new species were found in 1990 in the Hata deposits close to the village of Bouri and included a fragment of humerus and a mandible. From the tooth roots in the mandible it could be deduced that it did not belong to a robust australopith. The subsequent discovery of parts of a skull also showed that the species was not a robust one. The skull was partially washed out of a slope and 7 weeks were spent in digging tons of material from the slope and sieving it. The molar teeth are huge – larger than those of *Paranthropus robustus*, with the ratio of canine size to post canine (molars and premolars) size being large, resembling early *Homo*, rather than small as in *P. robustus*. The brain size, at 450 cc, is similar to *Au. afarensis* but the limited post-cranial material cannot be assigned definitely to *Au. garhi*. The femur suggests that like *Au. afarensis*, the femur was longer than the humerus, as it is in humans but not chimps (Asfaw *et al.*, 1999).

8.5 Tools and tool technologies

8.5.1 Is there evidence for tool use by australopiths?

The first manufactured tools do not appear in the fossil record until 2.5 mya. It is important to note the use of the word 'manufactured', here. Hominins may well have been using stones as tools earlier, without the ability to shape them, but it is not easy to discern from the archaeological record that this was taking place. There is evidence that australopiths used stones for obtaining food. The fossils of *Australopithecus garhi* described in Section 8.4, were dated at 2.5 mya. They were found at Bouri, Ethiopia, relatively close to a site called Gona, where fossil antelope bones, had been smashed open with stones. There is no evidence that australopiths manufactured stone tools: equally we cannot say for certain that they did not. Chimpanzees have been observed using rocks to process food, using plant stems to fish for termites and broken tree branches in displays of aggression. Wood and plant tools are not generally preserved. Raymond Dart thought that australopiths at South African sites possessed an osteodontokeratic culture, using bones and horns as tools, but his evidence is not accepted today. Some bone fragments and horn cores have been found that appear polished.

◆ Suggest a possible use of these fragments that might lead to polishing?

◆ When first discovered, it was suggested that if they had been used for digging for tubers in sand or soil, they would take on a polished appearance.

The specimens come from Sterkfontein and Swartkrans and so could be associated with australopiths at these sites. Later analysis of the wear patterns on the specimens (Backwell and d'Errico, 2001) suggests that the wear is caused by digging for termites.

8.5.2 Tools in Olduvai Gorge

Olduvai Gorge is perhaps the most famous locality for fossil hominins. It is in the Serengeti Plain of Tanzania and is part of the Rift Valley. The first European scientist to visit it was a German entomologist, Professor Wilhelm Kattwinkel, who in 1911 while on a medical expedition, collected some fossils. A second German expedition in 1913, led by Hans Reck, had discovered a human skeleton. Louis Leakey led a third expedition to the Gorge in 1931, and Hans Reck was a member. Shortly after their arrival in the Gorge they found a hand axe and a further 76 in the next 4 days. Reck had missed seeing them on his previous visit as he had expected that any tools he found would be made of flint, which does not in fact occur there. There are five beds recognized in the gorge covering, as we now know, a period from 2 mya to 20 000 years ago. During his expedition Louis Leaky recovered stone tools from all five layers and from Bed 1 tools older than those of the **Acheulean** type that he had found elsewhere as well as higher up at Olduvai. These roughly trimmed pebbles and lumps of rock he called the '**Oldowan** Culture' and they were later recognized as the oldest stone tools.

8.6 Australopiths in the human lineage

Construction of a phylogeny for the human species is not easy and the group of australopiths illustrates this rather well. A genus should be monophyletic, that is composed

Box 8.2   Classifying tool technologies

The types of stone tools found are divided into 'modes' based both on their appearance and the methods used to form them. The Oldowan tools are the earliest known and are classified as 'Mode 1'.

Mode	Name(s) associated with the mode	Summary of features
Mode 1	Oldowan, Clactonian	Rough flake tools made by striking one stone with another. The flakes produced were sharp tools. The stone from which the flakes were struck may have been used as a chopping tool or simply discarded.
Mode 2	Acheulean, Biface	Wood or bone was used to remove small flakes and to shape both sides of a tool (hence the term 'biface'). Often the core was shaped rather than the flakes that were struck from it, unlike Mode 1.
Mode 3	Levallois, Mousterian (or later Mode 3)	A stone core technology in which the core is carefully struck so that a number of tools can be detached and then retouched to produce a continuous cutting edge. Tools were often re-sharpened and re-used.
Mode 4	Aurignacian	The tools are long, narrow blades derived from cylindrical, shaped stone cores and are much more standardized than tools of earlier modes.
Mode 5	Magdalenian	The tools from this period are characterized by the small blades (called microliths) some times derived from larger blades by deliberate breakage.

of a complete lineage that shares a common ancestor. This complete lineage is a clade. The australopiths considered as a whole are not monophyletic. A genus can also be defined as occupying a single adaptive zone, so the early species that developed bipedalism could form the genus *Australopithecus*, the 'robust' australopiths that moved onto the savannah and developed a specialized vegetable diet could form the genus *Paranthropus*, leaving the more gracile forms that developed a large brain and omnivorous diet who would form the genus *Homo*. This division leaves out *Kenyanthropus*, while *Ardipithecus* would be incorporated within *Australopithecus*.

A more radical approach to the australopiths has been taken by Cela-Conde and Ayala (2003) in their analysis of the genera that make up the human lineage. They propose three subfamilies and split the australopiths across two of them, transferring *Kenyanthropus* to the third sub family and placing it within the genus *Homo* (Figure 8.4).

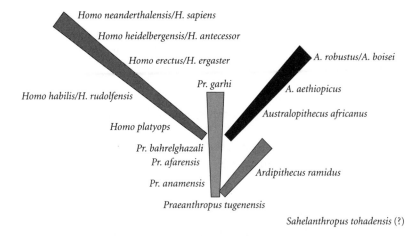

Homo neanderthalensis/H. sapiens

Homo heidelbergensis/H. antecessor

A. robustus/A. boisei

Homo erectus/H. ergaster

Pr. garhi

A. aethiopicus

Homo habilis/H. rudolfensis

Australopithecus africanus

Homo platyops

Pr. bahrelghazali

Pr. afarensis

Ardipithecus ramidus

Pr. anamensis

Praeanthropus tugenensis

Sahelanthropus tohadensis (?)

Figure 8.4 A radical approach to the human lineage. Reproduced from Cela-Conde and Ayala (2003). Genera of the human lineage. Proceedings of the National Academy of Sciences of the United States of America, 100, P7687.

They argue that there are only four genera of hominins (or perhaps five if you include *Sahelanthropus* as a hominin).

8.7 Early *Homo*

Almost a year after the discovery at Olduvai Gorge of the massive skull of *P. boisei* (Zinj), Louis and Mary Leakey discovered the first remains of another hominin, close to where they had found Zinj, but in slightly older strata of Bed I at the bottom of Olduvai Gorge. These specimens were a braincase, part of a lower jaw, most of a left foot and some hand bones. The foot is OH8 while the rest of the specimens are OH7. Subsequently further specimens were found in both Beds I and II, enabling Louis Leaky with Philip Tobias and John Napier to describe a new species of *Homo* who, they believed was the species responsible for the manufacture of the stone tools found in the gorge. The brain size was estimated at 640 ml, compared to the estimate of 500 ml for the average australopiths brain. The skulls showed no evidence of the large sagittal crest found in australopiths and both premolar and molar teeth were smaller. On this basis, they named the new species *Homo habilis*, meaning handy-man.

Now this new species was controversial even at the time, for although there were good indications that it differed from *P. boisei*, the primary driver for naming it appears to have been the link with the stone tools. So, the distinction between *Homo* and other species was taken as the ability to produce tools, rather than a set of strict morphological criteria.

The collection of *H. habilis* finds was augmented substantially by work carried out by Richard Leakey at Koobi Fora on the shores of Lake Turkana in Northern Kenya. Here in 1969 the team found a complete cranium of a robust australopith. Significantly, they also found stone tools that resembled those found at the lowest layers of Olduvai Gorge. So the search was on for another hominin in the area and in 1972 hundreds of fragments of a skull were found which, when reconstructed as far as was possible, proved to be a large brained individual – 750 ml – with a face which, depending upon how one viewed the reconstruction, was perhaps australopith.

◆ Name three features that you would look upon as typical of robust australopiths.

◆ You would look for a sagittal crest, a flat face and large teeth, although large teeth are a feature of australopiths in general.

Of these features, the skull lacks a prominent sagittal crest but does have a flat face. The tooth roots of the jaw suggest that the crowns would have been large. The skull has become famous as KNM-ER 1470 and was initially assigned to *H. habilis* (Figure 8.5).

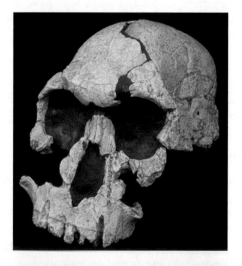

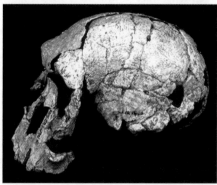

Figure 8.5   Front and side views of a cast of KNM-ER 1470.

Further finds at Koobi Fora have, if anything, been confusing rather than enlightening. In 1973 two more skulls were found, KNM-ER 1805 and KNM-ER 1813 (Figure 8.6).

KNM-ER 1813 is particularly interesting in that it has a brain size of 500 ml, more like *Au. afarensis*. The range of brain size for specimens assigned to *H. habilis* is 500 to nearly 800 ml, with an average of 610 ml.

◆ Suggest two possible explanations for this size range.

◆ One possibility is that there is an extreme form of sexual dimorphism in this species, as indeed was suggested by Clark Howell, with 1813 representing a female. Another possibility is that *H. habilis* is actually a mixture of more than one species.

KNM-ER 1805 is difficult to place. It could be that disease has altered its appearance. Originally thought to be *H. erectus*, the forward projection of the face and the prominent nuchal crest have led to it being assigned generally to *H. habilis*, but this remains an uncertain placing.

The Koobi Fora deposits from which 1470 and 1813 came are dated reliably to 1.9 mya. There are deposits at Swartkrans that are of similar age and have yielded a specimen of a species of *Homo* – SK 847. This specimen is similar to a cranium that may be *Homo erectus*, from East Turkana (KNM-ER 3733) dated to 1.8 mya, but there are sufficient differences to leave doubts about its precise status (Figure 8.7). SK 847 could be *Homo ergaster* or possibly *H. habilis*. Alternatively, it may belong in an as yet undescribed species of *Homo* found in Southern Africa but not East Africa (see Grine, Jungers and Schultz (1996)).

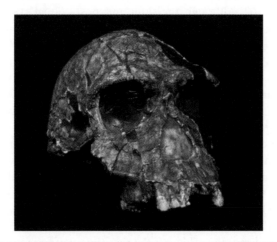

Figure 8.6 A cast of KNM-ER 1813.

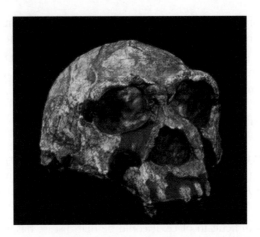

Figure 8.7   A cast of KNM-ER 3733.

The Sterkfontein site has stone tools (in Member 5) with a date of around 1.5 mya. A fragmentary cranium, Stw 53, from Sterkfontein has been assigned to *H. habilis*. The size of the brain is difficult to determine in this specimen, but probably it has a brain that is at the smaller end of the range for *H. habilis*. It looks similar to the reconstruction of the OH 24 cranium of *H. habilis* from Olduvai Gorge (Figure 8.8). OH 24 is one of the two most complete skulls found in Olduvai Gorge. It was named 'Twiggy' by the finders as it had been squashed flat (Twiggy was a famously slim female model, at the time of the discovery in 1968). The brain size has been estimated at 590 cc.

Shortly after arriving at Olduvai Gorge for a field season in 1986, Tim White discovered some pieces of the skeleton of a hominin. Eventually more than 18 000 fragments of bone were recovered and of these, 302 were identified as belonging to a hominin, now known as OH 62. Although the skull and post-cranial skeleton were so fragmented, it was possible to fit together 32 bits of bone from the maxilla (upper jaw). Sufficient of the right humerus, radius, ulna and left femur were found to enable the researchers to estimate the height of the individual and the proportions of its limbs.

◆ The third molar tooth had erupted in the jaw and showed signs of substantial wear. What conclusions could the researchers draw from this observation?

◆ The fact that the third molar had erupted suggested that the individual was adult and the substantial wear indicated that a long time had elapsed since the tooth came into use, so that the individual was likely to be an old adult.

The maxilla of OH62 bore a close resemblance to other *H. habilis* specimens from Olduvai Gorge and this fact, coupled with the lack of australopith features, placed OH62 in the *H. habilis* species. This was the first time that both upper and lower limb bones of *H. habilis* could be linked to one individual and an analysis of the proportions

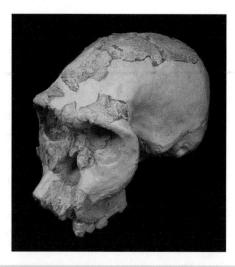

Figure 8.8 The cranium of *Homo habilis* from Olduvai Gorge. OH 24, was found in 1968 at Olduvai Gorge by Peter Nzube and is dated at 1.8 mya. Although the flattened condition of the cranium as originally found, makes if more difficult to estimate brain size, it was close to 600 ml, the minimum size normally attributed to the genus *Homo*.

threw up some unexpected results. In modern *Homo sapiens*, the humerus is shorter than the femur. The ratio of humerus length to femur length 3 100 gives a useful comparison of proportions – in *H. sapiens* the humero-femoral index is 70%.

♦ Thinking about modern apes, would you expect the humero-femoral index of a chimp to be greater than, or less than that of *H. sapiens*?

♦ The arms and legs of a chimp look similar in length, so you would expect the humero-femoral index to be greater than the 70% for *H. sapiens*. In fact, it is 100% in chimps.

Now the unexpected feature of OH62 was that the index was 95%, much closer to apes than humans, though the upper end of the human range does overlap the lower end of the chimp range. However, a recent analysis of the body proportions of *H. habilis* (2004) places OH62 in the area of overlap between chimps and humans and puts two other *H. habilis* specimens (KNM-ER 3735 and OH34) in the human range, along with *Au. afarensis*.

A further puzzle is the height of OH62. At 1 m (3 ft), it is the shortest adult hominin discovered so far. Yet, as you will read in Section 8.11, a skeleton of a hominin only 200 000 years younger than OH62 with an index close to that of *H. sapiens*, has an estimated adult height of 1.8 m. OH62 is thought to be female, based on the size and this would imply that *H. habilis* is a highly sexually dimorphic species, as are *Au. afarensis* and apes, though not chimps.

8.8 *Homo habilis* and *Homo rudolfensis*

In addition to the specimens of *H. habilis* discussed in the previous section, there are also some earlier specimens of *Homo* that are difficult to assign to any species. A maxilla collected in Ethiopia in the Hadar region in 1994, is dated at 2.3 mya. This specimen, A.L. 666-1, was found associated with stone tools of the Oldowan type. Although the shape of the palate is closer to *Homo* than *Australopithecus*, there is insufficient material to enable it to be assigned to a species. So there is a time range for early species of *Homo* of 2.3 mya to the last *H. habilis* at 1.6 mya. Within this time range the gracile specimens from Olduvai Gorge are *H. habilis*, but there are some provisos. OH62 with its archaic characters stands out and it is possible that there are two species at Olduvai. At Turkana there is at least one cranium, 1813, that appears to sit well with the *H. habilis* of Olduvai and there is 1470 which does not appear to fit, which leaves the possibility of two species there too. In 1975 a Russian anthropologist had assigned 1470 to a new species, *Pithecanthropus rudolfensis* (Rudolf is the old name for Lake Turkana). In a monograph on the Turkana specimens, Bernard Wood placed 1470, some other Turkana specimens and a fossil from Malawi in the same species *Homo rudolfensis*. This division seemed reasonable – it placed the small-brained and rather more archaic-bodied hominins in *H. habilis* and the larger, more modern-bodied hominins in *H. rudolfensis*.

In 2003 the discovery of a new specimen from Olduvai Gorge, OH 65, was announced and this specimen changed things (Figure 8.9). It is a portion of the upper face and jaw of a hominin, complete with all its teeth and it has similarities with 1470. It was found associated with stone tools and animal bones that showed cut marks (Blumenschine *et al.*, 2003) and is dated to 1.84 and 1.79 mya. Blumenschine argues for the re-grouping of *H. habilis*. Because OH65 appears to bear similarities to OH7 (the type specimen for *H. habilis*) and 1470, these three would form a single taxon. Placing 1470 firmly in the *habilis* species would invalidate the species *H. rudolfensis*, for which 1470 was the type specimen. However, the smaller brained specimens would be removed from *H. habilis* to a new, as yet un-named species (these would include, amongst others, OH24, OH 62 and KNM-ER 1813). Thus this group of early *Homo* still contains at least two species and possibly more.

Olduvai Gorge is a very rich site and will certainly yield further specimens in the future. The Turkana area and the South African sites are also likely to yield further fossils and so we can expect the relationships of the species of early *Homo* to be revised (certainly) and clarified (hopefully).

8.9 *Homo rudolfensis* and *Kenyanthropus platyops*

As you read in Section 7.4, there are similarities between the type specimen of *Kenyanthropus*, (KNM-WT 40000) dated at between 3.5 and 3.2 mya and the type specimen of *Homo rudolfensis* (KNM-ER 1470), dated at 1.9 mya (Figure 8.11). Despite this huge separation in time, there is similarity in the architecture of the face between

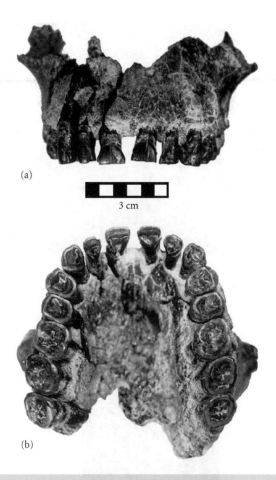

(a)

3 cm

(b)

Figure 8.9 A portion of the upper face and jaw of a hominin, OH 65. Reproduced from Blumenschine, R. J. *et al.* (2003). Late Pliocene *Homo* and Hominid Land Use from Western Olduvai Gorge, Tanzania. Science 299, P1219.

the two species. The face is flatter than in austropiths, in both species, and brow shape is very similar. The main differences are the more primitive nasal morphology and the size of the brain, which in *K. platyops*, appears to be similar to that of *Au. afarensis*. The difference in brain size means that they are unlikely to be the same species, but are the similarities sufficient for them to be placed in the same – and new – genus? The difficulty is in deciding whether the facial resemblances are inherited from a common ancestor, or have arisen separately. A further complication is the degree of post-mortem distortion in the *K. platyops* specimen which may have altered the morphology to a critical extent (for a discussion of this problem see a paper by Tim White in *Science* (White, 2003). So although some taxonomies and lineages, for example Cameron and Groves (2004), group KNM-ER 1470 and KNM-WT 40000 as separate species of *Kenyanthropus*, it seems unlikely that this is the last word on the matter.

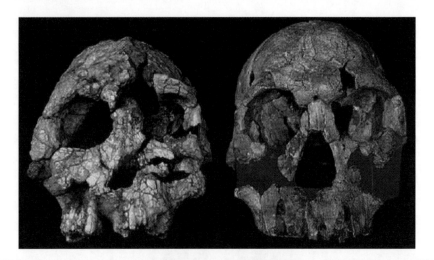

Figure 8.10   Two fossil skulls compared, on the left KNM-WT40000 and on the right KNM-ER 1470. Reprinted by permission from Macmillan Publishers Ltd: *Nature* (Lieberman, D E. Another face in our family tree. *Nature* 410, 419), copyright 2001.

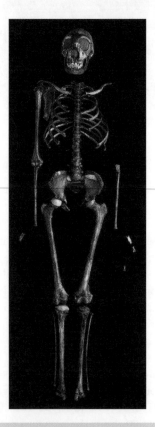

Figure 8.11   WT15000 – the Nariokotome boy
Photo David Brill.

8.10 Radiation of *Homo* species

A feature that unites hominins prior to 2 mya is their small stature, relative to modern *Homo sapiens*. Of course our information comes from relatively few specimens, all incomplete, but generally the picture is of individuals who were bipedal but with shorter legs than modern *H. sapiens*, with large – or very large – chewing teeth, smaller brains and a total body weight of 30–50 kg. They are recognizable as on, or linked to, the evolutionary path from apes to modern humans, but are sufficiently different from us to be taxonomically separate. Significantly, for the first time in this account, we are discussing specimens that were found outside Africa.

One of the major changes that must have begun with the australopiths, but really came to prominence with the emergence of *Homo* is the switch from diets that included seeds, fruit and nuts, to ones with an increasing meat content. This was not just a process of change in diet alone. Physiological and anatomical changes in the gut would have been associated with the diet change. Furthermore, a greater degree of co-operation between individuals would have been necessary for effective hunting, so with the change in diet would have come substantial changes in behaviour and greater social contact. There is evidence from studies using radio-isotopes (Sponheimer and Lee-Thorp, 1999) that around 2.5 mya some australopiths were consuming meat in quantity. The changes in the gut that would be associated with the diet might have already been occurring, in particular lengthening of the intestines, reduction in the size of the stomach and a shorter colon. These changes reflect a shift away from hind gut fermentation as the primary digestive process. At the time that the diet changes occur, the habitat was getting drier and more savannah-like. It may have been the environmental change that provided the selection pressure that drove the dietary shift. It is also arguable that the same selection pressure favoured the increasing tooth and jaw size of the robust lineage in the australopiths, which enabled them to cope with a diet of really hard fruit and seeds that would start to predominate in the increasingly dry environment (Schoeninger, Reeser and Hallin, 2003).

Analysis of enamel from molar teeth of *Au. africanus* specimens from Makapansgat (Sponheimer and Lee-Thorp, 1999) showed that the delta values for $^{13}C/^{12}C$ were significantly different from values for other grazers, browsers and mixed feeders at the site. However, they were not significantly different from that of a carnivore (hyena). The conclusion that we can draw from these results is that they are not consistent with a diet of only fruits and leaves (C3 plants) and *Au. africanus* was also obtaining dietary carbon from C4 plants, either directly or by eating the animals that had grazed on them, which could have been vertebrate animals and/or insects. As a comparison, modern chimps have a delta value that is indistinguishable from antelope eating C3 plants (Sponheimer *et al.*, 2005). The delta values for $^{13}C/^{12}C$ obtained from *Au. africanus*, *Paranthropus robustus* and early *Homo* are all very similar.

8.11 *Homo ergaster* and *Homo erectus*

At just about 2 mya the first fossils appear that have both a size and shape that is closer to modern humans than the australopiths or habilines. Proportionately, the jaw and

Box 8.3 Isotopes of carbon can help determine diet

Although archaeological evidence can show that hominins were feeding on animals, such evidence may often be absent and of course such evidence is unlikely to tell us anything about the plant content of the diet. Examination of the pattern of tooth wear can provide evidence of diet, as can the general size and structure of the dental arcade. However, isotopic analysis of dental enamel can provide direct evidence of diet. The analysis is based on the ratio of two stable isotopes of carbon. Of the three most abundant isotopes of carbon, ^{14}C which has eight protons and six neutrons in its nucleus, is unstable and decays at a predictable rate that enables it to be used for dating. ^{12}C (six protons and six neutrons) and ^{13}C (six protons and seven neutrons) are both stable. The ratio between the two isotopes is compared with the international standard (Pee Dee Belemnite formation) and the difference expressed as a delta value.

Plants fall into two groups, based on their photosynthesis biochemistry. Tress, shrubs, bushes and forbs (non- grass herbs) are C3 plants and tropical grasses and sedges are C4 plants. C3 plants discriminate against the heavier ^{13}C isotope when fixing carbon than do the C4 plants. So the amount of ^{13}C in the tooth enamel of animals can indicate the type of diet. Grazing animals will take in more ^{13}C than fruit eaters, as they feed predominately on grasses and sedges.

teeth are smaller relative to the body. The lower limbs are similar to those of modern humans. There are specimens from Africa, Europe and Asia that form this new group of hominins but, as you might imagine, fitting them into both a taxonomic and evolutionary framework is not easy. The dating of some of the specimens is difficult and remains controversial. There are four key groups of specimens that potentially date from just less than 2 mya that we need to consider. Although following our time line we ought to start with the African specimens, the type specimen of the genus *Homo erectus* comes from Asia.

Chronologically, the first of these groups of specimens to be discovered came from Trinil in Java, on the banks of the Solo River. Rene Dubois (See Box 9.1) discovered a molar tooth and a skull cap in 1891. The skull cap is of great interest as it is quite wide and low and the forehead slopes gently away from the eyebrow ridge. The skull suggested that the brain size was greater than that of any ape. In 1892 a femur was unearthed. These specimens were described by Dubois as a new species (which it clearly was), *Pithecanthropus*. Later it became *Homo erectus*, so the type specimen for *H. erectus* is the Trinil skull cap (calvaria). Specimens discovered subsequently need, of course, to be compared with the type specimen and being just a skull cap, it lacks the crucial taxonomic features of the facial region. Discovering significant morphological differences would raise questions over whether the new specimens did belong in the same species as the type. This is what has happened with a number of specimens that could, potentially, be *H. erectus*.

Following the discovery at Trinil there were substantial efforts to discover further specimens at the site, but without success. However, further discoveries were made in Java in the 1930s which appeared to be similar to the Trinil specimen, but younger and with larger brain volumes (1035–1255 ml, compared with 940 ml). The specimens came from the Solo River valley at Ngandong. The remains of 12 skulls were found, a quite unprecedented number, which were excavated under the direction of W. F. F. Oppennoorth of the Dutch Geological Survey. The larger brain and the younger age were considered to distinguish these specimens from (*Pithecanthropus*) *erectus*. The age and identity of the Ngandong specimens will be discussed in Chapter 9.

Ralph von Koenigswald, also of the Geological Survey received a skull found at Mojokerto and identified it as *P. erectus*. More specimens followed from Sangiran and by 1939 he felt it worth travelling to Beijing to compare his specimens with those found at a site near Beijing in China – Zhoukoudian (Box 9.1). In a joint paper for *Nature*, von Koenigswald and Weidenreich recognized similarities between the Java and China specimens and proposed that they were races of the same species. Thus the 'erectus' hominins demonstrably had a wide distribution across Asia and were at that stage restricted to Asia. Dating these finds has not been easy. The Zhoukoudian finds are from 500 K to 200 K years ago and we will consider them in the next chapter. The skull from Mojokerto, however, has been dated at 1.81 mya (Swisher, 1994) so there is a huge separation in time between this skull and the fossils from Zhoukoudian.

The date for the Mojokerto find is not a firm one, however, because the location data for the original find was not clear-cut. Recently, an attempt has been made to re-locate the exact site of the find (Huffman *et al.*, 2005, 2006) and this work places the site of the discovery 20 m above the layer dated by Carl Swisher (Swisher, 1994), casting doubt upon the date of 1.81 mya.

The most complete *Homo erectus* skull found in Java at Sangiran was dated to over 1 mya – possibly as much as 1.7 mya. Although the skull was distorted during fossilization, it is still possible to make a comparison with other skulls.

Despite the continuing dating problems, it seems likely that *H. erectus* was present in Asia at least 1 mya and possibly as much as 2 mya. In Africa, there are a number of specimens that might be *H. erectus*, but they are regarded as sufficiently distinct by some workers to warrant a separate species *Homo ergaster*. The type specimen for *H. ergaster* is a lower jaw (KNM-ER 992 dated approximately at 1.5 mya). This presents some problems when considering the affinity of other, more extensive specimens since the only true points of comparison are the lower jaw and teeth.

◆ Recall another type specimen that lacks some important features.

◆ The type specimen of *H. erectus*, the skull cap discovered by Dubois, lacks facial features, teeth and jaws.

The specimen of the lower jaw is in two parts. It is less robust than other *H. erectus* specimens and the molars are smaller (relative to the front teeth). Possibly belonging in the same genus is the skull KNM-ER 3733 dated to 1.8 mya, which was described earlier in Section 8.6 (Figure 8.7). A third specimen that has been grouped with these is one of the major fossil finds, the Turkana or Nariokotome boy. This is a 90% complete skeleton of a hominin discovered in 1984 by Kamoya Kimeu, working for Richard Leakey (Figure 8.12). The individual was immature at the time of death. From the fact that the canines and second molars had erupted, but the third molars had not, the age can be judged as around 12 years, using the time of eruption of modern human teeth as a guide.

♦ Does relating the eruption of the teeth to the time scale in modern humans provide a firm age?

♦ The age is not a firm one, because it is not possible to know that the eruption of teeth in this species follows exactly the same time course as in present day *Homo sapiens*.

Using the eruption pattern from chimps would give an age of 7.5 years. By comparing the pattern of eruption of all the teeth in modern humans and chimps, and then superimposing the observed pattern in the Nariokotome boy, it was possible to show that he

---

Box 8.4   The Nariokotome boy

When Richard Leakey and Alan Walker started to examine the sediments and volcanic ashes at Nariokotome on the western side of Lake Turkana, in 1984 only one ancient hominin had enough bones preserved to be described as a skeleton, and that was 'Lucy'. Shortly after starting work at the new site, Kamoya Kimeu found a small piece of cranium on the ground which, from its thickness, appeared to be *Homo erectus*. There was nothing more obviously visible on the surface, but they felt it was worth sieving the surface layers to see if any more bone could be recovered. More skull bones were recovered, and the reconstruction had started when the first post-cranial bone fragments were found. This was totally unexpected, given the rarity of post cranial fossils but as more and more bones were recovered it became apparent that the researchers had found the most complete skeleton of an ancient human ever found. A further four field seasons yielded more bones, but by 1988 little was being turned up and so the search was ended. Hand and foot bones are amongst the 10% or so of the skeleton that is still missing, but they could have disappeared in the past. It has been possible to date the volcanic ashes using the $^{40}K/^{40}Ar$ method (Section 2.5) to 1.56 to 1.51 mya. A full account of the discovery and its significance has been written by Alan Walker and Pat Shipman (Walker and Shipman, 1996).

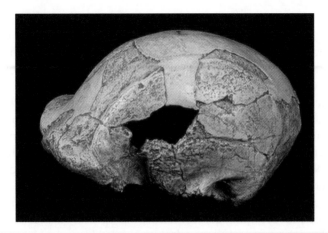

Figure 8.12 Cast of the partial braincase of *Homo erectus* from Olduvai Gorge (OH9).

matched neither modern humans nor chimps. His canine teeth were erupting later than in apes, but his molar teeth earlier than in modern humans. Thus, the Nariokotome boy appears on an evolutionary trajectory away from the ape pattern and towards that of modern humans.

After careful analysis of all the anatomical features, the age has been put at 9 years minimum. The skeleton suggests a height in life of 162 cm (5 ft 4 in) with a projected height at maturity of between 178 cm (5 ft 10 in) and 193 cm (6 ft 4 in). The volume of the cranium is 880 cm³, but of course when the boy reached adulthood his brain would have been slightly larger, around 910 cm³.

♦ Using your knowledge from earlier chapters how does this cranium volume compare with australopiths and modern humans?

♦ The equivalent figures would be about 1350 cm³ for a modern human and 600 cm³ for the largest known australopith volume, 'Mrs Ples' – see Section 7.5 (Figure 7.4).

With such a complete skeleton it has been possible to attempt to answer questions about both lifestyle and physiology. For example, could the Nariokotome boy speak? As the skull is largely complete it has been possible to obtain an endocast.

♦ What feature of the brain associated with speech would you expect an endocast to reveal?

♦ Broca's area (See the Introduction).

The presence of Broca's area does not in itself mean that the owner was capable of speech. Rather, the absence of Broca's area implies that the owner was incapable of speech. This is because Broca's area has other functions, as revealed by PET scans of humans performing motor tasks, and so, as it is not exclusively used for speech, its presence cannot be used as an infallible indicator of the presence of speech.

An analysis of the vertebrae of the skeleton revealed that the spinal cord, which passes through a canal in each vertebra, was narrower than in modern humans in the thoracic region, but not in the lumbar region. The canal in modern humans (and Neandertals) is wide in the neck region and for most of the spine, narrowing in the sacral region. If we had a tail, we would expect the canal in the sacral region to be wider to accommodate the nerves for the tail musculature. The narrowness of the spinal cord in the neck region of the Nariokotome boy is in line with that of other hominins and apes and is not narrow merely because the boy was not fully grown. In modern humans the thoracic spinal cord canal reaches the adult dimensions at about 10 years old. The canal of the Nariokotome boy is only 60% of that expected for a modern human and that is smaller than it would be in a modern human aged two years, so the small size of the canal cannot be attributed to immaturity. The thoracic canal carries nerve fibres involved in the fine breathing control needed for speech, suggesting that there were fewer nerve fibres present and as a result the boy would have had less fine control over the muscles, particularly those of the thoracic muscles and the vocal apparatus, which together enable speech.

The nasal bones of the face of the Nariokotome boy project (Figure 8.11) from the face and this suggests that the nasal passages containing the membranes that allow heat exchange were lengthened by comparison with earlier hominins. There is a possibility here that both heat and fluid exchange would have been more efficient, as a consequence of the increased length of the nasal passages. Interestingly, the nasal bones of KNM-ER 3733 also project (Figure 8.13) and you will encounter expanded nasal region in *Homo neanderthalesis* in Chapter 11.

Dated at 1.56–1.51 mya, this specimen is of a similar age to finds from Java and also fossils found in Georgia, which we will come to shortly. The skull has eyebrow ridges that are prominent but the face projects rather less than in *H. habilis*, while the nose is larger. The eyebrow ridges of Asian *H. erectus* and KNM-ER 3733 are more prominent than those of the Nariokotome boy.

By the time of the Nariokotome boy, hominins had already migrated out of Africa and into Asia. In 1991 a fossil hominin jaw was found during excavations at a medieval site at Dmanisi in Georgia. It was dated at 1.96–1.77 mya and was initially assigned to *Homo erectus*. Subsequently four skulls were excavated, further lower jaws and some post-cranial remains. Associated with the hominin remains are bones of vertebrates such as rhinoceros and giraffe.

The finds of such early hominins in that part of Asia was most unexpected. One of the skulls is almost complete, including a lower jaw. For all four it has been possible to measure the cranial capacity (Table 8.1).

♦ From your earlier reading, what species of hominin most closely matches these cranial capacities?

♦ These are close to the average for *Homo habilis* (610 ml), although the range of *H. habilis* is large: about 500–800 ml. The maximum size for an australopith is 600 ml ('Mrs Ples').

Table 8.1 The cranial capacities of the Dmanisi specimens.

Specimen number	Cranial capacity (ml)	Paired with separate jaw
D2700	600	D2735 lower jaw
D2280	750	
D2282	650	
D3444	625	D3900 lower jaw

So what species are the Dmanisi individuals? Although the first jaw found was assigned to *H. erectus*, there are problems with such an identification. The cranial capacity of African *H. ergaster* is larger: for WT-15000 it is 880 ml and KNM-ER 3773 it is 850 ml. *H. erectus* from Asia has a larger capacity still, with an estimated 940 for the type specimen and over 11 for other specimens. This makes the Dmanisi specimens very small-brained by comparison. Gabunia *et al.* (2002) in reporting the discovery of further fossils from Dmanisi proposed that all the fossils from the site belonged to a new species, *Homo georgicus*. Later, in 2006, it was proposed that all the specimens, with the exception of one jaw bone, be assigned to *H. erectus* (Rightmire, Lordkipanidze and Vekua, 2006). A detailed comparison of the features present in the Dmanisi hominins shows that they share a lot of features with the skull of *H. ergaster*, although the brain size makes them close to *H. habilis*. Opinions are divided as to the precise status of these first hominins found outside Africa, but it is possible that *H. georgicus* will eventually be merged into *H. ergaster*.

The tools found at the Dmanisi site are similar to the Oldowan tools that first appeared in Africa 2.5 mya. Oldowan technology is associated with *Homo habilis* and *H. rudolfensis*. Accumulations of fossil animal bones and Oldowan stone tools associated with early *Homo* have been found at Olduvai Gorge. Some of these tools appear to lie on a 'living floor', dated at 1.8 mya. Cut marks on bones are interpreted as evidence that hominins processed bones at the sites. Some carnivore tooth marks are overlapped by cut marks, indicating that hominins scavenged from carnivore kills. Other tooth marks overlap cut marks indicating that hominines used the bones first. The stone tools used were made by percussion knapping.

The Dmanisi tools have been made out of locally obtained basalt cobbles. The more advanced Acheulean technology appeared in Africa 1.5 mya and is also found in Europe and the Middle East, but it does not appear associated with *H. erectus* and *H. ergaster* in Asia. This strongly suggests that the first migration out of Africa started (and presumably finished) before the more advanced Acheulean technology had been developed. The key difference that lies behind the two technologies is the cognitive process needed to produce the tools. Oldowan tools are made from small cobbles which are struck by a hammer stone. The flakes struck off the cobble are the sharp tools that were used to butcher animal carcasses for food or cut up plants for food. There is skill required to hit the cobble in the right way but there is also skill required in choosing the cobble and the hammer stone in the first place. Furthermore, the hominins who used this technology carried suitable cobbles for some distance and did not just rely on picking up a suitable cobble when they needed to make a flake tool. About 1.5 mya hand axes first appeared amongst the stone tools. The axes are shaped and are obviously made from cobbles or selected from flakes according to a general mental pattern for an axe. These new Acheulean tools are found alongside the flake tools.

Once developed, the Acheulean technology spread quite fast. In Israel, a large number of Acheulean tools have been found at the Ubeidiya site that date from 1.4 mya. By 1 mya

---

Box 8.5   Early *Homo* in Georgia

Dmanisi was a flourishing medieval town in Georgia that was subsequently abandoned. During archaeological excavations of the old town, which started in 1936, bronze age layers were uncovered and they contained animal remains, including the tooth of an early Pleistocene rhinoceros. In 1984 stone tools were excavated and then, in 1991, a hominin mandible (D211) with a full set of teeth. Subsequently, other hominin skull bones were found. The significance of the finds was that when dated, they were half a million years older than any other hominins found outside Africa. In 2007, the finding of postcranial material added to the picture of these early representatives of the migrants from Africa and showed that they possessed a mixture of primitive and derived features. For example, the primitive small body and cranial capacity contrast with the derived modern human body proportions and lower limb adaptations to prolonged travel (Lordkipanidze *et al.*, 2007). The stature and body mass of the Dmanisi individuals would have been smaller than that of the Nariokotome boy.

---

hand axes were being made in France, and later at St Acheul from where the technology gets its name. You will meet the Acheulean technology again in Section 10.2.2.

8.12 Did *Homo erectus* return to Africa?

There are a number of hominin fossils found outside Asia that appear to belong to *Homo erectus*. The more recent (<1 mya) fossils are discussed in the next chapter, but a fossil from Olduvai Gorge dated to 1.5 mya is morphologically similar to the Asian *H. erectus* and may represent a group of *H. erectus* that migrated into Africa from Asia. This fossil, OH9, was discovered in 1960 by Louis Leakey. The brain size is estimated at 1065 ml (compare with the Nariokotome boy of roughly the same age and a cranial capacity of 880 ml).

Looking at the group of fossils that comprise *Homo erectus* and *Homo ergaster*, there is a lot of variability and it is difficult to be sure how many species are truly present in this large and geographically wide-ranging assemblage. It is arguable that the degree of variation is comparable with the variation seen in the whole of the *H. sapiens* species. If we accept this argument, then it is possible to view all the specimens of *H. erectus*, *H. ergaster* and *H georgicus* as one species, *H. erectus*. In this account we have separated *H. ergaster* and *H. erectus*, as this is quite a widely used distinction, but with the reservation that the taxonomy of the whole *erectus/eragster* group awaits clarification.

8.13 Conclusion

During the period 3–1 mya the climate got cooler and conditions in Africa became more arid, with savannah and grassland replacing much of the forest area in which hominins lived. At some time around 2 mya the first members of the genus *Homo* appeared in Africa and with this genus came the first large-scale migration which took *Homo ergaster* out of Africa and into Asia. The dates, details and routes of this migration are far from clear yet, but Figure 8.14 illustrates the current view. In addition to the migration out of Africa, there appears to have been migration into Africa too, although the evidence is fairly slender. However, it is unlikely that a migrating species would always travel in one direction only, so it is not impossible to imagine migration back into Africa.

The events of the transition from the *Australopithecus/Paranthropus* genera to *Homo* are not at all clear. Not enough is known about *H. habilis*. It appears to be the ancestor of *H. erectus*, but there is a period of half a million years or so when both species co-existed in East Africa (Spoor *et al.*, 2007). To coexist over this long period the species must have occupied different niches, perhaps with dietary or social differences, arguing against a linear progression from one species to another, at least in that geographical location.

The distinction between species of *Homo* at this time is a great area of uncertainty. Lumping all the species of *Homo* from this period, apart from *H. habilis*, into *H. erectus* and treating them all as one species that spread out across the continents is certainly a taxonomic possibility. Whether you stick with the separate species or lump them together really depends upon how you view the degree of variability shown by the *ergaster/erectus/georgicus* group. It can be described as the natural variability within one species or sufficient variability to warrant division into several species. As you will see later in Section 10.4, lumping of *Homo* species can been taken even further (see, for example, Curnoe and Thorne, 2003) as part of the multiregional hypothesis and all *Homo* specimens could be regarded as just showing variability within the single species *H. sapiens*.

Questions and activities

Question 8.1

Classify the following statements as true or false, giving reasons:

  a   Natural selection may result in evolution of similar dentition in species eating similar diets; therefore teeth and jaws are susceptible to homoplasy.

b   *Australopithecus afarensis*, the earliest hominine, is the ancestor of *Homo*.

c   *Australopithecus afarensis* is the founding species of the hominin clade.

Question 8.2

It has been argued that the capacity for language first appeared with the australopiths. What evidence would you look for to convince you of the validity or otherwise of such a claim?

References

Asfaw ,B.,White, T., Lovejoy, O., Latimer, B., Simpson, S., and Suwa, G. (1999) *Australopithecus garhi*: A new species of early hominid from Ethiopia. *Science*, **284**, 629–635.

Backwell, L.R. and d'Errico, F. (2001) Evidence of termite foraging by Swartkrans early hominids. *Proceedings of the National Academy of Sciences of the United States of America*, **98**, 1358–9200.

Blumenschine, R.J., Peters, C.R., Masao, F.T., Clarke, R.J., Deino, A.L., Hay, R.L., Swisher, C.C., Stanistreet, I.G., Ashley, G.M., McHenry, L.J. *et al.* (2003) Late Pliocene *Homo* and Hominid land use from Western Olduvai Gorge, Tanzania. *Science*, **299**, 1217–1222.

Broom, R. (1938) The Pleistocene anthropoid apes of South Africa. *Nature*, **142**, 377–379.

Cameron, D.W. and Groves, C.P. (2004) *Bones, Stones and Molecules*, Elsevier Academic Press, Burlington, MA.

Cela-Conde, C.J. and Ayala, F.J. (2003) Genera of the human lineage. *Proceedings of the National Academy of Sciences of the United States of America*, **100**, 7684–7689.

Curnoe, D. and Thorne, A. (2003) Number of ancestral human species: A molecular perspective. *HOMO – Journal of Comparative Human Biology*, **53**, 201–224.

Grine, F.E., Jungers, W.L., and Schultz, J. (1996) Phenetic affinities among early *Homo* crania from East and South Africa. *Journal of Human Evolution*, **30**, 189–225.

Huffman, O.F., Shipman, P., Hertler, C., de Vos, J., and Aziz, F. (2005) Historical evidence of the 1936 Mojokerto skull discovery, East Java. *Journal of Human Evolution*, **48**, 321–363.

Huffman, O.F., Zaim, Y., Kappelman, J., Ruez, J.D.R., de Vos, J., Rizal, Y., Aziz, F., and Hertler, C. (2006) Relocation of the 1936 Mojokerto skull discovery site near Perning, East Java. *Journal of Human Evolution*, **50**, 431–451.

Keyser, A.W. (2000) The Drimolen skull: the most complete australopithecine cranium and mandible to date. *South African Journal of Science*, **96**, 189–193.

Lordkipanidze, D., Jashashvili, T., Vekua, A., de Lean, M.S.P., Zollikofer, C.P.E., Rightmire, G.P., Pontzer, H., Ferring, R., Oms, O., Tappen, M. *et al.* (2007) Postcranial evidence from early *Homo* from Dmanisi, Georgia. *Nature*, **449**, 305–310.

Rightmire, G.P., Lordkipanidze, D., and Vekua, A. (2006) Anatomical descriptions, comparative studies and evolutionary significance of the hominin skulls from Dmanisi, Republic of Georgia. *Journal of Human Evolution*, **50**, 115–141.

Schoeninger, M.J., Reeser, H., and Hallin, K. (2003) Paleoenvironment of *Australopithecus anamensis* at Allia Bay, East Turkana, Kenya: evidence from mammalian herbivore enamel stable isotopes. *Journal of Anthropological Archaeology*, **22**, 200–207.

Semaw, S. (2000) The World's Oldest Stone Artefacts from Gona, Ethiopia: their implications for understanding stone technology and patterns of human evolution between 2.6–1.5 million years ago. *Journal of Archaeological Science*, **27**, 1197–1214.

Sponheimer, M. and Lee-Thorp, J.A. (1999) Isotopic evidence for the diet of an early hominid, *Australopithecus africanus*. *Science*, **283**, 368–370.

Sponheimer, M., Lee-Thorp, J., de Ruiter, D., Codron, D., Codron, J., Baugh, A.T., and Thackeray, F. (2005) Hominins, sedges, and termites: New carbon isotope data from the Sterkfontein valley and Kruger National Park. *Journal of Human Evolution*, **48**, 301–312.

Spoor, F., Leakey, M.G., Gathogo, P.N., Brown, F.H., Anton, S.C., McDougall, I., Kiarie, C., Manthi, F.K., and Leakey, L.N. (2007) Implications of new early *Homo* fossils from Ileret, east of Lake Turkana, Kenya. *Nature*, **448**, 688–691.

Stringer, C. and McKie, R. (1996) *African Exodus: The Origins of Modern Humanity*, Jonathan Cape.

Swisher, C.C., Curtis, G.H., Jacob, T., Getty, A.G., Suprijo, A., Widiasmoro. (1994) Age of the Earliest Known Hominids in Java, Indonesia. *Science* 263(5150):1118–1121.

Tattersall, I. and Schwartz, J.H. (2000) *Extinct Humans*, Westview Press, Boulder Colarado.

Ungar, P.S., Grine, F.E., and Teaford, M.F. (2008) Dental microwear and diet of the Plio-Pleistocene hominin *Paranthropus boisei*. *PLoS ONE* 3(4): e2044. doi:10.1371/journal.pone.0002044.

Walker, A. and Shipman, P. (1996) *The Wisdom of Bones*, Weidenfeld and Nicholson, London.

White, T.D. (2002) Earliest hominids, in *The Primate Fossil Record*, (ed. W.G.Hartwig), Cambridge University Press, Cambridge, UK, pp.407–417.

White, T.D. (2003) Early hominids – diversity or distortion. *Science*, **299**, 1994–1997.

9

1.0 mya – 700 000 Years Ago

The period 1.0 mya–700 kya is complex, and includes at least one speciation event which occurred in southern Europe. The new species discovered in Atapuerca in Spain is dated at 780 000 years old and named as *Homo antecessor*. Fossils of *Homo* species dated during this time period include finds identified as *Homo erectus* in East Asia, Africa and Europe, so *Homo erectus* had spread to, and persisted, in at least three continents.

9.1 Introduction

One million years ago the world was passing through a warm peak of the cycle of glacial and interglacial periods known as the Great Ice Age. This age started at about 1.8 mya and continues to the present, so it is also current. The Great Ice Age spans the Pleistocene, which is the epoch during which our ancestors, and our own species, undertook substantial journeys which spread the hominin group out across Asia and Europe. In Africa one million years ago the last members of the *Paranthropus* genus had probably died, leaving Africa populated by possibly just one species of hominin, *Homo ergaster/erectus*. In Asia *Homo erectus* was well established in Java and expanding further eastwards. The species was also present in China. *H. erectus* fossils have also been found at more than one site in Africa dated to around 1 Ma and more recently. It is possible that these fossils represent migrations into Africa from Europe or Asia. Western Europe was probably largely untouched by hominins, but *Homo antecessor*, whose early history is unknown at present, may have just started to enter Europe one million years ago. So the once bushy hominin tree had become pared down to two or three species, but subsequent speciation would produce a new set of branches to the tree.

The Emergence of Humans Patricia Ash and David Robinson
© 2010 John Wiley & Sons, Ltd

For anthropologists it is also a period where the interpretation of the events that occurred is deeply controversial. Every new find of fossils adds to our knowledge, of course, but the specimen that will settle the controversy about hominin evolution during this period has yet to be found and, almost certainly, one single specimen or locality won't be sufficient.

The importance of accurate dating was stressed earlier in the discussion of australopiths and in this chapter you will discover how refining the dates of particular specimens has radically changed views of the sequence of evolutionary events. As dating gets more reliable, the picture should become clearer, but some revised dates have thrown up apparent inconsistencies which have yet to be explained.

As the ice advanced and retreated cyclically, hominins moved with it. So, much of the evolutionary history of hominins during the last million years, particularly in Europe, must be seen against the backdrop of the ice sheets advancing and retreating. It is not just because the temperature changes affected the physiology of the hominins themselves, but because the distribution of animals they hunted and the plants that some of those animals fed on, was also influenced by the ice. During glacial periods, as the cold became more severe, the Earth's climate also became drier and areas unaffected by ice became more arid. Forests gave way to grassland and some grassland became semi-arid desert. These changes were a consequence of rainfall being less. In cold conditions, the water cycle of evaporation from the surface and re-precipitation is reduced. The resulting habitat changes would have provided significant selection pressures on hominin species and may have triggered the dispersals of hominins that are such a feature of this period of human evolution.

9.1.1 The Pleistocene

The Pleistocene had begun by about 1.8 mya, and research studies demonstrate that the epoch is split into cycles, each of which comprises a glacial and an interglacial part. Figure 9.1 shows ages and lengths for each cycle. The cycles were identified originally by Cesar Emiliani (University of Chicago), who studied fossil **Foraminifera**, specifically, ***Globigerina***, a planktonic micro-organisms with a calcium carbonate skeletons, found in deep-sea sediments. Millions of these unicellular organisms live in the upper layers of sea water forming periodic blooms, a process that has been continuing. The life cycle of *Globigerina* is short and when the vast numbers of these micro-organisms in a bloom die, they sink to the bottom of the sea. Over millions of years, sediments made up mainly of calcium carbonate build up, forming a sedimentary rock such as chalk or limestone. Living *Globigerina* accumulate two isotopes of oxygen, ^{18}O and ^{16}O from sea water. Water containing the lighter isotope evaporates more readily than that containing the heavier one. Atmospheric water vapour from equatorial regions that moves towards the poles eventually falls as snow which is depleted in ^{18}O relative to the oceans. During glaciations, more land ice is formed and the water that freezes to form it contains a higher proportion of ^{16}O, leaving sea water that has relatively high levels of ^{18}O. When the temperature increases again, ^{16}O from the melting land ice is released and finds its way back into the seawater, which consequently becomes richer in ^{16}O.

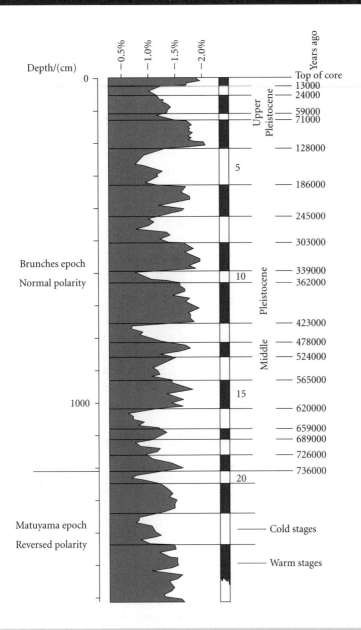

Figure 9.1 The Pleistocene climate, derived from measurements of heavy oxygen, ^{18}O in deep sea core V28–238 drilled from the bed of the Pacific Ocean. The shaded area shows how the amount of ^{18}O varies according to depth. At 1200 cm depth, these sediments record a change in magnetic polarity, dated by absolute techniques to around 730 000 years ago. Other dates indicated are based on their depths in the core.

Therefore during a warm period, foraminiferans accumulate relatively more ^{16}O; during glaciation the organisms accumulate relatively more ^{18}O.

Samples of deep sea sediments are obtained by boring into the sediment and extracting a column or core, which provides a layer by layer record. The deeper the layer the older it is. The levels of each oxygen isotope contained in foraminiferans from the various layers of sediment in the cores were measured by Emiliani. Layers corresponding to warm and cold periods were identified by calculating the ratios $^{18}O:{}^{16}O$; the ratios obtained were plotted against the age of each layer. The measurements can be calibrated against the value for the defined standard mean ocean water. Figure 9.1 is a summary of the findings, which includes information, from the use of absolute dating techniques (Section 1.3), that was not available to Emiliani at the time he carried out his research. The left side of Figure 9.1 shows the timing of major epochs of reversals in the earth's polarity; the timing of such reversals in volcanic rocks. Extrapolation from the known dates of the volcanic rocks enabled the ages of the marine sediment layers to be worked out. Note the boundary between two major magnetic reversals, **Matuyama** and **Brunhes**, which marks the end of the early and the beginning of the Middle Pleistocene.

During the late Pleistocene, climate fluctuated rapidly. Changes in climate match changes in the pollen record (Figures 9.2a and 2b), in that periods where tree pollen is scarce match glaciations – see for example 70–50kya.

From about 70 000 to 10 000 years ago mean surface temperature were 6–10°C lower than they are now – the full glacial lasted from 75 000–30 000 years ago. Most of the Pleistocene comprised periods of interglacial and early glacial climates, which in northern Europe meant open landscapes with rich herbaceous vegetation. There were also periods of glaciation when ice sheets covered much of Europe and North America. Figure 9.3 shows the glacial maxima for the middle and late Pleistocene glacial/interglacial cycles.

9.2 Persistence of *Homo erectus* in Africa and East Asia

We saw in Chapter 8 that it was *Homo ergaster* that became the first hominin to migrate out of Africa, the earliest dated specimens, 1.8 mya, being found at Koobi Fora, Kenya. At some point *Homo erectus* had probably arisen from *Homo ergaster*. The wanderlust of *Homo erectus* resulted in a wide distribution of the species, which reached many parts of Asia, including China and Java as well as North and South Africa. In this chapter we will see that *Homo erectus*, whose earliest date in Asia is the contested date of 1.8 mya for the Mojokerto site, persisted in Africa to at least 700 kya and probably survived much later in Asia. As we shall see in Chapter 11, some fossil evidence suggests that *Homo erectus* was still present in Java as recently as 30 000 years ago. In this chapter we examine evidence for the spread of *Homo erectus* in East Asia, and the possibility that the species returned to Africa from Asia. We will study fossil specimens from each of the main locations and where possible, draw conclusions about the way of life of *Homo erectus* from associated faunal remains and artefacts.

9.2.1 Late African *Homo erectus*

Intriguing evidence that *Homo erectus* either persisted in Africa or spread back into Africa from Asia was discovered by Asfaw and colleagues close to Bouri in Ethiopia.

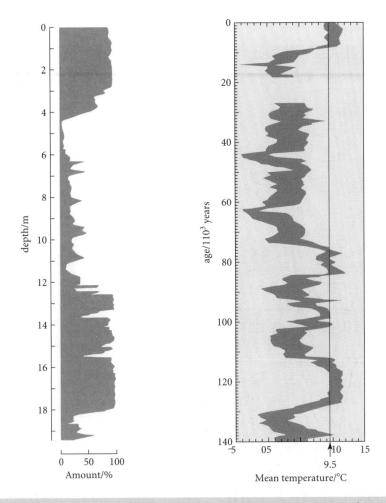

Figure 9.2 **(a)** A pollen diagram for Grande Pile, France, showing the percentage of tree pollen in successively deeper layers of pollen. **(b)** Long-term mean temperatures inferred from the Grande Pile pollen record. A gap in the core results from mixing of sediments during deposition which means that it is impossible to calculate temperature. Note the current mean long term temperature is 9.5°C. Reproduced from Discovering Science Book 2 P40 and 41. © The Open University.

The early Pleistocene Daka (Dakanihylo) **member** comprises 22–45 m of sediment above the Pliocene Hata (Hataye) member of the Bouri formation.

◆ Recall from Chapter 8 that important fossil hominin remains were found in sediments dated at 2.5 mya in the Hata member close to Bouri by Asfaw and his colleagues. What were these remains?

◆ Fossils of *Australopithecus garhi* were found there, with fossil animal bones that had been cut and smashed by stones.

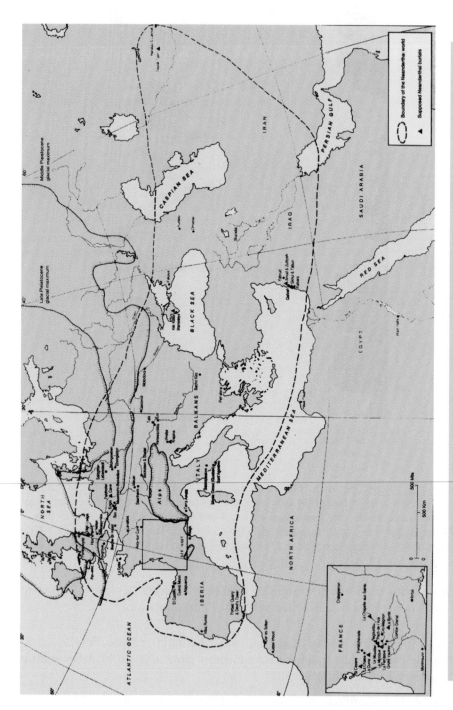

Figure 9.3 Glacial maxima for the Middle and late Pleistocene glacial/interglacial cycles. The boundary of the Neanderthal 'world' is shown and also key sites where fossils and/or artefacts were found. Reproduced from Lewin, 1999 P161.

As with the Hata member, the later Daka deposits link to ancient lakeside beaches on shallow slow-flowing water channels.

◆ Why do such areas provide fossil and archaeological remains of extinct *Homo*?

◆ Extinct *Homo* needed water supplies, so must have spent time around accessible bodies of water. Prey animals such as large herbivores require water too, and are vulnerable whilst drinking, thereby providing hunting opportunities for hominins. It is likely that meat would have been consumed fairly close to where it was captured, so it is possible that *Homo* spent much time around freshwater. Slow-flowing water promotes settling of sediments and consequent laying down of sedimentary deposits, conditions which favour processes of fossilization.

A huge number of fossils of vertebrates were discovered in the Daka member, close to Bouri. Bovids were particularly abundant (377 out of 713 specimens), and include three *Kobus* species (waterbuck), *Connochaetes* (wildebeest), *Pelorovis antiquus* (giant buffalo), *Megalotragus kattwinkeli* (giant hartebeest) and *Gazella* sp (gazelle). Giraffes, elephants, rhinoceros hippopotamus and pigs were also common. Primate fossils include *Colobus spp*, unidentifiable cercopithecine species, and *Theropithecus oswaldi* (baboon). So for the meat-eating *Homo erectus*, the area provided abundant food resources. However carnivores were also present such as *Panthera leo*, lion and *Pachycrocuta breviristris* (hyaena).

The fossil skull cap, BOU-VP-2/66, a **calvaria**, was found in silty sand by W H Gilbert[3] in December 1997. The skull was positioned base down and encrusted by fossilized root casts. The bones show signs of post-mortem scraping; the frontal and **parietal bones** bear striations consistent with defleshing activities by the gnawing of animals. Stone tool assemblages found in the Daka member are early Acheulean (Mode 2) and include handaxes and cleavers.

The endocranial volume was measured at $995\,cm^3$ by filling the calvaria with **teff** seed. The eyebrow ridges are large (Figure 9.4) and arched, and depressed between the nose. There is a weak **sagittal keel** on the **frontal squama** and **parietal bones**. The **mastoid processes** (part of the temporal bones) are small. The **occipital torus *is not*** delineated superiorly by a **supratoral sulcus**. Three femora and a tibia were also found in the Daka deposits, quite far away from the calvaria. The femora show the marked **platymeria** (a flattening in cross-section rather than a round cross section) and the extremely thick midshaft cortex typical of *Homo erectus*.

Measurements made on the Daka calvaria overlap with those of both Asian *H.erectus* and African *H.ergaster*. The researchers carried out a cladistic analysis (see Chapter 5) of calvarial anatomy in African and Asian *erectus* fossil anatomical features and concluded that that there is no deep separation of the two groups into distinct clades. OH9, an Africa *erectus* fossil, bearing features similar to those of the Asian fossils (see Chapter 8) was considered to be an evolutionary intermediate between *ergaster* and *erectus*. The Daka fossil has the same derived characters as the Asian fossils (Figure 9.4).

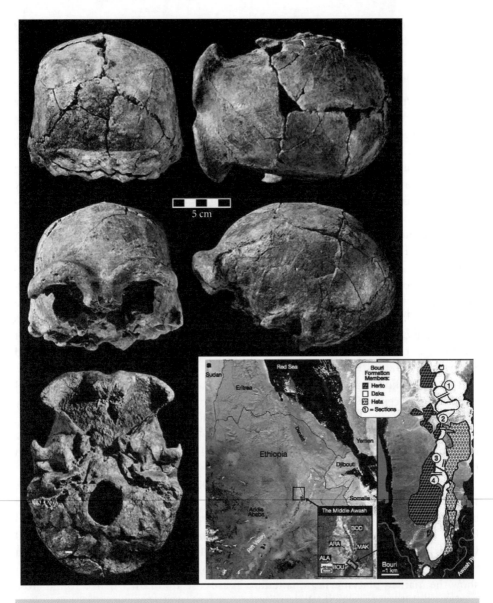

Figure 9.4 Views of the Daka calvaria. a) Views of the Daka calvaria. Note the prominent eyebrow ridges, shallow sloped forehead and elongated brain case. (b) Landsat and aerial photography of Middle Awash study earea. The 1.0 mya Daka member is shown in white. Reprinted by permission from Macmillan Publishers Ltd: Nature (Asfaw, et al. (2002).

The authors suggest that the Daka calvaria is consistent with the view that *Homo erectus* was a moderately polymorphic and widespread species (like modern *Homo sapiens*). Their view that *erectus* was not a solely Asian clade is supported by the find of another cranium UA 31, two pelvic fragments (UA 31) and 2 lower incisors (UA 222 and UA 369), in the Daka member near the village of Buia in Eritrea (Abbate, 1998). The same layers in which the *Homo* fossils were found includes many animal fossils, similar species to those found by Asfaw and colleagues at Bouri. Species include *Elephas recki*, (elephant), *Ceratotherium simum* (rhinoceros), *Hipparion sp* and *Equus sp* (unidentified horses), unidentified rhinoceros, *Pelorovis sp* (buffalo), *Hippopotamus gogops* (hippo potamus) *Hexaprotodon karumensis* (pygmy hippopotamus). Carnivores include hyaena and crocodile.

One million years ago, *Homo erectus* appears to have been living the life of a hunter and scavenger in Africa. Around Bouri there was fresh water, and large game species were diverse and abundant. *Homo erectus* may have hunted these animals, which would have required co-ordinated and planned group work. It is possible that *Homo erectus* was also an opportunistic scavenger of carcasses resulting from carnivore kills. Acheulean stone tools, in particular hand-axes, were in use for butchering carcasses. We will examine the manufacture of Acheulean hand-axes and their use for butchery and hide cutting later, in Chapter 10.

9.2.2 Chinese Homo erectus

A **karst** cave (Figure 9.5), on Dragon Bone Hill (Longgu-Shan) in the town of Zhoukoudian, China, yielded the most abundant group of *Homo erectus* fossils to be found. Excavation of the 30m depth of sediment layers deposited in the cave began in 1921. Fossil remains of 45 individuals, men, women and children, have been found, as well as stone tools, debris from stone tool manufacture, and animal bones. The hominin remains were named originally in 1927, as *Sinanthropus pekinensis* (Chinese man of Peking) by the anatomist Davidson Black of Peiping Union Medical College. In 1944 the species was identified as *Homo erectus*. The *Homo erectus* fossils were found in the lower cave designated as 'Locality 1' and divided into 17 stratigraphic layers. Layers 1–13 contained combinations of hominin fossils, artefacts, animal bones and black ash. As Layers 1–13 are within the Brunhes **Chron**, and the Brunhes/Matuyama boundary occurs between Level 13 and 14, 780 000 years is regarded as a limiting age for the fossils. ESR carried out by Rainer Grun and his colleagues[13], on fossil teeth suggest an age of 300–550 000 years for *Homo erectus* remains from Layers 3,6/7 and 10 in the cave. More recently, Shen et al. (2008) re-dated the Zhoukoudian *Homo erectus* fossils using a relatively new technique, ^{26}Al/Be^{10} burial dating, applied to stratigraphic layers 7–10 in the cave. The re–dating provided a date of 770 kya (range 850–690 kya) for Zhoukoudian *Homo erectus*.

The hominin fossils comprised a large collection of fragmented skulls and post cranial bones. Most of the collection, including five calvariae, cranial and facial fragments, mandibles and 147 isolated teeth, disappeared in the chaos of World War II (Box 9.1). Fortunately casts and photographs of the fossils had been prepared before they disappeared, and much research has been carried out on the casts. Franz Weidenreich prepared a reconstructed skull using replica pieces of fossil skull from Zhoukoudian (Figure 9.6). A more recent re-construction by Tattersall and Sawyer[(1996)] was built using pieces of skull considered to derive from a male only and may be more realistic. Features of this skull are those of 'classic *Homo erectus*', and include prominent arched eyebrow ridges, and a marked occipital torus. The parietal bones are flat and

Figure 9.5   The Zhoukoudian cave site.

Box 9.1   'Peking man'

Between 1921 and 1923 a cave site at Zhoukoudian near Beijing was excavated by a Swedish palaeontologist – Gunnar Andersson. During laboratory work on the fossils he found two human teeth – the first human fossils to be discovered in China. Further excavations were undertaken during the 1920's, yielding two lower jaws and numerous skull and teeth fragments, and in December 1929 the most important discovery was made. A young Chinese geologist, Wenzhong Pei discovered an almost complete skull cap in red sandy clay, partly embedded in **travertine**. Subsequently, four more skull caps were found during the 1930's, together with other human fossil remains, fossil animals and stone tools. Casts were made of the key finds before the Second World War, which was fortunate as the entire collection disappeared while being transported by US marines to a port for shipment away from the war zone. The loss of the specimens is perhaps the greatest tragedy in palaeontology. At the time of writing a Chinese government commission is trying to trace the fossils. Few believe that they will be successful.

Figure 9.6 A cast of the reconstruction of one of the Peking man fossil skulls, prepared from replicas of the original fossils.

thick; the frontal bone is receding, so there is no real forehead. Overall the facial bones are massive, as are the mandibles. The lower part of the face shows **prognathism**. In general, the Chinese fossils are more robust than African specimens such as OH 7. The five calvaria found at Zhoukoudian have a mean cranial capacity of 1043 cm³, a value at the top end of the range of brain size for *Homo erectus*.

The assemblages of tools and animal bones and *Homo* fossils were interpreted as suggesting that the cave was a home base for the hominins. The French palaeoanthropologists, Pierre Teilhard de Chardin (1937), and Henri Breuil (1938) suggested that the ancient extensive ash deposits in the cave were the remains of ancient hearths. Breuil interpreted damage to skulls and post-cranial skeleton as attributable to cannibalism. In the 1930s, Franz Weidenreich, the German anatomist, claimed that marks on the skulls were the result of blows with clubs and sharp stone tools aimed at extraction of the brain for food. Large splits in long bones were interpreted as attempts by the hominins to gain access to the marrow. So Weidenreich agreed with de Chardin's and Breuil's view, and for a long time, *Homo erectus* was regarded as a violent cannibalistic species.

Current opinion is that *Homo erectus* was not cannibalistic, and that giant hyaenas were responsible for breaking up the hominin bones at Zhoukoudian. A reassessment by Chinese palaeoanthropologists Liu Jinyi and Xu Qinqi and colleagues was based on the premise that the most common fossil bones at a site are those of the species that occupied the site for the most time (Boaz et al. 2000). In this context it is interesting that *Homo erectus* bones make up only 0.5% of the total bones. The bones of the giant hyaena, *Pachycrocuta brevirostris*, are the most abundant. It is possible that at least some of the *erectus* fossils belonged to victims of the hyaena, because about two thirds of the *erectus* bones bear puncture marks from large carnivore teeth, as well as long U-shaped grooves suggesting gnawing. Splitting of long bones such as femur is also characteristic hyaena behaviour. The position of bite marks on the hominin calvariae suggest the hominins were gripped around the face, whereby the hyaena could crack the edges of the facial bones for opening up the skull for access to the lipid rich brain.

Thick layers of black ash, up to several metres thick, in the sediments have suggested to some palaeoanthropologists that *H. erectus* may have used fire inside the cave.

◆ Suggest the uses of fire for *Homo erectus*.

◆ Fire would frighten off predators; giant hyaena appeared to have been frequent visitors to the cave. Fires also provide warmth, and a source of light at night. It is possible that *Homo erectus* may have cooked meat.

Some fossil animal bones found within the ash layers were blackened, suggesting they had been heated. However there are no signs of hearths, and the layers of ash are so thick, that many massive fires inside the caves would have been needed to accumulate so much ash. Furthermore, evidence suggests that many of the ash deposits were laid down under water suggesting that they were washed into the cave after a natural fire outside. Therefore it seems unlikely that Zhoukoudian could have been a home base for *Homo erectus* given the lack of evidence for hearths and the abundant evidence for the presence of giant hyaena in the cave.

Other locations in China where fossils of *Homo erectus* were discovered include Gongwangling village, near Lantian. Here cranial fragments, a molar tooth and bones of other mammal species were found. The date of the fossils is uncertain with values of 750 kya–1.15 mya obtained by palaeomagnetic dating (An and Ho, 1989). Fossil incisors of *H. erectus* found at Yuanmou in China were dated at 700 kya by use of palaeomagnetic techniques (Hyodo et al. 2002).

Homo erectus persisted for a long time in China. The oldest fossils known are dated at 1.8 mya and the most recent specimens are dated at 150–190 kya, (Chapter 10). We learned in Section 8.11 that *H. erectus* also migrated to Java soon after the origin of the species and in the following section we shall examine the persistence of *H. erectus* in Java.

9.2.3 Javan *Homo erectus*

The first Asian hominin fossil was found in Java in 1891 and other important fossil finds were made in the area during the 1930's concurrently with the major Chinese finds. In this section we will examine just two of the Javan *Homo erectus* fossils with attributed dates falling within 1.0 mya–130 kya. It is important to appreciate that the dating of the Javan specimens is difficult. Many of the important fossil specimens were collected by local people who were paid a sum of money per fossil found by palaeoanthropologists, so controlled excavation of sites did not take place. As a result, it was not possible to determine the precise layer in which the fossils were located. However in recent years palaeoanthropologists have returned to a number of the most important sites and attempted to identify the correct layers in which fossils were located originally so that modern dating techniques could be applied.

Box 9.2 Eugene Dubois

Eugene Dubois, a Dutch physician, discovered the type specimen for *Homo erectus* in Java in 1891. Although Dubois had graduated in medicine in 1884, his major interest was human evolution. As a boy and a young man, Dubois had collected animal fossils, and even after graduation, and working as a lecturer in anatomy, he attended lectures on human evolution whenever possible. Dubois supported Darwin's view of evolution by natural selection, and like Darwin, he was convinced that ancient human fossils were most likely to be found in tropical regions. This view derived from the hypothesis that natural selection in hot climates would promote loss of body hair in apes. We should be aware that Dubois, view of human evolution was coloured, inevitably, by the scientific thought prevailing in the late nineteenth and early twentieth centuries. The view of human evolution was based not on interpretation of fossil evidence but on studies of the fetal development of humans and apes. The ancestor of humans was regarded as being ape-like and any fossils that resembled humans were regarded as *Homo sapiens*, albeit a member of a 'primitive' race. Hence Dubois was determined to find the 'missing link' between apes and humans.

Disliking his teaching job, Dubois decided to join the Dutch Colonial Army as a medical officer stationed in the East Indies. The rationale for this momentous decision was that while employed as a medical officer, he would have sufficient spare time available for fossil hunting. Dubois, his wife and baby left Amsterdam and travelled to Sumatra in December 1887. Dubois soon found many animal fossils when he dug through sediments in caves and consequently made an eloquent appeal to the Dutch government for help. His appeal was successful, and he was transferred to the Department of Education, Religion and Industry in order to work full-time on fossil hunting. Although Dubois had high hopes of finding fossils of ancient human ancestors in Sumatra, he was unsuccessful, even with the help of two army engineers and 50 local forced convict labourers.

In 1890 Dubois obtained a transfer to the Ngawi region of Java, where he searched for fossils, again with two army engineers and 50 forced labourers. Close to the village of Trinil, on the banks of the river Solo, the group excavated a huge pit more than 20 m deep, which yielded numerous fossils of animal remains. In 1891, Dubois discovered an upper jaw molar of what he thought was a fossil ape and, a month later, the calvaria (skull cap) that later became then

(continued)

type specimen of *Homo erectus*. Later, in 1892, Dubois discovered a human-like femur, prompting him to name the fossil remains as *Pithecanthropus erectus* (upright ape man), and to identify it as the 'missing link' between apes and humans, an ancestor of modern man. In 1895 Dubois and his family left Java and returned to the Netherlands for reasons of health. Dubois' interpretation of the fossils provoked controversy and criticism from the church and the scientific community.

Dubois defended his view vigorously but eventually withdrew from the argument. It is likely that he also wanted to prevent anyone else from publishing descriptions of his fossils. Dubois had been upset when another scientist, Gustav Schwalbe, who had studied Dubois' fossil finds, published a description of *Pithecanthropus*. It was important to Dubois that only his name should be associated with *Pithecanthropus*. At some time around 1900, Dubois put away his fossil discoveries until he had time to study them in detail and publish the results, which he did eventually in 1926. One of several stories has him storing the fossils in a wooden box under his house where they stayed for nearly 30 years, but this is likely to be one of the popular myths that still surround Dubois (Curtis, *et al.*, 2001).

Dubois interpreted the fossil calvaria he had found at Trinil as the missing link between apes and humans and defended his view with much vigour and a dash of vitriol. In 1935 he set out these views in an article in the proceedings of the Amsterdam Royal Academy, 'On the gibbon-like appearance of *Pithecanthropus erectus*'.

◆ Examine Figure 9.7 which is the interpretation by Eugene Dubois[11], of the *Pithecanthropus* fossils he discovered at Trinil. How does his sketch reflect his view of the fossils as being the remains of an upright ape man?

◆ The marked prognathism of the face is ape-like; modern interpretations of the skull suggest forwardly projecting jaws only. The canine teeth are relatively large too, as would be expected for an ape.

However other finds in Java, including the Mojokerto child and Sangiran 2, and also the finds in China, were pointing towards a different interpretation. In the 1930s, the German anatomist, Franz Weidenreich, suggested that the similarities between the Javan and Chinese fossil finds indicated that they should be classified within the same group. Dubois was very much against this idea as it would remove the special status of the Trinil calvaria as the 'missing link'.

In 1944 Ernst Mayr, one of the original creators of the modern synthesis of evolution (Chapter 3), proposed that the Chinese *Sinanthropus* and the Javan *Pithecanthropus* were in fact members of the same species, *Homo erectus*. Currently, the calvaria found by Dubois, is the type specimen for *Homo erectus*, denoted as Trinil 2, and dated at 1.0–0.7 mya (Curtis et al.,2001). The calvaria is long with a low, sloping,

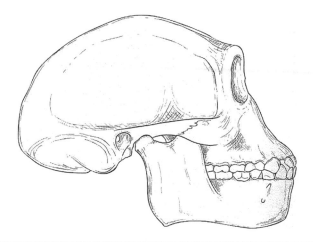

Figure 9.7 The initial interpretation by Eugene Dubois of the *Pithecanthropus* fossils that he discovered at Trinil. Reproduced from Lewin, 1999 P138.

flat forehead and a heavy brow ridge, There is a sagittal keel and also a characteristic protruberance at the back, the transverse or occipital torus. The widest part of the skull is close to the base and each side of the skull slopes inwardly towards the top.

Another Javan *Homo erectus* specimen that may fit into this section of our timeline is Sangiran 2. Sangiran 2 was discovered at Sangiran, Java in 1937 by GHR Von Koenigswald, helped by local people. The skull is small for *H. erectus*, with a cranial capacity of just 815 cm³. However features of Sangiran 2 are typical of *H. erectus* and include a marked transverse torus, and prominent eyebrow ridges (only the left one is intact in the fossil). Palaeoanthropologists interpret the small size and the *H. erectus* features as indicating that Sangiran 2 is an immature individual. Von Koenigswald estimated the age of the skull as 700 000 years and although dates as old as 1.6 mya have been suggested (Curtis, et al., 2001) currently an age range of 1.6–0.7 mya is the closest we can get. More work on the dating of Sangiran and Trinil *H. erectus* fossils would be needed for more precise date ranges.

Tattersall and Schwartz (2000) highlight the complex picture of human evolution in Java and suggest that the placing of all or most of the fossil specimens as *Homo erectus* may prove to be an over simplification.

9.2.4 Stone tool technology of *Homo erectus*

◆ What type of tool technology would you expect to find associated with the Javan *Homo erectus* fossils?

◆ The dates attributed to the Trinil and Sangiran *Homo erectus*, 1.6–0.7 mya, suggest that we might expect to find Acheulean technology associated with the fossil remains.

In fact, no Acheulean tools have been found in Java even though *Homo erectus* in Africa was using such tools by 1.5 mya. The few tools found so far in Java resemble the Mode 1 tools - the chopper-core type similar to those found in Olduvai Gorge. Oldowan technology persisted in Asia for a long time. Hallam Movius, an archaeologist based at Harvard, was the first person to draw attention to the lack of Acheulean tool technology in Asia and drew a line, the so-called Movius line on the world map showing the boundary between regions with and without Acheulean technology. The Movius Line, boundary ran along the border of northern India, and north straddling the eastern border of western Europe to indicate the stone tool technology difference between East and West. Acheulean technology had emerged by 1.5 mya in Africa and spread to Europe by about 600 kya but Oldowan chopping tool technology apparently persisted in Asia.

A number of explanations for the lack of Acheulean technology have been proposed. It was suggested by Geoffrey Pope that bamboo may have been used to make cutting tools, instead of stone. This hypothesis is difficult to test as bamboo does not fossilise. Nevertheless it is possible to make sharp knives out of bamboo. Garniss Curtis and Carl Swisher proposed another explanation and their reasoning can be followed by working through the following sequence of questions.

◆ What are the dates attributed to the oldest known *Homo ergaster* fossils in Africa and Asia? You will need to refer back to Chapter 6 to answer this.

◆ The oldest known African *Homo ergaster*, KNM-ER 3733, was found at Koobi Fora, Kenya, and is dated at 1.8 mya. The oldest known Asian H. *erectus* is the Modjokerto child re-dated at 1.81 mya by Garniss Curtis and Carl Swisher.

◆ What type of stone tool technology is associated with African *Homo ergaster* 1.9–1.5mya?

◆ Early H. *ergaster* used Oldowan stone tool technology.

Therefore, *Homo erectus* arrived in Asia soon after the origin of the species.

◆ What type of stone tool technology would the emigrating African *Homo ergaster* have taken with them to Asia?

◆ African *Homo ergaster* migrating to Asia 1.8 mya would have taken Oldowan tool technology.

Hence Curtis and Swisher propose that the reason that Acheulean tool technology has not been found in Asia is because it had not been invented when *Homo erectus* arrived in Asia.

However recent finds have provided a twist to the neat story proposed by Movius. Yamei and his colleagues (2000) reported their discovery of Acheulean style tools during excavations of mid-Pleistocene sediments in the Bose basin, South China. The tools were found in sediments deposited as one of seven river terraces, terrace 4. The stone tools were manufactured from cobbles of **quartz, quartzite** sandstone and **chert**.

The cobbles appear to have been obtained from deeper layers of sediments. The technology shows clear differences from Oldowan (Mode 1) and has features of Acheulean (Mode 2) technology. There are bifacial handaxes, many large in size, and flakes >10 cm in size. The tools show signs of planned manipulation and shaping, including largeflake scar facets and high numbers of flake scars. Some specimens look fresh with sharp striking platforms. The handaxes have the typical ovate shape, with thin converging tip ends and thick unmodified butt ends. Of 991 artefacts that were collected; 58% of these were unifacial or bifacial large cutting tools. The researchers point out that that as 65% of the large cutting tools (handaxes) showed unifacial flaking, the artefacts are distinguishable from those made by soft hammer thinning. The sediments in which the tools were found are dated at 803 000 years ago and are the oldest known large cutting tools found in China.

So far there is no evidence to suggest that *Homo erectus* was in Europe although the population of *H. georgicus* in Georgia (Chapter 8) was on the border of Europe and Asia around 1.7 mya. In the following section we examine the oldest known hominin inhabitants of Europe, discovered at the Gran Dolina cave site.

9.3 *Homo antecessor* in Spain

While so far there is no unequivocal fossil evidence for the presence of *Homo erectus* in Europe, there are finds of fossils of other species of *Homo* in Europe of similar age. The most ancient of these, dated at around 780 000 years ago[2], were contemporary with *Homo erectus* in Asia and possibly Africa too (Arsuaga, et al., 1999). Excavations at the Gran Dolina site in the Sierra Atapuerca, Spain have proved to be of crucial importance (de Castro, et al., 1997) Sierra Atapuerca is a small limestone hill peaking at 1079 m, located 15 km south east of Burgos in Spain. The Sierra is a karstic complex, consisting of cave and tunnel systemsformed by dissolution of the limestone by percolating acidic rainwater. These caves were attractive sites for hominins for hundreds of thousands of years, providing shelter and areas where meat was butchered and consumed. The Gran Dolina site, was discovered in the late nineteenth century when a trench was dug for a railway line for transport of minerals from a mine. The railway also provided services for passengers but it was never economically viable and closed down in 1910. Although the Gran Dolina site was partly destroyed by the railway construction work, the remaining sediments have yielded rich finds. Gran Dolina was a limestone cave about 20 m in depth. Continued dissolution of limestone by percolating rainwater had opened up the cave to the exterior and provided easy access for the ancient hominins. Systematic archaeological excavation of the site began in 1981. Sedimentary infilling of Gran Dolina is 18 m thick, and 11 layers have been identified, numbered from TD1, the oldest, to TD 11, the most recent. Detailed study of a 6 m² survey pit began in 1993 and level TD6, was exposed in 1994. Four years of excavation of TD6 have yielded hominin fossils, stone tools and animals bones, all dated at >780 kya. **Palaeomagnetic dating** showed that TD6 has reversed polarity corresponding to the Matumaya reversal dated at >780 kya (Figure 9.3). Other dating techniques used were ESR and U-series (Chapter 2)carried out on teeth, which confirmed the date of 780 kya years.

9.3.1 The hominin finds

Excavation of the TD6 layer indicates several occupations by hominins; a layer denoted the Aurora stratum in the upper part of TD6 contains >80 fossil remains of 6 individual hominins. The type specimen, ATD6-69, comprises bones from a child aged around 10 years old, including the fragmentary reconstructed frontal bone, part of the left orbit, nasal bones and part of the maxilla.

◆ What is the significance of designating bones from a child as the type specimen?

◆ When making comparisons with type specimens of other species, any differences would have to be viewed in the light of the relative immaturity of the individual from whom one of the type specimens came.

The features of the type specimen, and of the other adult specimens, were considered to justify the designation of a new species, *Homo antecessor*, distinct from *Homo erectus*. Salient features include a marked double arched eyebrow ridge, similar to that seen in *Homo erectus*. There is moderate taurodontism of the teeth, which have a low root apex and an expanded pulp cavity, similarities to *Homo erectus* and *Homo heidelbergensis*. Post-canine dentition is reduced, in that molar 3 is reduced in comparison to molar 1, a feature also characteristic of *Homo heidelbergensis*. The shovel-like maxillary incisors of the Gran Dolina hominins are thought to be a primitive feature. The second incisors (I2) are large, a similarity to *Homo heidelbergensis*. In contrast to *Homo erectus*, ATD6-69 has a human-like mid-face topography, showing mid-face prognathism and maxillary hollowing (hollow cheeks). Fossil remains of older individuals show expansion of the maxillary sinus which filling the maxillary hollow. A **canine fossa** is present, also seen in the Yunxian *Homo erectus* (Chapter 10) but not in other specimens such as Sangiran 17. It is suggested that *Homo antecessor* may have evolved in Africa from *Homo erectus* and could represent the last common ancestor for Neanderthals and modern humans (de Castro et al., 1997). However the similarities to *Homo heidelbergensis* suggest to other palaeoanthropologists that the Gran Dolina fossils should be assigned to this species rather than to *antecessor*.

Nevertheless, Tattersall and Schwarz agree that the Gran Dolina fossils are a distinct species because of their unique combination of features. They suggest that *Homo antecessor* in Europe may represent a colonisation that was successful for a time and then died out without leaving any descendants.

9.3.2 Stone tool technology

Most of the tools found with the *Homo antecessor* fossils were made of flint; others were made of quartzite, limestone, sandstone and quartz. All of these rocks are accessible within 2–5 km of Gran Dolina. The technology was Oldowan, which is fascinating as Acheulean technology had been present in Africa for over half a million years prior to these Oldowan tools being made. Acheulean tools came late to Europe, but the hominin colonisation of Europe also came late, by comparison with the spreading of

---

Box 9.3 Features of *Homo antecessor*

Has a marked double-arched browridge (like later Neanderthals and Chinese erectus).

Has a canine fossa, with no expanded maxilla (however, this is likely due to the individual's young age, since other older individuals (e.g., ATD 6–58) do have an expanded maxilla).

An approximate brain size of 1000 cc.

Reduced mandibular corpus thickness when compared to *ergaster* or early *erectus*.

Has small postcanines that resemble those of the habilines (*habilis* and *rudolfensis*), but they are still within the *ergaster/erectus* range.

Shovel-shaped maxillary incisors (ancestral condition).

M_3 is reduced relative to M_1.

Has moderate taurodontism: low root apex, expanded pulp cavity (characteristic of *erectus* and *heidelbergensis*).

Large I^2 dimensions that resemble *heidelbergensis*.

◆ Sharp nasal margin.

Shallow maxillary notch.

---

hominins from Africa into Asia. The failure of Acheulean technology to reach Western Asia can be seen as a consequence of early migrants from Africa departing before the development of the new technology. However, this argument does not apply to Europe.

At Gran Dolina, there are no large cutting tools such as the bifacial handaxes typical of Acheulean technology. Simple chopping tools and flakes typical of Oldowan technology are abundant. Such tools can be used for a variety of functions. Carbonell and others,[8] grouped the tools into four size categories: micro, <30 mm; small, 31–60 mm; medium, 61–100 mm and large, >100 mm (Figure 9.8). Small and medium-sized tools were the most abundant, and different sized tools were available for different purposes. The researchers were fortunate to have found a set of flakes representing an initial flaking sequence, made during the process of tool making. Furthermore they point out that all the structural categories shown in Figure 9.8 have been found at the site. Some tools had been retouched and most of these were made of the best quality Cretaceous flint. The artefactual evidence suggests that the rocks and cobbles used for knapping were taken into the cave where they were worked. Flakes apparently removed from a boulder by throwing rocks at it were also transported to Gran Dolina. Re-touching may have been done outside the cave.

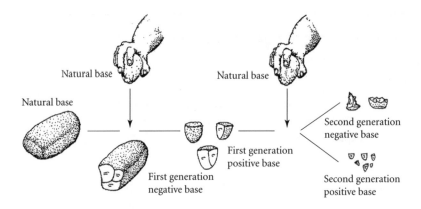

Definition using logical analytical system	Description of stone artefacts
Natural base	Cobbles, pebbles or block selected for flaking or use as hammers.
First generation negative base (1GNB)	Flaked cobbles, pebbles or blocks which show the scars of flakes detached from their surfaces. They can be both tools and cores.
First generation positive base (1GPB)	Flakes detached from the IGNB
Second generation negative base (2GNB)	Retouched flakes whose blanks were 1GPB. These flakes, (1GPB), were detached from the 1GNB and then retouched. The commonest are denticulates, notches, and side-scrapers.
Second generation positive base (2GPB)	Debris, mostly small flakes, detached from from 1GPB.

Figure 9.8 Structural and size categories of stone artefacts from Gran Dolina. The structural categories were defined using a logical analytical system for identifying the stages of tool manufacture. Reproduced from Carbonell et al., 1999 P655.

The researchers carried out detailed use-wear analyses of 43 stone artefacts; 24 showed signs of use-wear. Use-wear on blades and scrapers is manifested in two ways. Modifications of the crystalline structure of the rock results in striations, polishes, breakages and compression. Transformations of the mineral crystals result in chemical modifications, dissolution and generation of deposits on the edge surface. So, use-wear analysis involves detailed study of the sharp edges of tools using microscopy. Table 9.1 includes a summary of the observations made on a representative sample of the artefacts. Note that certain types of use-wear can be identified from features on stone tool edges. For example meat processing is associated with a strip of use wear comprising little alteration of surface topography, but compression and chemical corrosion can be seen resulting from the edge hitting bone. Bone processing itself is associated with dense deep homogenous wear usually with corrosion, abrasion and/or compression. Woodworking causes localised compression, and striations caused by abrasion, resulting in dense localised wear. One of the artefacts may have been used for cutting hide

Table 9.1 Results of use-wear analysis for 9 representative examples of artefacts found at Gran Dolina. Adapted from (Carbonell et al., 1999).

Category (See Fig 9.8 for details)	Raw material	Dimensions/mm	Deformation	Movement when in use	Worked material
2GNB	Neogene flint	54 × 16 × 14	Discontinuous; compression; striation; deposit	Oblique	Wood
2GNB	Cretaceous flint	38 × 33 × 16	Marginal with convex deposit	Transverse	Wood?
PB	Quartzite	77 × 37 × 23	Dispersed, convex dense deposit; abrasion, compression	Longitudinal	Wood?
PB	Quartzite	28 × 21 × 07	Marginal convex dense deposit		Wood?
PB	Quartzite	39 × 28 × 08	Discontinuous; convex very dense deposit, corrosion	Transverse	Bone
2GNB	Cretaceous flint	33 × 27 × 14	Marginal convex and low density deposit	Longitudinal	Meat
PB	Quartzite	65 × 50 × 14	Marginal convex dense deposit; corrosion	Longitudinal	Meat
PB	Quartzite	69 × 55 × 21	Discontinuous splitting; convex dense deposit, compression and corrosion	Longitudinal	Butchery (meat and bone)
PB	Quartzite	45 × 38 × 17	Low density deposit; splitting; compression striation	Transverse	Hide?

as the edge has a dense convex deposit and shows splitting, striations, corrosion and compression. Scraping fat from hide provided fat for consumption and also cleaned the hide for other uses.

An interesting feature of the used stone tools is that where there were number of sharp edges, the hominins had apparently not selected the best edge for the job, for example, one stone that had been used for wood-working showed use-wear on two edges. One of the edges had been re-touched, the other not. It appeared that the edges on stone tools were used until all had been exhausted. The advantage of Oldowan type tools for *Homo antecessor* was that their edges can be used to perform many tasks.

◆ Compare and contrast stone tool technology used by *Homo erectus* in Africa 1.0 mya with that used by *Homo antecessor*.

◆ The find of the *Homo erectus* calvaria in the 1.0 million year old sediment of the Daka member in Ethiopia was associated with early Acheulean tools, including hand-axes and cleavers. In contrast *Homo antecessor*, dated at 750 kya is associated with Oldowan stone tool technology.

◆ Using Curtis and Swisher's suggested explanation for the persistence of Oldowan technology in Asia as a guide, suggest an explanation for the association of this technology with *Homo antecessor* in Europe 750 kya.

◆ *Homo antecessor* may be descended from an immigrant African population that had never invented or come across Acheulean technology.

We now move on to examine the fossil fauna of Gran Dolina and to put together the lines of fossil and artefactual evidence for deducing the way of life of *Homo antecessor*.

9.3.3 Animal fossils found in the TD6 layer at Gran Dolina

Bird, ungulate and carnivore animal bones have been found at Gran Dolina. The avian species have been studied in detail and their habitat preferences reconstructed from what is known about communities of similar modern species. The study suggests that the environment consisted of open country with a wet climate.

Ungulate bones are abundant and include *Stephanorhinus etruscus* (rhinoceros), *Equus altidens* (horse), *Sus scrofa* (pig), *Dama nestii* (deer), *Cervus elaphus* (red deer), *Bison voightstedtensis, and Eucladoceros giuliani* (large deer). This is a faunal assemblage that is characteristic of the latter part of the early Pleistocene or the earliest Middle Pleistocene. Bones of young horses and deer are the most abundant, suggesting that meat from these species was preferred. The absence of typical glacial species suggests that the climate in Spain during the Late and middle Pleistocene was not severely affected by the extreme cold and glaciation experienced in northern Europe. Carnivore bones include *Ursus sp* (bear), *Crocuta crocuta* (hyaena), *Mustela palerminea* (weasel), *Lynx* sp, *Canis mosbachensis* (ancient wolf), and *Vulpes praeglacialis* (fox).

9.3.4 How did *Homo antecessor* live?

We saw in section 9.3.2 that the stone tools found at Gran Dolina appear to have been manufactured inside the cave. Use-wear analyses suggest that the stone tools were used for butchering carcasses, cutting meat and bones. Cut marks on animal bones confirm that stone tools were used for defleshing bone and gaining access to bone marrow, activities carried out inside the cave. The range and abundance of animal bones suggest that *Homo antecessor* preferred horse and deer flesh, but how the hominins trapped and killed such active and swift animals is not known. *Homo antecessor*, like *Homo erectus* would have needed to work in groups and plan a strategy but we have no evidence for what that strategy was. Modern day hunter gatherers hunt large mammal prey on foot. Initially the leader of the hunting group selects an animal from the herd that appears weaker than the other individuals; this may be an elderly animal, or an inexperienced calf or adolescent. The hunters separate the chosen prey from the group of animals and then drive the animal away and follow it relentlessly for a day or two, not allowing it to eat or drink. When the animal appears to be tiring a poisoned arrow is shot. Further tracking of the animal ensues until the animal collapses. The animal is killed and the carcass butchered into quarters, which are carried back to the camp-site where butchery is completed.

Fossil bones of *Homo antecessor* bore cut marks similar to those observed on the animal bones; the marks are consistent with de-fleshing. The researchers suggest that *Homo antecessor* was cannibalistic. Whether cannibalism was cultural or used as a survival strategy during times of food shortage is unknown. Another explanation is that possibly de-fleshing of bones of the dead may have been part of the species' culture.

There is evidence for working with hide in that one of the tools studied shows signs of the characteristic use-wear. Edges of other stone tools showed signs of wood-working. The uses made of hides and wood by *Homo antecessor* have not been identified, but we can speculate that hides were used as a form of clothing or possibly coverings for sleeping. There is no evidence at Gran Dolina for the use of wood for fire; if fire was not used by *Homo antecessor* then cooking was not possible and meat would have been eaten raw. The researchers suggest that Gran Dolina cave was an important cave site during the Lower Pleistocene that was used frequently by the hominins for carrying out a number of activities that included tool-making, butchery of animals and members of their own species, and probably meat consumption. Therefore it is likely that occupation and/or use of the site was long-term, but could have been sporadic. So the researchers do not assert that the cave was a central camp-site for *Homo antecessor*.

9.4 The Ceprano hominin calvaria

A hominin calvaria discovered close to Ceprano (Latium province) in Italy is even older than the Gran Dolina hominins. The fossil was dated at 800–900 000 years old using ^{40}Ar/^{39}Ar dating of adjacent layers of volcanic deposits. The fossil may be associated with nearby assemblages of Oldowan style stone tools. There are conflicting views on which species is represented by the Ceprano calvaria. Mallegni et al. (2003) suggest that it represents a new species, *Homo cepranensis*. However, Manzi et al. (2001) had suggested that it might be attributed to *Homo antecessor*. Studies of the features of the Ceprano calvaria suggest that it may represent a bridge between African *Homo erectus* and *Homo heidelbergensis*, the latter species being more recent than known fossils of *antecessor*. Cameron and Groves (2004) point out that the Ceprano specimen is the closest European specimen to *Homo erectus* and it also looks very similar to the African OH9 specimen from Olduvai Gorge, which is dated at 1.2 mya, and resembles other fossils of *erectus*, including OH12 from younger sediments dated at 700 kya. They suggest that the Ceprano specimen belongs with a group of *H. erectus* that spread into Western Europe and thence to Africa from Eurasia.

9.5 Conclusion

Fossils of *Homo erectus* have been known for more than a hundred years. Those specimens dated from 1.0 mya–700 kya have come predominantly from Asia but also from Africa. African *Homo erectus* dated from 1.0 mya was using Acheulean technology and finds of animal bones and Acheulan tools associated with the Daka cranium indicate a hunter-gatherer/scavenger life style. Where stone tool technology was found associated with *Homo erectus* fossils in China and Java dated from 1.0–0.7 mya, it comprised chopping tools characteristic of Oldowan technology. However, the find in the Bose Basin in China of Acheulean tools dated at about 803 kya showed that in fact there was Acheulean technology in use in Asia. Furthermore, *Homo antecessor* dated at 750 kya was in Spain using Oldowan technology, albeit with variants. So it is unwise to generalize about the spread of hominin stone tool technologies. The likelihood of multiple dispersals of *Homo erectus* from 1.8 to at least 1.0 mya, both out of Africa to Asia, and back into Africa from Asia, would have affected the types of technology used by their descendants. Other controversies link to the position of fossil finds in the evolutionary tree for *Homo*. The position of *H. antecessor* is still controversial, with some published evolutionary trees not including the species at all. The status of the Ceprano cranium is not agreed, with some views supporting it's classification as *Homo erectus*, and other views favouring its designation as a new species, *Homo cepranensis*. In Chapter 10 we move into a complex phase of human evolution during which there was the emergence of at least three new species of *Homo*.

9.6   Questions

Question 9.1

Collating information in a table is a useful way of identifying links between disparate lines of evidence. SAQs for earlier chapters have asked you to fill in blanks in provided tables. Now we ask you to design your own table that summarizes some of the finds of *Homo erectus* fossils dated at 1.0 mya–700 000 years ago. Include the location of each find, what it was e.g. partial cranium, teeth, and the date range, for each fossil find.

Organize your table so that there is one row per fossil find. Write a title for your table. *(Learning outcome C4)*

Question 9.2

Classify the following statements as true, or false, giving reasons:

a   'Lumping' is the correct strategy for classifying fossil hominines because members of the only species living today, *Homo sapiens*, show considerable variation in anatomy.

b   Natural selection may result in evolution of similar dentition in species eating similar diets; therefore teeth and jaws are susceptible to homoplasy.

c   Lines of evidence from dates and fossil finds are consistent with the view that African *Homo erectus* is the ancestor of *Homo antecessor*.

d   Neandertals are the ancestors of *Homo antecessor*.

e   *Homo erectus* emerged at about 1.8 million years, and this species had the longest known span of existence known for a *Homo* species. *(Learning outcome C1)*

Question 9.3

Oldowan technology persisted as the only type of technology used by *Homo* for about a million years, from 2.5–1.5 mya. Outline how the uses of the Oldowan tools by *Homo antecessor* enabled the hominins to obtain and process food and other resources. *(Learning outcome A3)*

Question 9.4

What anatomical features distinguish *Homo antecessor* from *Homo erectus* and are therefore quoted as the justification for a separate species? *(Learning outcome A3)*

References

Abbate, E., Albianelli, A., Azzaroli, A., Benvenuti, M., Tesfamariam, B., Bruni, P., Cipriani, N., Clarke, R. J., Ficcarelli, G., Macchiarelli, R. et al. (1998) A one-million-year-old *Homo* cranium from the Danakil (Afar) Depression of Eritrea. *Nature* **393**, 458–60.

An, Z. and Kun, H. C. (1989) New magnetostratigraphic dates of Lantian *Homo erectus* Quaternary Research **32**, 213–21.

Arsuaga, J. L., Martinez, I., Lorenzo, C., Gracia, A., Munoz, A., Alonso, O. and Gallego, J. (1999) The human cranial remains from Gran Dolina Lower Pleistocene site (Sierra de Atapuerca, Spain). *Journal of Human Evolution* **37**, 431–57.

Asfaw, B., Gilbert, W. H., Beyenne, Y., Hart, W. K., Renne, P. R., Woldegabriel, G., Vrba, E. S. and White, T. (1997) Remains of *Homo erectus* from Bouri, Middle Awash, Ethiopia. *Nature* **416**, 317–20.

Asfaw, B., Gilbert, W. H., Beyenne, Y., Hart, W. K., Renne PR, WoldeGabriel G, Vrba, E. and White, T. D. (2002) Remains of *Homo erectus* from Bouri, Middle, Ethiopia. Nature 416:317–320.

Black, D. (1927) Further hominid remains of Lower Quaternary age from the Chou Kou Tien deposit. *Nature* **120**:954.

Black, D. (1927) *Sinanthropus pekinensis*: the recovery of further fossil remains of this early hominid from the Choou Kou Tien deposit. *Science* **69**, 674–76.

Boaz, N. T., Ciochon, R. L., Xu, Q. and Liu, J. (2000) Large mammalian carnivores as a taphonomic factor in the bone accumulation at Zhoukoudian. *Acta Anthropologica Sinica Supplement to Volume* **19**, 224–34.

Breuil, H. (1939) Bone and antler industry of the Choukoutien *Sinanthropus* site. Palaeontologica Sinica. *N Ser, D* **6**.

Cameron, D. W. and Groves, C. P. (2004) Bones stones and molecules,. Elsevier Academic Press.

Carbonell, E., Garcia-Anton, M. D., Mallol, C., Mosquera, M., Olle, A., Rodriguez, X. P., Sahnoumi, M., Sala, R. and Maria, J. (1999) The TD6 level lithic industry from gran Dolina Atapuerca (Burgos Spain): production and use. *Journal of Human Evolution* **37**, 653–93.

Curtis, G. H., Swisher, C. C. and Lewin, R. (2001) *Java Man*. London: Little, Brown and Co.

de Castro, J. M. B., Arsuaga, J. L., Carbonell, E., Rosas, A., Martinez, I. and Mosquera, M. (1997) A hominid from the lower Pleistocene of Atapuerca, Spain: Possible ancestor to Neanderthals and modern humans. *Science* **276**, 1392–395.

Dubois, M. E. F. T. (1896) The place of '*Pithecanthropus*' in the genealogical tree. *Nature* **53**, 245–47.

Grün, R., Huang, P. H., Wu, X., Stringer, C. B. and Thorne, A. (1997) ESR analysis of teeth from the palaeoanthropological site of Zhokoudian. *China Journal of Human Evolution* **32**, 83–91.

Hyodo, M., Nakaya, H., Urabe, A., Saegusa, H., Shunrong, X., Jiyun, Y., Xuepin, J. (2002) Palaeomagnetic dates of hominid remains from Yuanmou, China, and other Asian sites. *Journal of Human Evolution* **43**, 27–41.

Mallegni, F., Carnieri, E., Bisconti, M., Tartarelli, G., Ricci, S. and Biddittu, I. a. S., A. (2003) *Homo cepranensis* sp nov and the evolution of African-European Middle Pleistocene hominids. *Comptes Rendus Palevol* **2**, 153–59.

Manzi, G., Mallegni and Ascenzi, A. (2001) A cranium for the earliest Europeans: Phylogenetic position of the hominid from Ceprano, Italy. *Proceedings of the National Academy of Sciences of the United States of America* **98 no 17**, 10011–16.

Shen, G., Gao, X., Gao, B., Granger, D. E. (2009) Age of Zhoukoudian *Homo erectus* determined with [26]Al/[10]Be burial dating *Nature* **458,** 198–200.

Tattersall, I. and Sawyer, G. J. (1996) The skull of *Sinanthropus* from Zhoukoudian, China: a new reconstruction. http://www.modernhumanorigins.com/erectus.html.

Tattersall, I. and Schwartz, J. H. (2000) *Extinct Humans*. Boulder Colarado: Westview Press.

Teilhard de Chardin, T. (1937) The discovery of *Sinanthropus*. *Etudes* **July 5th**.

Weidenreich, F. (1941). The Extremity Bones of *Sinanthropus pekinensis*. Palaeontologica Sinica. *Palaeontologica Sinica* **N Ser, D**, 5.

Weidenreich, F. (1943) The skull of *Sinanthropus pekinensis*; A Comparative Study on a Primitive Hominid Skull. *Palaeontologica Sinica* **N Ser, D**, 10.

Yamei, H., Potts, R., Baoyin, Y., Zhengtang, G., Deini, A., Wei, W., Clark, J., Guanghmao, X. and Weiven, H. (2000) Mid-Pleistocene Acheulen-like Stone technology of the Bose basin South China. *Science* **287**, 1622–626.

10

700 000 ya–130 000 ya. Emergence of new species of *Homo*

Fossil evidence indicates that from 130–700 kya, there was the emergence of at least three new species of *Homo*, while *Homo erectus* persisted in South East Asia and China. An African speciation event produced *Homo heidelbergensis*, more than 600 000 years ago. Fossil evidence suggests that *H. heidelbergensis*, like *H. ergaster*, wandered out of Africa but instead of spreading eastwards, moved North and westwards reaching Europe by about 500 000 years ago. Neandertals emerged around 250 kya and the oldest known fossils of this species were discovered in Germany and France. Finally, a further speciation event in Africa resulted in the emergence of modern *Homo sapiens* about 200 000–150 000 years ago.

10.1 Introduction

Homo erectus persisted for a long time in at least two continents, Africa and Asia. Evidence for the persistence of *erectus* includes a mandible dated at ~650 kya found at Chenjiawo near Lantian, China (An and Kun 1989). More recent fossils include a partial cranium found at Sale, Morocco, dated at about 400 kya, and a cranium discovered at Hexian China, dated at ~400 kya. However, in this chapter, we focus on three new *Homo*

The Emergence of Humans   Patricia Ash and David Robinson
© 2010 John Wiley & Sons, Ltd

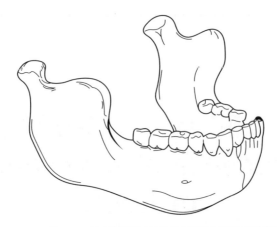

Figure 10.1   The Mauer mandible. This is the type specimen for *Homo erectus*. Reproduced from Lewin (1999) P170.

species that emerged over this time span, *H. heidelbergensis*, Neandertals and *H. sapiens*. Evidence obtained from fossil and artefactual finds throws some light on the anatomy and behaviours of these three species. Fossils of skulls, teeth and post-cranial bones of *Homo heidelbergensis*, were discovered in Africa and Europe. Their fossil anatomy is variable and it is possible that in the future, *H. heidelbergensis* may be split into two or more species. The type specimen for *H. heidelbergensis*, is the Mauer mandible (Figure 10.1) found in 1907 by a workman in the Rosch sandpit north of the village of Mauer close to Heidelberg in Germany. The workman took the mandible to the anatomist, Otto Schoentensack, who in 1908 proposed the name *Homo heidelbergensis*. Subsequently other researchers suggested the term 'archaic'*Homo sapiens*, but this is confusing as it suggests that the species was an early form of *Homo sapiens*. Hence Schoentensack's suggested name is favoured, as the species is neither *Homo erectus* nor *Homo sapiens*. *Homo heidelbergensis* was using Acheulean tools as we shall see in Section 10.2. Fossil finds of Neandertals are so far restricted to Europe, Western Asia and the Levant (Middle East), with the oldest known fossils dated at about 250 kya. The anatomy of Neandertals distinguishes them clearly from *Homo heidelbergensis*, as does their Middle Palaeolithic stone tool technology, named Mousterian, after Le Moustier in France, a site where Neandertal fossils were found. The oldest known fossils of *Homo sapiens* dated at 160–150 kya, were discovered at Herto, in association with a mix of Acheulean tools and **Middle Stone Age** technology. As we shall see in section 11.2, genetic evidence suggests similar dates for the emergence of modern humans.

10.2 The emergence and migration of *Homo heidelbergensis*

Since the initial find of Mauer mandible in Germany, other fossils of *Homo heidelbergensis* were discovered. The dates attributed to fossil finds of *Homo heidelbergensis*

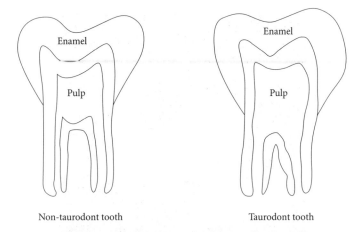

Non-taurodont tooth   Taurodont tooth

Figure 10.2 (a) Structure of a taurodont tooth seen in cross section; (b) structure of non-taurodont tooth. Reproduced from Stringer and Gamble (1993) P78.

range from 600–200 kya, with the oldest known fossil, the Bodo cranium, discovered in Africa.

◆ Outline the global climate from 600–200 kya drawing on information in Chapter 9.

◆ The Middle Pleistocene was a time of massive climatic fluctuation, and included four glacial and five interglacial periods (Figure 9.1).

Nevertheless despite the climatic fluctuations, *Homo heidelbergensis* spread out of Africa into Europe, reaching northern areas by at least about 500 kya.

The anatomy of *Homo heidelbergensis* is distinctive. The Mauer mandible is large and robust, and has no projecting chin. The **ramus**, the part that connects the mandible to the cranium, is unusually broad, and provided attachments for strong jaw muscles, suggesting an ability for heavy chewing. Tooth morphology is closer to modern *H sapiens* than *H. erectus* with molars having large pulp cavities and reduced roots, a structure known as **taurodont** (Figure 10.2), although taurodont teeth are not typical of all specimens of *H. heidelbergensis*. Other fossils found at Rosch sand pit in the same sedimentary layer as the Mauer mandible, include bones of Pleistocene species such as bear, horse, deer and rhino, which enabled the use of faunal correlation to date the mandible at 500 000 years. The animal bones indicate an abundant supply of food.

The oldest known fossil of *H. heidelbergensis*, the Bodo cranium, was discovered in Bodo d'Ar Ethiopia in 1978, and is dated at 600 kya. It is the most complete skull available and its endocranial capacity has been determined at 1200–1325 cm^3 (Conroy, *et al.*, 2000). This is within the range for modern humans, suggesting rapid brain expansion

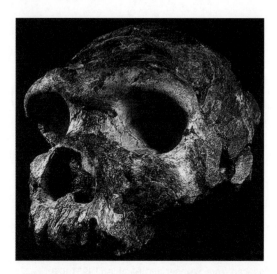

Figure 10.3   The Bodo cranium, found at Bodo in Ethiopia and dated at 600 000 years old. This thick skull with a massive and large face, is attributed to *Homo heidelbergensis.* Reproduced from https://www.msu.edu/~heslipst/contents/ANP440/heidelbergensis.htm, accessed 02/12/09.

in *Homo* from the Lower to the early Middle Pleistocene[3]. However the encephalization quotient for the Bodo cranium is below that for Neandertals and modern humans so the brain size expansion found in *Homo sapiens* was not complete in *heidelbergensis.* The Bodo cranium (Figure 10.3), has a broad massive face that is pushed outwards by the presence of spacious nasal sinuses. The cranium is high and rounded, being broadest in the lower parietal region. The nose is broad, and the frontal bone forms a low forehead, that slopes backward, like that of *Homo erectus.* There are prominent double-arched eyebrow ridges, and a small sagittal keel, although this is not present in all specimens.

Another specimen assigned to *Homo heidelbergensis* is the Kabwe cranium found in Kabwe, Zambia. Faunal correlation suggests an age of at least 125 000 years and possibly up to 300 000 years. The skull has marked eyebrow ridges and a slight sagittal keel like that seen in African *Homo erectus.* There is a partially healed wound close to the left ear, possibly the site of an infection.

◆ Certain features are identified as characteristic of *Homo heidelbergensis.* Using information from the descriptions of the fossils, and the pictures of the Kabwe cranium in Figure 10.4, summarise the characteristic features as a bulleted list.

◆ Answer:

- *Homo heidelbergensis* has a cranial capacity of about 1200–1325 cm³.

- The forehead is low and slopes backward.

- There are prominent double-arched eyebrow ridges and a slight sagittal keel.

Figure 10.4   Cast of the Broken Hill cranium.

- The ramus, the part that connects the mandible to the cranium, is broad, and has attachments for strong jaw muscles, which suggesting heavy chewing.

- The face is broad and massive.

- The cranium is high and rounded, and is broadest in the lower parietal region.

- The molars are taurodont.

Box 10.1   The first early human fossil from Africa

The first human fossil to be discovered in Africa was a cranium found in 1921 at Kabwe in Zambia, also known as 'Broken Hill'. The specimen is remarkably well preserved. Miners working the local limestone for lead ore broke into a lower cavern within a cave and found the cranium. Sir Arthur Smith Woodward described the find in a paper in Nature and named it 'Rhodesian man' – *Homo rhodesiensis*. The precise location and relationship to any other specimens isn't recorded, although animal bones have been found in the cave. The animal bones are mostly from species that are still found in the area today and include predators such as leopards and hyenas as well as grazing animals like kudu and zebra. A few extinct species have been found too. There are also some worked stone tools. Dating the cranium has been a problem. The estimated dates are based on faunal correlation and have a large uncertainty associated with them.

Hand axes and cleavers, characteristic of Acheulean stone tool technology, were found with the Bodo cranium and also hippopotamus, baboon and antelope bones. Cut marks on the animal bones suggest butchery. The Bodo cranium itself bears cut marks suggesting de-fleshing either before or shortly after death. The date and age of Bodo support the view that the species originated in Africa and then migrated out of Africa into Europe. *H. antecessor* in Europe was using Oldowan tools (Section 9.3.2), and although evidence is sparse, it appears that *H. heidelbergensis* brought Acheulean tool technology to Europe. Up to the late 1980s it was assumed that there were no hominids in Britain until after the Anglian glaciations (478 kya to 424 kya). We move on to study evidence that demonstrates that this view was incorrect.

10.2.1 *Case study: Boxgrove; a fair-weather Eden*

Much of what we know about the behaviours and tool technology of *Homo heidelbergensis* comes from a few key sites. The Boxgrove site is especially important and comprises an area within the Eartham quarries in Sussex close to the English Channel (Figures 10.5–10.7). The site is currently owned by English Heritage, who are providing the funding for further research work.

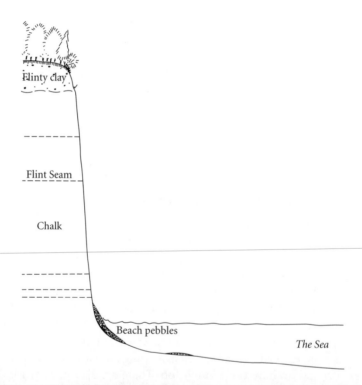

Figure 10.5 Simplified interpretation of the geology of the Boxgrove quarries. During the early Pleistocene, the sea eroded and cut back an ancient chalk cliff that was 75–100 m high. Flint layers from the chalk broke up and the flints plus the overlying clays fell into deposits of beach pebbles and shingle which mixed with chalk from cliff falls. Heavily eroded fish bones (flatfish, sardine/pilchard type and conger eel, all species that feed in the intertidal zone) have been found amongst blocks of chalk on the old sea bed. Uplift of these ancient beaches means that they now lie about 40 m above sea level. Reproduced from Pitts and Roberts (1998) P110.

The quarries overlie a floor of chalk rock, which comprises the remains of an ancient eroded chalk cliff. Figure 10.5 shows that initially the sea had cut back the chalk cliff, which was about 75–100 m high. As the cliff eroded, flints and chalk fragments fell onto deposits of pebbles, forming beaches. These beaches now lie at about 40 m above sea level because of uplift. The Slindon sands, a layer of brownish yellow sand up to 6 metres deep, were deposited on top of the beach and the chalk (Figure 10.6). This sand was deposited under a shallow sea and contains fossil burrows of worms and crustaceans. Above the sand there are sediments of fine silts and mud, the Slindon silts, deposited when the area was a quiet intertidal lagoon. The top of the silts eventually dried and the soil that formed subsequently supported grasslands. By this time, about 524 000 years ago, the climate warmed, marking the onset of an interglacial period.

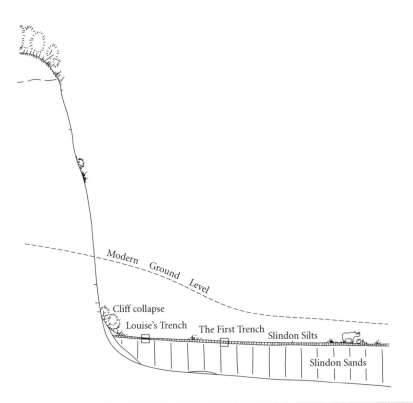

Figure 10.6 While the area was submerged by the sea, up to 6 m of sand was deposited on the eroded base of the ancient cliff. The sand, known as the Slindon sands, is overlain by a metre of very fine silt, the Slindon silts. Fish bones found in the silts include salmon, eels and flatfish. Eventually soil formed on top of the exposed Slindon silts and supported grassy plains. Fossil evidence indicates that the plains were grazed by large and small herbivores, including rhinoceros and beaver. Predators included lion and hyaena. Reproduced from Pitts and Roberts (1998) P110.

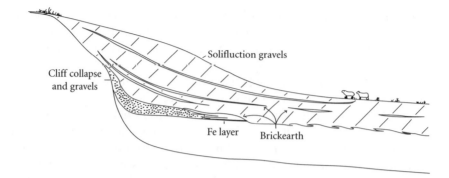

Figure 10.7 The grassland turned into marsh as the deteriorating climate associated with the onset of the Anglian glaciation set in. In the relatively hypoxic conditions in the marsh soil and water, a thin layer of silt rich in iron was deposited (the Fe layer). During the glacial, when subsoil was frozen (permafrost), the top of the cliff split and in the summer thaws, debris fell off the cliff and buried the grassland plain. Around the base of the ancient sea cliff, the silts and sands were preserved in an intermittent band 100–200 m wide. Further away from the cliff base, mud and gravel flows destroyed the silts. Occasional layers of brickearth within the gravels suggest short periods of warming climate. Reproduced from Pitts and Roberts (1998).

(Figure 9.1). So Pitts and Roberts (1998) describe Boxgrove 500 000 years ago as a fair weather Eden because at this time, the climate was pleasantly warm. We know from their fossil bones that the fauna included lions, bears, rhinoceros, beaver and various water birds and amphibians. Unusually, fossil skeletons of animal carcasses remained where they had died, or were chewed by hyaena, or butchered by hominids. Flint tools found in the silt appear to be close to or at the place where they were dropped. The end of the interglacial by about 478 000 years ago is marked by a thin overlying layer, stained in places by iron, and so known as the 'Fe layer'[7] (Figure 10.7). As the Boxgrove area was never covered fully by ice sheets, (Figure 9.3), the flint tools and the animal bones, remained where they were deposited, resulting in the rich finds some 500 000 years later.[7]

10.2.2 *Artefacts: an abundance of hand-axes*

A spectacular feature of Boxgrove is the large quantity of Acheulean hand-axes found on the firm surface of the Slindon silts. Silt deposition left the land surfaces perfectly preserved, with hand-axes left where they were dropped about 500 000 years ago. An idea of their abundance can be gauged from the observation that in the 1996 dig season, more than 250 hand axes were found.[7] Surfaces where fragments of flint were scattered during manufacture of hand-axes were preserved too. One trench excavated by Louise Austin in 1988 contained an area of < 0.25 m², in which she found a spread of 1715 pieces of flint. Outside that area there was clean silt without flint

Figure 10.8 A dense scatter of flint flakes in Louise's trench is interpreted as an area where a hominid had sat to make a hand-axe. Reproduced from Pitts and Roberts (1998).

fragments, apart from a group of larger flakes about 20 cm to the right that appeared to have been selected and placed deliberately. The overall pattern of distribution of flint fragments was a triangle of debris gradually thinning out in one direction and but abruptly limited on the other two sides. A thick accumulation of flint flakes was found on the right side of the area; some of these were standing vertically in the sediment where they had landed nearly 500 000 years ago (Figure 10.8). This unique and carefully recorded pattern of flint debris was the result of a flint knapper's work, about 500 000 years ago.

The initial stages of stone tool manufacture involve flint knapping and result in a rough-cut hand-axe, as well as flint debris. Finer detailed knapping requires use of 'soft hammers', pieces of bone antler or horn. The soft hammer is used to hit the edge of the rough hand-axe for removal of wide thin flakes from the surface. Use of a stone hammer would remove a thick flake or damage the thin edge of the axe. Why a soft hammer removes thin flakes without damaging the sharp edge of an axe is not fully understood. It is possible that a stone hit by a soft hammer sinks slightly into it, so spreading the impact. Soft hammers become pitted with use as contact with hard flint causes pits and depressions in the surface (Figure 10.9). Use of soft hammers requires forward planning, because a suitable antler or bone from a carcass has to be obtained before making the hand-axe. Many soft hammers found at Boxgrove show evidence of long-term use, suggesting that soft hammers were 'possessions'.

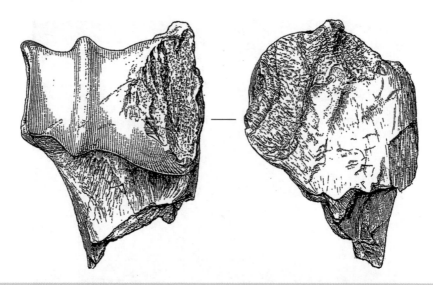

Figure 10.9   Examples of 'soft' hammers found at Boxgrove. Soft hammers are as common as stone hammers at Boxgrove because of the excellent conditions for preservation at the site. (a) Elbow joint (length 8.5 cm), of the humerus of a bison showing heavy wear on the right hand side due to heavy battering. Tiny slivers of flint are embedded in the battered surfaces. Reproduced from Pitts and Roberts (1998) P222.

10.2.3 *Who made and used the hand-axes found at Boxgrove?*

Roger Pederson's find[7] of a hominid tibia at Boxgrove in November 1993 confirmed the view that *Homo heidelbergensis* was living around Boxgrove 400–500 000 years ago, just before the cold climate of the Anglian glacial gripped the landscape. Ancient bones at Boxgrove are not the dense fossils in which bone mineral is replaced by harder denser minerals. Animal and hominid bones at Boxgrove were preserved by the high calcium carbonate content of water percolating the silt and gravel. The preserved bones become crumbly so careful treatment was required to conserve them. The Boxgrove tibia comprises a shaft in two parts; the ends were missing, apparently gnawed away by scavengers. The robusticity of the tibia, and its' estimated total length of 35.5 cm, indicate a height of about 2 metres, suggesting a male individual (if female the male would have been impossibly tall). **CT scanning** and microscopy of a thin section of the bone suggest that the Boxgrove hominid was in his twenties when he died. He appeared to have lived an active life-style as well-developed muscle attachments on the bone indicate that his leg was well-muscled.

◆ What evidence, other than the tibia, supports the view that *Homo heidelbergensis* was the hominid species living at the Boxgrove site around 500 000 years ago?

◆ The date attributed to the tibia, 500 000 years ago, and the tool technology are consistent with *Homo heidelbergensis* but do not provide definitive evidence as *Homo erectus* is also associated with Acheulean technology.

As hand-axes are abundant at Boxgrove and a number of flint knapping sites were found there, it is reasonable to suggest that hand-axes were the tools used for obtaining and processing meat.

Box 10.2 Hominin fossil finds at Boxgrove

Excavations at Boxgrove started in 1982 and plenty of evidence of human activity was found, but it wasn't until 1993 that any traces of the humans responsible appeared. In fact the excavation budget was nearly exhausted but a final winter dig, using a mechanical excavator, turned up a large limb bone that was subsequently identified as a human tibia. The tibia is a massive one, with very thick walls. Two lower incisors found in 1995, in a layer about 100 years older than that in which the tibia was found are from one individual as shown by a deep scratch mark extending across both teeth. The incisors are about 50% longer than those of *Homo sapiens*, have thick enamel and are similar to the incisors in the Mauer jaw.

10.2.4 *What was the function of the hand-axes?*

Cut marks found on the animal bones, including horse, bear, rhino, giant deer, and red deer bones suggest that they were butchered with stone tools (Figure 10.10).

A trench excavated by Indira Mann and James Mackenzie contained the remains of the butchery of a horse. The locations of every scrap of bone from the horse and every fragment of flint were recorded. Six or seven distinct knapping areas were identified; one contained flakes that could be re-fitted to form a flint with a cavity inside having the shape of a hand-axe. The horse bones, soft and fragile, were spread around the centre of the site. No complete hand-axes were found at the horse butchery site; it appeared that the hand-axes were made and used for butchery at the site and then taken away (possibly for re-use). The scatter of bones and flint fragments found in the trench provide us with a picture of a group of hominids sitting around a dead horse and butchering the carcass. There must have been social interaction between individuals as they were busy butchering the horse, but there is no evidence for a camp or of fires.

Recall from Chapter 8, the assemblages of animal bones and stone tools found at Olduvai Gorge and Koobi Fora and dated at 1.8 mya and 1.5 mya respectively. There is argument among palaeoanthropologists about whether the animals used for meat and marrow were scavenged or hunted. The same issues are argued for the Boxgrove sites. Was the horse in Indira's trench scavenged or hunted? A scapula from the butchered horse has a hole about 4 cm in diameter. The edges were clean suggesting a high velocity impact possibly made by penetration of a spear. Tests on an equine scapula pierced by a yew point made a similar hole in the bone. There is no way of proving that *Homo heidelbergensis* at Boxgrove were using spears for hunting but there is much circumstantial evidence that supports this view. Some of the butchery marks on the scapula run across the hole passing over the edge of the break

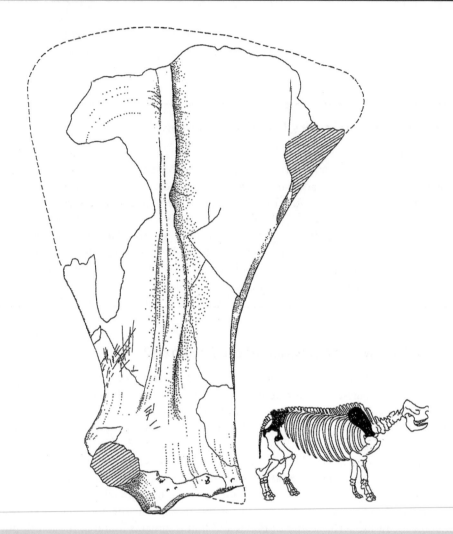

Figure 10.10 Evidence for butchery at Boxgrove. (a) This fossil rhinoceros scapula shows filleting marks, similar both in position and direction, to those that would be found on a large herbivore scapula butchered today. At the base the flint tool has scored the bone as it was used to disarticulate the scapula from the humerus. Two sets of marks on the top and bottom of the left side, suggest slicing through blocks of muscle attached to the scapula. Reproduced from Pitts and Roberts (1998) P196.

suggesting that the hole was made between before removal of flesh with a hand-axe. In 1911 a yew spear tip was found on the foreshore in Clacton Essex; it is dated at between 420 000–360 000 years old. Three spruce wood spears found in coal mines at Schoningen Germany by Hartmut Thieme are dated at 300 000 to 400 000 years old and shaped like modern javelins[13] (Figure 10.11).

Hand-axes are so abundant at Boxgrove that they must have been the equivalent of the 'Swiss Army knife'. Acheulean technology has been described as primitive, but it

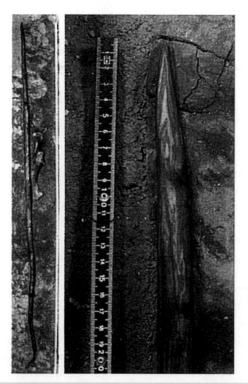

Figure 10.11 The Schoningen spears. The spears are made of spruce wood hardened by exposure to fire. The spear, which is 2.30m in length is shown on the left and details of the tip on the right. Reprinted by permission from Macmillan Publishers Ltd: Nature (Thieme (1997). Lower Palaeolithic hunting spear from Germany) Nature 385 P810, copyright 1997.

remained in use for a long time. Pitts and Roberts suggest that rather than regarding the persistence of the hand-axe as an indication of a 'lack of progress' in technology, long-term use of hand-axes should be attributed to their usefulness for the hominids. For groups of hominids living by hunting scavenging and gathering the hand-axe provided a means of rapid butchering of a fresh (or scavenged) carcass. The horse butchery site demonstrates that hand axes could be made as required at the site of a kill. The sharp edges of hand-axes suggest they were formidable cutting tools, but proof was required. A butcher from Oxford, Peter Dawson, was persuaded to skin and cut up a roe deer carcass using a set of 16 hand-axes made by an expert flint knapper to the design of those found at Boxgrove. Holding a hand-axe between his thumb and fingers in his right hand, Dawson separated the deer hide cleanly from the rest of the body. He used the sharp edges of the hand-axes to cut cleanly through the meat; they also were efficient tools for separating meat neatly from the bone. So the Acheulean hand-axe was an efficient butchery tool as well as possibly an item used in rituals or a weapon that could be thrown (Pitts and Roberts, 1998).

There is much we do not know about the lifestyle of *Homo heidelbergensis* at Boxgrove. We do not know where the hominids slept, what other foods, if any, were eaten apart from meat, or how the social structure and rituals of the groups were organised. The discovery of multiple fossil bones of *H. heidelbergensis* at Atapuerca (Box 10.3) provides more clues.

Box 10.3   The largest collection of ancient hominin fossils

The site of Sierra de Atapuerca in Northern Spain (Section 9.3) has proved to be an exceptionally rich site. Deep within a cave system lies Sima de los Huesos – the cave of bones – from which thousands of hominin bones have been excavated, along with the bones of animals from the same period, over 350000 years ago. Although geographically close to the Gran Dolina site where *Homo antecessor* has been found, the hominins of Sima de los Huesos are a different species, *H. heidelbergensis*. At least 30 individuals are represented by bones recovered so far, and examination of the teeth has shown that the majority were young adults or adolescents. Some bones show evidence of disease and injury. The re-assembled skull of one individual, known as Skull 5, shows evidence of past injuries and there is a broken tooth that became infected and may have been the cause of death. The reconstructed skull is one of the most complete known from this period.

Only one stone tool has been found so far at Sima de los Huesos. It is a hand-axe in the Mode 2 style, made from red quartzite, which is a very unusual material to be used in tool making. It has been suggested that the tool might have had some ritual significance. The suggestion is linked to the hypothesis that the bones came to be aggregated as a consequence of deliberate burial (Arsuaga, *et al.*, 1993).

10.1.5 *Language ability of Homo heidelbergensis*

There is argument about when language capacity was developed in the *Homo* lineage, and also whether language emerged slowly, beginning early in hominine history, or developed rapidly. We have no direct way of assessing the language ability of *Homo heidelbergensis*, or indeed of any other extinct *Homo* species. Language is invisible in the archeological record, but a few clues have been gleaned from brain endocasts, in that certain areas of the brain are known to be linked to language ability. However language capability cannot be located precisely to a particular part of the brain. However, there is some anatomical evidence that *Homo heidelbergensis* was capable of language. For coherent speech, fine control of the tongue is essential and this is the role of the hypoglossal nerve. This nerve branches from the brain and crosses the base of the cranium via a canal in the base of the cranium. In the Kabwe cranium this canal appears to be as wide as it is in modern humans, so there is a possible link to enhanced fine control of the tongue. Furthermore, the endocast of the Kabwe cranium shows signs of a Broca's area, the area of the brain that is associated with language. (Coolidge and Wynn 2009).

♦ Outline how fossil and artefactual evidence from Boxgrove suggest that communication was important for *Homo heidelbergensis*.

♦ The horse butchery site indicates that a group of individuals were working together, manufacturing hand axes and using them to butcher the horse carcass. Some form of language must have been required to communicate to others the skills required for butchery and hand-axe manufacture. Co-operation in hunting requires precise communication, which would be facilitated by language.

The selective pressures for evolution of language and intelligence relate to communication, particularly in a social group setting. Different lines of evidence suggest language ability, but to be certain about this, direct evidence is required, which we do not have.

10.3 The discovery of Neandertals

The Neandertals are the best-known 'cave-men', because this is the species for which there is the most fossil evidence available. Overall, since 1830, fossils representing about 500 individuals have been found. Fossil discoveries have provided sufficient information for drawing a map of the distribution of the species (Figure 9.3), but note that the map overlays their distribution on the current geography. The earliest Neandertals dated at around 200 000 years ago would have been able to migrate overland to what is now Britain, and then back to mainland Europe, as the English Channel was not flooded at this time. The name 'Neandertal' is derived from the location of the find of the first skull to be identified, which was found in the Neander Valley in Germany in 1856 (See Chapter 1 Box 3). Further discoveries were made in Belgium, Croatia, Germany and France (Table 10.1), and fossils found previously, such as the Forbes Quarry skull, were re-examined and identified as Neandertals too. For a long time

Table 10.1 Summary of some finds of Neandertal fossils dated from 230–33 kya grouped according to location (adapted from Stringer and Gamble, 1993).

Country	Location	Date of discovery	Age of fossil remains/kyrs	Nature of fossil remains
Belgium	Engis	1829	70	Partial cranium
	Spy caves	1886	60	2 skeletons & part crania
Croatia	Krapina	1889	130	~900 fossil bone fragments from which 2 skulls were put together.
Gibraltar	Forbes Quarry	1848	Uncertain; artefacts in Vanguard cave dated at ~40	A skull, including bones around nasal cavity.
Germany	Ehringsdorf	1908	200–225	Mixed adult & adolescent remains
France	Biache St Vaast	1976	150–195	Cranial fragments e.g. partial neurocranium, maxillary fragment,

(Continued)

Table 10.1   (Continued)

Country	Location	Date of discovery	Age of fossil remains/kyrs	Nature of fossil remains
	Bau de l'Aubesier	2000	180	2 incisors; a molar and half a mandible with loss of teeth and degenerative disease.
	Baume Moula-Guercy	1991	100	**Skeletal elements from 12 individuals**
	La Ferrassie 1	1909	70	Male & female skeletons + 5 juveniles
	La Chapelle-aux-Saintes	1908	50	Nearly complete adult skeleton
	Le Moustier	1908	<45	Partial skeleton adolescent
	Le Moustier 2	1914	40	Skeleton of baby; <4 months old
	Neander Valley TYPE SPECIMEN	1856	40	Partial skeleton; calotte is type specimen. More fragments e.g. thigh bone, found in 2002
	Saint-Césaire	1979	36	The most recent, largely complete specimen found so far. The stone tools found with this specimen are Châtelperronian.
	La Quina	1911	33	Remains of 2 individuals
Crimea	Kiik Koba	1924–26	undated	Adult hand & 2 feet; child bones
Israel	Tabun cave	1929	120	Partial skeleton; 5 limb bones; one mandible; one premolar
	Kebara	1983	60	Skeleton complete from mandible downwards
	Amud	1961/64	45	A fairly complete skeleton, the tallest known, at 6ft.
Iraq	Shanidar	1953 to 57	70–40	Nine skeletons
Italy	Saccopastore	1929–35	120	2 adult crania, a male and a female
Central Asia	Teshik Tash	1938	70	Burial: 8-9 year old child
United Kingdom	La Cotte de St Brelade Jersey	1910	180	13 teeth
Wales	Pontnewydd Cave	1978–1995	230	19 teeth

Figure 10.12 Marcellin Boule's interpretation of the Neandertal way of life (Henry Fairfield Osborn supervised the drawing of this image in 1915).

perception of how Neandertals looked and behaved was dominated by just one man's view. Marcellin Boule of the Paris Museum of Natural History made a detailed study of the Neandertal skeleton found in the cave at La Chapelle-aux-Saintes in France. Boule classified the skeleton, known colloquially as the 'Old man', as *Homo neanderthalensis*.

He wanted a clear separation between modern humans and Neandertals, believing that the latter were not ancestral to humans, but on a separate evolutionary branch. Boule's interpretation of the 'Old man' skeleton was that the Neandertal was a hunched and bow–legged individual of very low intelligence, verging on idiocy (Figure 10.12), and living a low-grade simple life. Neandertals were viewed as an evolutionary dead-end.

Who were the Neandertals? They lived in Europe, western Asia and the Middle East from around 230 000–30 000 years ago. The precise time span for the species is difficult to define, as the earliest dated fossils show some of the features specifed as Neandertal but not all. Chris Stringer calls the oldest dated fossils 'early Neandertals' and suggests that they had evolved in Europe by 230 kya. From Figure 9.1, we can see that although the Neandertals lived through a substantial part of the Pleistocene Ice Age, there were sharp fluctuations in climate during this time. The earliest Neandertals lived during a relatively warm interglacial which began about 245 000 years ago, but this ended about 186 000 years ago, when a long cold glacial period began, lasting up to about 128 000 years ago. Fossils defined as 'classic Neandertals' by Stringer, date from about 130 000–27 000 years ago, time spanning an interglacial from 128 000– 71 000 years ago, and a long cold spell from 71 000–59 000 years ago when a glacial period within the Late Pleistocene Ice Age gripped Europe. The timeline for climate change during Neandertal times is shown in Table 10.2.

Table 10.2 Timeline for climate change and location of known Neandertal and modern human populations in Europe and Asia. For an explanation of the oxygen isotope stage see Section 9.1.1. Adapted from Stringer and Gamble (1993) P47.

Estimated time period/ years ago	Oxygen isotope stage	Climate	Europe & western Asia	Middle East
303 000–250 000	9a-8	Glacial *Small oceans; large ice caps*	*Homo heidelbergensis* in Europe e.g. Atapuerca 300 kya	
250 000–186 000	7	Mainly cool or temperate with some glacial intervals. *Large oceans; small ice caps*	*Homo heidelbergensis* in Europe e.g. Steinheim ~250 kya Neandertals in Europe e.g. Ehringsdorf Germany 200–225 kya; Biache Saint-Vaast France 160–195 kya	
186 000–128 000	6	Glacial with some milder intervals. *Small oceans; large ice caps*	Neandertals in Europe e.g. Bau de l'Aubesier 180 kya	
130 000–115 000	5e	Interglacial with warm climate *Large oceans; small ice caps*	Neandertals in Europe e.g. Krapina, Saccopastore Italy	Neandertals and humans in Israel Neandertals in Tabun. Modern humans at Qafzeh and Skhull
115 000 – 75 000	5d-a	Temperate/cool	Neandertals in Europe e.g. Moula Guercy France ~100 kya	Neandertals (Kebara) & modern humans in Israel (Skhul)
75 000–30 000	4-3	Initially warm, cooling to glacial from 71–59 kya *Ice caps increasing*	By 60 kya modern humans & Neandertals in central Asia & western & eastern Europe;	Neandertals in Israel 48 kya (Kebara) Modern humans in many sites
30 000–13 000	3-2	Full glacial	Neandertals decline in Asia, & western & eastern Europe; extinct by ~25 kya	Neandertals extinct in Middle East

10.3.1 *How can we recognise a Neandertal?*

Fossil material indicates that Neandertals were of stocky robust build, with barrel-shaped chests, a long back, short legs and short forearms. The estimated mass of males is 65 kg and for females, 50 kg. Palaeoanthropologists link the stocky body shape of Neandertals to adaptation for life in a cold climate (Box 10.4).

BOX 10.4   Climate and body proportions

Climate is an important factor that affects anatomical differences between human populations living in different geographical regions. Two ecogeographical rules, Allen's and Bergmann's rules, can be applied to variation in human and animal populations.

Allen's rule states that populations of the same species living in warm areas of the species range, will have longer limbs than those living in cold areas

Bergmann's rule states that populations of a widely distributed species living in warm areas of the species range will have smaller bodies than those living in cold areas.

Christopher Ruff (John Hopkins University), describes the human body as a cylinder, its diameter is the width of the pelvis, and its length is trunk length (Ruff, 1994). As mammals, the high metabolic rate of *Homo* species results in release of much heat, which maintains the body temperature at a high level. The larger the ratio of surface area to body mass of a person, the greater the potential rate of loss of body heat. Low values for surface area to volume ratios facilitate heat retention. A simple mathematical calculation shows that when a cylinder is wide, the ratio of body surface area to volume is low. For a narrow cylinder, the ratio of body surface area to volume is high.

Therefore, in theory, those people living in high latitudes would have wide bodies and a stocky stature; in contrast to those living at low latitudes who would have narrow bodies and a slimmer stature. Ruff's survey of 71 human populations around the world supported the predictions of both rules. For example the tall Nilotic people of the hot African savannah with their long thin limbs, contrast with the Inuit of northern Canada who tend to have short limbs. Body width, the key feature of Bergmann's rule for *Homo*, is similar in individuals living in similar climatic zones, even for people of different heights. Nilotic people, whose average height is more than 2 m have a similar body width to Mbuti pygmies, who are about 2/3 m shorter. Nilotic people live in the open savannah, and cool by sweating. Mbuti pygmies live in humid forest where sweating is ineffective and their reduced height and therefore reduced body volume, help to limit the amount of metabolic heat generated. However, as Ruff points out, differences in the height of the body, when the body width remains the same, do not affect the lateral surface area to body mass ratio (Figure 10.13). So despite their short stature, Mbuti pygmies also have a relatively high body surface area to body mass ratio.

(continued)

> The short robust bodies of Neandertals, their short limbs, and their wide bodies, may reflect adaptation linked to cold climates during glacial periods of the Pleistocene Ice Age. However as can be seen in Figure 9.1, the climate during the Pleistocene fluctuated sharply so the relationship between body shape and climate is not a simple one. They would also have needed cultural adaptations, for example the use of shelters and clothing, in order to survive the colder periods.

The Krapina Neandertal fossils, from Croatia (Table10.1), provide a large sample of a population on the borderline between Stringer's groupings of 'early' and 'classic' Neandertals. Overall they show the features typical of Neandertals, but are not quite so robust (described in Johanson and Edgar 1996). The limb bones of Neandertals are thick, with large areas of muscle attachments, features compatible with an active lifestyle. The knee, elbow and hip joints are very wide. The limb bones are bowed, a feature that indicates massive muscularity and not a disease such as rickets. The collar bones and the pubic bones of the pelvis are very long. The head of Neandertals was relatively large with a long cranium, flattened on top. The base of the cranium is broader at the base than in the parietal regions. The back of the skull has a marked occipital bulge or 'bun' (Figure 10.14a). A depressed and pitted area at the back of the skull, the **suprainiac fossa** is also characteristic (Figure 10.14b). The mastoid

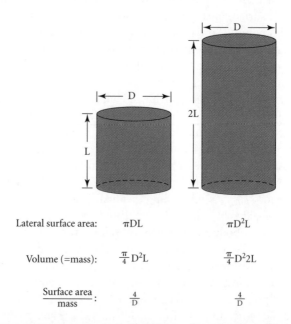

Lateral surface area:	πDL	πD^2L
Volume (=mass):	$\frac{\pi}{4}D^2L$	$\frac{\pi}{4}D^2 2L$
$\dfrac{\text{Surface area}}{\text{mass}}$:	$\dfrac{4}{D}$	$\dfrac{4}{D}$

Figure 10.13   A cylindrical model of body shape. An increase in length (L) of the trunk has no effect on the ratio of the body's lateral surface area to body mass when the cylinder width remains the same. Reproduced from Lewin, 1999, P59.

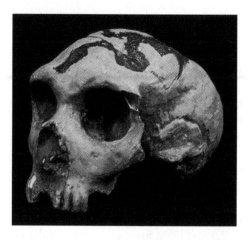

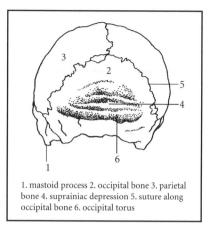

1. mastoid process 2. occipital bone 3. parietal bone 4. suprainiac depression 5. suture along occipital bone 6. occipital torus

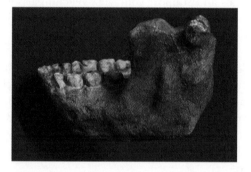

Figure 10.14 The Forbe's Quarry Neandertal skull. (a) Side view of a cast; (b) posterior view; (c) side view of a cast of a Neandertal mandible. (b) reproduced from Tattersall and Schwartz (2000) P195.

processes are small. Adult Neandertal brain sizes, determined from crania of classic Neandertals, was up to 1600–1740 cm³ (e.g. Amud 1 dated at 40–50 000 years, described in Johanson and Edgar, 1996).

As in *Homo erectus*, there were brow ridges comprising two arches, one over each eye, but in most fossil specimens the brow ridges are reduced at the sides of the head in comparison to *H. erectus*, and contained air spaces. The Neandertal nose was prominent and had a huge nasal opening (Figure 10.14c). The face was large with the middle part pushed outwards by the huge nasal cavities and maxillary sinuses. Just inside, and on each side of the nasal opening there is a large bony projection and behind each projection is a distinct swelling of the inside wall of the nasal cavity. These features were discovered by Tattersall and Schwartz (2000) who carried out a detailed re-examination of the Neandertal skull found at Forbe's quarry in Gibraltar. Subsequent examination of other Neandertal skulls confirmed the view that the nasal swellings are always present and provide a diagnostic feature for Neandertals.

The forward position of the face correlates with the forward position of the front teeth, both in the maxilla and mandible. The mandible does not have a mental eminence (chin). The forward position of the teeth in the lower mandible explains why there is a gap, a **retromolar** space, between the back of the 3rd molar and the vertical part of the mandible behind it (Figure 10.14d).

Neandertal front teeth are very large and, because of ridges on the sides, are shovel-shaped. Scratches on the front teeth of Neandertal fossils are common and suggest that something must have been held in the teeth while being cut with a stone tool. When the sharp edge of the stone tool penetrated what was being cut, a scratch mark was left on the teeth. The scratch indicated the direction of the cut, which in turn showed that Neandertals were holding the tool in the right hand.

♦ Palaeoanthrologists suggest that *Homo heidelbergensis* was the ancestral species for Neandertals. Evidence for this view is derived from fossil anatomy and dating. State whether you consider there are anatomical similarities between *H. heidelbergensis* and Neandertals and support your view by comparisons of the anatomical features of the two species. Are the dates for each species consistent with the palaeoanthropologists view?

♦ There are anatomical similarities between *Homo heidelbergensis* and Neandertals that suggest the two species may have an evolutionary relationship. Features the two species share include robusticity, large brain size, a protruding face, large nasal cavities, eyebrow ridges, taurodont molars and a broad ramus in the mandible. Dates for known fossils of *Homo heidelbergensis* in Europe, e.g 500 kyrs for the Mauer mandible, are consistent with a subsequent emergence of Neandertals around 250 kyrs ago.

10.3.2 *Mousterian tool technology*

The timing of the emergence of the Neandertals, around 250 000 years ago, coincides broadly with the start of the Middle Palaeolithic. At the beginning of the Early Middle Palaeolithic, Acheulean hand-axes were being made and used by Neandertals, but were gradually replaced by stone tools manufactured by the Levallois technique, or Mode 3, prepared core technology. However, there was not a clear 'progress' from Acheulean to Levallois technology, nor is the Levallois associated only with Neandertals. There is much variability in stone tool assemblages, but the difference between Acheulean and Levallois technology is clear. The Levallois technique involves preparation of a core from a stone cobble, so that flakes of a pre-determined shape and size can be made (Schlanger, 1996). The nodule is struck so two surfaces are obtained. Initially, the cortex (outer layer) of the nodule is removed. Flakes are then removed by striking with a flint to make a domed profile on one surface, and a striking platform on the opposite surface. The striking platform consists of a central protrusion, which aligns with the axis of the Y shaped ridge on the dorsal side of the core (Figure 10.15).

(1) The core is rounded in outline by removing flakes around the edges

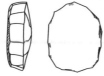

(2)then flakes are removes from the core surface towrds the centre

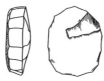

flaking continues from the edge to the middle

(3) until the entire surface of the core has been shaped and prepared

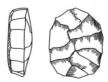

(4) A striking platform is prepared at one end
The platform is then struck

(5) a flake is removed to a predetermined shape
with sharp edges all around

Figure 10.15 Stages of the Levallois technique. Institute of Archaeology, University of Oslo. http://www.hf.uio.no/iakh/forskning/sarc/iakh/lithic/LEV/Lev.html accessed 20/11/09

Modern day flint knappers point out that flakes cannot be removed from nodule or core by sticking to a set list of instructions. Each nodule has unique properties so the knapper needs to plan the angle and location of strikes as the core develops, according to visual and tactile clues from the stone itself (Schlanger, 1996). The Levallois technique requires greater technical skills than those required to make hand-axes (Figure 10.15). However in comparison to modern humans, Neandertals made and used a restricted range of tools; Francois Bordes identified about 60 different types, each with its own function, such as scraping cutting and piercing. The tools included points, flakes, hand-axes, scrapers of various shapes and backed knives (Figure 10.16).

There is evidence that triangular stone points were hafted and may have been used in arrows or spears. Subsequently researchers discovered that many of the supposed tool types resulted from re-touching and re-sharpening of the tools so that there were in fact fewer categories; 20–40 tool types have been suggested. Re-touched tools were inevitably smaller than the originals and often a different shape. Such tools are found more commonly in areas where suitable rocks, especially flints, were scarce, such as La Cotte, Jersey, which is a cave formed in granite.

Sediments containing fragmentary Neandertal fossils in Pontnewydd Cave in North Wales are dated at around 200000 years old, within the warm interglacial phase 7 (Figure 9.1). Burnt flints were also found there, as well as hand-axes and Mousterian

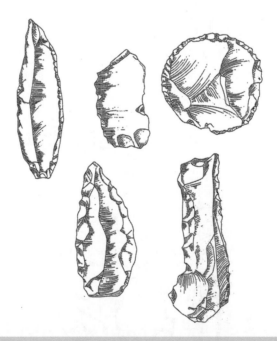

Figure 10.16 Mousterian tools. Top row left to right: Backed knife; Two scrapers. Bottom row: left to right: Mousterian bifacial point; Double straight edged scraper. Reproduced from Lewin, 1999, P158

stone tools (Stringer and Gamble, 1998). The tools are made of coarse-grained rock including rhyolites and volcanic tuffs. Their structure suggests that they are older than 200 000 years; however the structure and design of the tools was limited by the properties of the rocks used for their manufacture. It appears that Neandertals did not travel far in search of suitable rock for tool manufacture but relied on local sources. This is just one of the factors that demonstrate the difficulty of identifying a precise date for the beginning of the Middle Palaeolithic!

It is surprising that neither bone nor antler appear to have been used by Neandertals for tool-making. However, pieces of fossil animal bone found at Neandertal sites suggest that they were being used as soft hammers in a similar way to that by *Homo heidelbergensis*. Marks on Mousterian tools suggest that wood was being cut with them (Soressi, 2005). The typical polish left on edges used for cutting wood remains on stone tools and has been found on Mousterian tools. Wood may have been cut up for burning; evidence for fire is common in Neandertal sites.

♦ Drawing on evidence from your reading of previous sections, suggest other ways that wood that could have been used by Neandertals.

♦ The Schoningen spears (dated at 300–400 000 years ago are made of wood hardened by exposure to fire. They would have made formidable weapons for hunting ice Age mammals. It is possible that Neandertals used such weapons too, at least during periods when the climate was suitable for growth of trees. They may have followed the climate so that they lived within open woodlands.

10.3.3 *Language ability of Neandertals*

There is great controversy about the language ability of Neandertals. On one level, we know, as we do for *Homo heidelbergensis* and other extinct *Homo* species, that they must have communicated with each other, as do all social animals. One argument for use of language is that for hominids leading complex lives, communication was of utmost importance. Planned co-operation and strategy, facilitated by rapid and precise communication, would be essential for a group of relatively small hominids, hunting and capturing large and dangerous prey animals such as Irish elk, rhinoceros and mammoth. In adult humans, the larynx is located low in the neck and brief closure of the airway is necessary during swallowing to prevent choking. The low position of the larynx enlarges the space above it, which enables its emitted sounds to be modified. The movements of the tongue during speech modify the shape and volume of the mouth and pharynx. The degree of basicranial flexion (arching of the **basicranium**), in humans reflects the position of the larynx (Figure 10.17).

In human babies the larynx is high up in the neck, which allows simultaneous swallowing and breathing during suckling. In the first few years of life the pharynx, that connects the larynx to the oral cavity, extends and the basicranium flexes downwards. The larynx ends up lower in the throat and adults lose the ability to breath and swallow at the same time. However, the longer and looped pharynx, which the bending of

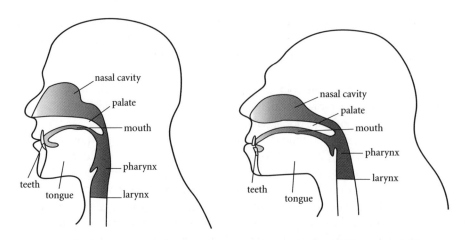

Figure 10.17 Comparison of arrangement of larynx and basicranium of adult modern humans with that of Neandertals. a) Adult human. Note the degree of basicranial flexion, and the relatively low position of the larynx in the throat. b) Neandertal. The basicranium is relatively flat and the larynx sits deeper in the throat. Reproduced from Stringer and Gamble (1993) P89.

the basicranium allows room for, enables the throat muscles to produce the full range of sounds that is needed for speech.

◆ How could evidence for the language ability of Neandertals be obtained from the study of a fossil skull?

◆ The degree of basicranial flexion in the skull would provide an indication of language ability. A flat basicranium would suggest poor language ability; a fully arched basicranium would support the view that Neandertals were capable of speech.

However, the capability of Neandertals for speech would have been limited by their long tongue (suggested by study of fossil skull anatomy), which appeared to have rested entirely in the mouth rather than in the throat. Therefore, movement of the tongue in Neandertals could have only altered the volume of the mouth, not the pharynx. Stringer and Gamble suggest that the consequent single chamber acoustical system would have restricted Neandertals to slow and simple speech. There is some evidence that basicranial flexion was a feature of *H. heidelbergensis*. The relatively flat basicranium, seen in Neandertal skulls, suggests an unusual 'backward step' in evolution. It can be argued that while a relatively flat basicranium would limit the range of vowel sounds produced, nevertheless language would be possible.

A major problem with interpretation of fossil skulls is that their precise shape depends on how fragments of the skull were pieced together. If hundreds of small fragments had to be put together to make up a skull, then its final shape depends on the precise way in which the palaeoanthropologist put the pieces together. The original reconstruction of a well-known Neandertal fossil, the La Chapelle aux Saintes skull, indicated a flattened basicranium. However, David Frayer (University of Kansas) argues that a new reconstruction of the skull indicates a degree of basicranial flexion similar to that in Upper Palaeolithic and Mesolithic Human populations in Europe. The discovery of an intact **hyoid bone** in a partial skeleton of a Neandertal provided further evidence to fuel the debate. Baruch Arensburg of Tel Aviv University, found a hyoid bone in a partial skeleton excavated at Kebara. The hyoid bone lies between the root of the tongue and the larynx and has attachments for jaw, larynx and tongue muscles. As the Kebara hyoid bears a close resemblance to the hyoid of modern humans, Arensburg and his team argue that this suggests that Neandertals were capable of language to a similar degree as *Homo sapiens* (Arensburg *et al.*, 1989). However other researchers have countered Arensburg's view by pointing out that as pigs have a similar hyoid bone to modern humans, it cannot be concluded that possession of a human-like hyoid implies language ability (Lieberman, 1993). Although the basicranium of Neandertals is not flexed, Lieberman argues that Neandertal technology suggests that these hominins had some form of language. However the mere possession of a hyoid bone does not mean that an ancient hominin was capable of using language. Neandertals must have had a communication system and it was probably largely a vocal one, but the evidence from their way of life does not suggest a level of sophistication in communication that would be equivalent to *H. sapiens*.

10.3.4 *How the 'early' Neandertals lived*

Neandertals were meat-eaters and obtained their food by hunting and opportunistic scavenging. Sites where remains of early Neandertals and signs of their activities have been found are rare; they include caves, open sites and rock shelters.

La Cotte de Sainte Brelade in Jersey contains a sequence of Lower and Middle Palaeolithic deposits. Two heaps of large animal bones, mixed rhinoceros and mammoth, were found beneath a rock overhang in sediments dated at 180 000 years. The heaps of bones were interpreted by Katherine Scott (1980), as the result of hunting drives in which the animals were driven over the rock overhang deliberately by a group of Neandertal hunters (Stringer and Gamble, 1998). If this is a correct interpretation of the site, this implies a high degree of planning and co-operation within a group. Fossil remains of Neandertals found at La Cotte include just 13 teeth.

A large rock shelter at Bau de l'Aubesier, Vaucluse, France, contains a series of Pleistocene sedimentary deposits. The contents of three layers designated as H-1, I-2, I-3 and K-1 are of particular relevance (Lebel, *et al.*, 2001). Excavation of H1, the 55 cm thick uppermost layer, revealed many animal bones, Mousterian stone tools, wood charcoal and ash; some of the stone tools and animal bones were burnt. Layers I-2, I-3 and K-1, deeper in the stratigraphic sequence, contained hominid fossils identified as early Neandertal, and large quantities of fossil bones of large herbivores, and flint artefacts. The stone tool assemblages are Mousterian with high concentrations of side-scrapers, Levallois flakes and Levallois blades. The fossil animal bones include those of bear, *Ursus arctos*, horse, *Equus mosbachensis*, pig, *Dicerorhinus hemioechus*, rhinoceros, *Sus scrofa*, elk, *Cervus elaphus*, gazelle, *Dama dama*, Irish elk *Megaceros giganteus*, auroch, *Bos primigenius* and tahr, *Hemitragus cedrenis*. Forty-three percent of the bones were identified as *Equus* and 31% as *Bos*. No finds of carnivore bones are reported. The layers of sediments at Bau de l'Aubesier suggest repeated phases of occupation of the site rather than a long-term set-tlement, a typical behaviour deduced for Neandertals at other sites too.

The flints from layer H-1 were dated by thermoluminescence which provided a mean minimum age of $169\,000 \pm 17\,000$ years and a maximum age of $191\,000 \pm 15\,000$ years. **Biostratigraphic** indicators suggest a younger age. The Neandertal remains comprise a mandible (Figure 10.18), and an incisor and molar. Neither tooth shows signs of degenerative disease.

♦ Suggest how the incisor and molar were identified as Neandertal.

◆ The incisor would show the marked shovelling typical of Neandertals. The molar's roots would be taurondont typical of Neandertals (but not unique to them).

The Aubesier mandible has classic Neandertal features but shows clear evidence of disease. Nevertheless, the Neandertal retromolar space can be discerned, and there is no distinct chin. Much of the alveolar bone (the bone forming the tooth sockets) of the jaw is missing so the sockets for most of the teeth have disappeared. Sockets of the incisors are enlarged radially, typical damage associated with abscesses. A few teeth are present e.g. right canine and third premolar, but all that is left of these teeth are the surfaces of the roots. Therefore very few teeth, if any, could have been functional. Chewing food would have been difficult and very painful. An individual with such severely diseased and damaged jaw and teeth would have had great difficulty eating and in chewing food. Lebel and his colleagues suggest that members of the group helped the individual with the diseased jaw and teeth to survive. The individual must have been provided with a major share of the soft food from animal carcasses such as

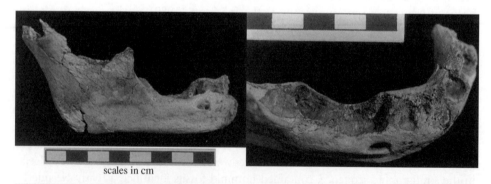

scales in cm

Figure 10.18   Mandible from Bau de l'Aubesier Neandertal (a) View from the right side (b) View from above showing alveolar resorption (bone in tooth sockets has been resorbed). Reproduced from Lebel, *et al.*, 2001 P11099.

the liver, brain, bone marrow and pancreas, and also given soft fruits. Meat may have been macerated or even cooked – layer H-1 at Bau de l'Aubesier consists of charcoal burnt bones and heated artefacts. However there is no evidence of hearths so we do not know to what extent fires were controlled and used for cooking.

Tools made of local rock, fossils of cave bears and Neandertal teeth from at least 5 and up to 15, individuals were found in Pontnewydd Cave in North Wales, in sediments dated at 225 kya. Stephen Aldhouse-Green interprets Pontnewydd as a site where bodies were cached but not actually buried (Petit, 2002). Whether Neandertals buried their dead deliberately has been a topic of hot dispute, which has not been resolved.

Signs of injuries and disease in Neandertal fossils indicate that the lifestyle of these hominids was hard and physically demanding. The Krapina Neandertals, dated at 135–130 000 years old consist of more than 850 fragmentary fossils from about 80 individuals. Their estimated ages at death range from about 16–24 years (See Johanson and Edgar, 2001). Some of the pieces of bone show signs of healed injury or signs of degenerative disease. For example, they include a healed broken arm bone, as well as bones bearing signs of osteoarthritis.

10.4 The emergence of modern *Homo sapiens*

Anatomically modern humans evolved towards the end of the Pleistocene epoch, and the final part of this chapter examines fossil, archaeological and genetic evidence that throws some light on the early evolutionary history of our species. We begin with a brief overview of African finds of skulls dating from 260–150 kyrs, with features suggesting they are close to modern humans. Our main focus on fossil finds includes the Herto skulls, discovered in Ethiopia, in 1997, and the Omo Kibish I cranium, discovered in 1967. The Herto skulls were discovered by Berhane Asfaw and excavated by a team of archaeologists led by Tim White (University of California, Berkeley).[14] Their finds are especially interesting, as they were discovered in sediment layers overlying those that had previously yielded a 1.0 million year old cranium and postcranial remains of *Homo erectus* (section 7.5.2). Yet deeper layers of sediment in the same locality had yielded fossil remains of *Australopithecus garhi* (Chapter 5).

The Omo Kibish I skull was discovered by Richard Leakey on the banks of the river Kibish in Ethiopia. Before we examine these and other finds, we need to understand the concepts behind the two major theories for the evolution of modern *Homo sapiens*.

10.4.1 *Out of Africa and Multiregional hypotheses*

In Chapter 7 (Box 7.1) you read about the 'single-species hypothesis' which claims, in essence, that there could only be one species with a tool-making culture at one time. The fact that there is clear evidence for more than one species of hominin being present at the same place and time falsified the hypothesis. Franz Weidenreich produced an argument for regional continuity in which he saw the *Homo erectus* species in Java as giving rise to aboriginal Australians, the Peking man fossils as giving rise to modern Chinese and, in Europe, Neandertals being ancestral to modern Europeans. His ideas influenced the development of the Multireigonal hypothesis for the origin of modern *Homo sapiens*. There are two major theories currently for the emergence of modern *Homo sapiens* known respectively as the 'Out of Africa' hypothesis, and the 'multiregional' hypothesis (Figure 10.19), which we compare in this section.

The roots of the 'Out of Africa' hypothesis may have originated in 1838, when Charles Darwin met an orangutan, Jenny, who was the first ape to be displayed at London Zoo. Jenny's human-like behaviour impressed Darwin, who subsequently hinted in 'The origin of species' that the principles of natural selection should be applied to human evolution too. Darwin, supported by Thomas Huxley's book, 'Evidence as to man's place in nature' suggested subsequently that the African apes have the closest evolutionary relationship to humans, with the Asian great apes being more distant. The evidence for this view was based mainly on anatomical studies; little fossil evidence was available at that time.

Darwin and Huxley's view was supported more than 100 years later in the 1960s by Louis Leakey's fossil finds in Africa which suggested to him that early and Middle Pleistocene hominids in Africa were likely to be the ancestors of *Homo sapiens*. Chris Stringer (Natural History Museum, London) developed such ideas further, drawing on fossil evidence accumulated not only from Africa but also from Europe, the Near East, the

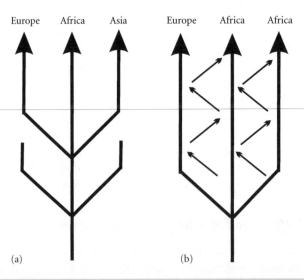

Figure 10.19 Hypotheses for the origin of modern humans (a) The 'Out of Africa' hypothesis proposes that modern humans evolved in Africa and then migrating populations replaced 'archaic' human populations all over the world. (b) The 'Multiregional Hypothesis' proposes that modern humans evolved at about the same time all over the Old World, and although there was gene flow between separate geographical regions, there were regional differences in detailed anatomy linked to features seen in local archaic populations.

Middle East, the Americas, Asia and Australasia. Stringer formulated the 'Out of Africa hypothesis', which states that modern humans evolved in Africa and that successive waves of migration of modern humans out of Africa resulted eventually in worldwide colonisation of our planet (Stringer and McKie, 1996). As modern humans moved into an area they displaced resident populations of archaic *Homo sapiens,* which became extinct. The theory does not rule out the possibility of limited hybridization of local archaic populations with incoming modern populations. We shall see in Chapter 11, that molecular biology studies indicate that modern *Homo sapiens* evolved around 150 000 years ago. If the Out of Africa theory is correct, we would expect to find the oldest fossils of modern humans in Africa, dated at around 150 000 years ago. Furthermore fossils with features transitional between those observed in archaic *Homo* and modern *Homo sapiens* would only be found in Africa. As modern humans were immigrants into areas such as the Near East, their anatomy will show clear differences from that of the local 'archaic' population.

In contrast, the multiregional hypothesis, developed mainly by Alan Thorne (Australian National University, Canberra) and Milford Wolpoff (University of Michigan) states that modern humans evolved at broadly the same times in a number of separate areas of the world during the Pleistocene. The theory assumes that there must have been sufficient contact between widespread populations to maintain gene flow. Fossils of local transitional forms, which may include hybrids of modern and archaic humans would be found over specific geographic areas. Within a particular area, there would be regional continuity of anatomical features, with local populations of modern humans showing similar features to those found in local archaic fossils. Supporters of the multiregional hypothesis claim to have identified regional continuity between archaic and modern human populations.

♦ Palaeoanthropologists working in Java have identified transitional fossil skulls which have a number of features found in both local modern human and archaic human fossils. What further information would be needed to support the view that the fossils could have been genuine transitional forms intermediate between local archaic and modern humans?

♦ The respective dates for the three sets of fossils are required. If the local modern human population was derived from a local archaic population then the archaic population should be older than the modern population, and the age of the transitional population should be between the dates for the archaic and modern fossils.

In the following sections, we examine fossil finds of *Homo* skulls from Africa dating from 260–130 kya; each provides evidence relevant for our investigation of the emergence of modern humans.

10.4.2 *Middle Pleistocene African Homo*

Fossil remains of *Homo* in Africa dating from the Middle Pleistocene are not all readily classified into species categories. The Florisbad (South Africa) skull was found in 1932 on the site of an ancient spring. Although the Florisbad skull, re-dated recently at 260 000 years old, is clearly *Homo* sp, it is not possible to identify the species conclusively from the available fragments, the cranium and part of the front of the face. Features that are similar to *Homo sapiens* include an evenly curved forehead; orbits that are set far apart, and teeth that are moderately sized. The cranium bears chew marks made by hyaenas and other bite marks suggest that the individual, or his/her remains were carried by a leopard. Stringer interprets the Florisbad remains as a possible early *sapiens*. The Singa calvaria, found in Sudan in 1924, is dated at 130 kya and shows a mixture of archaic and modern human features. The skull shows signs of disease, suggested by Spoor *et al.* (1998) to be possibly the result of an acoustic neuroma, a tumour of the nerve connecting the inner ear to the brain. The bony labyrinth on the right side of the skull is missing having been replaced by solid bone. Such a disease process would have caused disturbances in balance and an expanding acoustic neuroma would have put pressure on the brain causing headaches, facial numbness and mental confusion. The left side of the **temporal bone** contains a normal bony labyrinth similar in structure to that found in *Homo sapiens*. Other human-like features include a rounded skull, a high forehead and reduced brow ridges. Other African skulls interpreted as early *Homo sapiens* are not securely dated so our focus now is on two skulls considered to provide crucial evidence for the origin of *Homo sapiens* in Africa.

10.4.3 *Homo sapiens idaltu*

The earliest known fossils identified as *Homo sapiens* were discovered in 1997, close to the village of Herto in Ethiopia. Herto is located on the floor of the Afar Rift valley. The fossil remains of hominids, animal bones and stone artefacts were found in Pliocene Hatayae member sediments at the base of the Bouri formation. Fossils and artefacts were dated by application of the $^{40}Ar/^{39}Ar$ technique to layers of volcanic rock below and above and to **pumice** and **obsidian** in the same layer as the finds (Desmond Clark *et al.*, 2003). Dates obtained were between 160–150 kya, which is within the late Pleistocene. At this time Europe was in the grip of a full glacial, with thick ice sheets extending down to what is now the Midlands of Britain, Wales, Scandinavia, and northern Russia (Figure 9.3) Neandertals were living in Europe (but not Britain), and hunting large mammals typical of cold climates such as mammoth (Table 10.2). In contrast, the climate around Herto was warm and a large shallow freshwater lake there attracted animals, including *Kobus* (waterbuck), hippopotami and crocodiles. Grassland species were found there too including *Thryomys*, the grasscutter, *Equus*, horse and *Connochaetes*, wildebeest. The water contained abundant fish, including catfish. The hominid fossils include three skulls, two adult, BOU-VP-16/1 (Figure 10.20) and BOU-VP-16/2 and one juvenile BOU-VP-16/5 (White, *et al.*, 2003).

The exposed half of the skull, BOU-VP-16/1 was missing, presumably smashed into tiny pieces and scattered by the hooves of cattle and herbivores. Cranial capacity

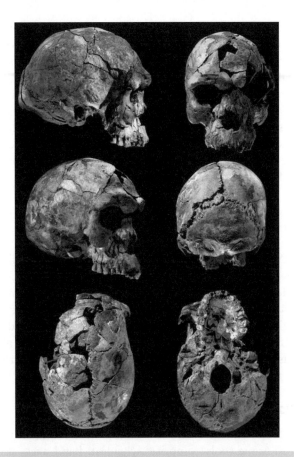

Figure 10.20 Reconstruction of Herto skull BOU-VP-16/1. Reprinted by permission from Macmillan Publishers Ltd: Nature (White *et al.*, 2003), copyright 2003.

of the intact half of the calvarium, estimated by filling it with teff seed, is 1450 cm³. The adult skulls are very large and robust in comparison to those of present-day modern humans, with the orbits and cheek bones relatively smaller (Figure 10.20). The crania and foreheads are tall. However comparison of the robusticity of the large cranium and its height, with the same measurements taken from several thousand human skulls from all over the world did not find any matches so for these features at least the Herto hominids are different from anatomically modern humans. The eyebrow ridges are reduced in comparison to those of Neandertals and *Homo heidelbergensis*. There is no occipital bun or suprainiac fossa. The mastoid processes are large and projecting, more so than in Neandertals or living humans. The zygomatic bones are robust around the infraorbital region. The face is broad with moderate prognathism below the nose. The mid-face nasal bones are narrow. The juvenile cranium is worn smooth, possibly by repeated handling and the back of the basicranium is broken away with the broken edge apparently polished. White *et al* interpret the anatomy of the Herto fossils as encompassing derived features not seen in *H. erectus* or *H. heidelbergensis*. There is no resemblance to Neandertals. As the Herto fossils are so similar to modern humans, White *et al* have classified them as a subspecies of modern humans designated *Homo sapiens idaltu* (idaltu means 'elder' in the Afar language).

White *et al.* conclude that the Herto fossils provide support for the Out of Africa hypothesis. They point out that the finds in and around the Awash valley indicate an evolutionary sequence that supports the emergence of humans in Africa. The sequence includes *Homo erectus*, the Daka cranium from the Middle Awash dated at 1.0 mya. Later members of the sequence include the 600 000 year old Bodo cranium, also found in the Middle Awash and finally the Herto crania.

◆ How does the anatomy of the Herto fossils provide evidence that supports the 'Out of Africa' hypothesis?

◆ The 'Out of Africa' hypothesis requires that the earliest fossils of anatomically modern humans should be found in Africa. This requirement is met by the anatomy of the Herto fossil remains, and the location, Ethiopia in which the fossils were found. Furthermore as a few of the features of the Herto skulls are not quite the same as those of modern humans, they may be regarded as a transitional form, which is very close to modern humans. Therefore as the oldest known such find which was discovered in Africa, the Herto fossils meet the criteria.

10.4.4 *Behaviour of Herto Homo*

Abundant stone tools and fossil animal remains were found in the same layers as the fossil remains. Stone tools comprise Acheulean hand axes, also Levallois tools including flakes and points suggesting that transition to Middle Stone Age technology was not yet complete. Most of the tools were made of fine-grained basalt; points and the few blades found were made of obsidian. Blades were rare making up just 1% of the tools found. Most of the scrapers were simple side scrapers; few were double-sided. Most of the scrapers had been retouched. Some of the scrapers resemble Aurignacian types found in Europe. The tools were used to catch and butcher large mammal prey especially hippopotami. Cut-marked fossil hippopotamus and bovine bones are common. Clark *et al.* (2003) describe an area in the sand layer immediately above the erosional surface where remains of several hippo calves and butchered adults were found.

The skulls bear cut and scrape marks suggesting post-mortem de-fleshing. BOU-VP-16/2 is a skull cap only that was re-constructed painstakingly from numerous fragments, many of which bore marks suggesting de-fleshing and superficial scratches, suggesting a repetitive scraping motion on the bone, not a feature found normally in bones that had been de-fleshed for meat. This skull lacks the bone around the foramen magnum and the broken edges are smooth and polished. The surfaces of the parietal bone are also polished. The juvenile cranium bears cut marks suggesting defleshing, probably by means of an obsidian flake edge. Post-mortem modification of human remains is indicated in later human cultures too, so the Herto fossils are not unique in this respect.

The largest skull of a male in his late 20s to 30s has more pronounced brow ridges and a longer cranium than that of most modern humans and has therefore been designated as *Homo sapiens idaltu.* It is suggested that the Herto skulls have some similarities to *Homo heidelbergensis* as well as having modern features. The Herto skulls appear to be intermediate between *heidelbergensis* and modern *Homo sapiens* and could well be the direct ancestors of modern *Homo sapiens.*

Evidence for the presence of modern humans can also be gleaned from tool technology. Modern humans are associated with stone blades and tools made from bone and ivory. Tools bearing the signature of modern humans, dated as contemporary with the most ancient modern human fossils have been found in Africa. For example bone harpoons dated at 90–160 000 years were found in Katanda, Zaire (section 7.6.3).

10.4.5 *Modern Homo sapiens*

The earliest known fossils of modern *Homo sapiens* were found in Ethiopia. Two *Homo sapiens* skulls, the Omo Kibish skulls, 1 and 2, were found on the banks of the river Kibish in Ethiopia in 1967 by Richard Leakey (Leakey, *et al.*, 1969). The bones were stained blue and brown after their long burial in the soil. The fossils were not found in layers close to volcanic rocks which made dating difficult, but samples of mollusc shells collected from the same layer in which the bones were found were dated by the uranium series technique, at 130 000 years old. Omo Kibish I has an expanded cranium with long curved parietal bones, a short broad face and a high straight forehead (Day, 1969). Reconstruction of the maxilla showed that the palate is typically U-shaped. The front of the mandible forms a well-defined chin. A break in the temporal bone prior to fossilization resulted in formation of a cast showing the shape of the structures of the middle ear, the cochlea and semicircular canals, showing a typical modern human structure. There are insufficient cranial remains for a reliable estimate of brain size, although it does appear that brain size is within the range for modern humans.

The finding of Omo Kibish I was of great importance as the date attributed to it doubled the known length of time for existence of modern humans. However in 2005 a re-dating of Omo Kibish was carried out using Ar/Ar dating from the relevant stratigraphic layers in the Kibish formation and the extraordinary date of 195 ± 5 kyr was obtained (McDougall *et al.*, 2005). The authors re-iterate the view that the Omo 1 and Omo II are the oldest known anatomically modern fossils.

10.5 Conclusion

The time range of 700 to 130 000 years ago is a complex period in human evolution. It is not easy to sort out the affinities of fossil specimens that are very rare but occur over a huge geographical range, and are generally fragmentary remains rather than complete skulls or skeletons. Although we can be fairly sure that all the species of hominid that were extant during this period belong to the genus *Homo*, the number of species is difficult to establish. At the start of the period, 700kya, *Homo ergaster* was probably extinct in Africa. *Homo erectus*, persisted in Asia and also in Africa .The radiation in the hominids that occurred after 1.0 mya produced *H. heidlebergenis* in Africa, which migrated to Europe. However, another view is that *H. antecessor* is the ancestor of *H. heidelbergensis* and that the African specimens of *H. heidelbergensis* represent a migration back into Africa from Europe. The origin of Neandertals and their ancestors are not known for certain. There are views that *Homo heidelbergensis* was the ancestor of Neandertals There is also debate over the extent to which the Neandertals are a natural grouping of a single species or whether there are more than one species in the group who share a common ancestor. In the next chapter we examine the behaviours and technology of *H. sapiens* and the spread of modern humans out of Africa.

10.6 Questions

Question 10.1

Summarise at least three of the selective advantages of increased brain size and complexity for *Homo*, using a set of bullet points. You will need to draw on material in Chapters 9 to 10 to complete your list. (*Learning outcome A1*)

Question 10.2

Sima de los Huesos, the 'pit of bones' is a small chamber lying at the bottom of a 15 metre deep shaft in the Sierra de Atapuerca. Fossil remains of at least 30 individual hominids have been found there and were dated by uranium series technique at 300–350 000 years old. Two complete calvaria, Cranium 4 and 5 respectively, provide a great deal of information about the skull anatomy of the hominids of the Sima de los Huesos. Their salient features are summarised in Table 10.3.

    a   Complete the columns for *Homo heidelbergensis* and Neandertals as far as possible using information from Chapter 10. There will be some blanks in your completed table so do not attempt to fill all the spaces. (*Learning outcome C4*)

    b   How many similarities can you identify between the Sima de los Huesos hominids and i) *Homo heidelbergensis*; ii) Neandertals? Do the similarities you have identified justify classifying the Sima de los Huesos crania as either *heidelbergensis* or Neandertals? Explain your reasoning. (*Learning outcome B2*)

    c   Suggest evolutionary relationships if any, between the three sets of fossil crania. (*Learning outcome A4*)

Table 10.3 Comparison of cranial features of Sima de los Huesos hominids, *Homo heidelbergensis* and Neandertals

Feature in crania from Sima de los Huesos 350–400 kya	Feature in crania of *Homo heidelbergensis* 600–125 kya	Feature in crania of Neandertals 240–30 kya
Crania 4 & 5: cranial capacities 1390 cm³ & 1125 cm³		
Slight sagittal keel on cranium		No sagittal keel
Double-arched brow ridge		
Crania high and rounded		
Crania broadest at the base		
Mastoid process prominent	Unknown	
Retromolar space on mandible		Retromolar space on mandible
Taurodont molars		
Occipital torus		Pronounced occipital bun
No true suprainiac fossa but pitted area present at back of occipital bone	Suprainiac fossa absent	
Middle of face pulled forward		Middle of face pulled forward

Question 10.3

Section 10.1 points out that there is much that we do not know about the lifestyle of *Homo heidelbergensis*. Drawing on fossil and artefactual evidence, and your understanding of primate social structure from Chapter 5, write a paragraph of no more than 250 words, suggesting features of the lifestyle of the Boxgrove *Homo heidelbergensis*, drawing on the evidence in section 10.1. Your main focus should be on social structure, and on how the hominids obtained their food. (*Learning outcomes B5 and C4*).

Question 10.4

What were the likely advantages for Neandertals of group living? Hint: Apply information about primate social structures from Chapters 2 and 3 to Neandertals. (*Learning outcome B5*).

References

An, Z. and Kun, H. C. (1989) New magnetostratigraphic dates of Lantian *Homo erectus. Quaternary research* **32**, 213–21.

Arensburg, B., Tillier, A. M., Vandermeersch, B., Duday, H. S., L A and Rak, Y. (1989). A Middle Palaeolithic human hyoid bone. *Nature* **338**, 758–60.

Arsuaga, J-L., Martiniz, I., Gracia, A., Carretero, J. M. and Carbonell, E. (1993) Three new human skulls from the Sima de los Huesos Middle Pleistocene Site in Sierra de Atapuerca site, Spain. *Nature* **362** 534–537

Clark, J. D., Beyene, Y., WoldeGabriel, G., Hart, W. K., Renne, P. R., Gilbert, H., Defleur, A., Suwa, G., Katoh, S., Ludwig, K. R., Boisserie, J-R., Asfaw, B. and White, T. D. (2003). Stratigraphic, chronological and behavioural contexts of Pleistocene *Homo sapiens* from Middle Awash, Ethiopia. *Nature* **423** 747–752

Conroy, G. C., Jolly, C. J., Cramer, D. and Kalb, J. E. (1978). Newly discovered fossil hominid skull from the Afar depression Ethiopia. *Nature* **276**, 67–70.

Conroy, G. C., Weber, G. W., Seidler, H., Recheis, W., Zur Nedden, D. and Mariam, J. H. (2000). Endocranial capacity of the Bodo cranium determined from three-dimensional computed tomography. *American Journal of Physical Anthropology* **113**, 111–118.

Coolidge, F. L. and Wynn, T. (2009) *The rise of Homo sapiens. The evolution of modern thinking.* Wiley-Blackwell.

Day, M. H., (1969). Omo human skeletal remains. *Nature* **222** 1140–1143

De Lumley, H. and de Lumley, M.-A. (1972). Découverte de restes humains anténéandertaliens datés au début de Riss a la Caune de l'Arago. *Tautavel, Pyrénées-Orientales* **Comptes rendus Academie de Sciences Paris, 272**.

Green, H. D., Stringer, C. B., Collcut, S. N., Currant, A. P., Huxtable, J., Schwartz, H. P., Debenham, N., Embleton, C., Bull, P., Molleson, T. I. and Bevins, R. E. (1981). Pontnewydd cave in Wales: a new middle Pleistocene hominid site. *Nature* **294** 707–713

Grün, R., Huang, P. H., Huang, W., McDermott, F., Stringer, C. B., Thorne, A. and Yan, G. (1998). ESR and U-series analyses of teeth from the palaeoanthropological site of Hexian, Anhui Province.China. *Journal of Human Evolution* **34**, 555–64.

Johansson, D. and Edgar, B. (2001) *From Lucy to Language.* Cassell paperbacks.

Leakey, R. E. F., Butzer, K. W., and Day, M. H. (1969). Early *Homo sapiens* from the Omo River region of southwest Ethiopia. *Nature* **222** 1132–1133

Lebel, S., Trinkaus, E., Faure, M., Fernandez, P., Guerin, C., Richter, D., Mercier, N., Valladas, H. and Wagner, G. (2001). Comparative morphology and paleobiology of Middle Pleistocene human remains from the Bau de l'Aubesier, Vaucluse, France. *Proceedings of the National Academy of Sciences of the United States of America* **98**, 11097–11102.

Lieberman, P. (1993) On the Kebara KMH Hyoid and Neanderthal speech. *Current Anthropology* **34**, 172–75.

MacDougall, I., Brown, F. H. and Fleagle, J. G. (2005). Stratigraphic placement and age of modern humans from Kibish, Ethiopia. *Nature* **433** 733–736

Mithen, S. (1998). *The Prehistory of the Mind.* London: Orion.

Pettit, P. (2002) When burial begins. *British Journal of Archaeology* **66** August

Pitts, M. and Roberts, M. (1998). *Fairweather Eden.* London: Arrow Books Ltd.

Ruff, C. (1993). Climatic adaptation and hominid evolution: the thermoregulatory imperative. *Evolutionary anthropology* 2.2 53–60

Schlanger, N. (1996). Understanding Levallois: lithic technology and cognitive archaeology. *Cambridge Archaelogical Journal* **6**.

Shen, G., Gao, X., Gao, B. and Granger, D. E. (2008). Age of Zhoukoudian *Homo erectus* determined with ^{26}Al/^{10}Be burial dating. *Nature* **458** 198 – 200

Soressi, M. (2005) Late Mousterian lithic technology: its implications for the pace of the emergence of behavioural modernity and the relationship between behavioural modernity and biological modernity. In *From Tools to Symbols* ed L Backwell and F d'Errico Witwatersrand University press Johannesburg.

Spoor, F., Stringer, C. and Zonneveld, F. (1998). Rare temporal bone pathology of the Singa calvaria from Sudan. *American Journal of Physical Anthropology* **107**, 41–50.

Stringer, C. and McKie, R. (1996). *African Exodus: the Origins of Modern Humanity.* Jonathan Cape.

Stringer, C. B. and Gamble, C. (1993). *In Search of the Neanderthals.* Thames and Hudson.

Tattersall, I. and Schwartz, J. H. (2000). *Extinct Humans.* Boulder Colorado: Westview Press.

Thieme, H. (1997). Lower Palaeolithic hunting spears from Germany. *Nature* **385**, 807.

White, T. D., Asfaw, B., DeGusta, D., Gibbert, H., Richards, G. D. and Suwa, G. a. H., F C. (2003). Pleistocene *Homo sapiens* from Middle Awash Ethiopia. *Nature* **423**, 742-747.

Woodward, A. S. (1921). A new cave man from Rhodesia, South Africa. *Nature* **108**, 371–72.

Wu, X., Schepartz, L., Falk, D. and Liu, W. (2006). Endocranial cast of Hexian *Homo erectus* from South China. *American Journal of Physical Anthropology* **130** 445–454

Yellen, J. E., Brooks, A. S., Cornelissen, E., Mehlman, M. J. and Stewart, K. (1995). A middle stone age worked bone industry from Katanda Upper Semlik Valley, Zaire. *Science* **268**, 553–536.

11

130 000 – 10 000 Years Ago
Homo sapiens Out of Africa

One view of this time period is that it was dominated by the proliferation and migration of modern *Homo sapiens* out of Africa. Following a successful migration out of Africa, modern humans dispersed, giving rise to populations of modem humans in the Middle East, Europe, Asia and Australasia and the Americas. This interpretation of the available evidence is known as the 'Out of Africa' hypothesis, and was suggested by Chris Stringer. An alternative theory for events over this time period, is the proposal that modern *H. sapiens* evolved in a number of different geographical areas, from local populations of archaic *Homo* species, with some gene flow between the regions. This is known as the multiregional hypothesis. Another model, a mixture of incoming modern human populations and local archaic humans, especially Neandertals, is propounded by Erik Trinkhaus. Fossil anatomy, study of tools and artwork, and accurate dating of fossils and artefacts, have provided critical evidence, which has been further enhanced by genetic studies. Inevitably the evidence can be interpreted in different ways.

11.1 Introduction

The mid-Pleistocene glaciation dating from 186 000–128 000 years ago had ended by 120 000 years ago, and the global climate was warming. The locations and dates of finds of modern human fossils and the associated technology and art work provide important evidence for the subsequent history of human migrations and technological innovation. The available evidence suggests that a group of modern humans migrated out of Africa about 60–80 kya and this successful migration was

The Emergence of Humans Patricia Ash and David Robinson
© 2010 John Wiley & Sons, Ltd

followed by a spread of modern humans to the Middle East, Europe, Asia, the Americas, Australasia and the Pacific Islands. This view links to the 'Out of Africa' hypothesis, which proposes that modern humans evolved in Africa (Section 10.4). Groups of modern humans leaving Africa would have come into contact with other species of *Homo* as they reached other continents. From fossil evidence we know that up to about 28 000 years ago, groups of modern humans coexisted with other hominids, sometimes known as 'archaic' *Homo* and including Neandertals in Europe, the Near East and western and central Asia, and *Homo erectus* in East Asia.

♦ Not all palaeoanthropologists interpret the fossil evidence as indicating that modern humans evolved in Africa. Outline the other main hypothesis proposed to explain the origin of modern *Homo sapiens*.

♦ The multiregional hypothesis proposes that modern *Homo sapiens* evolved in a number of different geographical areas from local populations of archaic *Homo*, such as Neandertals and *Homo erectus*, with limited gene flow between regions.

♦ How do supporters of the multiregional hypothesis interpret the fossil anatomy of *Homo* dated 120–30 000 years ago in the Middle East, Europe, Asia and Australasia.

♦ Archaic *Homo*, for example Neandertals and *Homo erectus*, evolved locally into modern humans and there was gene flow between the dispersed *Homo* populations. Therefore local populations of modern humans had some similar features to the local archaic *Homo*, especially in the skull anatomy.

As we shall see, fossil anatomy and accurate dating, together with study of artefacts such as stone tools and portable art, have provided valuable evidence that is used by both those supporting the 'Out of Africa Hypothesis' and those supporting a multiregional origin of modern humans.

Neandertals were living 120 000 years ago in southern Europe and the Middle East As we saw in Chapter 10, long cold periods of glaciation, including that stretching from 303 000–245 000 years ago would have shaped the evolution of the suite of features seen in Neandertal skeletons. These features are seen in Neandertals dated from around 200 000 years ago (Section 10.2) and persisted right up to their final extinction by about 27–28 000 years ago.

♦ What features of the Neandertal skeleton suggest that these hominids evolved over a long period in cold, even glacial climates?

♦ The short stocky body shape, and barrel chest, indicated by the post-cranial skeleton minimizes the surface area of the body exposed to cold ambient temperature. The large nasal cavity would warm the intake of cold air and also be a heat exchanger with warm exhaled air.

The skeletal anatomy of Neandertals means that their fossil remains can be distinguished from those of modern humans. Fossil remains of *Homo erectus* can also be distinguished from those of modern humans.

♦ What features of the skull of *Homo erectus* distinguish it from a modern human skull?

♦ The face of *Homo erectus* is characterized by clear eyebrow ridges, prognathism and lack of a forehead or chin. There is a sagittal keel, and the top of the skull is not domed like that of modern humans.

So study of fossil anatomy is essential for distinguishing *Homo* species, and has proved useful in identifying where there was coexistence of modern humans with archaic *Homo*. Technology and artwork have proved of crucial importance both in tracking migrations of modern humans and in gaining some understanding of early modern human behaviour and social structures.

11.2 The role of genetic studies

Recently genetic studies have complemented the fossil and artefactual evidence in tracing both the emergence and migration routes of early modern humans. Molecular geneticists can use samples taken from an extant population to trace all alleles of a specified gene down to a single ancestral copy shared by all members of a population. The ancestral copy is known as the most recent common ancestor, or **MRCA**. In this way an ancestral genotype, known as the **coalescent**, for the population is obtained. The **coalescence time** is defined as the time when that gene appeared in the population. In order to determine the coalescence time for a gene, a molecular clock based on mutation rate is used. So there will be different coalescence times for genes within a species, but some will be older than the species, others will be more recent and coincide within the time span of that species. Such studies have consistently resulted in dates of 100–200 000 years ago for the origin of modern humans.

Mitochondrial DNA (mtDNA) has proved useful for genetic studies. There is a ring of DNA comprising 16 569 base pairs located within the mitochondrial matrix (Figure 11.1). The ring DNA includes genes for most of the protein electron carriers in the electron transport chain, ribosomal and transfer RNAs, as well as a non-coding regulatory fragment of about 1100 base pairs of DNA, known as the control region.

The advantage of using mtDNA to trace human prehistory is that it is passed through the female line only, because after fertilization of the oocyte (egg cell), the sperm mitochondria are destroyed within the oocyte. Hence only mitochondria from the mother are passed on to her offspring. Rare cases of individuals having some paternal mtDNA as well as maternal mtDNA have been reported in the literature but these are interpreted as being caused by a breakdown in the normal processes of destruction of paternal mitochondria in the fertilized oocyte (egg cell). So researchers

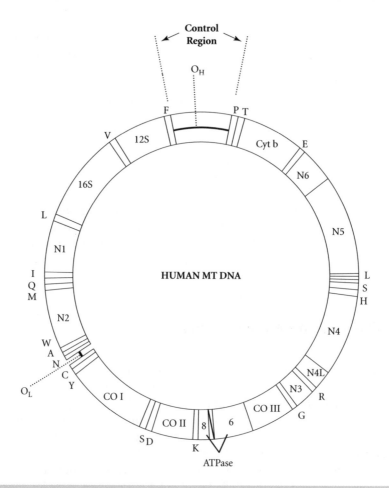

Figure 11.1 Sketch showing genome of human mtDNA Reproduced from Pakendorf and Stoneking, 2005 P166.

have likened mtDNA as being like a female 'surname' to be passed on to a woman's descendents. As mtDNA is present in all the mitochondria in most body cells, there are vast numbers of copies in an individual and many hundreds in individual cells. Therefore it is relatively easy to obtain samples of mtDNA from individuals and even feasible to obtain samples from suitable fossil bones. In most people the multiple copies of mtDNA are identical, so mtDNA does not undergo recombination during meiosis, except possibly in rare cases where paternal mtDNA is also present.

◆ Why is the lack of recombination in mtDNA so important for investigating the genetic history of human populations?

◆ The lack of recombination in mtDNA means that gene sequences are not re-shuffled and changes in gene sequence are due to mutation (Section 3.2.1.).

The mutation rate of a gene provides a molecular clock which can be used to trace the date of a particular mutant gene. Two DNA sequences in the control region of mtDNA, the D-loops, are the hypervariable regions, **HVR1** and **HVR2**, which are used in mtDNA analysis. Mutations in HVR1 and HVR2, occur at a relatively rapid rate, with estimates ranging from $0.075–1.463 \times 10^{-6}$ substitutions site^{-1} year^{-1}. Pakendorf and Stoneking (2005) quote an average mutation rate based on observations of mtDNA mutations in families and deep rooted pedigrees is 0.473×10^{-6} substitutions site^{-1} year^{-1}.

The calculated age for a population of modern humans, and dates for migrations to a particular region depend on the value selected for mutation rate, and so will vary according to the mutation rate that is used. To put it simply, the age of a mutation can be calculated from the number of mutations and the mutation rate.

Analysis of mtDNA is used to develop the history of mtDNA lineages which are known as **haplogroups**. Each haplogroup is itself defined by related groups of DNA sequences, defined as **haplotypes**, originating from shared mutations. Haplogroups tend to be specific to regions. The most ancient mtDNA lineage has been traced back to about 130 kya and the individual concerned named as '**Mitochondrial Eve**'. This does not mean that there was only one woman living at this time, although the population at that time was likely to have been quite small. Many of the women living in the ancestral population would have had offspring but only the daughters would be passing on their mtDNA to their offspring. Sons would not be passing on their mtDNA. So a family mtDNA lineage that produced sons only, or in which the daughters produced no surviving female offspring, would die out. As other lineages died out, only the descendants of mitochondrial Eve remained and survive today. The situation is similar to the loss of surnames in a European society – only male surnames are passed on to offspring but in families where a generation produces no male children, the surname will die out.

The earliest known mtDNA lineages are classified as L1 and are found only in Africa and also rarely, in Arabia and Mediterranean countries. Studies of mtDNA sequences indicate that maternal lineages of modern humans coalesce in a 'mitochondrial Eve' born in East or South Africa at least 130 kya.

◆ What is the significance of the date 130 kya in the context of the origin of modern *Homo sapiens*? (**Hint:** *Refer back to the modern human fossils described in Chapter 10.*)

◆ The date of 130 kya is similar to that attributed to the finds of fossils of *Homo sapiens* at Herto in Ethiopia. Dates obtained were between 160–150 kya, a time range within the late Pleistocene.

Evolutionary geneticists suggest that the population of breeding females was quite low, probably just a few thousand, around the time of the emergence of modern humans. It is helpful to imagine a scenario at this point. A woman living many tens of thousands of years ago around the time of the emergence of modern humans, may have had a high breeding success because she lived in an environment where food was plentiful, and she was very healthy. Her mtDNA would be passed on to all her offspring and her daughters and granddaughters in turn would be passing on the mtDNA to their offspring.

Many generations later some of the woman's descendents would have some mutant base sequences within the mtDNA forming one or more variants of the original mtDNA. The pattern can be represented by a star-like cluster although this isn't always the case, for example, if the ancient lineage has disappeared. In some cases, the star-like clusters have been used for dating and locating geographical areas of increased incidence and divergence of a specific mtDNA type. From this star-like cluster, the founder mtDNA type or types can be located and identified. Certain descendent types might increase in number; others might die out, and even the founder type may have disappeared.

Where a star-like tree is available and a founder mtDNA type is known, dates can be calculated for both the founder and the branches. The length of each branch represents its age measured as the number of mutations. So if the mutation rates are known, the numbers of mutant genes in mtDNA provide a molecular clock, but not all of the sequences in mtDNA behave like clocks so caution is needed in interpreting the star-like clusters. Where sequences do behave in a clock-like manner, dividing the number of mutations by the mutation rate provides a measure of the length of time the population have lived in a particular area. So the more mutations in the mtDNA, the longer the population have been in a particular area. The founder type of mtDNA may represent the ancestral type, the coalescent (Figure 11.2).

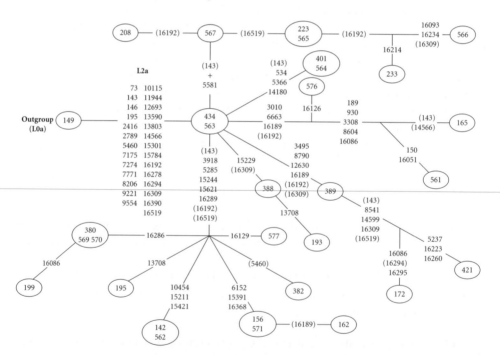

Figure 11.2   The numbers in this chart identify positions in the mtDNA sequences where mutations have occurred. Note how L0a, the initial mtDNA sequence, gives rise to L2a. In turn this ancestral node, marked by sequences 434 and 563, diverges into a total of 6 branches, forming two star-like clusters. Adapted from Howell *et al.*, (2004), P1851.

So phylogenetic comparisons rely on observed differences in mtDNA sequences and their timings. Forster (2004) points out that as so few ancient mtDNA lineages survive including L1 mtDNAs found in various parts of Africa, this suggests that the population of breeding females at the time of the origin of modern humans was small. The L1 mtDNAs gave rise to L1c, L1d, L1e, L1f and L1k, and eventually branched to L2 and L3 mtDNAs. (Figure 11.3). There is the most diversity of sub-haplogroups within Africa, supporting the view that the L1 coalescent is the most ancient.

Genetic studies using the Y chromosome have also yielded much useful information about human migrations. Recent research has identified the entire gene sequence within the Y chromosome. Y chromosome genetic variation has proved useful for tracking the evolution and migrations of modern humans. Half of the Y chromosome comprises tandem repeats of satellite DNA, and the rest comprises a few genes.

♦ What are the male and female genotypes in humans with respect to the sex chromosomes?

♦ Females do not have a Y chromosome, so the female genotype is *XX*. Males have one X chromosome and one Y chromosome, so the male genotype is *XY*.

As with mtDNA, a major advantage of using the gene sequences in the Y chromosome is that it does not undergo recombination.

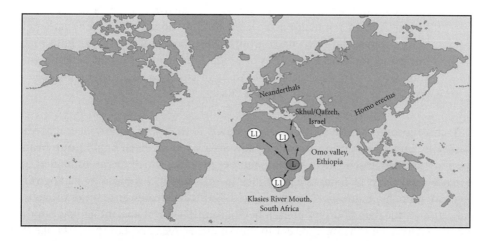

Figure 11.3 Expansion of ancient mtDNA lineages known in Africa in the period 200–100 kya. Reproduced with kind permission of Dr Peter Forster, Cambridge University. Forster, (2004) P258.

- Why is there no recombination involving the Y chromosome during meiosis?

- Recombination involves crossing over of genes between the two homologues of each chromosome. As there is only one Y chromosome in male cells, by definition recombination is not possible.

Recombination during meiosis causes reshuffling of the allele gene sequences. So the consequence of the lack of recombination is that the DNA sequence in the Y chromosome is usually passed on unchanged to the succeeding generation. Any changes in the DNA sequence are caused by mutations, and the consequent variations are themselves passed on to sons and their descendents.

Two types of variation in the Y chromosome are used for tracing human evolution and migration patterns.

- **Short tandem repeats, STRs**, of sequences of nucleotides. The number of repeats defines an allele and varies greatly between individuals. Each STR on a Y chromosome has a number that corresponds to the number of repeat. The number of repeats in a **Y-STR** may change after just a few generations so the variation rates of STRs are high. A specific set of a variant's Y-STRs provides an individual male's **haplotype**, which is present in a relatively small number of men. A few known large scale deletions have occurred in a Y-STR causing a big reduction in repeat number which is a unique change within a group of lineages. (e.g. this type of change distinguishes two sub-groups in **Y-DNA** haplogroup J).

- Y-specific **single nucleotide polymorphisms SNPs**. An SNP is a single change to just a single nucleotide. The significance of the low mutation rate for SNPs is that it is likely that all those males who have a specific SNP marker would have shared the same single mutation event which was inherited from the same common ancestor. Therefore detailed analyses of SNPs reflect the history of human populations. Specific combinations of SNPs are markers for both mtDNA and DNA haplogroups, which are used to analyze both matrilineal and patrilineal ancestries of modern humans organized as family trees. Haplogroups are essentially collections of closely related haplotypes that are grouped together according to Y-STRs.

Y chromosome haplogroups are designated A to R and subdivided according to specific mutations as appropriate by lower case letters. Each haplogroup bears a specific mutation, essentially a specific number of STRs, which has an estimated coalescence date. Table 11.1 shows a simplified list of some Y chromosome haplogroups; there are more haplogroups than those listed. Estimated coalescence times provide an indication of the date of origin of each haplogroup. The most ancient haplogroups are found in Africa, and the most recent in the Americas, Asia and Europe. Data like that in Table 11.1 is used to map migration patterns of modern humans out of Africa and to most parts of the world.

Table 11.1 Simplified summary of some examples of Y chromosome haplogroups and their distribution worldwide. (collated from [1]ISOGG and other sources).

Y Haplogroup	Defining mutation	[1]Location/s	Notes & examples of peoples with Y haplogroup
A	M91	Africa	[1]Dates from ~ 60 kya. Common in hunter gatherer groups in Ethiopia & Sudan e.g. Khoisan
B	M60	Africa	[1]Dates from ~ 50 kya. African pygmies; Sudanese; Ethiopians; central African pygmies
[1]Haplogroups with mutation M168 dated at about 55 kya.			
C	M216 M130	Arabian peninsula; India: SE Asia.	[1]C originated ~50kya
C3 Jobling& Tyler Smith[2]	M217	Central Asia; Siberia; Americas.	
C4	M327	Australia	[1]Unique to aborigines
D [3]Shi et al	M174	Central & SE Asia; Japan; Tibet; Mongolia; Andaman islands.	[1]DE haplogroup originated ~50kya in N Africa . D may represent earliest migration of modern humans to East Asia[3].
E [2]Jobling & Tyler Smith; Karafet et al	[4]M96 the most diverse haplogroup (Karafet et al)	Africa; Middle East; S Europe	Bantu
Groups with mutation M89			
F Jobling & Tyler Smith; Karafet et al	P14, M89	Indian subcontinent	[1]F may have appeared 80–60 kya. Parent of haplogroups G - T
G Jobling & Tyler Smith; Karafet et al	M201 P257	Mediterranean; Caucasus; Middle East; rare in Europe.	[1]Founder probably lived in Middle East about 30 kya.
H Jobling & Tyler Smith; Karafet et al	M69, M370	Indian subcontinent; Roma people in W Europe.	[1]Founder with M69 mutation probably lived in Indian subcontinent 40–30 kya
I [2]Jobling & Tyler Smith; Karafet et al	M170	NW, E Europe, Sardinia, Balkans Georgia; Turkey.	[1]Founder probably in Europe; split to 2 main subgroups from ~28kya
J1 [4]Karafet et al	M267	Middle & Near East: North Africa;	Iranians; Sudanese;
J2 [4]Karafet et al	M172	Central Asia; India Pakistan; Europe.	[1]J2 distribution may link to spread of Neolithic peoples.
Groups with mutation M9 40 000 years			

(Continued)

Table 11.1 Simplified summary of some examples of Y chromosome haplogroups and their distribution worldwide. (collated from [1]ISOGG and other sources).

K1-K4 [4]Karafet et al	So far no clear defining SNPs available	Africa; Australia; Eurasia; S Pacific.	[1]Origin ~40kya in SW Asia
L	M11 M20	[1]India; Pakistan; Mediterranean coast; Middle East;	
M Karafet et al	P256 M4	Papua New Guinea; E Indonesia.	[1]M is present in 33% males in Papua New Guinea
N	M231	China; Korea; Baltic regions; N Europe; Siberia.	[1]May originate from China & Mongolia
O	M175	Taiwan; Indonesia; Melanesia; Polynesia.	[1]Originated E Asia then spread to S Pacific
O2 Shi et al	P31	Japan; Korea; Indonesia.	
O3 [5]Shi et al	M122	China	[5]Northward migrations of M122 lineage 25-30 kya
Examples of groups with mutation M45			
P	M45		[1]Originated in central Asia ~35kya. P has 2 subclades, Q & R.
Q	M242	North Eurasia,; North America.	[1]Sub-group Q1a3a found in First Nation Americans
Examples of groups with mutation M207			
R	M207	NW Asia; Europe.	Originated in Asia ~27 kya
R1	M173	E & W Europe; W & central Asia.	[1]Originated in SW Asia ~18.5 kya
S	M230	Papua new Guinea	
T	M70	Middle East; Europe; N & W Africa.	

[1]International Society of Genetic Genealogy (2009) Y-DNA Haplogroup Tree 2009 version 2 December 2009 http://www.isogg.org/tree/ISOGG_HapgrpK09.html

[2]Jobling, M. A. and Tyler-Smith, C. (2003). The human Y chromosome: an evolutionary marker comes of age. *Nature Reviews* **4** 598–612.

[3] Shi, H., Zhong, H., Peng, Y., Dong, Y-L., Qi, X-B., Zhang, F., Liu, L-F., Tan, S-J., Ma, R. Z., Xiao, C-J., Wells, S., Jin, L. and Su, B. (2008). Y chromosome evidence of earliest modern human settlement in East Asia and multiple origins of Tibetan and Japanese populations. *BMC Biology* **6** 45–54.

[4]Karafet, T., Mendez, F. L., Meilerman, M. B., Underhill, P. A., Zegura, S. L. and Hammer, M. F. (2008). New binary polymorphisms reshape and increase resolution of the human Y chromosomal haplogroup tree. *Genome research.*

[5]Shi, H., Dong, Y-L., Wen, B., Xiao, C-J., Underhill, P. A., Shen, P-D., Chakraborty, R., Jin, L. and Su, B. (2005). Y chromosome evidence of southern origin of the East-Asian specific haplogroup, O3 M122. *American Journal of human genetics* **77** (3) 408–419.

11.3 Studying Artefacts

The third major line of evidence for studying the evolution and migration of modern humans is derived from artefacts. The relative scarcity of finds of art in Africa was interpreted by some palaeoanthropologists as indicating that the arrival of modern humans in Europe was followed by an explosion of symbolic expression and refinement of artistic skills, characteristic behaviours of modern humans. Some palaeoanthropologists support the hypothesis that the explosion of artistic ability in Europe 40 kya ago, derived from a spontaneous mutation causing a change in the neural organization of the human brain.

◆ Can the hypothesis that a spontaneous mutation caused a change in the neural organization of the human brain be tested? Explain your answer.

◆ As brains cannot be fossilized, and fossil endocasts of the brain provide only details of the surface of the brain (e.g. brain endocast of Taung child, Box 7.3.) details of neural organization cannot be distinguished. So we cannot tell whether there was a change in the brain of modern humans in Europe ~40 kya.

Nevertheless, the idea of a modern human behaviour persists and includes a number of distinct features. These include the use of bone, ivory and antler for making tools, and the creation of artwork such as cave art and carved artifacts of ivory or stone. Personal adornment is regarded as being characteristic of modern human behaviour too.

About 120 kya ago there were at least three species of *Homo*, including Neandertals, *Homo erectus*, and our own species. We will examine the fossil and the archaeological evidence for the migrations of modern humans and the development of modern human behaviour as we study the spread of modern humans over most of the world. Where available, evidence from genetic studies will be used to complement that from fossils and archaeology. For simplicity we examine each continent in turn, so each has its own timeline. The story is complex, as we also need to consider other *Homo* species that co-existed with modern *Homo sapiens*.

11.4 Modern *Homo sapiens* in Africa

Fossil anatomy, study of artefacts and genetic evidence together provide evidence for the origin of modern humans in Africa. In Chapter 10 we examined the oldest known fossils of modern humans, the Omo-Kibish skulls dated at about 130 kya years and the Herto skulls at 150–160 kya. Finds of more recently dated fossils of modern humans in South Africa include the skeletal fragments, four mandibles, and several pieces of cranium from Klasies River Mouth dated at 80–100 kya old. Modern human skull fragments discovered in Border cave, were dated at around 70–80 kya years old (Grun, Shackleton and Deacon, 1990). Seven human milk teeth dated at ~70 kya, were found at Blombos cave indicating that children, and therefore their adult parents were there in the Middle Stone Age (Grine and Henshilwood, 2002).

Evidence from artefacts and artwork, coupled with the development of reliable dating techniques supports the view of the onset of modern human behaviour up to 120 kya. In 1988 Alison Brooks (George Washington University), and John Yellen (National Science Foundation) discovered worked bone tools at a site at Katanda, by the Semliki river. They were exploring Middle Stone Age sediments dated then at 40–50 kya. In total they discovered seven carved barbed bone points, two unbarbed points and a large dagger-like tool (Figure 11.4), made from ribs or long bones of large mammals (Yellen *et al.*, 1995). The barbed points were made by cutting a row of barbs on one side of a bone point and cutting rings around its base so that it could be hafted to a wooden shaft, making a spear. Numerous mammal and fish bones were found in the same sediment layer as the bone tools, but adult catfish bones were particularly common. The evidence suggests that the people were catching catfish seasonally during the catfish spawning season. Catfish spawn in shallow rivers during the rainy season and the people at Katanda were likely to have planned their fishing accordingly. The Katanda bone tools are dated at about 80–120 Kya (Brooks *et al.*, 1995). One set of dates for the bone tools was obtained by applying the **thermoluminescence technique** to a sample from a layer of sand immediately above the tools. Another set of older dates was obtained by applying electron spin resonance to hippopotamus teeth discovered by the bone tools, but located about 50 cm deeper. The design of the harpoons is sophisticated and similar to Magdelenian harpoons dated between 18–10 kya old discovered in Tursac, in the Dordogne, France.

Detailed investigation of sediments in African caves that were used by people from 140–70 kya ago have provided much evidence about early modern human behaviour, and indicate that the early modern humans had much the same abilities as those living

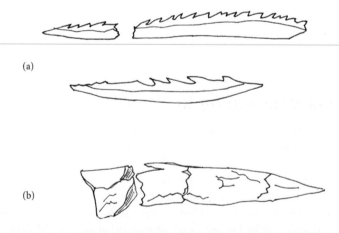

(a)

(b)

Figure 11.4   Discoveries at Katanda Zaire: (a) sketch of barbed bone harpoon; (b) sketch of bone point.
Drawings based on Yellen *et al.*, 1995 P555.

40 kya in Europe. Fossil remains of modern humans dating from 110–80 kya were found in the cave at Klasies River Mouth, Port Elizabeth (Grine *et al.*, 1998). Four mandibles and cranial fragments of *Homo sapiens* dated at 100–80 kya were discovered in sediments in the caves and cliff face. Scientific study of the site started in 1967–68 by Ronald Singer and John Wymer and continues currently. The sediments contain substantial deposits of stone tools and butchered animal bones. The oldest deposits dated at 110 kya include quartzite blades more than 100 mm in length, but deposits dated at 100 kya include shorter, wider flakes prepared by the Levallois technique. Short blades are typical of deposits dated at 70 kya and these are distinctive, having geometric shapes such as crescents. Bone tools are rare and are simple points or notched pieces. Hearths are common and they are simple hollows about 30 cm in diameter, containing burnt shells and bone fragments. Richard Milo's detailed study of 5400 animal bones from Klasies River Mouth identified clear signs of butchery including cut marks, and evidence of disarticulation of long bones, for example at hip and knee joints (Milo, 1998). Milo had also discovered the broken tip of a stone point in a bone of a giant buffalo.

Blombos cave located on the southern cape of South Africa, has revealed more aspects of modern human behaviour dating as far back as 100 kya. The cave is set back at about 100 m from the coast and 35 m above sea level and was used by people as recently as 290 years ago. The cave floor was covered by layers of deposited sediments ~4–5 m deep. Researchers led by Prof. Chris Henshilwood, (African Research Institute, Cape Town) are excavating the sediments systematically (Henshilwood, 2005).

Henshilwood's team have identified an upper Late Stone Age layer dating from ~2000 years ago underlain by a layer of compacted dune sand, a hiatus in the record. Below the hiatus are **Middle Stone Age**, MSA, layers. These MSA layers are divided into M1, M2 and M3 (Figure 11.5). The most recent layers, M1, dated at ~75 000 years ago, contain large numbers of bifacial points many with a point at both ends and resembling in shape Middle Palaeolithic bifacial blades. Double edged scrapers made of **silcrete** are found too, which suggest that the cave was a site where preparation of hides was carried out. The deeper layer, M2 dated from ~78 kya contains a lower density of bifacial silcrete tools, but more retouched quartz tools. Thirty bone tools were found at in M2 layers dated at 82 kya old (Figure 11.6). They include awls, and points which may have been hafted to use as spears or arrows. Manufacture of tools from bone and ivory is considered by some paleaoanthropologists to be a signature for modern human behaviour.

The oldest MSA layer dated at 140 kya old contains many lithics but no bifacial points. The re-touched tools have mostly denticulate or notched edges and most are made of quartz.

As well as hunting animals on land, the people at Blombos were fishing by about 120 Kya. More than 1200 fish bones were found in sediment layers in the cave dated from 75 to 120 ky old. Fish species identified from the bones are still found in the seas around the cave, for example, red stumpnose, White Sea catfish and kob. The people living in the Southern Cape may have lured fish close to shore by spreading bait, and then killed the fish with spears tipped with bone or stone points, many of which have been found in the cave sediments. Distinct basin-shaped hearths have also been

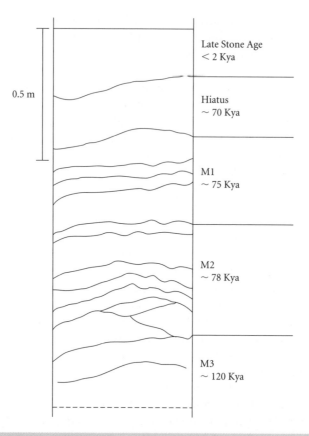

0.5 m

Late Stone Age
< 2 Kya

Hiatus
~ 70 Kya

M1
~ 75 Kya

M2
~ 78 Kya

M3
~ 120 Kya

Figure 11.5 Summary of Middle Stone Age layers M1, M2, and M3 in Blombos cave. M1 sediment layers include basin shaped hearths containing ash and carbon. Bifacial points, bone tools engraved ochre and shell beads were also found in this layer. M2 sediments contained few bifacial points. Bone tools, including awls and points were also found in these sediments. The M3 sediments contained a few bifacial stone points, as well as bone tools and many ochre pieces. (Drawn and adapted from Figure 2 Henshilwood (2005)

found, and burnt stones were dated at 77ky old. Bones of eland, rock hyrax, grysbok, tortoise and dune mole rat are found in LSA and MSA layers suggest that animals were trapped or hunted. Other bones found, seals, dolphin and whale, suggesting scavenging of beached whales, and possibly clubbing of seals. A shell midden in sediments about 140000 years old, contains limpet, brown mussel and turbo shells, indicating that the inhabitants of Blombos cave enjoyed eating molluscs as well as fish and meat.

Personal adornment was important to the people who used Blombos cave. Henshilwood's team discovered more than 8000 pieces of ochre in the MSA layers. Ochre has been used by modern humans for a long time for painting the body, and is still in use. Maasai men and women may paint their faces with ochre when preparing for ceremonies. Maasai men may also paint their braided hair with a red paste made

(ai)

(b)

(aii)

3 cm

1 cm

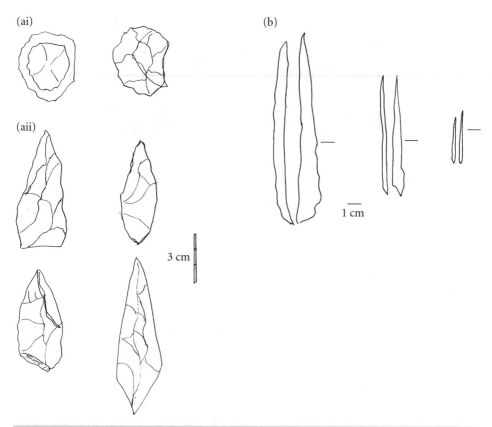

Figure 11.6 (a) Stone tools found at Blombos cave. ai) scrapers aii) bifacial points. Sketched from Figure 5 Henshilwood, 2005 P446. (b) Bone tools found at Blombos cave. (Drawn from Figure 8 Henshilwood C S, *et al.,* 2001 P647.

from ochre powder mixed with fat. So where pieces of ochre are found in cave sites known to have been used by early modern humans, the assumption is made that the ochre was used for body adornment. The importance of ochre for the people who used Blombos was highlighted by finds of crayon-shaped pieces of ochre with scratch marks, suggesting they had been used to make ochre powder (Figure 11.7). Two of the pieces were found close to hearths and were marked by cross hatched lines making a sequence of diamond shapes, with horizontal lines bisecting the shapes. These finds were dated by applying the thermoluminescence technique to burnt lithic samples which gave an age of 77 kya years.

One of the most exciting finds was 39 pierced shells of a small estuarine snail, the tick shell, *Nassaria*, in sediment dated at about 75 kya. The shells are all of similar size and were probably selected to be so. Tick shells are too small to eat, so it is likely that

Figure 11.7   A piece of ochre from Blombos cave with etched pattern.
Reproduced from Henshilwood *et al.*, 2002 P1279.

the Blombos people gathered the shells for making decorative beadwork, as people do now (d'Errico *et al.*, 2005).

♦ Suggest the significance in terms of modern human behaviour of the find of bone tools, decorative beadwork and carved ochre at Blombos cave.

♦ The dates of the artefacts found at Blombos cave show that personal adornment was established in Africa by about 80 kya.

Discoveries of beautiful and complex cave paintings in Europe from 1868–1923 had led archaeologists to conclude that there was an explosion of modern human behaviour co-inciding with the arrival of modern humans in Europe about 45 kya ago. The discoveries made by Henshilwood's team at Blombos cave demonstrate that people in Africa were using ochre and beadwork for body adornment by up to 100–74 kya.

It is tempting to interpret sites such as Klasies River Mouth and Blombos as base camps for modern human hunters. Lewis Binford (1984) had interpreted Klasies River Mouth as being an area where scavenged dead game derived from lion kills was dumped and processed with stone tools, so that it could be consumed by the hunters and their families. However he also suggested that smaller and juvenile animals were hunted and may have been partly consumed at the kill site.

♦ How does the evidence collected by Milo (1998) refute Binford's hypothesis that the people at Klasies River Mouth were scavenging carcasses left by large carnivores?

♦ Milo's study showed that many of the bones had been butchered with stone tools and that they showed little damage by carnivore teeth. Milo had also found the broken tip of a spear point in a giant buffalo bone.

Milo suggested that the people worked in groups to hunt and butcher the prey. He interprets Klasies River Mouth as a site where people gathered with their families to process meat, and eat. The hearths suggest a domestic scene where food was prepared and people sat around the fire eating. Ochre pencils found in the sediments suggest the people had time for body painting or other artwork. The artefacts found at Blombos cave suggest a similar use of a site where a group of people gathered many times to process meat, manufacture tools and make items for personal adornment, such as ochre crayons (Figure 11.7) and shell necklaces. The caves may not have provided permanent settled homes, but appear to have been used regularly as home bases.

Finds of ancient artwork in Africa are rare and up to the end of the twentieth century, the oldest known African cave art, dated at ~27 000 years old, was discovered in Apollo 11 cave, Namibia (Wendt, 1976). Charcoal and ochre drawings of animals including black rhino and zebra, were discovered on seven stone slabs found in sediments in the cave floor.

Genetic studies have complemented the evidence from fossils and artefacts. Analyses of mtDNA samples show that clades derived from L1 type mtDNA are found in Africa only today (Forster, 2004). Clade L1c is found in central and western African people, in particular in the Biaka people (West African pygmies). L1d and L1k occur in southern Africa in the Khiosan people (bushmen). L1e and L1f are typical of some East African people. This distribution pattern represents the initial spread of modern humans throughout Africa between 130–100 kya when there was a brief exodus to the near East which had petered out by about 100–90 kya (Section 11.2). This was followed by a major expansion from 60–80 kya (Figure 11.8).

By ~60 kya modern humans had migrated out of Africa and as far as is known, M and N haplogroups derived from L3 types gave rise to all non-Africans. Forster points out that we don't know if M and N mtDNA originated in Africa or after migration, but both M and N are found in Africa, and had reached the Arabian peninsula and

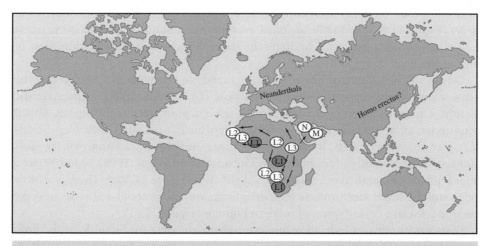

Figure 11.8 Distribution of clades of modern humans based on mtDNA analyses from 80–60 kya. Reproduced with kind permission of Dr Peter Forster, Cambridge University. Forster, (2004) P258.

Eastern Europe, India and Australia by 60–30 kya. Within Africa today there are many sub-haplogroups of the clades L0, L2, L3, L4 and L5, reflecting the ancient origin of the L lineage, with the date of the MRCA for L1 estimated at 100–170 kya.

The findings from studies of gene sequences in the Y chromosome support those from the mtDNA studies. The most ancient haplogroups, A and B, with coalescent dated at > 50 kya, are still found in Africa today, but they are rare. Type A YDNAs are found in the Khiosan, Ethiopian and Nilotes peoples, and type B in Pygmy and Hadze peoples. The picture is complicated though by more recent migrations, as haplogroup E Y chromosomes are prevalent in most of Africa. Haplogroup E was probably spread by Bantu-speaking iron workers from West Africa who travelled and settled all over the African continent around 2700 years ago (Jobling and Tyler-Smith, 2003). The picture is further complicated by ancient migrations back to Africa, which may explain the finding of haplogroup-R1b Y chromosomes in North Africa and northern Cameroon.

We now move on to investigate the migration of modern humans all over the world, including the Levantine, Europe, Central Asia, the Far East, South East Asia Australasia and the Americas. The picture is complicated so we can only examine a fraction of the evidence available.

11.5 Neandertals and modern *Homo sapiens* in Western Asia and Middle East

As we have seen, by 140–120 kya modern humans in Africa were using caves as shelter, probably sporadically, as these hunters moved on from site to site. At the same time, groups of modern humans spread northwards, with at least one group spreading out of Africa to the Middle East. There is evidence for this migration from fossil remains of modern humans with their stone tools at Mount Carmelin Israel.

In the 1930s, modern human fossils were found at Skhul cave Mount Carmel in Israel (Figure 11.9). The fossils included an adult male, Skhul V aged 30–40 years, as well as nine other adults and children. The skeletons had been buried deliberately in nine graves.

One of the skeletons was buried with the mandible of a wild boar enclosed in the arms, a find which suggests a symbolic purpose (Grün *et al.*, 2005), a characteristic feature of modern human behaviour. In the same deposit layer as the burials, 10000 Mousterian stone tools were found, which are usually associated with Neandertals (Chapter 10). Nevertheless, Johansson and Edgar interpret the anatomy of the skeletons as predominantly modern human (Johanson and Edgar, 1996). Skhul V has a high forehead, a rounded occipital and a slight chin (Figure 11.10a). There is a brow ridge and the lower face projects forwards. Brain volume is about 1518 cm^3, and the endocast reveals a brain typical of modern humans (Figure 11.11).

Post-cranial remains indicate a modern human anatomy for Skhul V, as the limb bones are long and slender.

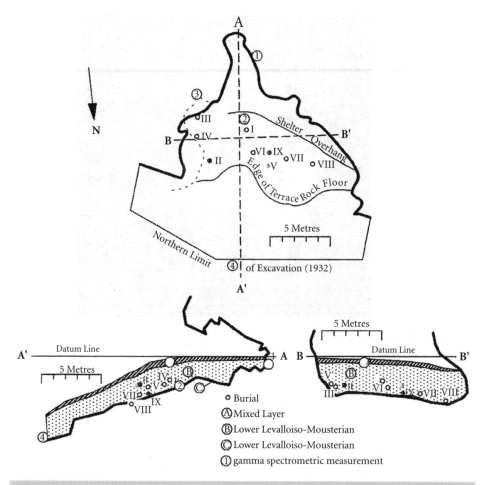

Figure 11.9 Sketch of Skhul Cave site and locations of burials.
Reproduced from Grun *et al.*, 2002 P317.

♦ Compare the features described for the Skhul skull and the post-cranial skeleton
of Neandertals.

♦ Neandertals were stocky and short and had thick limb bones. The bones of the legs
are thick and bowed. In contrast, Skhul V, has long slender limb bones. The
Neandertal skull has a distinct occipital bun whereas the modern human skull has
a rounded occipital. Neandertals have marked brow ridges, whereas those of Skhul
V are slight (Figure 11.10).

(a)

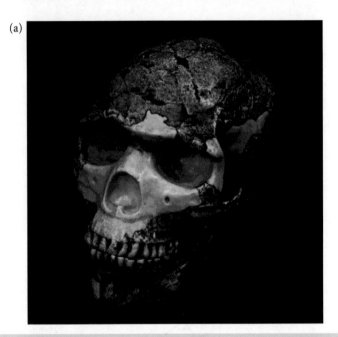

Figure 11.10   Cast of Skhul V skull.

Grun and others carried out new U-series and ESR analyses of the human fossil material from four of the Skhul burials, and concluded that 100–135000 years ago was a best estimate, assuming the bodies were all buried within a short time span (Grün *et al.*, 2005).

In 1969 partial skeletons of modern humans were found in deliberate burials in and around Qafzeh Cave Israel. The most complete skeleton, Qafzeh IX, was that of a young adult male (about 20 years old), dated at 92000 years by thermoluminescence and 120000 years by electron spin resonance (Valladas *et al.*, 1988). The Qafzeh IX skull (Figure 11.11), has a slight bony chin, a high flat forehead, a flat mid-face, much reduced brow ridges and a high flat-sided cranium (Tattersall and Schwartz, 2000). There is no retromolar gap, and a canine fossa is present. Brain volume was estimated at 1554 cm³, slightly larger than that of modern humans today.

Stone tools found at Qafzeh cave include Mousterian scrapers, disc cores and points made by the Levallois technique. The human fossils and artefacts were associated with bones of horse, fallow deer, gazelle, rhinoceros and auroch.

Palaeoanthropologists who support the multiregional hypothesis had interpreted features of the Qafzeh and Skhul skeletons as being intermediate between those of Neandertals and modern humans. For example the lower faces of both Qafzeh IX and Skhul V project forward. Although a chin is present, it is slight and Skhul V has brow ridges. In contrast those who support the 'Out of Africa' hypothesis focus on the features of the fossil skulls that are clearly those of modern humans. They also point

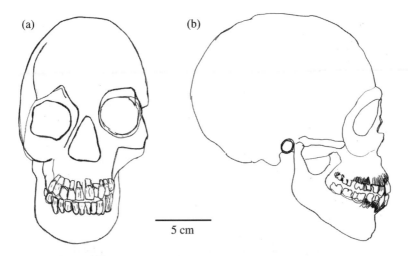

Figure 11.11 The Quafzeh skull. (a) Anterior view; (b) lateral view.

out that the remains of post-cranial skeletons from Qafzeh show similarities to modern human skeletons in that they are much more gracile than those of Neandertals. The long slender limb bones are characteristic modern humans adapted to warm climates (Chapter 10). Artefactual evidence of adornment suggests modern human behaviour too. Two shell beads were found at Skhul Cave in sediment layers dated at 100–135 000 years ago (Vanhaeren *et al.*, 2006).

Neandertal fossils were also found in Israel close to the sites where the modern human fossils were found. In 1932, fossil remains of a Neandertal woman were discovered by Dorothy Garrod in the Tabun cave on the edge of Mount Carmel. Different dating techniques have assigned varying dates to the skeleton, but a date of 120 000 years was indicated obtained by ESR analysis of a tooth (Grun and Stringer, 2000). This date suggests that the modern human and Neandertal populations were coexisting about 120–100 000 years ago. Previously the dates of 120–100 000 years for the Mount Carmel Neandertals and earlier estimates of 40 000 years BP for the Skhull and Qafzeh fossils had been used by supporters of the multiregional hypothesis for modern human origin as evidence for evolution of modern humans from Neandertals in the Near East. The dates were consistent with the view that modern humans in the Middle East evolved from the local population of Neandertals. However as we have seen, more recent dating studies put the dates of the modern humans at Skhull and Qafzeh much closer to 100–90 000 years (Table 11.2).

Other Neandertal remains found at Mount Carmel are dated more recently from about 48–70 kya ago. No indication of any modern human presence between about 48–90 kya ago has been found.

Table 11.2   The timelines for Neandertals and modern humans at Mount Carmel and Boker Tachtit

Time line	Dates obtained for fossils	
	Neandertals	Modern humans
140		
130		Skhul (Grün *et al.*, 2005)
120	Tabun (Grun and Stringer, 2000)	Skhul (Grün *et al.*, 2005) and Qafzeh (Grün *et al.*, 2005;
100		Valladas *et al.*, 1988)
90		
70		
60	Kebara (Schwartz *et al.*, 1989) Amud 7 (Valladas *et al.*, 1999)	
50	Amud 1 (Rink *et al.*, 2001)	Kebara (Bar-Yosef *et al.*, 1996) Boker-Tachtit (Gilead and Bar-Yosef, 1993)
40		Kebara (Bar-Yosef *et al.*, 1996)

♦ What can be concluded from the lack of evidence for the presence of modern humans around Mount Carmel from ~90–48 kya?

♦ The evidence suggests that the modern human population died out or migrated elsewhere, and was replaced by Neandertals.

In 1982, Bar-Josef discovered the skeleton of an adult male, Kebara 2, aged between 25 and 35 in an apparent burial in Kebara Cave. Kebara 2 was dated at about 48–60000 years old by application of the thermoluminescence technique to 38 burnt flints (Valladas *et al.*, 1987). This individual was unusually tall at 1.7 m. The skeleton is almost complete from the mandible down, and includes the pelvis, ribs and vertebrae. Kebara 2 is the only Neandertal skeleton so far discovered having an intact hyoid bone. This bone is embedded in cartilage that supports the larynx (voice box) and provides attachments for those throat muscles involved in speech. The Kebara 2 hyoid resembles that of modern humans in shape, which suggests that Neandertals were capable of speech. However, unlike in adult modern humans, the larynx of Neandertals is located relatively high up in the throat at a position more like that seen in young modern human children. For this reason, and others, palaeoanthropologists do not all agree that the presence of the hyoid bone in Neandertals indicates that they could speak. It has been argued that as modern human children with their elevated position of the larynx, are well capable of speaking, then Neandertals would have been capable too.

There was also disagreement about the interpretation of the thousands of Mousterian stone tools associated with the Qafzeh and Skhul fossils. One view linked to the multiregional hypothesis, is that the Qafzeh and Skhul people had evolved from the local Neandertals and were therefore still using Mousterian tools.

♦ Suggest an alternative interpretation of the finds of Mousterian tools associated with modern humans at Qafzeh and Skhul. (*Hint: Examine the tools discovered at Blombos cave (Figure* 1.6)).

♦ The similarities in stone tool assemblages derive from the use of traditional methodologies by a population of modern humans that had migrated to central Asia from Africa relatively soon after the origin of the species. Middle Stone Age technologies in Africa, for example Blombos cave, used variants of the Levallois method for tool making so inevitably these assemblages resemble Mousterian tools. For example at Blombos, bifacial points are found dated at 78 000 years old but not in layers dated 100–140 000 years, where tools with ventral flaking or notched edges are found, as well as denticulate scrapers. There are similarities between the African tools and those used by the people at Qafzeh and Skhul.

Klein *et al.* (2004), suggest that the similarities between the Mousterian tools and the MSA tools in Africa indicate that Neandertals and early modern humans may share a common African ancestor. The researchers also suggest that early LSA peoples moving northwards developed Upper Paleolithic technology and brought these skills with them when they expanded into the Near East. There is no evidence from genetic studies to suggest that the early modern humans who colonized the Near East about 120–100 kya left any descendents so the population appears to have died out.

Amud cave which is also in the Mount Carmel area, was occupied by Neandertals from about 70 to 55 kya. This cave is important because fossils of 15 Neandertal individuals and abundant Mousterian stone tools were found there as well as fossil remains of animals and plants. Amud 1 is the skeleton of an adult male, which has the largest brain size, 1740 cm³, so far measured in fossil hominins. There is also the skeleton of a 10-month-old baby, Amud 7, which may be a deliberate burial because of the apparent planned positioning of the baby's hands and feet and the placing of a red deer's upper jaw on the pelvis.

Fossils and archaeological evidence from Western Asia and the Middle East suggest that modern humans had returned to Western Asia and the Middle East by about 60 kya (Figure 11.3). Forster's review of the genetic evidence from mtDNA analysis suggests that there was an expansion of the modern human population in Africa from about 60–80 mya, which was followed by successful migration out of Africa. Forster points out that there are two views of how modern humans reached the Arabian peninsula and from there the Levant. Evidence from mtDNA analysis suggests that type L3 mtDNA is ancestral to all mtDNA genotypes. M and N genotypes are direct descendents of type L3 and they had reached the Arabian peninsula by about 60–80 kya. Modern humans had returned to the Levant by the late Middle Palaeolithic, about 30–60 kya, a time roughly spanning the late Middle Palaeolithic and the Early Upper Palaeolithic. Evidence from Late Middle to Upper Palaeolithic sites indicates that modern humans were using the Mediterranean coastal areas, the Galilee and Judean mountains as well as the Sinai, the Negev and Syrian deserts, and Jordan. The Levantine climate was quite dry during the transition between late Middle and early Upper Palaeolithic, spanning about 55–40 kya, but by 40–32 kya conditions were becoming more humid, especially in the Mediterranean zone (Gilead, 1998).

Interpretation of assemblages of animal bones and stone tools suggests that during the Middle and Upper Palaeolithic, the modern humans in the Levant were subsisting on all available resources (Gilead, 1998). Meat was a key resource and animal bones in both cave and open sites indicate the species that were used for meat. In the Mediterranean zone they included gazelle, deer, onager, horses, as well as tortoise, and large lizards. In Palaeolithic sites in Lebanon, about two thirds of the bones found are those of fallow deer. In contrast, in the drier areas of Galilee and Carmel, gazelle bones (*Dama mesopotamia*), are dominant. In marginal areas that had a dry climate in Palaeolithic times, fewer mammal bones were found in the sites but ostrich egg shell fragments are common.

From the 1930s to the 1950s various excavations of sedimentary deposits in cave sites in Israel and Palestine had revealed assemblages of stone tools and other artefacts as well as hearths and animal bones. Archaeologists classified these assemblages in terms of unique tool shapes which indicated the cultural history of the people who were using the area (Gilead, 1998). Researchers working in the 1930s to the 1950s had identified a transitional technology characterized by assemblages including high frequencies of Emireh points. More recently assemblages have been discovered in open air sites that were apparently occupied briefly, possibly seasonally. Boker Tachtit is an open air site in the Central Negev desert in Israel and sediments there date from about 47–33 kya. The deposits are about 7 m above the floor of a water channel. The discovery of the Boker Tachtit site and the subsequent excavation of the sediments revealed that initially the occupants produced mostly blades and Levallois points. More recent deposits contain longer blades produced from a single platform core and also a high frequency of Emireh points (Figure 11.12) supporting the view that these are

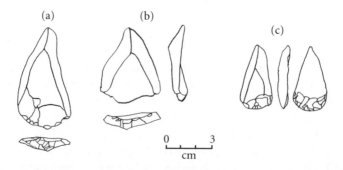

Figure 11.12 Sketches of projectile points from Israel: a) Levallois point (Qafzeh cave) b) Levallois point (Kebara) c) Emireh point (Boker Tachtit)
Reproduced from Shea, (2006) P831.

characteristic of the Middle to Upper Palaeolithic transition, which at Boker Tachtit appeared between 47 and 46 kya (Bar-Yosef *et al.*, 1996).

More examples of assemblages in open air sites are known including those in the Qadesh Barnea area in NE Sinai (Gilead and Bar-Yosef, 1993). The open air sites were apparently occupied briefly, possibly seasonally. The more recent discoveries demonstrated that assemblages of tools do not follow a sequential pattern with time, as there is frequent overlap between types of assemblages.

The picture is by no means simple as there appear to have been two types of early Upper Palaeolithic technologies in the Levant. Overall, the evidence supports the view that the Middle Palaeolithic local Levallois (Mousterian) technologies gave rise to the transitional assemblages characterized by Emireh points (Figure 11.12) which in turn developed into a local technology, known as Ahmarian. This is characterized by blank blades, core blades and backed blades and bladelets. Ahmarian sites include the open air sites of Gebel Maghara and Kadesh Barnea.

The other Upper Palaeolithic assemblages known as the Levantine Aurignacian may have been brought into the Levant by incoming groups of modern humans descended from a population that was also spreading into Europe (Gilead, 1998). Excavations at Kebara Cave revealed Ahmarian artefacts dated at 43–36 kya and Levantine Aurignacian artefacts dated from 36–32 kya (Bar-Yosef *et al.*, 1996), suggesting that incoming modern humans moved into the cave about 36 kya. The Levantine Aurignacian is characterized by burins and endscrapers, and very few blades. There is agreement among some palaeoanthropologists that the Levantine Aurignacian technology was brought in by groups of modern humans from possibly Europe or Asia.

Upper Palaeolithic sites are abundant elsewhere in the Levant, and were studied extensively when political circumstances allowed. Marcel Otte (Liege University) and his colleagues have studied Upper Palaeolithic sites in Iran, for example Yafteh cave, which contains Aurignacian sediments >2 m deep. An excavation of a previously undisturbed part of the sediment layers was carried out in 2005 (Otte *et al.*, 2007). Up to 2007 the deepest sediment layer dated by the researchers was 240 cm deep and dated at $35\,450 \pm 600$ years. Work was still in progress in 2007 with deeper layers being dated.

The flint tools at Yafteh are made from river cobbles and also from fine-grained flints obtained from distant sources as yet unknown suggesting that these flints were traded. Some of these are unfinished. Other indications of trade are perforated marine shells, which may have been transported from the Persian Gulf, 350 km from Yafteh. The stone tools are dominated by bladelets, which make up 48% of the lithics so far found. There are also typical Aurignacian blades and endscrapers on some retouched blades, as well as burins, some of these being carinated or keeled. Bone tools were also found, including awls, piercers, and remarkably, part of the end of a **sagaie** (spear).

◆ What were the following tools used for?

   i) Burins and (ii) Scrapers

◆ A burin is a tool that is used for engraving or cutting materials such as wood, antler and bone. Scrapers were used for cleaning and preparing hide.

Ochre appeared to have been spread over the cave floor surface and in some places this layer was 20 cm thick. Items used for personal adornment included two perforated deer canines, two perforated shells, and a haematite pendant carved to resemble a canine tooth. The perforated marine shells suggested trading activity, because the closest location that the shells could have been obtained was the Persian Gulf, 350 km away. Bones of small animals found at Yafteh Cave were 96% rabbit and 4% gazelle. Larger prey included mostly goats, some sheep and very few pigs. Most bones were fragmented probably due to trampling, and many were burnt.

Otte proposes that the high density of Aurignacian sites in Iran suggest that the vast area of central Asia stretching from the Caucasus to Afghanistan was a centre for the spreading of Aurignacian culture to Eurasia and the Levant (Otte *et al.*, 2007). This is an intriguing idea. Modern humans originating from Africa could have travelled to Europe via the Middle East. Once in the Middle East and Europe, modern humans would have encountered local groups of Neandertals.

11.6 Neandertals and modern *Homo sapiens* in Europe

Neandertals were living in southern Europe, and the Middle East 120 kya. As we saw in Chapter 10, long cold periods of glaciation, including that stretching from 303 to 245 kya are likely to have shaped the evolution of the suite of features seen in Neandertal skeletons. These features are seen in Neandertals dated from around 200 kya (Section 10.2) and persisted right up to their final extinction about 27–28 kya.

◆ What features of the Neandertal skeleton suggest that these hominids evolved over a long period in cold, even glacial climates?

◆ The short stocky body shape, and barrel chest, indicated by the post-cranial skeleton minimizes the surface area of the body exposed to cold ambient temperature. The large nasal cavity would warm the intake of cold air and also be a heat exchanger with warm exhaled air.

The suite of Neandertal features means that their fossil remains can be distinguished from those of modern humans. Fossil evidence indicates that Neandertals were driven south by successive glaciations, and that these hominids migrated northwards as the ice sheets melted. There were two cold periods or glaciations that affected populations of hominids in Europe from 120 kya, one lasting from 70 kya to 59 kya and the most recent from about 26 kya to 13 kya.

From about 75 kya the climate had cooled and herds of bison and reindeer inhabited Europe and the Near East. As the climate warmed, Neandertals moved northwards and had returned to northern Europe by 60 kya. There are numerous sites in Europe where Neandertal fossils and/or Mousterian artefacts and assemblages of animal bones have been found. Discoveries of accumulations of animal bones, plant remains and Mousterian tools at Lynford Quarry in Norfolk show that Neandertals were in Britain by 60 kya. One of the earliest discoveries was the find in 1829 of a partial infant cranium at Awir cave II near Engis in Belgium, but the cranium was not recognized as a different *Homo* species. Lt Edmund Flint made another early discovery of a Neandertal skull (Figure 1.1) at Forbes Quarry in Gibraltar in 1848, but again the skull was not recognized as a different species of *Homo*. Unfortunately, as the provenance of the skull is unknown it cannot be dated precisely.

♦ Suggest a dating method that could be used on the Forbes Quarry skull.

♦ Coupled ESR/**Uranium series** dating on a fragment of tooth enamel (see Section 2.5) and also direct gamma ray dating.

The first Neandertal fossils to be recognized as a separate species of *Homo* were those found by limestone miners in 1856 in the Feldhofer Grotto above the Neander Valley Germany. A local schoolteacher, Carl Fuhlrott, realized that the bones were not those of a cave bear and collected a calotte and 15 bones from the miners. In 1864 William King designated the fossils as the holotype specimen for *Homo neanderthalensis*, Neandertal 1. Unfortunately the site was excavated extensively, with clay deposits being removed and thrown on to the valley floor, so much information and fossil fragments were lost. As the cave and its sequence of sediments were destroyed, dating of the Neandertal fossils was impossible. Fortunately some of the sediments were rediscovered by Schmitz and Thissen (Schmitz *et al.*, 2002). The researchers subsequently excavated the sediment spoil heap further and found more fossil bone fragments and Middle Palaeolithic artefacts. Two of the cranial bone fragments were found to fit precisely into holes in the Neandertal 1 calotte. Schmitz and colleagues applied Accelerator Mass Spectrometry (AMS) radiocarbon technique to the new bone fragments and obtained dates centred around 40 kya.

In 1886 M. de Puydt and Maximin Lohest discovered fossil skeletons of two adult Neandertals in the grotto Spy located on the bank of the river Orneau in Belgium. The fossils were associated with Mousterian tools and animal bones. The fossils were dated recently (2008) by the radiocarbon (^{14}C) technique to 36 000 years old (Semal *et al.*, 2009).

Neandertals were still living in Europe when modern humans arrived in Eastern and Western Europe by about 40 000 years ago, bringing new technology known as Aurignacian. Both Neandertals and modern humans were subsisting as hunter-gatherers and it is possible that the two species were competing for the same food resources, and the shelter provided by caves and overhanging rock formations. The interpretation of evidence from Middle and Upper Palaeolithic sites is often the subject of disagreement between palaeoanthropologists.

Anikovich and his group described their findings at the archaeological site of Kostenki (Don River, Russia), where they investigated sediment layers dated at 45–40 kya (Anikovich *et al.*, 2007). These layers underlie a layer of volcanic ash dated at 41–38 500 years ago (the Campanian Ignimbrite, C1 **tephra**). The layers beneath the C1 tephra contain typical Aurignacian artefacts including end scrapers bladelets, blade cores, burins and small bifaces (Figure 11.13). Most of the stone tools were made from

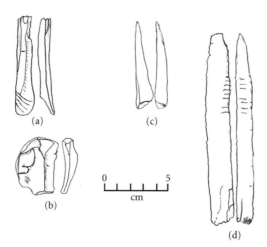

Figure 11.13   Examples of Aurignacian tools and other artefacts found in the lowest Upper Palaeolithic sediment layer at Kostenki. (a)burin, (b) blade core, (c) bone awl and (d) bone point. Drawings based on Anikovich, et al., (2007). Science 315 P225.

stone brought in from sources 100–150 km distant. Bone points, awls, antler mattocks and worked ivory were found. Perforated shells found at the site that would have been items of personal adornment could only have been brought in from the Black Sea, 500 km distant. So overall this is an Aurignacian assemblage dated at 42–40 kya discovered in Eastern Europe. Animal bones found in the sediments included those of hare, Arctic fox, wolf and birds, and less commonly, reindeer and horse. In addition, the sediment layers beneath the C1 tephra also contained some Middle Palaeolithic assemblages characterized by side scrapers and bifaces, and made from local stone. These assemblages do not contain ivory and bone tools, and they may have been produced by local Neandertals.

Anikovch interprets the artefactual evidence as indicating an abrupt change from a local Middle Palaeolithic industry to an Aurignacian technology brought in by modern humans moving into the central East European Plain. However, John Hawks (University of Wisconsin, Madison), is sceptical about Anikovich's interpretation, which is based on the date for the C1 tephra. **Tephra** is the name for airborne ejecta from an erupting volcano, for example ash falls, bombs.

Other disagreements in interpretation relate to the origin of modern humans. In 2002 a robust modern human mandible was found by three cavers in Pestera cu Oase, a cave in Romania. The mandible, Oase 1 was dated by accelerator mass spectrometry ^{14}C to 34–36 000 ^{14}C years old, equivalent to 40.5 kya and so was described as the oldest modern human skull in Europe. Oase 1 was an adult, with unusually large molar teeth, a feature of archaic humans such as Neandertals. By 2005, fragments of an early modern human cranium found in the cave had been sorted and joined successfully to make up a cranium, Oase 2. This individual was probably about 15 years old judging from tooth development – the third molars (M3) were still within their crypts (Rougier, et al. 2007). In contrast Oase 1 had fully erupted third molars.

Oase 2 has derived features of a modern human including lack of eyebrow ridges, prominent canine fossae, narrow nasal aperture, anteriorly oriented cheek bones and a high neurocranium, with no occipital bun. There is no suprainiac fossa or nuchal torus (a prominent attachment site at the back of the Neandertal skull for neck muscles). Archaic human (Neandertal) features include a flat frontal arc (flat forehead) and very large molars that increase in size from the back to the front of the mouth. The ramus of the mandible is much wider than would be expected in a modern human. So the researchers interpret the skull as being 'modern' in having a suite of derived modern human traits but point out that the skull does have some archaic features. The authors suggest that the skull could represent one of the variants within a diverse Middle Palaeolithic early modern human population. They also suggest that Oase 2 may be the result of admixture with Neandertal populations as modern humans moved into Eurasia. However, this suggestion is not supported by the genetic data, which we explore later in this section.

We leave the central Russian plain and Eastern Europe at this point and move into Western Europe. The earliest modern humans moving into Western Europe are known as Cro-Magnons, named after the rock shelter in France where Louis Lartet discovered them in 1868. The fossils comprise four adult skeletons and one infant and are dated at about 32–30 000 years old. Animal shells and teeth found with the fossils suggested deliberate burial. Cro-Magnon 1 is the skeleton of a middle-aged man with pitted facial bones, indicating a fungal infection. The Cro-Magnon people brought a distinct Upper Palaeolithic industry to Europe, known as Aurignacian and characterized by bladelets and long blades struck from pre-prepared cylindrical stone cores (Figure 11.14).

Carinated and nosed scrapers are also characteristic. Bone, antler and ivory points were made as well as portable art, and beads. The relative proportions of the types of artefact vary from site to site. Cave sites containing Aurignacian artefacts are found all over Europe, including France, Spain and Eastern Europe. Riparo Mochi, one of the Grimaldi caves in Italy contains sediments dated at 35 000 years which contain Aurignacian artefacts, including shell ornaments and bladelets (Kuhn and Stiner, 1998). The bladelets were made of flint obtained from sources up to 200 km away. The pace of change in stone tool technology and art in Europe from 35–11 kya led to a range of characteristic styles of tool technologies and artwork of increasing complexity (Table 11.3).

The concept of modern human behaviour was defined by specific signatures linked to artefactual evidence, and in turn this led to the view that there was rapid development of human cognitive ability about 45–40 000 years ago. Examples of ancient art and decorative body adornment, both signatures of modern human behaviour, were first discovered in Europe. Modern human skulls dated at ~30 000 years old, as well as pendants made of pierced shells and teeth, were discovered in 1868 at the Cro-Magnon rock shelter in Les Eyzies, France. Chauvet Cave at Pont d'Arc in France was discovered in 1994, and the art there is dated at 32 410 years. There are paintings of

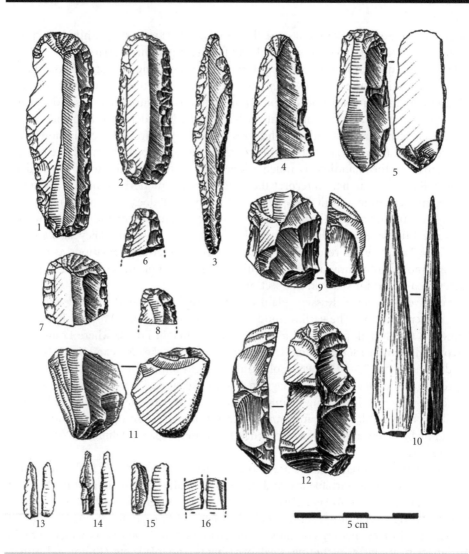

Figure 11.14 Examples of Aurgnacian tools discovered at the Grotte des Fees at Chatelperron, France. Key: 1-8 retouched Aurignacian blades; 9 and 12 carinated (keeled) end scrapers; 10antler or bone point; 11) bladelet core; 13-16 bladelets. Reproduced from Gravina, et al., (2005) P53.

hyaena and leopard, as well as mammoth, reindeer, bison. A finger tracing of an owl was made in the soft outer layer of the cave wall.

However, the recent discoveries of artefacts in Africa have demonstrated that modern humans in Africa from about 120–100 kya showed similar patterns of skills and behaviours as the Cro-Magnon people and their descendents in Europe about 40–30 kya.

Pendants of pierced shells discovered at Blombos cave and dated at abut 80 kya, are similar in concept to the pierced shell and tooth discovered in the Cro-Magnon rock shelter, dated at about 30 kya. Evidence for the use of ochre for body painting

Table 11.3 Summary of technologies and art work in Europe

Date range/years	Name	Examples	Sites
35 000–30 000	Aurignacian	Blades; bone points burins; pendants; mammoth ivory Vogelherd horse; cave art	France: Chauvet cave; Cro-magnon rock shelter; Germany Vogelherd Cave
30 000–22 000	Gravettian	Cave art; burials with ochre and pierced shell ornaments	Portugal: Lago do Lager Velho (Duarte *et al.*, 1999); Wales: Paviland (Aldhouse-Green, 1998); France: Pech-Merle (Walter and Aubrey, 2001)
22 000–18 000	Solutrean	Laurel leaf blades; cave art	France Abri-Pataud rock shelter; Pech-Merle cave; Les Maitreux (Walter and Aubrey, 2001)
18 000–11 000	Magdalenian	Cave art; complex carvings, for example le bison se lechant	France: Lascaux cave; L'abri de la Madelaine

discovered at Blombos cave indicates that body painting was established in modern humans in Africa by about 100–70 kya. A number of ochre crayons decorated with etched patterns were also found at Blombos in sediments dated at 70–78 kya The use of bone tools including awls and points was established at Blombos by about 100 kya. Other African finds include the crafted bone harpoons dated at 80–120 kya which were found at Katanda in Africa.

As far as is known, Neandertals never achieved the artistic skills demonstrated in cave sites such as Chauvet and Les Eyzies, or skills for designing and making items for personal adornment. However, late Neandertals in western France and northern Spain are associated with a new technology named Chatelperronian after the discovery site, in the Grotte des Fees de Chatelperron in east-central France. This technology is characterized by points, blades and knives, as well as Mousterian technology, scrapers on flakes, and denticulate flakes (Figure 11.15).

The blades are slender and more than twice as long as wide, like those made by modern humans in Africa 70 000 years ago. After the discovery of the cave in the 1840s, excavations of the sediments and collection of artefacts removed most of the deposits in the centre of the cave without any recording of the sediment layers. Later excavations by Henri Delporte from 1951–55 were carried out with care and identified at least eight levels. The bottom three layers of deposits contained Mousterian artefacts including bifaces. The upper five layers contained Chatelperronian artefacts. Gravina noted that the Chatelperronian tools were made from poor quality brown flint obtained from a site 14 km northeast of the

0   cm   5

Figure 11.15   Examples of Chatelperronian stone tools. From left to right: Top row: point; backed knife; scraper Bottom row: Convergent scraper; burin (Reproduced from Lewin, 1999, page 159).

2 cm

Figure 11.16   Perforated animal teeth from Grotte des Fees, France: (a) fox canine; (b) feline canine Reproduced from (Gravina, Mellars and Ramsey, 2005), P54.

cave (Gravina, Mellars and Ramsey, 2005). The Chatelperronian layers, contained Aurignacian tools including blades, bladelets and scrapers made of either high quality Chalcedony flint sourced from at least 100 km to the north or from local high quality flint. Two beads, perforated canine teeth, respectively fox and feline were also found (Figure 11.16).

Table 11.4 Results of accelerator mass spectrometry dating of sediment layers at the Grotte des Fees de Chatelperron

Layer	Date/years	Aurignacian or Chatelperronian	Rock type used for tool making
B5	$40\,650 \pm 600$–$39\,150 \pm 600$	Chatelperronian	Most made of local poor quality brown flint
B4	$39\,780 \pm 350$–$35\,540 \pm 280$	Aurignacian	Most made of high quality local flint and Chalcedony flint from 100 km away
B3–B1	$36\,340 \pm 320$–$34\,550 \pm 550$	Chatelperronian	Most made of local poor quality brown flint

Source: Adapted from Gravina, Mellars and Ramsey, 2005).

The way the perforations were carried out is typical of Aurignacian beads found elsewhere in that first the tooth root was scraped to thin it and then a hole was bored. Gravina *et al.* interpret these finds as interstratification of Neandertal and modern human occupations, resulting from intermittent use of the cave by Neandertals and modern humans. Collagen from fossil animal bone samples collected in three sediment layers (stored at the National Museum of Antiquities at St Germain-en-Laye), were subjected to dating using Accelerator Mass Spectroscopy (Table 11.4) Layer B4, containing Aurignacian artefacts, and dated at 39 750 – 35 540 years was sandwiched between two layers containing Chatelperronian artefacts, B3 – B1 dated at 36 340 -34 550 years and B5 dated at 40 650 – 39150 years. The dates of the layers support Gravina et al's hypothesis that there is interstratification of Chatelperronian and Aurignacian technology.

However, Zilhao *et al.* (2006) argue that Gravina *et al.*'s interpretation of the sediment layers in the cave is incorrect, and that the Chatelperronian technology is earlier than the Aurignacian. There is a practical problem with resolving the argument, because it is difficult to tell whether objects from specific layers penetrated into deeper or shallower layers. Such mixing can occur by means of disturbance by human activity or by burrowing animals.

By about 25 000 years ago Neandertals had disappeared from Europe and Central Asia. Chris Stringer and his team have spent much time excavating the Neandertal sites of Vanguard and Gorham's caves in Gibraltar (Stringer, et al., 2008). A Middle Palaeolithic layer in Vanguard cave, dated at about 45 000 years BP contains charred mussel shells cut marked ibex and tortoise bones and Mousterian artefacts. The stone tools include large blade-like flakes made by the Levallois technique. More recent layers dated at around 31–33 000 years BP contain hearths with charcoal and also Mousterian discoidal cores and flakes. Gorham's cave was clearly a favoured site in which natural light penetrated the cave and smoke from the fires was dissipated in the high cave ceiling. In 2006, Finlayson *et al.* presented data and observations from

Gorham's cave that indicated survival of Neandertals up to 28 kya. The researchers took samples from the hearths and obtained dates suggesting a stratigraphic sequence running from 31–24 kya. They report that while the date of 24 kya is not well supported, they are confident that the date of 28 kya is the most recent date that Neandertals used the cave. They suggest that the Neandertals living in southern Iberia were likely to have had limited contact with modern humans, a view consistent with the lack of a Chatelperronian style of tool technology (Finlayson *et al.*, 2006).

There has been much speculation about the possibility that Neandertals interbred with modern humans. Duarte and other palaeoanthropologists interpret a fossil skeleton of a Middle Palaeolithic child found in Abrido do Lagar Velho in Portugal as a Neandertal/modern human hybrid (Duarte *et al.*, 1999). The child was aged about 4 years and dated at 24500 years BP. The relative proportions of the femur and tibia as well as the robusticity of the femur are more typical of Neandertals rather than modern humans. Yet modern human features, including a well-developed chin, are also present. Duarte *et al.* interpret the Lapedo child's anatomy as representing a mixture between the local populations of Neandertals and modern humans. The authors also advise that strict application of the criteria for species of reproductive isolation is not appropriate for Neandertals and modern humans. Yet the evidence from mtDNA studies does not support Duarte's view.

Studies of Neandertal mtDNA provide useful information relevant to the relationship between modern humans and Neandertals. Researchers have succeeded in extracting mtDNA from fossilized Neandertal bones. One of the first published studies was Krings *et al.*'s (1999) report of the extraction of a 333 base pair sequence from the HVRI region of mtDNA extracted from the Neander Valley skeleton. Since then there have been at least 16 other studies of mtDNA sequences obtained from fossil Neandertal bones and overall the data indicated no contribution of Neandertal mtDNA to that of modern humans. A recent study (Green *et al.*, 2008), examined the entire base sequence of mtDNA extracted from a Neandertal bone from Vindija Croatia dated at 38000 years ago, which was a remarkable achievement. The Neandertal mtDNA was reassembled from fragments and in total comprised 8341 base sequences. Green *et al.* identified 206 differences between the Neandertal and reference human mtDNA. The non-coding control region of the mtDNA sequence includes a deletion of four base pairs, CACA and an insertion of one base pair. Green *et al.* also compared pairwise sequence differences in mtDNA from 53 human samples from around the world, with their own Neandertal sample and also with chimpanzee mtDNA. They found that the 53 human mtDNA samples showed differences ranging from 2–118 and the Neandertal mtDNA showed 201–234 differences from the human samples, indicating that Neandertal mtDNA variation is outside the range for human mtDNA variation. Green *et al.* estimated a divergence time for human and Neandertal mtDNA of 520000–800000 years. Examination of mtDNA samples from 10000 Europeans did not show any mtDNA type that could have been derived from a Neandertal.

Overall the evidence, both fossil and genetic can be interpreted to support the view that Neandertals and modern humans did not interbreed, which is consistent with the divergence time of 520–800000 years ago. However, Trinkaus argues that insufficient

DNA sequences have been studied for conclusions to be drawn (Trinkaus, 2005). As so few mtDNA sequences from Neandertals have been obtained so far, Trinkaus asserts that the conclusion to be drawn is that some Neandertal DNA sequences are different from those of modern humans, which he suggests is to be expected since Neandertals are so different anatomically from modern humans. Trinkaus argues that the studies of the ancient DNA sequences are in fact compatible with both a replacement model and a model that incorporates a mixture.

So by about 25 000 years ago modern humans were the only species of *Homo* living in Europe. Modern humans developed more complex stone tool technologies, as well as bone and ivory tools and complex items of personal adornment. Artwork and other artefacts found in graves indicate the importance of ritual.

The ceremonial burial of a young man in Goat's Hole at Paviland Wales is a Gravettian burial dated at 26–27 000 years ago (Aldhouse-Green, 1998). The bones were coloured red with ochre and mammoth ivory ornaments were with the body. At that time the Devensian glaciation was beginning to take effect, and as the ice sheets were building up to the glacial maxima by 18 000 years ago, modern humans left Britain and moved southwards. This was the last occasion on which humans left Britain.

Now we examine the prehistory of Central Asia, where our time line starts at 70 kya.

11.7 Modern Humans and Neandertals in Central Asia

The Baisun region of Uzbekistan, is far distant from Western Europe yet it was within the geographical range of Neandertals. In 1938, the skeleton of a 9-year-old Neandertal boy was discovered by Alexei Okladinov and his colleague in the Teshik-Tash cave in the Gissar mountains in Baisun. The remoteness of this area for homini nds that had no means of travelling apart from walking can be gauged by the distance of about 1600 km from the Neandertals in Europe and the altitude of the cave, almost 1600 m. The grave of the Neandertal boy was in a shallow pit surrounded by six pairs of ibex horns. There was evidence of a small fire close by, and this, together with the ibex horns led to the suggestion that the burial was ritualistic. The finding of 761 more ibex bones in the cave, suggest that the Neandertal group was subsisting on ibex, abundant game in the area. The ibex horns around the cave could have been used as tools for digging the grave. Evidence that the child is a Neandertal derives from the skull, which was re-constructed from 150 fragments. The skull is long and has a receding forehead, a developing brow ridge and lacks a chin. The date of the Teshik-Tash child is estimated at 70 kya (Johanson and Edgar, 1996).

The find of fossil remains at Okladnikov Cave in the Altai region in Siberia includes some bones from a Neandertal subadult, from which a subadult humerus, was dated at about 29 900–37 800 years old. In 2007 Krause extracted mtDNA from the HVR1 region from the Okladnikov subadult humerus and also from samples taken from the left femur of the Teshik Tash child (Krause *et al.*, 2007). The mtDNA was sequenced, and the results showed that the mtDNAs of both the Okladnikov subadult and the Teshik-Tash child are Neandertal. These samples were matched up to Neandertal mtDNA by a laboratory in Paris, who confirmed that the samples were Neandertal mtDNA. Three hundred base pairs from each of the Teshik Tash child and the Okladnikov subadult mtDNA were compared to the same HVR1 sequences from seven other Neandertals and they only differed in six bases, providing a 98% similarity. The significance of the identification of the subadult humerus in Okladnikov Cave in Western Siberia is that it pushed the boundary of the Neandertal world 2000 km beyond Baisun, further to the East.

A recent excavation of a Middle Palaeolithic site in Uzbekistan was at the Anghilak cave in the Kashkasariya region. Michelle Glantz and her colleagues discovered, in 2003, 485 stone artefacts including bladelets, Mousterian stone tools, and >2200 animal bones in sediments at 30–85 cm deep. About half of the animal bones are tortoise and the remainder sheep and goats. Two hearths containing burnt animal bone were found. The authors point out that the presence of Upper Palaeolithic artefacts amongst Middle Palaeolithic assemblages means that dating of the sediments must be carried out in order to work out the chronology of the stone tool technology. Glantz later (2008) reported a date range of 43 900–38 100 years obtained by preliminary ^{14}C dating of the site (Glantz *et al.*, 2008). Just one hominin bone, a metatarsal, has been found in the cave so as yet it isn't possible to link either Neandertals or modern humans to the site. Overall, Upper Palaeolithic sites are scarce in central Asia, but in contrast, more Middle Palaeolithic sites are known and investigation of these sites is continuing.

So far there is no direct evidence that Neandertals reached East Asia or South East Asia, but as we saw in previous chapters, *Homo erectus* had dispersed to these areas and evidence indicates that this hominin persisted there for a long time.

11.8 South East Asia and Australasia

It is likely that *Homo erectus* had arrived in South East Asia by about 1.8 million years ago. The evidence includes the finds of the Modjokerto child, dated at 1.8 mya and the cranium Sangiran 17 dated at 1.7 mya (Curtis, et al., 2001). *Homo erectus* appears to have persisted for more than a million years in South East Asia if we accept that brain cases found at Ngandong on the Solo River in Java are indeed H. *erectus*. In 1931, the geologist, C. ter Haar was surveying the area around the Solo River for producing a geological map. He noticed a layer of sand and gravel at about 20 m height in the steep river bank. He found a piece of fossil bone protruding from this layer, and organized a survey of the site which unearthed thousands of animal bones, 12 *Homo* crania and 2 *Homo* leg bones. Ralph von Koenigswald, a palaeoanthropologist who spent many years researching human evolution in Java, studied the fossils. The huge numbers of animal bones included those of elephant, rhinoceros, hippopotamus, pigs, cattle, deer tigers and panthers. The finds of these modern mammalian species suggested to von Koenigswald that the sediment layer was recent, possibly Late Pleistocene, at the time of a glaciation, giving a date range of 30–150 000 years for the Solo people. The crania have proved difficult to identify, with contrasting views held by various palaeoanthropologists. The names given to the crania include *Homo soloensis*, *Homo neandethalensis soloensis*, *Homo erectus erectus*, *Homo erectus* and *Homo sapiens*. In 1945, Franz Weidenreich interpreted the Java finds as suggesting an evolutionary line from *H. erectus* (*Pithecanthropus*) through *H. soloensis* to the Australian aboriginals.

♦ Which hypothesis for the origin of modern humans would be supported by fossil evidence for Weidenreich's view?

♦ The multiregional hypothesis is supported if there is an evolutionary line from *Homo erectus* through *H. soloensis* to the Australian aboriginals. The multiregional hypothesis proposes regional continuity in that populations of *H. erectus* in various regions evolved into modern humans and variations between human populations are accounted for by variations in the ancestral populations and the environments they lived in.

Weidenreich suggested that the Ngandong crania are 100 000 years old, which would make regional continuity feasible in South East Asia. Both Von Koenigswald and Weidenreich thought that the large brain sizes of the Ngandong crania, on average around 1100 cm³ suggested that the Solo people were more advanced than *Homo erectus*.

The skulls found at Ngandong were in a bone bed that was part of an ancient river terrace. It is possible that post-cranial material was also present, but un-recognized amongst the approximately 25 000 bones recovered from the bone bed. In a later excavation at the same site, post-cranial fragments were recovered. All 25 000 bones were lost during the Second World War, though all the hominin skulls survived. Carl Swisher (Swisher *et al.*, 1996) has attempted to date the skulls by using samples from animal teeth in the bone bed. The date he and his co-workers have come up with – 40 kya with a range of 53–27 kya – is (of course) controversial for, if correct, it suggests that in Asia *Homo erectus* survived long enough to be contemporaneous with *Homo sapiens*. With such a recent date, there is a second point to consider and that is whether the Ngandong skulls really are *H. erectus* rather than *H. sapiens*. The skull is bigger than the skulls of earlier *H. erectus* but retains essentially the same anatomical features and so most workers would regard them as genuine *H. erectus*. In fact, although the Ngandong crania are larger overall than the more ancient *erectus*, their thick bones, low broad braincase, continuous brow ridge, and lack of the globularization in modern human skulls, do indicate *erectus* rather than *sapiens* (Curtis, *et al.*, 2001).

These dates are disputed by those who support the multiregional hypothesis. For example, Grun and Thorne argue that the fossil mammal teeth used for Swisher *et al.*'s study may not be the same age as the Ngandong crania (Grun and Thorne, 1997).

♦ What natural processes may mix fossil bones of different ages together?

♦ The water flow of rivers cuts through layers of soft sediments exposing hard fossils deposited in several layers of different ages. Subsequent sorting by water currents can cause accumulations of fossil bones of different ages.

Curtis *et al.* argued that re-sorted fossils show signs of damage such as scratches and wear, but damage is not seen in the Ngandong crania. Von Koenigswald, who had witnessed the digging up of the Ngandong crania, pointed out: 'That the human remains from Ngandong were contemporary with the laying down of the sediments is evident from their preservation which is exactly the same as in the numerous animal bones found in the same deposit'. Furthermore, although it is unusual to have found only crania rather than other bones, this was not due to previous re-sorting by river flow, but due to the selection of pieces by those who were digging up the fossils. The eminent Indonesian anthropologist, Teuku Jacob had found post-cranial hominid material, including a leg bone, when digging in the 1970s.

If we accept that the Ngandong crania are *Homo erectus*, dated at 27000–53000 years old, this would indicate that *H. erectus* persisted for much longer than had previously been thought. The date implies that the Ngandong people could not have been the ancestors of the ancient human populations in Australia. As Curtis *et al.* point out this makes the multiregional theory for the origin of modern humans in Australasia untenable. Furthermore the recent date shows that *H. erectus* in Java was still living as a contemporary of modern *H. sapiens* in East Asia.

The available genetic evidence (YDNA), suggests that modern humans reached East Asia by about 60 kya which was followed by a northward migration, as ice sheets were retreating (Su *et al.*, 1999).

Fossil bones of ancient people have been found in Australia where one of the richest areas for such finds is Mungo National Park in New South Wales, about 987 km west of Sydney. 50000–25000 years ago there were lakes and lush vegetation in the area, although the climate was gradually becoming more arid. Lake Mungo had dried up by about 14000 thousand years ago but vegetation was still growing on the dunes up to the end of the nineteenth century, when it was over-grazed and wiped out by colonists' sheep and rabbits. The resulting erosion of the dunes exposed fossil human remains. Mungo lady (Mungo I) is a cremated human skeleton discovered by Jim Bowler (University of Melbourne) in 1969 on the old shore of Lake Mungo. This skeleton is regarded as the oldest known human cremation. Mungo man is the name given to skeletal remains of a modern human, Mungo III, discovered by Jim Bowler in 1974 just 500 m away from where Mungo I, was found 5 years earlier. Mungo III's skeleton was covered with ochre and his hands had been folded over his groin. The fossil remains at Lake Mungo indicate a gracile people with relatively thin crania, rounded foreheads, small mandibles and weak brow ridges. Jim Bowler paints a picture of Lake Mungo surrounded by lush vegetation. Marsupial species, now extinct, lived around the lake and included Tasmanian tiger, giant kangaroo, hairy-nosed wombat and *Zygomatus*, an animal similar in size and appearance to the pygmy hippopotamus. Mungo man's people hunted game and fished for cod and perch, probably using nets, and collected mussels from the lake waters. The people practised ritual burial, which included covering the bodies with ochre, which coloured the bones red (Bowler *et al.*, 2003).

Following earlier attempts at dating Mungo man, Jim Bowler and his colleagues used optically stimulated luminescence (OSL) for dating sand grains in the sediment layer where the grave of Mungo III was found (Bowler *et al.*, 2003). The research team obtained dates of 40–42 kyr ago for Mungo man. In addition, Bowler's team dated the oldest sediment layer where stone tools, silcrete flakes and striking platforms, were found. They obtained dates of 50–46 kya, consistent with archaeological evidence from sites in North West Australia, suggesting human occupation from ~50–46 kyr ago. The route taken by the incoming people is unknown. There was no land bridge at that time between Australia and the land mass that is now the islands that include Indonesia. The resulting division between the fauna of Indonesia and Borneo and the marsupial fauna of Australia was recognized by Alfred Russell Wallace in (1859). A deep ocean trench divides Australia from South East Asia so even the changing sea levels could not have created a land bridge. Hence 50 kyr ago, modern humans had to travel by sea to Australia using boats or rafts. The ability of ancient peoples to cross the sea would not be surprising as humans living 50 kyrs ago are likely to have had much the same cognitive abilities as people living today. Unfortunately as there are no known remains of boats older than about 7000 years, or rafts older than about 11 000 years, there is no direct evidence of boat or raft use prior to those dates.

Genetic evidence from Y chromosome DNA and mtDNA has also been used to investigate dates for the colonization of Australia by modern humans. Hudjashov and his colleagues (2007), point out that so far all Y chromosomal DNA lineages in Australians and New Guinea are derived from types, C and F, which are proposed to be the earliest founder out of Africa types (Table 11.1). New Guinea and aboriginal Australian peoples share the mtDNA branches M and N, which are derived from the founder mtDNA type L3 and do not share any branches with Asian populations more recent than M, N and R (Figure 11.17).

♦ Does the genetic evidence from the Y chromosome and mtDNA studies support the multiregional hypothesis for the evolution of modern humans in Australasia? Outline the rationale for your view.

♦ The genetic evidence from YDNA indicates that aboriginal peoples descended from an African group with branches C and F that are probably the earliest out of Africa founder types. Similarly aboriginal peoples' mtDNA is derived from an African founder types M and N which are dated at 70–50 kya. So the genetic evidence supports the view that the aboriginal peoples are descended from modern humans who had migrated out of Africa. So the multiregional hypothesis and regional continuity in Australasia are not supported by the genetic evidence.

Hudjashov and his colleagues suggest that aborginal Australians and New Guinea peoples all descended from a founder group that spread out from Africa 50–70 000

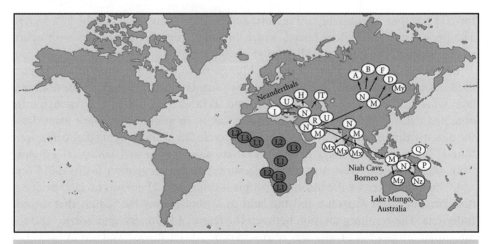

Figure 11.17   Expansion and migration of mtDNA types in Europe, Asia and Australasia 60–30 kya.
Reproduced with kind permission of Dr Peter Forster, Cambridge University. Forster, (2004), P258.

years ago, when the low sea levels meant that islands were consolidated into one land mass. This meant that the travellers had to cross just narrow sea straits in order to reach New Guinea and Australia. Subsequently the modern human populations were isolated for a long time, which Hudjashov suggests could explain the narrow range of stone and bone tools that were used by aboriginal peoples (Hudjashov *et al.*, 2007).

Some of the other fossils of modern humans discovered in Australia are more robust in anatomy than the Mungo people. They include those human fossils dated at about 12 kya, which were discovered at Kow swamp, also in South East Australia. The Kow swamp people have thick cranial bone, large mandibles, and prominent brow ridges. Hudjashov *et al.* agree with the view that the variation from gracile to robust anatomy could be explained by the divergence of a single founder population. Previous interpretation of this fossil evidence had suggested multiple colonization events.

11.9 A New Species of *Homo*?

Until recently, the available fossil and archaeological evidence indicated that by about 25 000 years ago, modern humans were the only remaining species of *Homo*. However this view was challenged in 2003, when Peter Brown (University of New England, Australia) and his team discovered some unusual hominid bones on the island of Flores in Indonesia (Brown *et al.*, 2004). While excavating sediments in the floor of a limestone cave, Liang Bua, the researchers found parts of a skeleton of a tiny hominid, denoted as LB1. The bones lay in sediments 5.9 m deep, and were fragile as they had not fossilized. They included much of a cranium and mandible, the right leg and the left hip bone (innominate), and fragments of the left leg and other bones. LB1 was identified as an adult by the wear on the teeth, and as female by the broad greater sciatic notch of the innominate. The estimated height of LB1 is 1.06 m, so within the range for *Australopithecus afarensis*. The bones were dated at about 18 000 years using various techniques including AMS (calibrated accelerator mass spectrometry) and luminescence. A second smaller mandible from another individual, LB6 was also found and dated at about 15 000 years. The distinctive hominin features of the bones and their resemblance to known fossil bones of *Homo*, led Brown and his co-workers to name LB1 as a new species, *Homo floresiensis*.

Brown *et al.* emphasize the unique combination of features *Homo floresiensis*. The calvarium is small with endocranial volume 380–417 cm³ so lower than that associated with *Homo* and also at the lower range for *Australopithecus*. The calculated EQ is 2.5, lower than that of other *Homo* species. Later Jacob recalculated EQ as 4.6. Low EQ is a symplesiomorphy (shared primitive character) for hominins. The face lacks a chin, and facial prognathism is much reduced. Eyebrow ridges are present but are not prominent (Figure 11.18).

The skeletal anatomy of LB1 supports the view that LB1 was bipedal. The foramen magnum is located centrally in the floor of the basicranium. The anatomy of the leg bones and the pelvic girdle suggest that LB1 was bipedal (Jungers *et al.*, in press). The ilium is broad and flared laterally, resembling that of Lucy, *Australopithecus afarensis*. Measurements of the leg bones showed that the femur head was relatively small and its neck relatively long, similar proportions as those observed in australopithecines and *Homo habilis*. The feet are unusual as they are wide and long, measuring about 70% of the length of the femur. In contrast, the feet of modern humans are about 55%

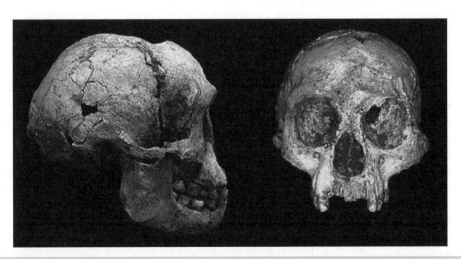

Figure 11.18   Skull of *Homo floresiensis* (LB1) (adapted from Figure 1; Brown *et al.*, 2004).

of the length of the femur. The big toe is much shorter than the other toes, but stiff and aligned with them so *H. floresiensis* could toe off when taking a step. Brown noted that while the anatomy of the cranial and post-cranial skeleton comprises a unique mix of primitive, unique and derived features, it is consistent with bipedalism like that in other *Homo* species (Brown *et al.*, 2004).

Bill Jungers (Stony Brook University New York) suggested that the long wide feet of *Homo floresiensis* would have restricted walking to a slow pace and awkward gait. Yet *H. floresiensis* is not unique in having longer, wider feet than would be expected for their body size and shape. A recent study carried out by Japanese researchers of the body proportions of a Polynesian population living on Tonga demonstrated that the people have a relatively heavy body build and wider, longer feet than European, Japanese, West African and Australian aborigine populations. The authors suggest that the ancestors of Polynesians probably suffered natural disasters and famine causing population bottlenecks. Subsequent natural selection produced the adaptive features of heavy body build and large hands and feet. The salient point here is that the Tongan islanders do not suffer any disadvantages linked to their feet (Gonda and Katayama, 2006).

Bones of other individuals found at Liang Bua include a very small radius dated at 12 000 years old, the most recent remains of *Homo floresiensis* so far (Morwood *et al.*, 1998). Additional parts of the skeleton of LB1 were found too, including a humerus, described as relatively thick in comparison to that of modern humans. Brown suggests that LB1 was part of a population of hominins who remained on Flores from about 95–74 up to about 12 000 years ago. The researchers concluded that the mix of primitive and derived features, the cranial morphology and skeletal proportions support the view that the small hominids are neither modern humans or *Homo erectus*, but are a new previously unknown species, *H. floresiensis*. This conclusion has led to much argument, which we will explore.

Interesting insights into the lifeway of *H. floresiensis* are provided by finds of artefacts, animal bones and hearths. Animal bones and stone tools discovered at Liang Bua were interpreted by Morwood as evidence for tool making and use (Morwood *et al.*, 1998). Bones found in the same sediment layers as the hominin bones, included those of *Stegodon*, a dwarfed elephant species now extinct, as well as those of Komodo dragon, rats and bats. Most of the *Stegodon* bones were those of juveniles and neonates. Morwood acknowledges that small faunal remains at least, for example fish, frog, lizard and bird bones could have accumulated in the cave by natural processes, but the larger bones were the remains of animals hunted or collected for food. A total of eight hearths were found, each a cluster of burnt volcanic pebbles arranged in a rough circle. Artefacts were found in all layers dating from 95–74 kyr to 12 kyr. They include simple flakes, points, blades and microblades, possibly hafted as barbs onto spears. Large quantities of the stone tools were found associated with *Stegodon* remains in deposit layers dated from around 95–74 kyr up to 12 kyr. Brown *et al.* (2004) interpret this evidence as indicating that *Homo floresiensis* was hunting juvenile *Stegodon* using a complex set of stone tools. Others have argued that these tools were made by modern humans.

♦ Suggest an explanation of why stone tools found at Liang Bua are unlikely to have been made and used by modern humans.

♦ Fossil evidence indicates that modern humans did not arrive in Java until about 60 000 years ago, which is more recent than the dates for the oldest stone artefacts.

Brown and his colleagues suggested that *Homo floresiensis* may have evolved from an ancestral population of *Homo erectus*. Their rationale was that as with other large ancestral mammalian species that were isolated on Flores, *H. erectus* may have undergone endemic dwarfing (Brown *et al.*, 2004). Brumm *et al.* (2006) argue that the stone tools that he and his team found in sediments at Mata Menge on Flores and dated at 840–740 kyr show close similarities to those found just 50 km to the west of at Liang Bua. These Mata Menge artefacts had in fact been transported by water and undergone sorting. The tools are attributed to *H. erectus*, and Brumm points out that the Mata Menge technology shows aspects of continuity with the Liang Bua technology (Brumm *et al.*, 2006). Both stone tool assemblages are based on volcanic cobbles which were prepared by freehand reduction of cores bifacially and radially. However bipolar reduction is common at Liang Bua but very rare at Mata Menge. Bipolar reduction involves placing the core on a hard stone and then striking it with a hammerstone, which may propagate a fracture from both ends of the core.

So we have a diminutive species of *Homo* that lived on Flores from about 94–75 000 to 15–20 000 years ago, but not all anthropologists interpret the evidence in this way. Teuku Jacob and colleagues pointed out that reduction in stature of human populations living on Flores was likely to be linked to the humid climate, the hilly topography and abundant undergrowth on Flores (Jacob *et al.*, 2006). Jacob *et al.* argue forcefully that *Homo floresiensis* was not a new species but rather a member of a pygmoid population of modern humans affected by a genetic developmental abnormality, microcephaly. Jacob also argued that the small stature of the individuals found at Liang Bua can be linked to the climate and vegetation on Flores. He described pygmy people living in the village of Rampasasa close to Liang Bua. The adults range in height from 130–155 cm, and mean brain size for females was measured at 1198 ml (41 samples) and 1354 ml (35 samples) for adult males, which are much larger values than the 430 ml for *floresiensis* (Jacob *et al.*, 2006). Ninety-three per cent of the Rampasasa villagers do not have a chin so Jacob argues that the absence of a chin is not necessarily a feature that separates *H. floresiensis* from modern humans. Jacob *et al.* also point out that there are populations of people with diminutive body size on many islands in the region, including the Andaman islands, Sulawesi and Papua.

Jacob's interpretation of the Liang Bua bones have been refuted by some palaeoanthropologists, who have examined the condition itself. Microcephaly is observed as an abnormally small head with a tiny brain. Individuals with true microcephaly have a narrow and sloping forehead and a pointed vertex. Microcephaly combined with extreme dwarfism is a classic feature of primordial dwarfism, a condition in which there is very little growth after birth. There are a number of different types of microcephaly with extreme dwarfism, making it a variable syndrome. Some types are non-lethal.

Debbie Argue *et al.* (Australian National University) carried out anatomical comparisons of the LB1 skull with those of ancient fossil hominins, *Homo habilis, ergaster* and *erectus* as well as skulls from microcephalic modern humans, including one individual dated at about 2 kya from Crete, and one from Sano Cave site in Japan also dated at about 2 kya. Argue *et al.* concluded that LB1 is unlikely to be a microcephalic modern human as the only feature they had in common with each other is the extremely small brain size. The skull dimensions of LB1 have little in common with microcephalic skulls. Argue *et al.* conclude that the morphology of LB1 is more like that of early *Homo*, but the combination of features is unique, justifying the species name, *Homo floresiensis* (Argue *et al.*, 2006).

♦ Suggest the reason why Argue *et al.* recommend that more detailed morphometric studies are needed on more microcephalic skulls so that they can be compared with LB1.

♦ Argue *et al.* examined only two fossil microcephalic skulls, which is a very small sample. Furthermore as microcephaly with primordial dwarfism is a very variable syndrome, examination of more skulls affected by this condition is essential to ensure that the spectrum of primordial dwarfism has been covered adequately.

Other palaeoanthropologists have put forward their interpretations of the finds at Liang Bua but we do not have the space to cover the arguments here. Discussion and argument about the interpretation of the fossils of *Homo floresiensis* are still continuing and no doubt will do so for a long time, as there are many controversies about the bones discovered at Ling Bua.

11.10 East Asia

The Chinese hominin fossil record is complex and its interpretation is disputed so there are views of those who support the multiregional hypothesis, the admixture model and the 'Out of Africa' hypothesis to consider. Here we present some examples of finds, but note that there are likely to be more in future. We begin with examining a fossil which was originally dated at about 30–20 kya, but now there are research data which suggest that the fossil could be much older.

The skull and some post-cranial bones of a modern human were discovered in 1958 by workers digging for fertilizer in Tongtianyan cave at Liujiang in China. The skull has a low cranial vault, an occipital bun and moderate eyebrow ridges. The face is short and broad. The teeth found with the skull are of moderate size and include a shovel shaped incisor, and interestingly, there is a congenital lack of a third molar. Trinkaus (2005) mentions that some features of the Liujian skull are archaic, but does not specify which ones. Bones of other mammals found at the site include *Stegodon orientalis*, (elephant-like mammal) *Rhinoceros sinensis*, (rhinoceros), *Pongo* sp. (orangutan) and *Ailuropoda* (giant panda) and *Sus* (pig), a typical Late Pleistocene fauna. The most frequently quoted date for the Liujiang hominin is ~20–30 kya which was estimated from ^{14}C dating of similar remains found in Japan. It would be difficult to identify the sediment layer in which the bones had been found because the sediment layers in Tongtianyan cave were lost by the digging operations in the cave. Nevertheless more recent research by Shen and co-workers involved investigating the residue of the sediment layers on the cave walls and a leftover intact cross section of the sediments. The researchers were thus able to re-investigate the stratigraphy of the cave and work out the most likely provenance for the fossils. Using U-series dating on calcite samples from the appropriate sediment layers they obtained dates of about 68 kya but noted that another older date range, 111–153 kya was also feasible (Shen *et al.*, 2007).

♦ If the Liujiang modern human was dated securely at 111–153 kya suggest any implications there would be for the 'Out of Africa' hypothesis.

♦ For the 'Out of Africa' hypothesis to be feasible an earlier date range than the postulated 150–200 kya for the origin for modern humans would be needed. Furthermore there would have to have been an earlier successful migration out of Africa possibly at least 160–120 kya.

Shen suggests that their dates for the Liujiang hominid are too early for modern humans to have arrived in China after spreading from Africa although the oldest date of 200 kya is just within the range of current estimates for the origin of modern humans in Africa. The date range for the origin of modern humans has also been worked out from genetic studies. Ingman *et al.* (2000) established a date range for the most recent common ancestor of modern humans using the entire mtDNA genome apart from the D-loop. Their rationale was that only sequences outside the D-loop evolve in a roughly clock-like manner. This molecular clock gave a date range for the most recent ancestor of modern humans of 171 ± 50 kya, which could be compatible with Liujiang being 111–153 kya. Nevertheless, the date for Liujiang does appear to be very early. One criticism of Shen *et al.*'s work is that rather than using a sample of the sediment that was stuck to the skull, the researchers used samples from the sediment layers thought to match the sediment layer in which the skull was found. These sediment layers could in fact be much older than the skull itself, and so may have provided a spurious date.

It is interesting that the Chinese fossil record provides evidence that is interpreted by some palaeoanthropologists as supporting the admixture of incoming early modern humans with local archaic populations. Thirty-four fossil bones of an early modern human were discovered at Tianyuan cave in Zoukhoudian in 2003 (Shang *et al.*, 2007). The bones appear to be those of one individual, and include part of the mandible with some teeth, the axis, both femora, both tibiae, both scapulae, both humeri, an ulna and radius, as well as others, for example hand and foot bones. Fossilized deer bones were found in the same sediment layer including those of red deer, Sika deer and Siberian musk deer. The human bones were dated to 42–39 kya by mass accelerator spectrometry ^{14}C dating. The authors agree that some of the bones have the derived morphology typical of recent humans. They note though that the relative length of the tibiae and their high robusticity suggest a combination of equatorial ancestry with an emphasis on mobility. The authors also draw attention to some archaic (Neandertal-like) features they observed in the teeth and bones. They point to the increased tibial robusticity which isn't normally seen in modern humans. They also mention the increased anteroposterior proportions of the crown breadths of the teeth. The hamulus (one of the hand bones) of Tianyuan 1 is enlarged, a feature that is typical of Neandertals. So the authors suggest that there was gene flow from earlier modern human populations around Tianyuan cave. Furthermore, Shang *et al.* suggest that the archaic features they observed indicate that a simple eastward spread of modern human features from Africa is unlikely.

Other fossils of modern humans found in China include those discovered at Laibin Guangxi in southern China dated at 44–38.5 kya by U-series dating (Shen *et al.*, 2007). More recently, dated fossils found in China include those found at Zhoukoudian. In 1933–34, fossil remains of modern humans were found in the upper part (Shandingdong) of the Zhoukoudian cave complex (Figure 9.5). The Upper cave is about 13.5 m long and 5.6 m wide. The bottom layer of the Upper cave was actually deposited above the top layer of the sediments in which 'Peking Man' was found. In 1933 and 1934, three modern human skulls UC101, UC102 and UC103 were found in the sediments of the Upper cave, as well as various pelvic and leg bones. Unfortunately, all three skulls and most of the bones were lost in 1941 during World War II, but casts and photographs of some the fossils are available. Items of personal adornment found in the sediments include perforated shells, animal teeth and stones. Fossils of fish, amphibians and mammals were found. Recently Christopher Norton and Xing Gao examined the artefactual and faunal remains that were originally discovered in the cave (Norton and Gao, 2008). Five sedimentary layers, labelled 1–5 had been identified by researchers in the 1930s. The three human crania and most of the human skeletal fossils were found in layer 4 but dates for layer 4 proved variable with values obtained from various techniques ranging from 10–34 kya. Chen, Hedges and Yuan (1989) used ^{14}C accelerator dating applied to samples from the lower sediments of layer 4 and obtained values of 33–34 kya, whereas Wu and Wang in 1985 used ^{14}C on the upper layers obtained dates of $10\,470 \pm 600$ BP. As at Liujang, bones of deer were the most abundant in the cave. Some of the cranial bones of deer had cut marks and others were burnt supporting the view that the human hunter gatherer groups were processing carcasses in the cave. Tooth marks on the deer bones indicated small carnivore activity; presumably the carnivores were scavenging the discarded remains of the deer carcasses.

It is important not to lose sight of the extraordinary fact that the Zhoukoudian cave complex has been occupied, albeit intermittently, by hominins for nearly 500 000 years!

As we have seen, the Chinese fossil record has been interpreted by some anthropologists as supporting a mixture of modern humans and local archaic humans. The presence of features identified as archaic in the Chinese human fossil record has also been interpreted as evidence for regional continuity, suggesting that modern humans may have evolved in China from Peking man (*Homo erectus*). Nevertheless, there is genetic evidence that supports an Out of Africa origin for Chinese peoples. Ke and others studied YDNA from samples taken from 12 127 male individuals living in East Asia. They investigated three YDNA markers, YAP, M89 and M130, of which all individuals sampled had one of the three. The three markers all coalesce to mutation M168 which originated in Africa about 40–80 kya (Table 11.1). This data was interpreted as strong support for the Out of Africa hypothesis (Ke *et al.*, 2001). Trinkaus (2005) contends that the genetic evidence is compatible with admixture and the Out of Africa hypothesis. He argues that it is unlikely that there will ever be sufficient genetic evidence to distinguish between the two models. Clearly the debate will be ongoing for a long time.

11.11 Modern Humans Arrive in the Americas

The only fossils of *Homo* found in the Americas are those of modern humans, and there is no evidence of any other species of *Homo*. Both the route and the timing of the arrival of modern humans have been the subject of much argument, so accurate dating techniques for fossils and artefacts are of crucial importance, as always. The earliest hypotheses suggesting migration routes and the origin of Native Americans and First Nations peoples in Canada were linked to similarities between the features of North American and Asian peoples. It was suggested that modern humans had arrived and spread in North America about 11 kya, having travelled across Beringia, which at that time was extended eastwards, providing a land bridge linking Siberia and North America. Thirteen thousand years ago ice sheets still covered vast areas of the northern hemisphere, as a period of glaciation, with a maxima at about 21–18 kya, was drawing slowly to an end. Most of Canada and part of the northern USA were covered by the Laurentide ice sheet, and the Cordilleran ice sheet in the eastern coastal area. The estimated thickness of the ice sheets was 3–4 km, so life was not sustainable there. Furthermore, the ice sheets would have provided an insurmountable barrier to travel. However it was this massive glaciation, named the Wisconsin, that enabled humans and other mammals to cross from Siberia to North America, using the Beringian land bridge.

♦ Suggest an explanation for the existence of a land bridge linking Siberia and North America.

♦ The land bridge was a result of the drop in sea level caused by the locking up of vast amounts of water into ice, much of it as ice sheets on land.

The effective drop in sea level has been estimated as about 100 m, which exposed the Beringian land bridge, so providing a route for modern humans and other animals to reach North America. Once modern humans reached North America their route southwards would have been blocked by the ice-sheets. However there appears to have been an ice-free corridor by about 12–11 kya, so linking Alaska, Canada's Yukon and Northwest territories to southern North America. The existence and date range of the inland ice-free corridor has been the focus of much dispute and an alternative ice-free coastal route is accepted by some palaeoanthropologists. In 2008 Ted Goebel (Texas A and M university) and colleagues, reviewed the recent evidence and pointed out that the coastal corridor was probably ice-free by about 15 kya whereas the inland corridor was probably ice-free by 13.5–14 kya. Nevertheless, people living and travelling on the Beringian land bridge, and those who had reached Alaska would have been subsisting in an extremely cold climate and a tundra habitat. Large mammals such as steppe bison, woolly mammoth and horse would have provided meat, skins, bones and ivory for the modern human hunters subsisting on the Beringian land bridge and Alaska.

Goebel *et al.* (2008) highlight the achievement of modern humans in learning to survive in the extremely cold climate of the Arctic more than 30 kya. Evidence for this view is provided by the finds at a site by Yana River in Siberia. Pitulko (Russian Academy of Sciences) describes a **foreshaft** made from a woolly rhinoceros horn which was discovered in Yana Valley in 1993 (Pitulko *et al.*, 2004). A foreshaft is a short, thinner shaft tipped with a point that can be inserted into the end of a longer shaft making a longer spear. Foreshafts with different tips can be inserted and fixed into the longer shafts providing a useful kit of projectiles for different uses. The site where the foreshaft was found subsequently became known as the Yana Rhinoceros Horn site, (Yana RHS).

Pitulko and his colleagues re-visited and investigated Yana RHS, and found two more foreshafts made of mammoth ivory, and stone tools including side and end scrapers, bifacial and unifacial tools, retouched flakes and a hammerstone (Pitulko *et al.*, 2004). Most tools were made of flinty slate and a few were made of quartz. Some small fragments of ochre were found. The cultural layer of the site was dated at about 30 kya. The date and the location of the Yana site in northwest Beringia placed the people who were there in a pole position to move further east and to cross the Beringia land bridge. However there is no direct evidence that suggests that the people using the site did travel across the land bridge. Nevertheless the success of the people in subsisting at Yana suggests that they would have been well-equipped to survive in North America. Once having crossed the Beringia land bridge, the people travelling from Siberia, would have arrived in what is now Alaska.

There are sites in Alaska with evidence of human occupation by 14 kya. Goebel *et al.* highlight the Swan point site in Alaska dated at 14 kya which has a microblade and burin technology. More recently dated sites included in Alaska contain varied combinations and technologies, which may be due to cultural differences between groups of people. Many of the earliest known sites of human occupation south of Alaska, are Clovis sites dated at 13.2–13.1 to 12.9–12.8 kya by new high precision accelerator mass spectrometry (AMS) ^{14}C dating (Waters and Stafford, 2007). According to these dates, the Clovis culture lasted only for a maximum of 400 years, and for as little as 200 years, but nevertheless, there is much evidence of their presence available from their lithic technology. Clovis stone tools are characterized by the fluted projectile point and long blade (Figure 11.19), and by foreshafts and projectile points made of ivory bone or antler.

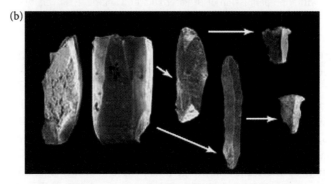

Figure 11.19 Stages in manufacture of Clovis tools: (a) Clovis fluted point; (b) Blades. Reproduced from Goebel, Waters and O'Rourke, 2008.

The Clovis people were considered to have been the first modern humans to settle in North America and pre-Clovis sites were regarded by many as controversial. The evidence for pre-Clovis sites can no longer be ignored since modern dating techniques have been available. Goebel points out the existence of earlier pre-Clovis sites in North America, such as the Schaefer and Hebior sites, where stone tools and a disarticulated mammoth carcass were encased in a matrix of pond sediments. Daniel Joyce described the two stone tools found at Schaefer as blade-like flakes made of chert (Joyce, 2006). The mammoth bones have cut marks supporting the view that the carcass was the remains of a hunting trip. The Schaefer site is dated at 14.8–14.2 kya, which is pre-Clovis. Goebel, Waters and O'Rourke (2008) also mention the Paisley 5 Mile Point Caves site in Oregon where human coprolites were found and dated by accelerator mass spectrometry at 14.27–14.0 kya (Gilbert *et al.*, 2008). There are other

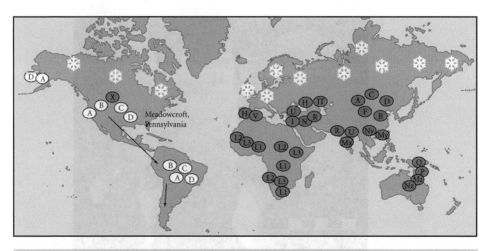

Figure 11.20   Expansion of mtDNA genotypes in the Americas: (a) 20–15 kya.
Reproduced with kind permission of Dr Peter Forster, Cambridge University. Forster, (2004) P258.

sites older than Clovis and overall the evidence supports the view that modern humans had reached the Americas by about 15 kya.

Genetic evidence from analysis of mtDNA and Y chromosome DNA supports the view that one group of people migrated from Siberia and crossed the Beringian land bridge between about 30–13 kya, although it's more likely that the migration occurred after 22 kya, the date of the late glacial maximum. Genetic studies support the hypothesis of a Siberian origin for North American peoples. So far mtDNA analyses (Figure 11.20) show that native Americans and indigenous people in South Siberia include five mtDNA haplogroups, A, B, C, D and X (Goebel, Waters and O'Rourke, 2008). Although the mtDNA haplogroup X is also found in Europe and central Asia it is diverse in these areas, and the Native American lineage of X is not the same as that in Eurasia.

Analyses of Y-DNA in native Americans have identified two YDNA haplogroups, C and sub-group C3, and Q and sub-group Q3 (Table 11.1).

♦ Summarize the information in Table 11.1 about YDNA haplogroups C and Q. What does this tell us about the ancient history of Native Americans?

♦ Haplogroup C has a coalescence date of 50–60 kya and is found in Australia, Siberia, Japan, N. America and India. The subclade, C3 has a coalescence date of 20 kya and is found in Mongolia, Central Asia, Siberia and N. America. The subclade of C3, C3b is found in na-Dene populations in N. America. Haplogroup Q has a coalescence of 15–20 kya, and was of Siberian origin. Haplogroup Q3 is unique to indigenous peoples in the Americas with a coalescence date of 8–12 kya.

The link between Siberian and native American Y-DNA haplogroups supports the hypothesis that migrants from Siberia were the likely ancestors of native

Americans. So the ancestors of native Americans peoples were most likely to have been Asian.

11.12 Conclusion

The timeline for the spread of hominins over the world is complex, and is a branching tree with each branch having its own timeline. Evidence from fossils and artefacts indicates the migration of a group of modern humans out of Africa to the Middle East at about 120 kya. Yet by about 90 kya modern humans were no longer in the Middle East, and some palaeoanthropologists interpret this evidence as a failed colonization. Neandertals were living in the Middle East from about 120 kya and by about 60 kya, modern humans had returned there. Around 70 kya Neandertals were living in Central Asia, as well as southern Europe. The picture became more complex as time moved on. Modern humans had reached South West Europe by 40 kya and spread to Eastern Europe as well, possibly from the Middle East. Neandertals appear to have persisted in the Middle East up to at least about 40 kya. *Homo erectus* was living in South East Asia up to about 27 kya. Recent discoveries in South East Asia added another hominin species, *Homo floresiensis*, that was extant on the island of Flores up to as recently as 18–15 000 years ago. There is a view that *floresiensis* is a dwarfed *H. erectus* but as with many topics in this chapter, this interpretation is controversial. Modern humans were in China by at least 45 kya but as yet it is difficult to pinpoint the timing of their arrival. In Europe, modern humans were forced to move southwards during the most recent glaciation that reached its maxima about 21–18 kya. However, modern humans were living successfully in Eastern Siberia 30 kya and moving into Beringia, and by about 15 kya were crossing the Beringian land bridge to Alaska. These peoples had somehow survived the glacial maxima possibly by subsisting on the large game. The oldest modern human sites in Alaska are dated at 14 kya, suggesting that by about 14 kya modern humans had colonized all of the continents with the exception of Antarctica.

Modern human cultures and societies have become diverse but genetic studies demonstrate that we all share the same African origin.

Questions and Activities

Question 11.1

Write six bullet points that identify six features of Qafzeh IX that distinguish the skull from those of Neandertals.

Question 11.2

What can you deduce about the way of life of the occupants of Yafteh cave from about 36 000–25 000 years ago? Explain your reasoning and the supporting evidence.

Question 11.3

Do the dates for the Ngangdong crania and Mungo man obtained by Swisher *et al.* (1996) support the multiregional hypothesis? Outline the rationale for your view.

Question 11.4

What features described for (a) the cranial and (b) the post-cranial skeleton would indicate that *Homo floresiensis* was walking bipedally?.

Question 11.5

Morwood *et al.* (2004) interpreted Liang Bua as a spot where carcasses were being processed by *Homo floresiensis* using stone tools. What other explanation could account for the grouping of stone tools and animal bones?

Question 11.6

What was Jacob *et al.*'s rationale for linking the small stature of LB1 and the other individuals discovered at Liang Bua to the climate and vegetation on Flores?

Question 11.7

Complete Table 11.5, which summarises some comparisons of the anatomy of *Homo floresiensis* with that of australopiths and *Homo erectus*. Write a summary of the comparisons and suggest how they might suggest evolutionary relationships between *H. floresiensis*, *H. erectus* and australopiths.

Question 11.8

(a) An intriguing theory about the original human colonization of America suggests that modern humans originating from south western Europe travelled along coast lines and the edge of the North Atlantic ice sheets reaching North America by about kya. The original observation that suggested this view was that stone tool technology resembling the Solutrean, was found at Clovis sites dated at around 13.2–12.8 kya.

What is the date range for Solutrean technology? Which European stone tool technology was current around 13 kya?

(b) Using the date ranges for Solutrean technology as a guide, estimate the time it would have taken for Solutrean technology to reach North America.

Question 11.9

Gilbert *et al.*'s genetic analysis of the human coprolites at Paisley Caves revealed mtDNA haplogroups A and B. What does this finding tell us about the origin of the population that was using the Paisley caves site?

Table 11.5 Some comparisons of the fossil anatomy of *Homo floresiensis* with that of australopithecines and *Homo erectus*

Feature described	*H. floresiensis*	*H.erectus*	Australopithecines
Estimated height			A. *afarensis* males ~1.51 m tall; females ~1.05 m. A. *africanus* males ~1.38 m tall; females ~1.15 m.
Overall shape of cranium and face			Face projecting (prognathic) below the orbits e.g. A. *afrarensis*, A. *africanus*. Eyebrow ridges prominent. Chin absent
Endocranial volume			*~375–550 cm³
Molars	Molars relatively larger than those of *H. sapiens* but relatively smaller than *Australopithecus*		Molars massive and ridged, & extremely so in *Paranthropus*
Encephalisation quotient E Q (Brown et al 2004)			EQ 2.5–3.0
Ilium (pelvic girdle) flared			Ilium (pelvic girdle) flared

*This is an estimated range, based on data for *A. afarensis, A. africanus, A. aethiopicus* and *A. robustus*.

References

Aldhouse-Green, S.H.R. (1998) Paviland Cave: Contextualising the 'Red lady'. *Antiquity*, **72**, 756–772.

Anikovich, M.V., Sinitsyn, A.A., Hoffecker, J.F., Holliday, V.T., Popov, V.V., Lisitsyn, S.N., Forman, S.L., Levkovskaya, G.M., Pospelova, G.A., Kuz'mina, I.E., *et al.* (2007) Early Upper Paleolithic in Eastern Europe and implications for the dispersal of modern humans. *Science*, **315**, 223–226.

Argue, D., Donlon, D., Groves, C., and Wright, R. (2006) *Homo floresiensis:* Microcephalic, pygmoid, Australopithecus, or *Homo? Journal of Human Evolution*, **51**, 360–374.

Bar-Yosef, O., Arnold, M., Mercier, N., Belfer-Cohen, A., Goldberg, P., Housley, R., Laville, H., Meignen, L., Vogel, J.C., and Vandermeersch, B. (1996) The dating of the Upper Paleolithic Layers in Kebara Cave, Mt Carmel. *Journal of Archaeological Science*, **23**, 297–306.

Binford, L. R. (1984) Faunal *remains from Klasies River Mouth.* New York: Academic Press.

Bowler, J.M., Johnston, H., Olley, J.M., Prescott, J.R., Roberts, R.G., Shawcross, W., and Spooner, N.A. (2003) New ages for human occupation and climatic change at Lake Mungo, Australia. *Nature,* **421,** 837–840.

Brooks, A.S., Helgren, D.M., Jon, S.C., Franklin, A., Hornyak, W., Keating, J.M., Klein, R.G., Rink, W.J., Schwarcz, H., Smith, J.N.L., *et al.* (1995) Dating and context of three middle stone age sites with bone points in the Upper Semliki Valley, Zaire. *Science,* **268,** 548–553.

Brown, P., Sutikna, T., Morwood, M.J., Soejono, R.P., Jatmiko, WayhuSaptomo, E., and Awe Due, R. (2004) A new small-bodied hominin from the Late Pleistocene of Flores, Indonesia. *Nature,* **431,** 1055–1061.

Brumm, A., Aziz, F., van den Bergh, G.D., Morwood, M.J., Moore, M.W., Kurniawan, I., Hobbs, D.R., and Fullagar, R. (2006) Early stone technology on Flores and its implications for *Homo floresiensis.,* **441,** 624–628.

Chen, F., Hedges, R.E.M., and Yuan, Z. (1989) Accelerator radiocarbon dating for the Upper cave of Zhoukoudian. *Acta Anthropologica Sinica,* **8,** 216–221.

Curtis, G., Swisher, C. and Lewin, R. (2001) *Java man.* Little and Brown.

d'Errico, F., Henshilwood, C., Vanhaeren, M., and van Niekerk, K. (2005) *Nassarius kraussianus* shell beads from Blombos Cave: Evidence for symbolic behaviour in the Middle Stone Age. *Journal of Human Evolution,* **48,** 3–24.

Duarte, C.L., Maurício, J.O., Pettitt, P.B., Souto, P., Trinkaus, E., van der Plicht, H., and Zilhão, J.O. (1999) The early Upper Paleolithic human skeleton from the Abrigo do Lagar Velho (Portugal) and modern human emergence in Iberia. *Proceedings of the National Academy of Sciences of the United States of America,* **96,** 7604–7609.

Fiedorczuk, J., Bratlund, B., Kostrup, E., and Schild, R. (2007) Late Magdelenian feminine flint palquettes from Poland. *Antiquity,* **81.**

Finlayson, C., Giles Pacheco, F., Rodriguez-Vidal, J., Fa, D.A., Maria Gutierrez Lopez, J., Santiago Perez, A., Finlayson, G., Allue, E., Baena Preysler, J., Caceres, I. *et al.* (2006) Late survival of Neanderthals at the south-ernmost extreme of Europe. *Nature,* **443,** 850–853.

Forster, P. (2004) Ice ages and the mitochondrial DNA chronology of human dispersals: A review. *Philosophical Transactions of the Royal Society B: Biological Sciences,* **359,** 255–264.

Gilbert, M.T.P., Jenkins, D.L., Gotherstrom, A., Naveran, N., Sanchez, J.J., Hofreiter, M., Thomsen, P.F., Binladen, J., Higham, T.F.G., Yohe, R.M.II. *et al.* (2008) DNA from Pre-Clovis Human Coprolites in Oregon, North America. *Science,* **320,** 786–789.

Gilead, I. (1998) *The foragers of the Upper Palaeolithic period, in The Archaeology of Society in the Holy Land* (ed. Levy), Continuum International Publishing Group.

Gilead, I. and Bar-Yosef, O. (1993) Early Upper Palaeolithic sites in the Qadesh Barnea area SE Sinai. *Journal Field Archaeology,* **20,** 265–280.

Gilead, I. and Bar-Yosef, O. (1993) Early Upper Paleolithic sites in the Qadesh Barnea Area, NE Sinai. *Journal of Field Archaeology,* **20,** 265–280.

Glantz, M., Viola, B., Wrinn, P., Chikisheva, T., Derevianko, A., Krivoshapkin, A., Islamov, U., Suleimanov, R., and Ritzman, T. (2008) New hominin remains from Uzbekistan. *Journal of Human Evolution,* **55,** 223–237.

Goebel, T., Waters, M.R. and O'Rourke, D.H. (2008) The Late Pleistocene dispersal of modern humans in the Americas. *Science,* **319,** 1497–1502.

Gonda, E. and Katayama, K. (2006) Big feet in Polynesia: A somatometric study of the Tongans. *Anthropological Science,* **114,** 127–131.

Gravina, B., Mellars, P., and Ramsey, C.B. (2005) Radiocarbon dating of interstratified Neanderthal and early modern human occupations at the Chatelperronian type-site. *Nature,* **438,** 51–56.

Green, R.E., Malaspinas, A.-S., Krause, J., Briggs, A.W., Johnson, P.L.F., Uhler, C., Meyer, M., Good, J.M., Maricic, T., Stenzel, U., *et al.* (2008) A complete neandertal mitochondrial genome sequence determined by high-throughput sequencing. *Cell,* **134,** 416–426.

Grine, F.E. and Henshilwood, C.S. (2002) Additional human remains from Blombos Cave, South Africa: (1999–2000 excavations). *Journal of Human Evolution,* **42,** 293–302.

Grun, R., Shackleton, N.J., and Deacon, H.J. (1990) Electron-spin-resonance dating of tooth enamel from Klasies River Mouth cave. *Current Anthropology,* **31,** 427–432.

Grun, R. and Stringer, C. (2000) Tabun revisited: Revised ESR chronology and new ESR and U-series analyses of dental material from Tabun C1. *Journal of Human Evolution,* **39,** 601–602.

Grün, R., Stringer, C., McDermott, F., Nathan, R., Porat, N., Robertson, S., Taylor, L., Mortimer, G., Eggins, S., and McCulloch, M. (2005) U-series and ESR analyses of bones and teeth relating to the human burials from Skhul. *Journal of Human Evolution*, **49**, 316–334.

Grun, R. and Thorne, A. (1997) Dating the Ngandong humans. *Science*, **276**, 1575–1576.

Henshilwood, C. S., D'errico, F., Marean, C. W., Milo, R. G. and Yates, R. (2001) An early bone tool industry from the Middle stone Age at Blombos Cave, South Africa: implications for the origins of human behaviour, symbolism and language. *Journal of Human Evolution* **41** Issue 6 631–638.

Henshilwood, C.S. (2005) Stratigraphic integrity of the Middle Stone Age levels at Blombos Cave, *in From Tools to Symbols: From Early Hominids to Modern Humans* (eds F. d'Errico and L. Blackwell), Witwatersrand University Press, Johannesburg, pp. 441–458.

Howell, N., Elson, J.L., Turnbull, D.M., and Herrnstadt, C. (2004) African haplogroup L mtDNA sequences show violations of clock-like evolution. *Molecular Biology and Evolution*, **21**, 1843–1854.

Hudjashov, G., Kivisild, T., Underhill, P.A., Endicott, P., Sanchez, J.J., Lin, A.A., Shen, P., Oefner, P., Renfrew, C., Villems, R., *et al.* (2007) Revealing the prehistoric settlement of Australia by Y chromosome and mtDNA analysis. *Proceedings of the National Academy of Sciences*, **104**, 8726–8730.

Ingman, M., Kaessmann, H., Paabo, S., and Gyllensten, U. (2000) Mitochondrial genome variation and the origin of modern humans. *Nature*, **408**, 708–713.

Jacob, T., Indriati, E., Soejono, R.P., Hsü, K., Frayer, D.W., Eckhardt, R.B., Kuperavage, A.J., Thorne, A., and Henneberg, M. (2006) Pygmoid Australomelanesian *Homo sapiens* skeletal remains from Liang Bua, Flores: Population affinities and pathological abnormalities. *Proceedings of the National Academy of Sciences*, **103**, 13421–13426.

Jobling, M.A. and Tyler-Smith, C. (2003) The human Y chromosome: An evolutionary marker comes of age. *Nature Reviews*, **4**.

Johanson, D. and Edgar, B. (1996) *From Lucy to Language*. Cassell and Co., London.

Joyce, D.J. (2006) Chronology and new research on the Schaefer mammoth (?*Mammuthus primigenius*) site, *Kenosha County, Wisconsin, USA. Quaternary International*, **142–143**, 44–57.

Jungers, W.L., Larson, S.G., Harcourt-Smith, W., Morwood, M.J., Sutikna, T., Awe Due, R., and Djubiantono, T. Descriptions of the lower limb skeleton of *Homo floresiensis. Journal of Human Evolution*, in press. Corrected Proof.

Ke, Y.H., Su, B., Song, X.F., Lu, D.R., Chen, L.F., Li, H.Y., Qi, C.J., Marzuki, S., Deka, R., Underhill, P., *et al.* (2001) African origin of modern humans in East Asia: A tale of 12 000 Y chromosomes. *Science*, **292**, 1151–1153.

Klein, R. G., Avery, G., Cruz-Aribe, K., Halket, D., Parkington, J. E., Steele, T., Volman, T. P. and Yates, R. (2004) The Ysterfontein I Middle Stone Age site, South Africa, and early human exploitation of coastal resources. *Proceedings of the National Academy of Sciences* **101**(16) 5708–5715.

Krause, J., Orlando, L., Serre, D., Viola, B., Prufer, K., Richards, M.P., Hublin, J.-J., Hanni, C., Derevianko, A.P., and Paabo, S. (2007) Neanderthals in central Asia and Siberia. *Nature*, **449**, 902–904.

Krings, M., Geisert, H., Schmitz, R. W., Krainitzki, H. and Paabo, S. (1999) DNA sequence of the mitochondrial hypervariable region II from the Neandertal type specimen. *Proceedings of the National Academy of Sciences* **96** no 10 5581–5585.

Kuhn, S.L. and Stiner, M.C. (1998) The earliest Aurignacian of Riparo Mochi (Liguria, Italy). *Current Anthropology*, **39**.

Milo, R.G. (1998) Evidence for hominid predation at Klasies River Mouth, South Africa, and its implications for the behaviour of early modern humans. *Journal of Archaeological Science*, **25**, 99–133.

Morwood, M.J., O'Sullivan, P.B., Aziz, F., and Raza, A. (1998) Fission-track ages of stone tools and fossils on the east Indonesian island of Flores. *Nature*, **392**, 173–176.

Norton, C.J., and Gao, X. (2008) Zhoukoudian Upper Cave revisited. *Current Anthropology*, **49**, 732–745.

Otte, M., Biglari, F., Flas, D., Shidrang, S., Zwyns, N., Mashkour, M., Naderi, R., Mohaseb, A., Hashemi, N., Darvish, J., *et al.* (2007) The Aurignacian in the Zagros region: New research at Yafteh Cave, Lorestan, Iran. *Antiquity*, **81**, 82–96.

Pakendorf, B. and Stoneking, M. (2005) Mitochondrial DNA and human evolution. *Annual Review of Genomics and Human Genetics*, **6**, 165–183.

Pitulko, V.V., Nikolsky, P.A., Girya, E.Y., Basilyan, A.E., Tumskoy, V.E., Koulakov, S.A., Astakhov, S.N., Pavlova, E.Y., and Anisimov, M.A. (2004) The Yana RHS Site: Humans in the Arctic before the last glacial maximum. *Science*, **303**, 52–56.

Rink, W.J., Schwartz, H.P., Lee, H.K., Rees-Jones, J., Rabinovich, R., and Hovers, E. (2001) Electron spin resonance (ESR) and thermal ionisation mass spectrometric (TIMS) dating of teeth in Middle Palaeolithic layers at Amud cave, Israel. *Geoarchaeology*, **16**, 701–717.

Rougier, H., Milota, S., Rodrigo, R., Gherase, M., Sarcina, L., Moldovan, O., Zilhao, J., Constantin, S., Franciscus, R. G., Zollikofer, C. P. E., Ponce de Leon, M., and Trinkhaus, E. (2007) Pestera cu Oase and the cranial morphology of early Europeans. Proceedings of the National Academy of Sciences 104 no. 4 1165–1170.

Schmitz, R.W., Serre, D., Bonani, G., Feine, S., Hillgruber, F., Krainitzki, H., Pääbo, S., and Smith, F.H. (2002) The Neandertal type site revisited: Interdisciplinary investigations of skeletal remains from the Neander Valley, Germany. *Proceedings of the National Academy of Sciences of the United States of America*, **99**, 13342–13347.

Schwartz, H.P., Buhay, W., Grun, R., Valladas, H., Tchernov, E., Bar-Yosef, O., and Vandermeersch, B. (1989) ESR dating of the Neanderthal site, Kebara cave, Israel. *Journal of Archaeological Science*, **16**, 653–659.

Semal, P., Rougier, H., Crevecoeur, I., Jungels, C., Flas, D., Hauzeur, A., Maureille, B., Germonpré, M., Bocherens, H., Pirson, S., *et al.* (2009) New data on the late Neandertals: Direct dating of the Belgian Spy fossils. *American Journal of Physical Anthropology*, **138**, 421–428.

Shang, H., Tong, H., Zhang, S., Chen, F., and Trinkaus, E. (2007) An early modern human from Tianyuan Cave, Zhoukoudian, China. *Proceedings of the National Academy of Sciences*, **104**, 6573–6578.

Shea, J. J. (2006) The origins of lithic projectile point technology: evidence from Africa, the Levant, and Europe. *Journal of archaeological science.* 33 issue 6 823–846.

Shen, G., Wang, W., Cheng, H., and Edwards, R.L. (2007) Mass spectrometric U-series dating of Laibin hominid site in Guangxi, southern China. *Journal of Archaeological Science*, **34**, 2109–2114.

Su, B., Xiao, J., Underhill, P., Deka, R., Zhang, W., Akey, J., Huang, W., Shen, D., Lu, D., Luo, J., *et al.* (1999) Y-Chromosome evidence for a Northward migration of Modern Humans into Eastern Asia during the Last Ice Age. *The American Journal of Human Genetics*, **65**, 1718–1724.

Tattersall, I. and Schwartz, J.H. (2000) *Extinct Humans*, Westview Press, Boulder, Colorado.

Trinkaus, E. (2005) Early modern humans. *Annual Review of Anthropology*, **34**, 207–230.

Trinkhaus, E., Moldovan, O., Milota, S., Bilgar, A., Sarcina, L., Athreya, S., Bailey, S. E., Rodrigo, R., Gherase, M., Higham, T., Ramsey, C. B. and van der Plicht, J. (2003) An early modern human from the Pestera cu Oase, Romania. *Proceedings of the National Academy of Sciences* 100 no.20 11231–11236.

Valladas, H., Joron, J.L., Valladas, G., Arensburg, B., Bar-Josef, O., Belfer-Cohen, A., Goldberg, P., Laville, H., Meignen, L., Rak, Y., *et al.* (1987) Thermoluminescence dates for the Neanderthal burial site at Kebara, Israel. *Nature*, **330**, 159–160.

Valladas, H., Mercier, N., Froget, L., Hovers, E., Joron, J.L., Kimbel, W.H., and Rak, Y. (1999) TL dates for the Neanderthal Site of the Amud Cave, Israel. *Journal of Archaeological Science*, **26**, 259–268.

Valladas, H., Reyss, J.L., Joron, J.L., Valladas, G., Bar-Josef, O., and Vandermeersch, B. (1988) Thermoluminescence dating of Mousterian Troto-Cro-Magnon remains from Israel and the origin of modern man. Nature, 108 (2716), **331**, 614–616.

Vanhaeren, M., d'Errico, F., Stringer, C., James, S.L., Todd, J.A., and Mienis, H.K. (2006) Middle Palaeolithic shell beads in Israel and Algeria. *Science*, **312**, 1785–1788.

Walter, B. and Aubrey, T. (2001) Le site solutreen des Maitreauz Bulletin des amis du Grand Pressigny. *Musee Antiquities Nationales*, **52**, 23–29.

Waters, M.R. and Stafford, T.W. Jr (2007) Redefining the age of Clovis: Implications for the peopling of the Americas. *Science*, **315**, 1122–1126.

Wendt, W.E. (1976) Art mobilier from the Apollo 11 cave, South West Africa: Africa's oldest dated works of art. *South African Archaeological Bulletin*, **31**, 5–11.

Yellen, J.E., Brooks, A.S., Cornelissen, E., Mehlman, M.J., and Stewart, K. (1995) A middle stone age worked bone industry from Katanda Upper Semlik Valley, Zaire. *Science*, **268**, 553–536.

Zilhao, J., d'Errico, F., Bordes, J.-G., Lenoble, A., Texier, J.-P., and Rigaud, J.-P. (2006) Analysis of Aurignacian interstratification at the Chatelperronian-type site and implications for the behavioral modernity of Neandertals. *Proceedings of the National Academy of Sciences*, **103**, 12643–12648.

12

Coda

Now that the time-line of the Emergence of Humans has been laid out, complete with the evidence, it is time to address the questions raised about the shape of the evolutionary tree. Although each chapter dealt with the relationships between species and the characters used to distinguish them, in drawing up the human evolutionary tree we need to take a broader view. The number of species and genera that are recognized is not agreed by everyone, of course and new finds will alter the picture too, but at the time of writing (2009) there are 25 species of 7 genera that we should *consider* in any evolutionary tree. These are listed in Table 12.1 and it should be noted that the status of some of these species is uncertain.

In Chapter 7 (Box 7.1) you read about the single-species hypothesis of Loring Brace and Milford Wolpoff, a hypothesis that was based on the idea that there was only one niche for hominins to occupy. Since only one species can occupy a niche at any one time, there was only one hominin species at any one time. Evolution, there-fore would be phyletic (also known as anagenesis), in which one species accumulated changes over time and became a different species.

♦ Is there an example from hominin history where phyletic evolution might have taken place?

♦ Yes. The sequence of species from the Middle Awash (Section 7.8) which shows *Ardipithecus ramidus*, *Australopithecus anamensis* and *Au. afarensis* in an accurately dated sequence with no overlap of the species in time.

Any time sequence has uncertainty associated with it, however, in that it isn't possible to be certain about what the time range of a species was. Absence of fossils that are as rare as hominin ones are does not mean that you can be certain that they were absent.

The Emergence of Humans Patricia Ash and David Robinson
© 2010 John Wiley & Sons, Ltd

Table 12.1 The genera and species of hominin that are currently part of the discussion of the human evolutionary tree

Earliest date/mya	genus	species	location comments	
7.2	Sahelanthropus	tchadensis	Chad	hominin status uncertain
6.0	Orrorin	tugenensis	Tugen Hills, Kenya	hominin status uncertain
5.8	Ardipithecus	kadabba	Middle Awash, Ethiopia	
4.4		ramidus	Middle Awash, Ethiopia	
4.2	Australopithecus	anamensis	Ethiopia and N Kenya	
3.9		afarensis	Ethiopia and Tanzania	
3.5		bahrelghazali	Chad	
3.3	Kenyanthropus	platyops	N Kenya	Has affinities with *H. rudolfensis*
2.5	Australopithecus	africanus	South Africa	
		garhi	Ethiopia	
2.4	Paranthropus	aethiopicus	Ethiopia and N Kenya	
		boisei	Ethiopia and N Tanzania	
	Homo	rudolfensis	East Africa	Regarded by some as an australopith. Has affinities with *K. platyops.*
2.0	Paranthropus	robustus	South Africa	Has also been split into two species, *P. robustus* and *P. crassidens*
1.9	Homo	habilis	East Africa	
1.8		erectus	Asia	
1.6		ergaster	East Africa and Georgia	Perhaps also Europe and Africa
		georgicus	Dmanisi, Georgia	
0.9		cepranensis	Ceprano, Italy	May be *H. ergaster*
0.8		antecessor	Atapuerca, Spain	May be *H. erectus*
0.7		heidelbergensis	Africa and Europe	May be *H. heidelbergensis*
0.3		helmei	Africa	
0.2		neanderthalensis	Europe and Asia	
0.16		sapiens	First found in East Africa	status uncertain
0.02		floresiensis	Flores, Indonesia	status uncertain

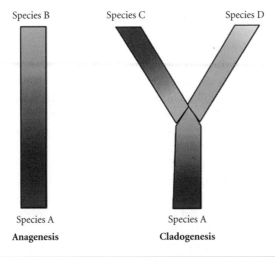

Species B   Species C   Species D

Species A   Species A

Anagenesis   **Cladogenesis**

Figure 12.1 Phyletic and branching evolution compared.

The single species hypothesis is falsified if more than one species of hominin occurs in the same place at the same time.

♦ Is there an example of more than one species of hominin occurring in the same place at the same time?

♦ Yes there are several examples. *Paranthropus boisei* (2.3–1.4) and *Homo habilis* (1.8–1.5 mya) occurred together. *Paranthropus robustus* and *Homo* sp. occur in the same sites and time range in South Africa (1.8–1.0 mya). There are also three species of australopith in the same time period: *Australopithecus africanus* (2.9–2.4 mya), *Australopithecus garhi* (2.5 mya) and *Paranthropus aethiopicus* (2.7–2.3 mya).

For several hominin species to be extant at the same time in the same region, evolution must have proceeded by branching, a process also known as cladogenesis (Figure 12.1). Neither of these processes need be mutually exclusive, so it is certainly possible that the early speciation of hominins in Africa was by anagenesis and subsequently by cladogenesis.

Looking at the diversity of the hominins, as set out in Table 12.1, a number of questions are raised. The most obvious one is whether these are *all* genuine species. Certainly you could increase the number slightly, or decrease it by quite a lot, but however much you decrease it you would still end up with over a dozen species, which is quite a significant diversity for a taxonomic group that is now only represented by one species. The oldest putative hominin, *Sahelanthropus*, is very close to the last common ancestor of hominins and chimpanzees, so we probably now have a clear idea of the period (7 million years) over which this diverse range of species evolved. We do not, of course, have anything like a complete fossil record. To illustrate just how this can cause problems let's consider the period 7–5 million years ago. There are three genera from that period, *Sahelanthropus*, *Orrorin* and *Ardipithecus*. It is possible to interpret these species as part of a diversity of forms that were a radiation from the Miocene apes and so part of a bushy expansion with side branches that didn't lead anywhere. It might even be, as Senut and Pickford suggested, that *Ardipithecus* is the ancestor of chimpanzees, *Sahelanthropus* the ancestor of an extinct ape line (or possibly gorillas) and *Orrorin* is the ancestor of hominins. Set against this, is the fact that the three genera almost certainly do not overlap in time and *Sahelanthropus* is the only genus known from a period of a million years. So, if there was a bushy radiation with diversity of species so early in the hominin evolutionary tree, as yet there is no evidence that supports the proposition. 'More fossils may fill the gaps' is one possible argument, but it is a difficult argument to sustain when, in essence, it runs – 'there might be more diversity if we had more specimens', for that will always be true!

A second question raised by the diversity shown in the table is the influence of the rarity of specimens. Is it possible that the diversity of species arises from the rarity of fossils? At one time it seemed that every new find was viewed by the finder as a new taxon. With so few finds being anywhere near complete skeletons, the defining features of a new species were, of necessity, limited. Also, because specimens were so rare, a comparative approach which took into account inter-individual variability, was generally impossible. Some more recent finds have included remains of several individuals, for example *Australopithecus afarensis*, so the establishment of species definitions can be more robust. However, there is one important proviso to make here which is that we are not dealing with a biological species definition based on ability to interbreed, but a species definition based on skeletal features and, for later species, tool technologies. It has been pointed out that skeletons of living monkeys are really quite similar, even though in appearance and behaviour the species are very different. It is doubtful if we could produce the same species divisions in present day monkeys if we only had the skeletons to work from. Nevertheless, although this sounds depressingly negative, we can make deductions about relationships from an analysis of the characteristics of the skeletal remains of hominins. Distinctive features can be separated from common anatomical ones and specimens grouped according to their shared primitive and derived characters. Functional deductions from structure, for example diet deduced from tooth type, provide information about particular adaptations shown by specimens. With the added geological and archaeological contexts, these can give information about the selective pressures that the specimens may have been subjected to and hence their evolutionary path.

A third question prompted by the diversity of hominin species is how far the diversity is a consequence of geographical distribution. Given the distribution of hominins across Europe, Africa and Asia, is it possible that geographical isolation could produce speciation? One possible example is *H. antecessor*, which appears to have originated in Spain from an early *H. ergaster* lineage that also gave rise to *H. georgicus*. Part of the support for this theory comes from the tool technology. All these species shard the Oldowan style of tools rather than the more advanced Acheulean technology of *H. heidelbergensis* and later *H. ergaster*.

There is an alternative view of the diversity of hominin species, which is that the number is far too high. After carrying out a genetic analysis of humans and chimps, Curnoe and Thorne (2003) argued that there had only been four species of *Homo* in the sequence leading to *Homo sapiens*, since the last common ancestor of chimps and humans, with the chimp being renamed *Homo troglodytes*. This last species would also include the bonobo, *Pan paniscus* (the pigmy chimp); hence all the chimps and fossil humans would be placed in the same genus as modern humans. Their argument is based on what they see as a short genetic distance between chimps and humans, coupled with an estimated 2 million years needed for sufficient genetic divergence to have occurred within the line to produce a branch into two species. Given that the last common ancestor of chimps and humans was around 7 million years ago, they argued that there has also been insufficient time for substantial speciation to have taken place.

The argument for insufficient time for extensive speciation comes, in part, from work on chimps. There are three subspecies of chimps:

♦ *Pan troglodytes schweinfurthii:* Eastern Common Chimpanzee

♦ *Pan troglodytes troglodytes:* Central Common Chimpanzee

♦ *Pan troglodytes verus:* Western Common Chimpanzee

It is estimated on the basis of genetic analysis that *P.t. verus* diverged from other chimps 1.58 mya (Morin *et al.*, 1994). However, there is no evidence of low fertility between the subspecies. Captive colonies in a zoo (Tama Park) appear to interbreed freely, with 48 cross-breeds existing there. This suggests that 1.6 million years is insufficient time for speciation to have occurred in chimps (see review by Hunt (2003)).

In a subsequent paper Curnoe, Thorne and Coate (2006) reconsidered the position of chimps and suggested that two other taxonomic frameworks were possible. The first would place the last common ancestor in its own genus and leave *Homo* and *Pan* as separate ones. The second would extend the genus containing the last common ancestor to include the first 2.0–4.0 million years of both the human and chimp lineages.

The alternative view coming, as it does, from a purely genetic analysis is not one that will be taken up un-critically by those building an evolutionary framework based on cladistic analysis of skull and skeletal features. The difference between the view of 1 genus and 4 species, versus 7 genera and 25 species is not likely to be easy to resolve. It will be difficult for many people to accept that, for example, *H. erectus*, Neandertals and *H. sapiens* are in fact one species, given the appearance of the skulls. However, with these widely differing views in mind, we need to attempt to draw up something approaching a consensus evolutionary tree (Figure 12.2).

The first hominins appeared in Africa about 7 mya and probably did not leave the continent. Whether the last common ancestor was *Orrorin*-like or *Sahelanthropus*-like (or neither) isn't clear, but that last common ancestor gave rise to the sequence *Ardipithecus ramidus* to *Australopithecus anamensis* to *Au. afarensis*. From the *Au. afarensis* line came the *Homo* and *Paranthropus* lines, as separate branches, with the species of *Paranthropus* dying out, perhaps as a result of competition with tool-using *Homo*. Also on side

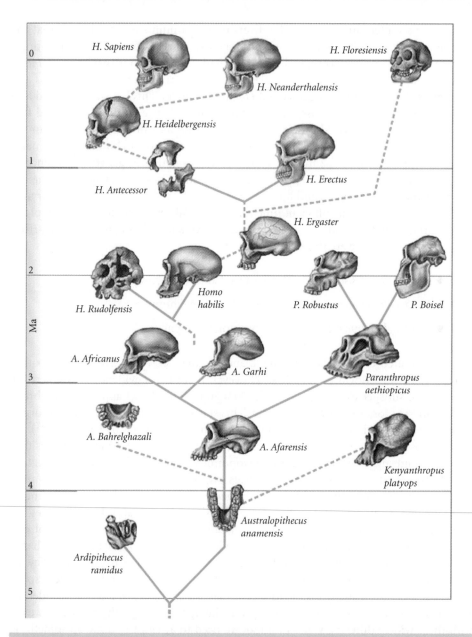

Figure 12.2 Summary of evolutionary relationships in the hominins. Reproduced from 99% Ape. The Natural History Museum. Debbie Maizels, adapted from Biology: The dynamics of life 2004 McGraw-Hill

branches are the other species of *Australopithecus* and *Kenyanthropus*. About 1.7 mya the first migration out of Africa occurred. *Homo ergaster* carried with it Oldowan tools and speciation took place outside Africa. In Africa, *H. ergaster* developed Acheulean tool technology, subsequently carried into Europe by *H. heidelbergensis*. *Homo erectus* appeared in Asia and migrated widely, appearing in Europe and Africa. Around 0.5 mya Neandertals appeared in Europe, which *H. heidelbergensis* had already reached from Africa. At some point, probably earlier than 0.2 mya, *Homo sapiens* emerged from a heidelbergensis stock in Africa and about 120 kya started a migration into Europe and Asia. The last Neanderthal died around 27 kya and *H. erectus* survived until around 40 kya. The rather controversial *H. floresiensis* would have been the final extinction at around 18 kya.

There will be new finds in the future that will undoubtedly modify accepted views of hominin evolution. There will also be refinement of dates and probably changes in the known geographical range of species. This information will improve our understanding of the details, but it does seem now that the timescale over which hominins evolved is more certain than it was in the past, with a relatively good agreement between anthropological and genetic estimates. The human lineage was thought to be hundreds of thousand of years long, before 1961, so when 'Zinj' was dated at 1.6 1.9 mya it transformed our understanding of the antiquity of humans. Gradually, the dates of specimens pushed the date further back. Now we can be more confident that we have reached the limit, with a date of 7.5 mya as the oldest possible date for the start of the human lineage. We can also have confidence that the search for our ancestors will continue into the future. There will always be the possibility of that one fantastic find that will both enhance our understanding of who we are and where we come from and bring great fame to the finder. With these twin goals beckoning, we can be sure that there will always be people prepared to pursue the quest for further fossils and an improved understanding of the emergence of humans.

References

Curnoe, D. and Thorne, A. (2003) Number of ancestral human species: a molecular perspective. *HOMO – Journal of Comparative Human Biology*, **53**, 201–224.

Curnoe, D., Thorne, A. and Coate, J.A. (2006) Timing and tempo of primate speciation. *Journal of Evolutionary Biology*, **19**, 59–65.

Hunt, K.D. (2003) The single species hypothesis: truly dead and pushing up bushes, or still twitching and ripe for resuscitation? *Human Biology*, **75**, 485–502.

Morin, P.A., Moore, J.J., Chakraborty, R., Jin, L., Goodall, J. and Woodruff, D.S. (1994) Kin selection, social structure, gene flow, and the evolution of Chimpanzees. *Science*, **265**, 1193–1201.

Answers to End of Chapter Questions

Chapter 1

Question 1.1

The brain of *Homo sapiens* is 2.1% of body mass and weighs around 1500 g. There are larger brains in larger animals. For example, the brain of an elephant has a mass of 7.5 kg which taking the mass of a typical elephant of 5000 kg, gives a relative mass of 0.15% of body mass. So, however we compare the intelligence of humans with that of elephants, neither mass nor relative size would be a good indicator of intelligence.

Question 1.2

1797	Report of presence of flint tools in gravel beds at Hoxne
1823	Discovery of 'Red Lady' at Paviland
1841	Discovery of tools in undisturbed strata in the Somme Valley
1848	Discovery of Gibraltar skull
1856	Discovery of human fossils in the Neander valley
1859	Publication of Darwin's *On the Origin of Species*
1863	Publication of Lyell's *Antiquity of Man*
1871	Publication of Darwin's *The Descent of Man*

Chapter 2

Question 2.1

Figure 2.1 shows that in the last 4 million years there have been six periods when the magnetic field has been in the normal direction and six when it has been in the reverse direction. Thus there have been 11 reversals in the period, the last occurring at 0.78 Ma.

Question 2.2

Pollen samples taken from sediment will consist of pollen shed by plants in the locality and pollen blown in from other areas. Beetles are not so dispersed, are quite sensitive to climate and an assemblage of species may allow an accurate assessment of the local climate. However, if the two types of pollen can be identified then pollen can still give a reasonable indication of local climate.

Question 2.3

The fossil was found in a bed that was closely related to a layer of volcanic ash. The ash could be dated by the potassium/argon method, which gives good precision.

Chapter 3

Question 3.1

DNA make RNA makes protein One gene – one protein

Question 3.2

- ♦ More offspring are produced than could possibly survive.
- ♦ There is a struggle for existence in which individuals best able to obtain food resources and avoid disease and predators have a greater chance of survival.
- ♦ Even within a particular species there is a considerable degree of variation e.g. in eye colour, size, musculature and
- ♦ Features of individuals that increase their likelihood of survival to produce offspring are heritable.

The offspring inherit features present in the parents.

Question 3.3

Fitness is defined as relative reproductive success which can include one or both of fecundity and offspring survival. So in this context greater fitness would be linked to the emergence of a mutant gene within a population of organisms. A dominant mutant gene would spread more rapidly in the population than a recessive gene.

Answers to in-text Questions

Table 3.1 (b) The mother and father have genotype *Aa*, and both have achondroplasia. The mother and father produce 50% gametes with the genotype *a*, that codes for normal skeletal growth and 50% with genotype *A* that codes for achondroplasia

So genotype of parental generation, **P**: mother *Aa* x father *Aa*		
Genotypes of gametes	Egg *A*	Egg *a*
Sperm *A*	*AA*	*Aa*
Sperm *a*	*Aa*	*aa*

Table 3.2 (b) Punnet square for calculating the proportion of offspring genotypes from a father with one albino gene, *Bb*, and a mother with two albino genes, *bb*

P generation: parent genotypes: father *BB* x *Bb*		
Genotypes of gametes	Egg *b*	Egg *b*
Sperm *b*	*bb*	*bb*
Sperm *B*	*Bb*	*Bb*

Chapter 4

Question 4.1

+ A primate is an arboreal animal living in tropical and sub-tropical forest; this does not apply to humans who live in a huge range of habitats, and are not arboreal.

+ Primates have grasping hands and feet with opposable thumbs and great toes. Hands and feet have ridged finger and toe pads; hands are touch sensitive. These features apply to humans. However, human feet are adapted for upright walking and have lost the grasping function.

+ Locomotion in primates is hind-limb dominated; this applies to bipedal humans!

+ Vision is highly developed with eyes at the front of the head producing stereoscopic vision. Olfactory sense is reduced. This applies to humans.

+ The snout is shortened; there is reduction of the number of incisors and front teeth. This applies to humans.

- ♦ Large brains reflect increased intelligence in primates, including humans. Reproductive output is low with greater longevity. This applies to humans.

- ♦ Gestation period is long with small litters, often just one. This applies to humans.

- ♦ Age at first reproduction is late; certainly true for humans.

Question 4.2

For each of the three species, *Adapis, Notharcus* and *Cantius*, the teeth on each half of the mandible include two incisors, one canine, four premolars and three molars. So the dental formula for the mandible of the three species of adapiformes is: 2 1 4 3 (using the convention outlined in Box 4.1).

Note that in these sketches it is difficult to distinguish the premolars from the molars.

Question 4.3

1 The fossil bones date from the Eocene, and so they are extremely old, dated at least 55.5–35.5 mya.

Absolute dating techniques are inappropriate, for Eocene limestone e.g. radio-potassium dating and fission track dating, can only be applied to volcanic rock, not to sedimentary rock. Relative and indirect dating techniques are the best option. Stratigraphy involves dating fossil bones by identifying fossils of other species in the same stratigraphic layer whose date is known. Faunal correlation draws on changes in groups of fossil animals e.g. horses, elephants. If fossils of *Eosimias* were found in a sediment layer sandwiched between two sediment layers containing fossils whose ages are known, then that date range could be attributed to *Eosimias*. (Section 2.4)

2 Comparisons of dates for fossil primates helps paleoanthropologists to build an evolutionary sequence e.g. neither of two fossil species of the same ages could be the ancestors of each other.

Chapter 5

Question 5.1

a

i Gibbons are monogamous, and pair for life. There is limited competition between males for females and body size and canine teeth size in the two sexes are the same.

ii In contrast male chimpanzees are about 30% larger than females, and the males have larger canine teeth than the females. Chimpanzees live in loose groups, a multimale-multifemale social grouping with polygynous mating. The group comprises related males, and both related and unrelated females and their offspring. Male chimpanzees in a group co-operate with each other to fend off rival groups, but within their group they compete with each other for females.

b   If there are sufficient fossil finds of an extinct hominoid species canine teeth dimensions and possibly body sizes of males and females can be compared. Fossil remains of *Proconsul africanus* at Rusinga Island show that the males had larger canine teeth than the females, suggesting a social structure that included polygyny.

Question 5.2

a   *Morotopithecus*, Hylobatids (gibbons) and *Pierolapithecus* and the great apes and humans are crown hominoids.

b   *Pierolapithecus* is a representative of the sister group to great apes and humans. The upright or **orthograde** body plan, along with its ape-like facial anatomy, places *Pierolapithecus* as a sister group for great apes and humans.

c   No. *Morotopithecus* is a genus that branched off at an early point from the line that resulted in the radiation of crown hominoids.

d   Great apes and humans are hominids.

Question 5.3

The teeth, including the cheek teeth, are coated with thin enamel. The incisors are of similar small size, and the canine teeth relatively small. Premolars and molars have broad rounded surfaces.

Question 5.4

The incisor that is visible is forward projecting and there is a gap, a diastema, between it and the canine tooth. The premolars and molars appear to be of similar size. The procumbent incisors could have been used to grasp fruit and cut into it. The pointed canines would have grasped the fruit and the molars with their thick enamel would have crushed and broken down the fruit.

Chapter 6

Question 6.1

In *Ardiptihecus ramidus* the foramen magnum is further forward than in apes, which would suggest that the head was on top of the spine and thus the species was bipedal. It has been suggested that bipedalism developed as the environment got drier and the habitat became more open and savannah-like. Bipedal hominins would have had a selective advantage. The evidence from the other fossil animals associated with *Ar. ramidus* suggests that it lived in a forest habitat, which does not accord with the theory of the direr habitat providing a selective advantage.

Chapter 7

Question 7.1

The single species hypothesis states that only one species of hominin existed at any one time. Evolution proceeded by steady improvements up a single ladder. The rationale for this view was that two species with similar adaptations cannot co-exist in the same environment – this is the principle of competitive exclusion. As culture was considered to be the defining adaptation in humans, the inevitable conclusion was that there could only be one species existing at any one time. The theory collapsed when the fossil evidence started to show that more than one species co-existed, for example at around 2.5 mya at least three species of hominins appear to have co-existed in Africa. *Australopithecus garhi*, (2.5 mya), *Australopithecus africanus* (2.9-2.4 mya) and *Paranthropus aethiopicus* (2.7–2.3 mya) were contemporary with each other.

Chapter 8

Question 8.1

a   True.

b   Untrue, or most unlikely. The evolutionary tree in **Figure 7.5** indicates that earlier species, *Ardipithecus ramidus* and *Australopithecus anamensis* gave rise to *Australopithecus afarensis*. Statement c is also untrue as *Ardipithecus* is a hominin.

Question 8.2

An endocast might show whether or not Broca's area of the brain was present. Presence does not indicate that speech was possible, but absence would mean that speech was not possible. The size of the thoracic spinal cord canal might indicate whether the nerves that would provide the fine control of musculature necessary for speech were present. The size would need to be compared with modern *Homo sapiens* (see section 8.11).

Chapter 9

Question 9.1 See Table 9.2.

Question 9.2

a   Untrue. 'Lumping' does on the face of it, seem to be reasonable and logical strategy. However, as we have only information available from fossil anatomy, and much of that is not very detailed, it is unwise to apply 'lumping' where small anatomical differences exist between fossils because by doing so we are likely to miss important speciation events. The human evolutionary tree is complex and probably evenmore bushy than we currently know.

b   True. There is a trend for the back teeth in *Homo* to be reduced in size in comparison to australopiths (Chapters 4 and 6). As this reduction in size links to the reduction of tough plant food in the diet, similar reductions in back teeth may be seen in species that do not have a close evolutionary relationship with hominins, such as cats, which have also lost molars, leaving just one on each side of the upper and lower jaws. Therefore similarities or differences in the dentition of two *Homo* species cannot be used in isolation to deduce evolutionary relationships.

c   True. The dates of later African *Homo erectus* are consistent with a speciation event about 1.0 mya–0.800 kya that produced *Homo antecessor* from *Homo erectus*. Some features of fossil anatomy identified in *Homo antecessor*, make the species distinct from *Homo erectus*, (but not all paleoanthropologists agree with this view). In contrast to *Homo erectus*, *H. antecessor* has a human-like mid-face topography, with prognathism and maxillary hollowing (hollow cheeks). *Homo antecessor* has a marked double arched eyebrow ridge, similar to that of *H. erectus*. The teeth of *Homo antecessor* show moderate taurodontism similar to that of *H. erectus*. The reduction of post-canine teeth in *H. antecessor*, especially that seen in molar 3 is found in both *H. erectus*, and *H. heidelbergensis*. So the dates, as well as the similarities and differences between *H. antecessor* and *H. erectus* are consistent with the view that *H. antecessor* may have evolved in Africa from *H. erectus*.

Table 9.2   Summary table of main sites where *H. erectus* dating between ~1.0 mya and 700 kya have been found.[1]

Region	Site	Fossil find	Approximate age range
Africa	Bouri	Calvaria; femora and tibia	1.0 mya
Java	Sangiran	skull	1.5–1.0 mya
	Trinil	calvaria	1.0 mya–700 kya
China	Lantian	Cranial fragments; a molar	1.15 mya–700 kya
	Zhoukoudian	5 calvariae, facial & cranial fragments, mandibles 7 teeth	550–750 kya
	Yuanmou	2 incisors.	700 kya

[1]Note that many of the dates for *Homo erectus* fossils in Java and China are uncertain. As far as possible we have provided the most likely date ranges, but further applications of new dating techniques are likely to provide more accurate dates in future.

d   Untrue. It's not possible for Neandertals to be the ancestors of *Homo antecessor*, because Neandertals had not emerged before 700 kya. (The earliest known Neandertals are dated at about 200 kya – see Chapter 10).

e   True. *Homo erectus* emerged at about 1.8 mya and from Chapter 9 we saw that the species was still extant by 700 kya. So even on that basis clearly *Homo erectus* had existed longer than any other known species of *Homo*. Chapter 11 includes evidence that suggests that *Homo erectus* may have persisted up to about 30 kya in Java.

Question 9.3

Oldowan tools found at Gran Dolina were used for butchering meat and defleshing bones. The tools had one or more sharp edges and some of them have use-wear on all of their sharp edges (Table 9.1). The sharp edge of a quartzite tool for example, showed discontinuous splitting, as well as compression and corrosion, and a dense convex deposit, suggesting that it had been used for butchering meat and cutting or scraping bone for de-fleshing. Different sizes of flakes and chopping tools could be selected as required. Use-wear analysis also suggested that the tools were used for cutting hide and wood. Scraping fat from hide enabled consumption of the fat and also use of the hide. So clearly the Oldowan technology was used for a variety of functions which were of crucial importance in processing food and other resources, including hide and wood. Oldowan technology persisted for a long time, more than a million years and was adequate for the subsistence of both *Homo erectus* and *Homo antecessor*.

Question 9.4

The main distinguishing feature of *Homo antecessor* was identified in the type specimen, ATD6-69, a juvenile aged about 10 years old. The available fossil fragments of the skull, indicate a human-like mid-face topography, showing mid-face prognathism and maxillary hollowing, i.e. hollow cheeks. Such features are not seen in *Homo erectus*.

Chapter 10

Question 10.1

Any of the following would be appropriate
- Increased brain size and complexity are associated with improved cognitive abilities, which in turn facilitate development of complex skills such as planning strategies for hunting large fast-moving animal prey.

♦ Improved cognitive abilities derived from increased brain size and complexity facilitate technological innovation, which for extinct *Homo* species, provided enhanced ability to obtain and process fresh meat.

♦ Increased brain complexity is linked to enhanced 'social intelligence' important for an individual's status within a social group.

♦ Increased brain size and complexity links to enhanced social intelligence whereby individuals skilled in making and maintaining alliances within a social group are more likely to be successful at producing offspring that themselves survive and produce offspring.

♦ Those individuals that have a higher status gained by alliances and/or prowess in obtaining meat, within a social group are more likely to leave offspring who survive to adulthood and produce viable offspring themselves.

Question 10.2a See Table 10.4 (overleaf).

Question 10.2b

There are nine similarities and no differences between the features listed for the Sima de los Huesos crania and those of *H. heidelbergensis*. Their similarities to *Homo heidelbergensis* may justify placing the Sima de los Huesos crania as *H.heidelbergensis* (a number of palaeoanthropologists do so). As the dates attributed to the Sima de los Huesos fossils fall within those for *H.heidelbergensis* it may be a reasonable to assume they are all the same species. However it is important to distinguish features that are homoplasies from those that are homologies and Table 8.2 does not do so.

There are four similarities and six differences between the Sima de los Huesos crania and Neandertal crania. Some of the differences relate to the prominence of a feature e.g. in Neandertals there is an occipital torus but it has become more prominent forming a 'bun'. There is a sharp increase in brain size in the Neandertal crania in comparison to those from Sima de los Huesos. The fossil anatomy and the dates (400–350 Kya) of the Sima de los Huesos hominins suggest that they were not Neandertals.

Question 10.2c

If the similarities between the Sima de los Huesos and Neandertal crania are homologous and not due to homoplasy, then the dates and location of the fossils are consistent with an evolutionary relationship between these two groups of fossil crania.

Question 10.3

The Boxgrove *Homo heidelbergensis* were probably nomadic and subsisted by hunting large mammal prey. To catch a fast-moving large mammal requires co-operation

Table 10.4 Comparison of cranial features of Sima de los Huesos hominids, *Homo heidelbergensis* and Neandertals

Feature in crania from Sima de los Huesos 350–400 kya	Feature in crania of *Homo heidelbergensis* 600–125 kya	Feature in crania of Neandertals 240–30 kya
Crania 4 & 5: cranial capacities 1390–cm³ & 1125–cm³	Cranial capacity up to 1200–1325–cm³	Cranial capacity up to 1600–1700 cm³
Slight sagittal keel on cranium	Slight sagittal keel on cranium	Absent
Double-arched brow ridge	Present e.g. Bodo	Present
Crania high and rounded	Crania high and rounded	Crania long and low
Crania broadest at the base	Cranium broadest at the base	Cranium broadest in parietal region, above the base
Mastoid process prominent	Unknown	Small mastoid processes
Retromolar space on mandible	Retromolar space on mandible	Retromolar space on mandible
Taurodont molars	Taurodont molars	Taurodont molars
Occipital torus	Occipital torus	Pronounced occipital bun
No true suprainiac fossa but pitted area present at back of occipital bone	Absent	Suprainiac fossa at back of occipital bone
Middle of face pulled forward	Middle of face pulled forward	Middle of face pulled forward

between individuals, so at least during hunting forays, *Homo heidelbergensis* would have worked in groups. The pronounced muscle attachments on the Boxgrove tibia support the view that the hominids were active. There is evidence that *Homo heidelbergensis* used spears. Discovery of a round hole in a horse scapula found at the Boxgrove horse butchery site, suggested a spear wound in the animal's shoulder. Cut marks on the scapula are above the level of the hole. Wooden spears dated at 300 – 400 000 years old and contemporary with European *Homo heidelbergensis*, have been found e.g. the Clacton spear tip; the Schoningen spears. The Boxgrove horse butchery site with six to seven flint knapping areas, suggests that a group of *H. heidelbergensis* were working together. Stones suitable for hand-axe manufacture had been taken to the horse butchery site. Experiments in which a butcher used newly made hand-axes for skinning and butchering a deer, demonstrated that they were efficient tools for removal of hide, and de-fleshing bones. No evidence for camp fires has been found at the horse butchery site, or elsewhere at Boxgrove. *Homo heidelbergensis* was either eating raw meat, or portions of carcass were taken elsewhere for cooking and consumption.

(You could also mention that the large brain size of *H. heidelbergensis* suggests a long period of infancy and childhood during which the mother would need support, so a social structure in which this was possible is indicated. Such a structure would require a degree of co-operation between males, albeit interlaced with competition for females, a situation that is typical of chimpanzee group structure, and indeed modern human behaviour.)

Question 10.4

A group of hominids can put up a better defence against rival groups and predators than individuals, both in terms of vigilance and beating off an attack. A group may be more effective than an individual at finding plant food and in locating and scavenging animal carcasses. Although Neandertals were robust and capable of heavy manual labour, like other hominids, they had no natural weapons such as claws and sharp teeth. Therefore the best chance of hunting large mammal prey successfully would have been for a group to co-operate and work together. Living as a group also meant that pregnant and nursing females could be supported by the group. Co-operation in a group is also beneficial when the group consists of relatives, which share genes. Those genes are more likely to be passed to future generations when offspring are reared within a stable social group.

Chapter 11

Question 11.1

The six bullet points are as follows although there are other features that could be mentioned.

- The Qafzeh skull has a high flat-sided cranium (Figure 11.11a) whereas the base of the Neandertal cranium is broader than in the upper part and there is a marked occipital bun at the back.

- Neandertal skulls have a suprainiac fossa, a depressed and pitted area at the back of the skull, a feature absent in Qafzeh IX.

- The mid-face of Qafzeh IX is flat (Figure 11.11b), in contrast to the Neandertal mid-face, which is pushed outwards by huge nasal cavities.

- Neandertal mandibles have a retromolar gap between the 3rd premolar and the vertical part of the mandible behind it (Figure 8.12d) but there is no such gap in the Qafzeh skull.

- The prominent eyebrow ridges in Neandertal skulls are absent in Quafzeh IX.

- A chin is present in Qafzeh IX but absent in a Neandertal face.

Question 11.2

The occupants of Yafteh cave were hunters, subsisting on large and small mammals. Stone tools at the site include bladelets, especially points, and the tip of a sagaie. These tools are used as projectiles for killing prey. Multiple bladelets can be hafted on to a spear making a weapon. There are also typical Aurignacian blades and endscrapers on some retouched blades, as well as burins. Scrapers would have been used to clean the hides. Fragmented animal bones found in the cave were 96% rabbit and 4% gazelle. Larger prey also included mostly goats, some sheep and very few pigs. Many of the bones were burnt. The thick layer of ochre spread on the floor suggests long-term occupation or repeated occupations. The users of the cave had the time to use personal adornment and possibly to make these items. They included perforated deer canines and shells, and a haematite pendant carved to resemble a canine tooth. Trading activity was likely because the closest location that the shells could have been obtained was the Persian Gulf, 350 km away.

Question 11.3

Re-dating the Ngandong crania and Mungo man at 27–53 kya means that *Homo erectus* was co-existing with *Homo sapiens* in Australasia and so was unlikely to be ancestral to *H.sapiens* in Java. So the re-dating does not provide support for the multiregional hypothesis and regional continuity.

Question 11.4

The foramen magnum of *Homo floresiensis* is located more centrally in the floor of the cranium, (basicranium), so the skull rests on the top of the vertebral column (Section 11.5). This indicates that *H. floresiensis* stood upright on two legs. b) The innominate is shorter and broader than that of apes and the ilium is flared, forming the iliac blade, (Section 11.5). The foot is platform-like and the big toe is aligned with the other toes.

Question 11.5

Water transportation and consequent hydraulic sorting could have caused the deposition of the animal bones and stone tools together at the same site (section X.X).

Question 11.6

People living in hot humid climates tend to be thin and short because this maximizes their surface to volume ratio and therefore their ability to lose heat. Furthermore, reduced body volume helps to reduce the amount of metabolic heat generated. In contrast, the maintenance of body temperature in hot humid climates is more difficult for taller robust individuals as they have a relatively low surface area to volume ratio. Selection for small size may link to a reduced requirement for food as smaller individuals have lower calorific requirements than large individuals. Smaller individuals use less energy when walking and running than do large individuals.

Question 11.7 Please see Table 11.6.

Table 11.6 Some comparisons of the skeletal anatomy of *Homo floresiensis* with that of australopiths and *Homo erectus*

Feature described	*H. floresiensis*	*H. erectus*	Australopiths
Estimated height	LB1 height was ~1.06 m	Java *Homo erectus* height ~1-7 –1.8 m	**A. afarensis* males ~1.51 m tall; females ~1.05 m. *A. africanus* males ~1.38 m tall; females ~1.15 m.
Overall shape & features of cranium and face	Skull has thick cranial walls. Occipital torus and eyebrow ridges present, & not prominent. Facial prognathism is reduced. Chin absent.	Skull is long, with thick cranial walls. An occipital torus is present. Eyebrow ridges prominent. Forehead low & flat. Facial prognathism is reduced. Chin absent	Face projecting (prognathic) below the orbits e.g. *A. afrarensis, A. africanus* Eyebrow ridges prominent. Chin absent
Endocranial volume	****380 cm³ (Brown et al 2004); 415– 430 cm³ (Jacob et al 2006)	About 900–1400 cm³	*** ~ 375–550 cm³
Molars	Molars relatively larger than those of *H. sapiens* but relatively smaller than *Australopithecus*	Tooth morphology similar to that of *H.sapiens* but relatively larger, with molars not as massive and ridged as those of australopiths.	Molars massive and ridged, & extremely so in *Paranthropus*
Encephalisation quotient E Q	E Q calculated as 2.5–4.6	EQ ~ 3.3–4.4	EQ 2.5–3.0
Ilium (pelvic girdle) flared	Ilium (pelvic girdle) flared	Ilium (pelvic girdle) flared	Ilium (pelvic girdle) flared

*Sexual dimorphism is assumed so two different average heights estimated from fossils, one for males and one for females.
**Estimate based on filling cranium with mustard seed (Brown, *et al.* 2004). Jacob *et al.* (2006) removed more sediment from inside skull and so obtained higher value.
***This is an estimated range, based on data for *A. afarensis, A. africanus, A. aethiopicus* and *A. robustus*.

H. floresiensis (LB1), H. erectus and australopiths were bipedal as indicated by various anatomical features including the flared ilium. LB1 was about 1.06 m tall, so within the range for *Australopithecus afarensis*. The skull of LB1 is very small with endocranial volume of about 380–430 cm³, which is within the range for *australopiths*. Estimated EQ values for *H. floresiensis*, 2.5–4.6, are similar to those for *H. erectus*. Although the LB1 skull is so small there are anatomical similarities with

H. erectus, in that the cranial bones are relatively thick, and there are eyebrow ridges and an occipital torus. The face of *H. floresiensis* shows much reduced prognathism, in contrast to the face of australopiths. The cheek teeth, molars and premolars of *H. floresiensis* and *H. erectus* are markedly reduced in size relative to those of australopiths.

The anatomy of the skull and teeth of *H. floresiensis* has many features in common with *H erectus*, which could suggest an evolutionary relationship between the two species. However the reduced stature of *H. floresiensis*, and the small brain size are features in common with australopiths.

Question 11.8

    a   Table 11.4 shows that Solutrean technology in south west France is dated at 22–18 kya. Clovis tool technology is dated at 13.2–12.8 kya at which time Magdelenian technology was current in south western Europe.

    b   It would have taken about 10–6 000 years for Solutrean technology to reach America.

Note: Straus et al. (2005) concluded that the differences between the Solutrean and Clovis technologies were too great to support colonization of the Americas by modern humans travelling from south western Europe. Straus et al. also point out that the large time difference between the two technologies makes it unlikely that Solutrean technology was brought to America from south western Europe.

Question 11.9

The mtDNA haplogroups A and B originated in Asia, so it is likely that the ancestors of the modern humans who were using the Paisley cave sites originated in Asia (see also Table 11.1).

Glossary

Acheulean A type of stone tool technology that typically includes bifacial hand-axes and cleavers, dating from about 1.4 mya in Africa and linked to *Homo erectus*.

Achondroplasia heritable type of dwarfism in which growth of the long bones is impaired causing short limbs and short stature.

Adaptive radiation The process by which a number of new types of organism arise from a single ancestral type.

Adaptation A heritable character of an organism that improves its survival and reproductive potential.

Alleles Alternative forms of a gene that codes for the same trait.

Allopatric speciation Speciation that is a consequence of physical separation of two populations, literally 'another country'.

Altricial A species whose young are so immature that they are unable to feed themselves.

Alveolus The socket into which a tooth root fits.

Analagous Those characters that perform the same or similar functions but are of different evolutionary origin, for example the primate eye and the squid eye.

Angiosperm radiation theory The theory that asserts that the adaptive radiation of primates occurred as angiosperms were undergoing radiation. However it has been pointed out that angiosperms had emerged long before primates but this does not necessarily negate the theory as there were multiple radiations of angiosperms as climates and habitats changed.

Apomorphies Derived features that evolved later in a group. For example, a postorbital bar is considered to be a derived feature for early primates that distinguishes them from a sister group.

Arboreal animals Animals adapted to a life in trees.

Arboreal hypothesis The hypothesis that the adaptations that are characteristic of primates have been selected for as a consequence of an aboreal lifestyle. Proposed by Elliot Smith and Jones in 1913, it is no longer widely accepted.

Ar^{40}/ Ar^{39} dating A dating technique in which a sample, e.g. rock, is irradiated initially with neutrons, which transform the stable K^{39} (potassium-49) into Ar^{39}. The rock sample is then heated and releases the Ar^{40} and Ar^{39} which are measured using gas chromatography. The Ar^{39} level gives a measure of the potassium originally present in the rock and the Ar^{40} gives a measure of the decay of K^{40} since the rock was erupted from the volcano. As the half-life of K^{40} is known the age of the rock sample can be calculated.

Basicranium   The base of the cranium, that forms a 'floor'.

Biostratigraphic indicators   Fossil species used to indicate the ages of particular sedimentary layers as they have previously been found in those layers elsewhere which have been dated. The most important of these species include elephants, pigs and horses.

Bovids   Those ruminants classified in the family Bovidae, which typically have a pair of permanent hollow horns. In about two thirds of bovids, both sexes have horns, but those of females are smaller than those of males. The Bovidae include cattle, *Bos spp.*, yak, water buffalo, guar and bison.

Broca's area   A region of the brain located on the side of the frontal lobe just above the temporal lobe that has a crucial role in speech. Damage to Broca's area causes speech impairment or loss.

Brunhes   One of two major magnetic reversals, a time span of normal magnetic polarity. This began at 730 kya, marking the end of the Early and the beginning of the Middle Pleistocene.

Calvaria   The skullcap, or the rounded dome of the skull. The term may also be used as a collective noun for the bones of the skull cap.

Canine fossa   A depression on the outer surface of the upper jaw which is above and towards the side of the canine tooth socket. When the **infraorbital** (below the eye socket) bone surface of the face slopes down and backward this results in a depressed area in the face known as the canine fossa.

Chert   A microcrystalline variety of quartz formed within a sedimentary context.

Chron   A major division or epoch of time marked by one magnetic polarity e.g. the current Brunhes chron, which has lasted from about 750 000 years ago.

Cingulum   A band of enamel circling a tooth. It is essentially a ridge of enamel at the base of the surface of the crown of a tooth – it can appear as a raised outside rim of a tooth.

Clade   A group of species including the common ancestor of the group and its descendants.

Cladistics   A biological classification system based on the quantitative analysis of comparative morphology, which is used to build up phylogenetic trees. The trees summarize what is known about evolutionary relationships between the sub-groups within a higher systematic group.

Cladogenesis   The splitting of an evolutionary line into a number of groups known as clades. The Haplorrhini, for example are a clade that branched from the ancestral primates. Their sister group is the Strepsirrhini, and the two clades split about 63 mya.

Cladogram   A chart showing the evolutionary relationships between groups of related organisms. A cladogram is built up from an analysis of derived features in each group, and can have various styles including that of an evolutionary tree.

Coalescence time   The time at which a gene appeared in a population.

Coalescent   An ancestral genotype obtained by tracing all alleles of a specified gene down to a single ancestral copy shared by all members of a population. Molecular geneticists can use samples taken from an extant population to find all of the known alleles and trace their evolutionary history by examining the DNA sequence of each allele. The ancestral copy is known as the most recent common ancestor, or **MRCA**.

Codon   A sequence of three bases in DNA or RNA that codes for a single amino acid.

Convergence   The development of similar morphological characters in un-related taxons, as a consequence of similar selection pressures.

Cranium The skull, not including the mandible.

CT scan A computerized tomography scan. A scan of a body part e.g. the head, is carried out using a computerized tomography scanner, which is a type of X-ray machine that sends out several beams of X rays simultaneously at different angles. The computer calculates the relative densities of the tissues and uses them to build up a set of images of cross sections, which can be linked to form a 3D image.

Dental formula This describes the number of incisors, canines, premolars and molars on each side of the upper and lower jaws.

Derived (character/feature) Whether a feature is 'derived' or 'primitive' depends on the comparison made. For example, fingernails are found in all primates so they are primitive characters that could not be used to distinguish hominoids from monkeys. In contrast, brow ridges are found only in hominoids not in other primates so they are a feature that is derived for hominoids.

Diastema A gap between two teeth. *Aegyptopithecus* for example, has a diastema between the second incisor and canine in the upper jaw.

Dominant gene or allele An allele that is expressed phenotypically when present in a heterozygote with another allele.

Emireh points The stone tools identified as a transitional technology marking the boundary between Middle and Upper Palaeolithic in Israel and Palestine.

Encephalization Quotient EQ For extinct and extant primates, the ratio of the mass of the brain to the expected mass of the body.

Endocast A cast made of the impression a mould makes from the internal surface of the cranium that gives an indication of the size and shape of the brain.

Epiphyses In juveniles these are cartilage growth plates at the ends of long bones such as the femur where growth in length and breadth are occurring by means of cell division and cell growth. Once sexual maturity is reached the epiphyses fuse with the bones and disappear.

ESR (Electron spin resonance) Excited electrons accumulate as they are trapped within the crystal lattice of certain minerals e.g. tooth enamel, flint, as a result of energy input from ionizing radiation emitted by radioisotopes in the soil. ESR detects these electrons by application of a magnetic field, which orientates the electrons, followed by microwave energy, which flips the orientation of the electrons, causing a signal. The signal strength provides a measure of the number of trapped excited electrons, which in turn provides a measure of the age of the sample.

Euarchonta A superorder of the Mammalia, that includes Scandentia (tree shrews), Dermoptera (colugos), Primates, Lagomorpha (hares and rabbits) and Rodentia.

F1 generation The first generation produced by crossing two parental lines.

Fitness Relative reproductive success, measured for example by fecundity or survival.

Foramen magnum The hole in the **basicranium** through which the spinal cord passes into the skull and joins to the brain.

Foraminifera A group of single celled organisms, less than about 1.0 mm in diameter, characterized by complex shaped shells usually made of calcium carbonate, (a few species have silica shells). Some species e.g. form massive blooms in the oceans and when they die en masse they fall to the sea bed, their shells forming layers of sediments, and ultimately, sedimentary rock.

Foreshaft   A short shaft tipped with a point that can be inserted into the hollowed tip of a much longer shaft, making an even longer spear of 1.8 m or more. A set of varied foreshafts with different tips plus the longer shaft, make up a flexible tool kit for hunting a variety of prey.

Frontal bone   The bone that forms the front of the cranium, which is a vertical forehead in modern *Homo sapiens*.

Frontal squama   The flat part of the frontal bone (that forms a forehead in modern *Homo sapiens*).

Frugivorous   The term frugivorous describes animals that subsist on a diet of fruit.

Fusion-fission   This term describes the social structure of chimpanzees. The social group consists of many members but sub-groups go off and forage together and maintain contact with each other by calling.

Gene fixation   The process by which the frequency of a mutant gene increases so much within a population of animals that it becomes the norm.

Genotype   The set of genes that an organism possesses.

Globigerina   Planktonic micro-organisms with calcium carbonate skeletons, that can form blooms in the upper waters of the oceans. When these organisms die, their shells sink to the bottom, and accumulations of this material over millions of years forms sedimentary rocks such as chalk and limestone.

Half-life   The time taken for half the nuclei in a sample of an isotope to undergo radioactive decay.

Hallux   The big toe.

Haplogroups   A haplogroup is itself defined by related groups of DNA sequences, defined as **haplotypes**, originating from shared mutations. So a haplogroup comprises a collection of closely related haplotypes.

Haplorhini   A clade of primates that includes tarsiers, Old World monkeys apes and humans. They have a short snout, dry noses, and unsplit nostrils. Their orbits are closed so the post orbital bar is not present. They are diurnal. The term 'Suborder Haplorhini' replaces the suborders Prosimian/Anthropoidea.

Haplotypes   A haplogroup is defined by a specific DNA sequence e.g. a specific set of variant short tandem repeats defines an individual male's **haplotype** which is present in a relatively small number of men.

Hominin (and hominid)   *Homo sapiens*, extinct *Homo* species, australopithecines, and any unknown evolutionary relative of *Homo*, extending back to the split between the chimpanzee and *Homo* evolutionary line.

Hominoid   A member of the superfamily Hominoidea which includes apes, australopithecines and *Homo* species.

Homologous   Two behavioural or morphological traits in different organisms that originate from the same ancestor. Only homologous characters can be used to work out evolutionary relationships between groups.

Homoplasies   Certain common characters of animals in two groups may not be linked to evolutionary relationships between those groups. The possession of wings in insects and birds does not imply an evolutionary relationship, as wings have a different origin in the two groups.

The possession of wings in birds and insects is regarded as an example of **convergence** and in cladistics convergent characters are known as **homoplasies**.

HVR1 and HVR2 The hypervariable regions of mtDNA, which are used in the analysis of the DNA sequences in mtDNA.

Hyoid bone A U-shaped bone that has attachments for the tongue muscles.

Karst A typical topography that overlays rocks, limestone, dolomite, and gypsum, that are soluble in rainwater, which is slightly acidic. The action of the percolating rainwater in dissolving the rock results in caves, sinkholes and cavities where roofs of caves have collapsed. Underground streams and rivers are typical. The term karst is derived from the Slovenian word 'kras' used to describe a world famous limestone region of the country.

Late Stone Age A period of time in Africa dating from about 40 000 years ago, coinciding with the Upper Palaeolithic in Asia and Europe.

Laurasia During the late Mesozoic, some 100–65 mya, the major continents of the northern hemisphere were joined together forming a supercontinent known as Laurasia.

Lordosis A curvature of the lumbar spine seen in humans.

Mandible The lower jaw bone, which articulates with the skull, enabling the moth to open. The ramus is the posterior vertical part, and the mandibular condyle at its end articulates with the skull forming a hinge joint that enables opening of the mouth. At the front, the two halves of the mandible meet and form a chin in *Homo sapiens*.

Matuyama A magnetic polarity epoch, in which polarity was reversed. The end of the Matuyama and the start of the **Brunhes** at 730 kya marked the end of the Early and the beginning of the Middle Pleistocene.

Maxilla The upper jaw bone, which is fused to the cranium.

Member In the context of geology, this is a subdivision of a rock formation.

Middle Palaeolithic A period of time in Asia and Europe dating from as long ago as 120 000 years ago to about 40 000 years ago. Middle Palaeolithic technologies include the Mousterian in Western Asia, the Middle East and Europe.

Middle Stone Age (MSA) A period of time in Africa dating from as long ago as 180 000 years ago to about 40 000 years ago and characterized by technology ranging from Levallois flakes to crescent shaped blades, double edged scrapers and even sophisticated bone harpoon heads. Evidence of the use of personal adornment has also been found including ochre pencils. The time span coincides with the Middle Palaeolithic in Asia and Europe.

Mitochondrial DNA The ring DNA located within a mitochondrion also known as mtDNA, that codes for many mitochondrial proteins.

Mitochondrial Eve The **coalescent** of mtDNA maternal lineages of modern humans who were born in East or South Africa at least 130 kya. The earliest known lineages, L1, are found only in Africa and rarely in Arabia and Mediterranean countries.

MRCA The 'Most Recent Common Ancestor' of a group of organisms is the most recent individual that was ancestral to that group of organisms. The MRCA is found by tracing gene alleles back until the ancestral genotype is determined.

MRI (Magnetic Resonance Imaging) A non destructive method which utilizes the properties of magnetism to create a three-dimensional, internal image of a biological object such as the skull, brain, spinal cord and muscle.

Multimale polygyny   This is a primate social structure in which the group comprises multiple males and females. Such groups include clans made up of families, with each family comprising a dominant breeding male and several females and their offspring.

Neogene   A period of time between the 23–1.63 mya that spans the Miocene and Pliocene epochs.

Niche   Place occupied by an organism in a particular ecological community. In any one community, only one species occupies each niche.

Node   (in a cladogram) A point of divergence in a cladogram, where there is a split of a cladogram line into two lines, each representing divergence from a common ancestor.

Obsidian   A shiny black volcanic rock formed from rock melted at high temperature that solidified into a glass; it is usually black, but may be greenish or banded.

Occipital torus (occipital bun, or chignon)   One of the defining features of Neandertals; a rounded bulge of the occipital bone, at the back of the skull.

Oldowan   The oldest known stone tool technology (dating to 2.4 mya in Africa) and characterized by chopping tools and small flakes made by percussion of cobbles with hard stone hammers.

Orthograde   The term used to describe upright ape locomotion either when climbing or standing and walking bipedally.

Outgroup   An organism that is related in evolutionary terms to another group of organisms but is not closely related that group. Primate species are more closely related to each other than they are to any species of rodents. So relative to primates, a rodent would form an outgroup in terms in a cladistic analysis.

Palaeomagnetic dating   A relative dating technique based on the known periodic reversals of the Earth's magnetic axis. During 'normal' polarity, a magnetic needle points northwards; during a magnetic reversal a magnetic needle would point southwards.

Paranasal sinuses   Air-filled spaces in the bones of the face that are connected with the nasal cavity.

Parietal bones   The bones that lie between the frontal and occipital bones forming the sides and top of the cranium.

Parsimony   The simplest interpretation of an evolutionary tree involving the lowest number of 'steps'.

Pentadactyl limb   The basic vertebrate limb which ends in five digits.

Phenotype   The physical and observable characteristics of an organism, determined by its genetic make-up.

Planum temporale   The posterior superior surface of the superior temporal gyrus in the cerebrum, a part of the brain involved with language.

Platyrrhine   A member of the Infraorder Platyrrhini, the new World monkeys.

Platymeria   A broadening and flattening of a long bone e.g. femur.

Plesiomorphic   The term used instead of primitive past that is no longer used by many biologists, who use the term **plesiomorphic** instead. Features described as primitive are those that were present in an ancestral group of animals and continue be present in living species of the group.

Plesiomorphy This is a plesiomorphic feature. For example, possession of nails in living primates is considered to be **plesiomorphy** in relation to ancient primates.

Polarity Identifying a feature as primitive or derived is described as deciding on the feature's **polarity.**

Polygynous A social grouping in which a male has access to more than one female for mating.

Precocial A species whose young are born relatively mature with a substantial degree of independence.

Primitive (character/feature) A feature in a species that was present in the ancestral group. Refer to definition for 'derived feature'.

Procumbent A term describing forward projection of a feature e.g. the procumbent front teeth of rodents and the Miocene ape, *Afropithecus.*

Prognathism A term describing forward projection of the face in hominids.

Pumice A light porous volcanic rock, with high silica content, formed by rapid cooling of a molten lava containing gas bubbles.

Quadripedal The term used to describe walking on all fours.

Quartz A mineral made of silicon dioxide; quartz may be found as hexagonal crystals in some rocks.

Quartzite A general time for sandstone that has been cemented or recrystallized.

Ramus The vertical part of the mandible which ends as the lower part of the hinged joint that articulates with the skull.

Recombination The re-arrangement of genes during meiosis that results in a new combination of chromosomes that produce a new gamete.

Retromolar space A gap between the final molar and the ramus in the lower jaw.

Sagaie A bone or ivory point, that forms the tip of a spear.

Sagittal keel A ridge of bone running along the midline of the top of the skull; in some fossil skulls it extends along the midline of the forehead (frontal squama).

Shared derived character The possession of a feature common to all members of a group and absent in nails in living primates would be regarded as derived in relation to other groups of mammals such as tree shrews and rodents. So, the possession of nails is a **shared derived character** found in primates, distinguishing them from other mammal groups such as tree shrews.

Silcrete A silica rich rock comprising sand and gravel cemented together by silica, commonly found in deserts and talus slopes.

Single nucleotide polymorphism (SNP) A single change to just a single nucleotide. The significance of the low mutation rate for SNPs in Y-DNA is probably all males who have a specific SNP marker share the same single mutation, inherited from the same common ancestor.

Sister groups Two groups that share a common ancestor.

Stratigraphy The study of layered deposits of rocks, fossils and archaeological remains. The information about particular fossils or artefacts found in specific layers of known ages can be applied to estimation of the ages of layers of rocks elsewhere.

Strepsirrhini   A clade of primates that includes lemurs and lorises. They have moist noses and split nostrils. The term 'Suborder Haplorhini' replaces the suborders Prosimian/Anthropoidea, but is no longer used in classification.

STR (Short tandem repeats)   Repeats of short sequences of nucleotides in a DNA sequence. The number of repetitions varies greatly between individuals, and defines an allele, Y-STR) on the human Y chromosome. Each Y-STR on a chromosome is given a DYS number that corresponds to the number of repetitions. For example, the DYS number of As the variation rate of STRs are high, the number of repeats in an Y-STR may change after just a few generations.

Suprainiac fossa   An elliptical pitted depression at the back of the skull (on the occipital bone). This is one of the defining features of Neanderthals.

Supraorbital torus   An eyebrow ridge, formed by a ridge of bone on the frontal bone above the eye socket.

Supramastoid crest   See entry for temporal bone.

Supratoral sulcus   A narrow groove in the skull that lies above a torus, typically in palaeoanthropology, the occipital torus.

Suspensory locomotion   A type of arboreal locomotion seen in some primates which involves hanging from branches and using the arms to move through the tree canopy, with the hands grasping tree branches at each 'step.'

Sympatric speciation   The evolution of a species within a subpopulation of the ancestral species that overlaps geographically with a population of the ancestral species.

Synapomorphy   A term used in cladistics to mean a shared derived character.

Taphonomy   The study of processes by which fossils form.

Taurodont; taurodontism   The term used for describing teeth, typically molars, that have enlarged pulp cavities, making the roots shorter in proportion to the rest of the tooth.

Teff   A grain crop grown in Ethiopia; individual grains are small and ideal for use in measuring endocranial volume of fossil skulls.

Temporal bone/s.   The two bones located on each side of the skull. Each temporal bone consists of five parts:

> The squama comprises the upper and anterior parts of the bone and is thin and translucent. The supramastoid crest, a curved line, runs backward and upward across the squama's posterior part.
>
> The petrous portion is thick and encloses the inner ear.
>
> The mastoid forms the posterior part of the frontal bone. The mastoid extends to form a conical process, the mastoid process.
>
> The tympanic part is a curved plate of bone lying below the squama.
>
> The styloid process projects downwards and outwards from the under surface of the temporal bone.

Tephra   This is solid material which may comprise small particles or larger pieces of rock that are ejected into the air from an active volcano.

Thermoluminescence dating technique   Excited electrons accumulate as they are trapped within the crystal lattice of certain minerals e.g. tooth enamel, flint, as a result of energy input from ionizing radiation emitted by radioisotopes in the soil. Exposure of the artefact or tooth to heat releases the trapped electrons, which return to the ground state releasing photons (light) that can be detected by special instruments. The number of photons emitted can be related to the age of the samples.

Torus A ring-like structure e.g. raising the surface of a bone; examples include the supraorbital torus and occipital torus.

Transcription The process by which mRNA (messenger RNA) is synthesized using the template provided by DNA. The mRNA is the means by which the genetic code for a protein can be applied to the synthesis of that protein.

Translation The process by which the genetic code in the mRNA is used as a template for synthesis of a protein.

Travertine A sedimentary rock formed by precipitation of calcium carbonate from slow moving water in springs or streams, which was saturated with calcium bicarbonate. Banding patterns in the rock formed from iron or organic impurities.

Uniformitarianism A theory proposed by Charles Lyell, that geological formations are produced by stages over long periods of time.

Uranium series dating technique A dating technique that is based on decay of uranium-238, uranium-235, and thorium-232, which decay to lead isotopes. The principle of the technique involves measuring the proportion of decay products, the daughters, in comparison to the original uranium isotope. As the half life or uranium isotopes is known, the age of the sample can be calculated from the calculated ratios. The technique can be applied to artefacts and fossil bones dated at around 1000 to one million years ago.

Vallesian Crisis A episode of global climate change, about 9.6 mya (Middle – Late Miocene), causing subsequent colder winters and dryer summers. The Climate change linked to mountain building in the Alpine Himalayan area.

Visual predation hypothesis Matt Cartmill (Duke University) noted that most arboreal mammals do not have the adaptations characteristic of primates. He suggested the visual predation hypothesis, which links primates' forward-facing eyes and grasping hands and feet to stalking insect prey and snatching them with the hands, while their feet cling to the tree branch.

Wernicke's area A region of the brain in the posterior temporal lobe of the left hemisphere involved in the recognition of spoken words.

Wild type The 'normal' allele of a gene, in the context of a population of organisms.

Y-DNA The DNA found in the Y chromosome.

Y-STRs Short tandem repeats, which are repeats of short sequences of nucleotides in the DNA sequence of the Y chromosome.

Index

Page numbers in *italics* represent figures, those in **bold** represent tables.